'The Sahel is one of the most harsh regions of Africa and yet it contains many of the most interesting and beautiful people. Peter Hudson's lyrical book about the village he has been visiting and helping for the last 20 years gives a rare insight to the problems these brave people face and genuine ways in which they can be helped to overcome them.'

Robin Hanbury-Tenison, explorer and founder of Survival International

'This is written by a man who knows the parts of Africa he writes of better than almost any other Western author. Peter Hudson addresses his experiences in Africa with a searing honesty and refreshing insight. He is not blind to the continent's difficulties and shortcomings. Nor does he fall prey to the simplistic romanticism of so many travellers. But he clearly loves Africa and his affection shines through his writing. Before packing their bags for Africa, development workers, charity workers, diplomats, journalists and travellers should read Hudson's account of his undertaking in West Africa and then ponder their own motives and mission.'

Alec Russell, an editor at the *Financial Times* and author of *After Mandela.*

'I loved this book and it stayed with me for a long time. His present-tense account of a visit to Mauritania to monitor the progress of his small-scale aid projects is vivid, humble, deeply felt and at times incredibly moving. He writes with a freshness and a lack of artifice that is beyond the pretence of most travel writing – as if he, and we, were seeing the world entirely afresh. The result is quietly wonderful.'

Roger Crowley, author of *Constantinople* and *Empires of the Sea.*

'Impoverished agricultural communities in Mauritania, and especially in marginal areas prone to desertification after the great droughts of the 1970s and 1980s, need to rely on "stable governments, stable market prices and a stable climate, none of which are currently very available". At the heart of Peter Hudson's book is a rallying cry for the restoration of trust and confidence in the people and land of Mauritania, together with a practical demonstration of how that can be achieved by the patience, sensitivity, idealism and determination of Mauritanians themselves working to overcome a despair that nothing will ever change. In the course of the book, the hot sweet metallic taste of the mint tea – over which a fascinating swirl of characters is conjured to give us insights into social life, cultural and religious outlooks and the conflicted history of Mauritania – becomes a taste for the people themselves, how much their pride and resilience, humility and hospitality are admired and trusted.'

Gabriel Gbadamosi, Nigerian poet, playwright and novelist, author of *Vauxhall*.

'An Englishman sets up a series of grassroots projects in Mauritania with a local friend... the question is: can things ever change? Hudson's account of rural life in Mauritania delivers a great cast of characters, the color and texture of their lives vibrantly described... the rituals of daily life of desert people lovingly and entertainingly conveyed. Off the beaten track doesn't begin to cover it: this is an unexpected, intimate view of village life, of people ravaged by war and drought, determined to survive.'

Clare Longrigg, author and *Guardian* editor.

UNDER AN AFRICAN SKY

A journey to the frontline of climate change

About the author

Peter Hudson has worked as a farmer, charity worker, travel writer and photographer. Over a period of 30 years, he has travelled extensively throughout Africa, visiting 31 countries, the majority of them seen from the back of a bush-taxi, donkey or moped. He has written three previous books about Africa. The first of these – *A Leaf in the Wind* (Columbus Books, 1988), which details a year-long journey made from Morocco to Egypt via West, Central and East Africa – was nominated for the 1989 Thomas Cook Travel Book of the Year award. His second book, *Travels in Mauritania*, was published in 1990 by Virgin Books. His third book, *Two Rivers*, recounts the story of following in the footsteps of British explorer Mungo Park, the first European to discover the Niger River in what is today Mali. Peter currently lives with his family on the Herefordshire/Wales border.

UNDER AN AFRICAN SKY

A journey to the frontline of climate change

PETER HUDSON

New Internationalist

Under An African Sky
First published in 2014 by
New Internationalist Publications Ltd
The Old Music Hall
106-108 Cowley Road
Oxford OX4 1JE, UK
newint.org

Front cover photos: Peter Hudson; Tony P Eveling/Alamy

Printed by TJ International Ltd, Cornwall, UK
who hold environmental accreditation ISO 14001.

MIX
Paper from
responsible sources
FSC® C013056

British Library Cataloguing-in-Publication Data
A catalogue record for this book is available from the British Library.

Library of Congress Cataloging-in-Publication Data
A catalog record for this book is available from the Library of Congress.

ISBN 978-1-78026-178-2

Dedication
For Marie, Ruby, Caitlin, Rosabel and Eile.

Acknowledgements

I would like to thank the people of the Islamic Republic of Mauritania for their unfailingly good-humored hospitality. I would like to thank all those many people who, over the years, I have seen and met on roadsides, in villages and on city streets from whom I have learned so much. In the UK, I would like to thank both Michael Marten and Laura Longrigg for reading my manuscript and giving me encouragement; Chris Brazier, my editor at New Internationalist for correcting my many mistakes (and bringing me up to date on certain matters of expression!); Veronica, my sister, for her brilliant drawings; and my wife, Marie, for her constant support (and her proofreading skills!). For reasons of anonymity and security the names of people and of some places mentioned in this book have been altered.

Donation

A portion of the royalties from the sales of this book will be used for our ongoing development work in southern Mauritania.

Contents

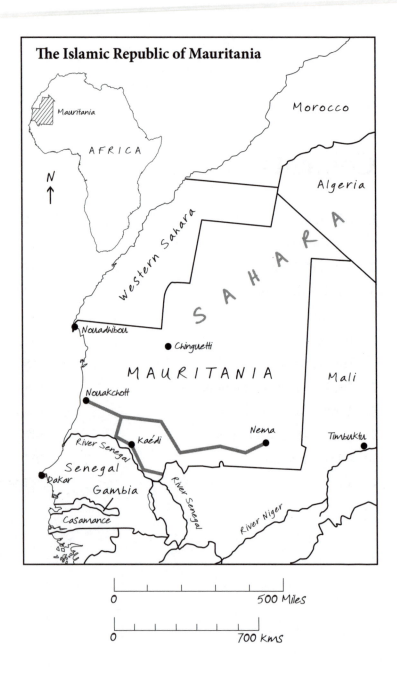

The Islamic Republic of Mauritania

Mauritania

AFRICA

N

Morocco

Algeria

Western Sahara

SAHARA

Nouadhibou

Chinguetti

MAURITANIA

Mali

Nouakchott

Nema

Timbuktu

Kaédi

River Senegal

Senegal

Dakar

Gambia

River Senegal

Casamance

River Niger

0   500 Miles

0   700 kms

Introduction

A bush taxi in the south of Mauritania, West Africa. Outside, wastes of sand and scrub; a fierce wind. This is the Sahel, the southern 'shore' of the Sahara: a region at the frontline of climate change. I am sandwiched in the back of the vehicle's three rows of seats between two large men. Up front sits a man of about my age: 28. He is clean-shaven, with a look of calm and gentleness about him. Beside him sits a girl of five or six, his daughter, perhaps: a picture of the prettiest and most composed perfection. With her hair plaited immaculately to her scalp, her African print dress wrapped neatly to the ankles and her hands folded demurely in her lap, she looks more like a mini-adult than a child. The man, I notice, treats her as such.

It is 1988 and I am travelling aimlessly: a well-stocked backpack, money in my pocket and time on my hands. I have taken the taxi south only because it is one of the few parts of Mauritania I have not yet seen. By camel, donkey, foot and bush-taxi, I have travelled the length and breadth of this desert country. I have been to the ancient caravan towns stuck far out in the desert with their ancient libraries and smells of the Maghreb. I have stayed with nomads, sharing their ghee and couscous, drinking milk last thing at night, warm from the udders of their cows. I have seen and experienced a great many aspects of this wild, dusty and difficult country, not least the 'White' Moors – those supreme desert opportunists now trying their hands at modernity and all the angles of gain and exploitation it can provide the quick-witted – and the 'Black' Moors, descendants of freed slaves, at best sharing the power and spoils of nationhood with their white-hued, clannish compatriots; at worst, subsisting at the bottom of the pile with a handful of goats and a scrap of tent.

In the towns and cities, the roux of black, white and brown, of traders, marketeers and shanty-dwellers, was infinite and infinitely fascinating. Here was a world turned inside-out: all the mechanisms of an economy and society – the industry, ingenuity, joy and suffering – displayed in all their raw vitality: a man hammering satellite dishes out of pieces of sheet metal; an entire street of blackened charcoal sellers; an alleyway of settees; water sellers; ragged madmen; letter writers by the post office; infants defecating on curbs; an anarchy of fuming vehicles swarming like an invasion of locusts down and into every passage, road and alleyway. And among them, I, a lone Westerner – for I only rarely saw another Westerner – wandered freely, never once threatened or alienated. Then I decided to travel south.

This was where the Black Africans lived, in country where more precipitation meant a degree of agriculture and so a different existence. These were the Bantu peoples of sub-Saharan Africa – as opposed to the desert-dwelling Moors, whose culture harks back to the Berbers of North Africa and the Yemeni Arabs who invaded Mauritania in the 17th century. These two peoples – the intensely clannish Moorish dwellers of the desert and the Bantu to their south – have been traditional rivals ever since, and the frontline of their rivalry

has always been the band of country along the southern edge of the Sahara: the Sahel. This is where desert finally gives way to scrub. It is where pastures, born of the annual rains, can take a better hold, where rain-fed agriculture is possible, and where seasonal rivers and streams can sometimes be found.

I had barely spoken to that young man during the journey south; perhaps just some pleasantries exchanged during one of the innumerable stops. Then, amid the swirling confusion of dusk and dust in Kaédi, the regional capital, where the bush taxi deposited us, the young man asked if I would like to accompany him to his village. I must have looked a little lost, standing beside my backpack in the taxi park.

'Yes,' I said, 'I'd like to very much.'

'My name is Salif,' he said, 'and this,' he indicated his pretty young daughter standing by his side, 'is Ramata.'

And, because Salif was an honest man – as even then I could see – I believed him when he told me his village was not far. Two hours later, after a nightmarish journey lurching along a concrete-hard track, squeezed into the back of a taxi-van with 30 other souls, we arrived. But I am glad I accepted Salif's offer. For it was here that I first became acquainted with Mustapha, Abu and Harouna... with Fama, Mariam and Aliou... with Amuna and Isa and Musa... all those many people whose lives in the 25 subsequent years – in most of which I have paid them a visit – have unfolded in step with my own. Some, at that time, were mere babes in arms. Some, who were youngsters, are now at the forefront of family affairs. Some have long gone grey and settled back into the quiet anonymity of elderhood; and some have died – too many. On that first trip, though, Mamadou, Amadou and Mohamedou were names I could not untangle, especially when their owners were little more than profiles in the darkness of the village night, only a sheen of expression visible in the starlight.

Images have stayed with me from that first trip to Salif's village: a naked child squatting by an open ditch of effluent, chewing on a dried chicken bone he had just picked up; a boy perched on a donkey-cart, setting about his poor, emaciated beast with a stick like a truncheon, beating its bruised and sore-covered back until its knees buckled and it crumpled up; Salif's mother, with a strong arm and a gleam in her eye, milking a cow whose ribs stuck out like a plate rack. But then this was poor country. It had been devastated by the great Sahelian droughts of the 1970s and 1980s, during which 90 per cent of the livestock of its pastoralist inhabitants had perished. Losing 90 per cent of herds that represented all a family's wealth and inheritance and have been built up over generations was devastating. At one fell swoop, these once proud livestock herders were robbed of the means and, indeed, the very purpose of existence. The herds they now had were pitiful reminders of what they had once possessed, and they relied instead on a rain-fed agriculture that even in good years could never pay the bills.

Yet Salif's family, despite the obvious difficulty of their condition, were the 'wealthy' ones. They and their like, I was to discover, were the ones to whom other families – those in the camps and hamlets in the bush – looked up. It was they who inhabited the large home-village where the markets, the schools, the medical center and the administrative representatives were to be found. It was to these bigger, patron

families that poorer cousins from the bush would send any promising children so they could study the Qu'ran or go to the primary school. It was to these families they would come when they were desperate: for support, assistance, food. Poverty, I realized – besides being highly subjective – was also relative.

I was struck by the hardship of the region in a way I never had been before, but I was also charmed by a culture that was gentler, subtler and more disciplined than the many cultures I had already been charmed by in the continent. Perhaps it was that special blend of Bantu Africa with Islam which is so clearly delineated in the Sahel, the first perhaps softening the sharper edges of the second, the second perhaps calming the more fiery temperament of the first. Perhaps it was the merging of the pastoral, semi-nomadic peoples of the plains with the more settled agrarian culture of those to the south. Perhaps it was the history of the cultured civilizations that had been born of the wealthy trans-Sahara trade at whose terminus the Sahel was situated – empires such as ancient Ghana, great Mali and Songhai. These had standing armies hundreds of thousands strong, universities to which students travelled from as far away as North Africa, and centralized bureaucracies: an inheritance that can be seen in the the

Sahelian peoples' bearing of inner confidence and calm. Or perhaps it was just the wide-open, fenceless country, softened at the edges by sand, with horizons, like those at sea, promising anonymity and a clear space in which to breathe.

Whichever, of all of the parts of Africa I have visited, it is to this dusty and, in many respects, unspectacular corner that, time and again, I have been drawn back. Salif and I now run small development projects there. And each year, grey winter approaching, I board a plane to emerge, four hours later, under a bright African sky.

1 The Capital

Morning in Nouakchott... Why I come back year after year... Salif's brave return home... Monsieur Adrosso and the de-husker dilemma... A visit to the Cinquième market

4.30am: I am jolted awake by a muezzin calling the early prayers – an overly amplified, ugly sound coming from the mosque just down the street. The sound wavers on, sometimes descending into a chant, at others, reasserting itself. I drift in and out of sleep.

5.45am: Amadou's radio bursts to life. Amadou is the owner of the house in which I am staying, out by the sand dunes on the edge of town. He is hard of hearing, so the French news program he listens to always each morning is played at full volume. I listen as he goes about preparing himself for work: the clink of tea glasses, a noisy hacking in the yard, mumbled conversations with his wife. In my room, it is pitch dark.

6.30am: The metal yard door scrapes open as Amadou leaves for work and a moment later his vehicle, parked directly outside the door, is gunned explosively to life. Shortly, the students wake up. I hear them move about: clumping, hacking, drawing water from the water jar just outside my door. There are always any number of students and other miscellaneous

family members staying at 'L'Auberge Amadou', as I call it. The students do not take breakfast and I soon hear the yard door scraping open again as they make off to the main thoroughfare into town beside which they will wait with all the other early morning wraiths for a taxi-van to pick them up. A thin light is just starting to illuminate my room.

Amadou's wife, Fama, begins cleaning pots and pans in the yard, clanking and banging them against each other. In my mind's eye I can see her, squatting on a small stool in the yard, dress stretched tightly between her knees, bent over the huge pots as she scrubs them inside and out. Fama is young with dark eyes and a shy manner. Beside her, Isata, her daughter, sits on the ground teething on a nice, sharp bottle top. For a while Fama sings a quiet song until interrupted by a man calling in the compound doorway. A loud, shouty conversation ensues, interspersed with periodic bursts of laughter, the babble of rounded, tumbling syllables going on and on. This is the Peul language, of which I understand little.

8.00am: A herd of sheep stops outside my window, bleating loudly.

8.15am: Ghettoblaster music erupts from a neighbor. God, I've forgotten how noisy Africa is.

I wake finally mid-morning but I do not immediately get

up, as it is my first day this year back in Nouakchott, capital of Mauritania, and I did not make it to bed until 4am. It is true, one part of me is itching to get going, as there is much to do on my first day back, and I am eager to get out and see the African day. Another part of me, though, is in a soft, holiday mode. The light in my shuttered room now, thin as it still is, has an orange hue that speaks of a tropical sun. Coming from grey, northern climes, I am conditioned to relax in such light.

I lie on my foam mattress and think about how it all started.

You could say it started in 1991, the year I received my first letter from Salif. His family were in a bad way at that time, a third successive year of poor-to-non-existent rains having left them virtually destitute, with nothing to fall back on. They had little left even to eat, and the wages Salif earned at the mining company where he worked in the north of the country could not feed the great many mouths there were back in the village. Not that Salif, typically, mentioned any of this in his letter. All he said then was that he wondered if I might help his family find the finances for an irrigation project, as they did not have the means to finance it themselves. I was very welcome, he said, to come and see them again, when he could further explain his plans to me. I was looking for an excuse to get back to Africa and so agreed to make the journey.

It turned out to be a bad moment for the people of southern Mauritania, for it had only been in 1989, two years previously, that the military dictatorship that then ruled the country had used a border dispute with its southerly neighbor, Senegal, as an excuse to impose a period of ethnic cleansing against its southern minority Black African population – expelling them from all positions of responsibility, imprisoning a great many, killing many hundreds, if not thousands, and ejecting another 100,000 from the country.

I arrived only some months after the end of this period but again, typically of Salif, and typically also of myself, I travelled all the way to the village in the south – into what was virtually a war zone at the time, with tensions on both sides very high and the army mounting roadblocks every few kilometers – completely ignorant of what had taken place. This was both because I was not at that time in the habit of finding out about places before I went to them, and because Salif's natural diffidence prohibited him from mentioning it. Indeed, it was not until many years later that I realized just how closely my trip had coincided with this traumatic period of oppression.

And so it began. I helped Salif's family purchase a water pump. Some time later, a second pump was added; then a tractor. And then, in the year 2000, Salif announced that he wished to give up his job in the north and return to his village to concentrate on agriculture. He wanted, he said, not only to develop his family's irrigation project but also to see what he could do to help agriculture in the region as a whole.

This was a move that made me nervous for Salif. He would be giving up a secure job and an income, both rarities in the country. And for what: the uncertainties of agriculture in one of the most marginalized, climatically challenged and poorest parts of the world. But he was adamant. He had no doubt. He did not want to pass away his life in an office on some meaningless clerical job where, because of his ethnicity, there was no hope of promotion.

'In the south I can be a farmer,' he said. 'Here, I am nothing.'

So it was that Salif returned to his village, which was an action of both courage and rarity in Africa, where those who have managed to get an education and a job do not often return to their homes. We agreed that if he looked for worthwhile agricultural projects, I would see if I could find funds to support them. And over the years this is more or less what has happened. Salif now runs a small development group based in his home village, or small town, of Keniéba; I help him create the projects and look for the funds for them.

It is Salif, of course, who has borne the brunt of this work. It is he who has had to juggle the many, often irreconcilable, requirements involved in our actions. It is easy to underestimate how difficult things can be in countries such as Mauritania. Small but often essential actions that we in the developed world take for granted – like walking into a garage and buying a new car tire, for example, or withdrawing some money from a bank, or popping over to discuss a matter with a neighbor – in developing countries can take on gargantuan proportions of effort that seemingly quite outweigh the gain. One time it took Salif six months to locate a replacement tire for our four-wheel drive, which cost him $450. A bank might, if you're lucky, let you open an account and put money into it, but when you come to withdraw it again you could well find yourself facing an extortionate 'fee' to do so. And the trip to see the neighbor – even if you are lucky enough to have access to a vehicle – might well involve having to first source some fuel, then negotiate a police post, and next an area swamped with flood waters, while all the time carrying in the back three family members with commissions of their own, meaning countless diversions, not to mention picking up on the way two men with six sheep who are relations of the driver's and need delivering somewhere else. Then you might get a puncture, and have no spare. And that's just the journey there.

So, planning and implementing projects that require participatory consultations, risk and impact assessments, log frames and baseline data, not to mention all the infrastructure development and financial or people management requirements. But Salif, despite his quiet, unassuming manner, is a resourceful man and somehow –

often I have no idea how – things just seem to work out. This has taken a lot of work, though, and for Salif by far the most intense and trying parts of this endeavor coincide with my annual visits.

By the time I open my bedroom door onto Amadou's small yard, the sun is already high. I perform my ablutions in the toilet cubicle by the yard door; then brush my teeth under the yard tree. Salif and his brother, Amadou Tall, who is our driver, are dozing on divans in the lounge, their *bobos* pulled over their heads against the flies. Salif sits up as I enter. He asks how I slept.

'Not so good,' I reply, speaking French, the language in which I communicate in Mauritania. 'The muezzin was up very early this morning.'

'Too early,' Salif agrees. Then his face darkens. 'These Islamists,' he spits out. 'They are not good Muslims. All they want to do is impress people with their devoutness. But the Qu'ran says only that we must pray before dawn, not in the middle of the night.'

There are not many things that outwardly stir Salif, but this, I have discovered, is one of them. He does not like Islam, his religion, to be misrepresented.

We take breakfast on the floor in the lounge – coffee and baguette – and discuss all that has to be accomplished during the 11 days of my visit. It is a long list: it is a year since I was here. We have a large seminar organized in Salif's village to which a Senegalese consultant will be coming, poled over the Senegal River in a dugout. This is a new direction for us: never before have we brought in outside help and we do not know how it will work out. We too will have to cross into Senegal by dugout – avoiding border posts, if we can – to see our Dohley Women's Market Garden project, with which there are issues related to 'mission drift'. There are also problems with our well-digging program and the provision – or rather lack – of donkeys for hauling. Then there are questions over the sustainability of certain tractor services we provide, school desks that have not materialized… there is much to fit in over the next few days.

As always in the capital, Salif is dressed in a smart white bobo, as the traditional Mauritanian gown is known: as brilliant and immaculate as some rare and elegant seabird. He hoists the excess folds of material over his shoulder and dips his baguette into his tea. We are discussing Ibrahim Tandia, the Senegalese development consultant who will be leading our seminar.

'He's coming over the river,' Salif says.

'He's arriving soon?' I ask.

'In four days' time,' Salif says.

'Coming to Kaédi?'

'Yes,' Salif replies. 'The Dohley women will bring him over the river.'

'So he will go to their village?' I ask.

'Yes, he'll go there first, arriving in the afternoon, and they'll bring him over.'

'At the official border crossing?'

Salif nods his head, chewing his bread: 'Yes, at the border crossing.'

'So he can get an official stamp in his passport?'

'Of course.'

'And we'll meet him in town?'

Salif smiles. 'Of course.' Not a flicker of impatience has crossed his face.

In all the years I have known Salif, he has changed little. He has put on a little weight; and at times his face has the puffy, strained look of the overworked, for, as well as having responsibility for all our development efforts and any number of income-generating and agricultural activities, Salif is also head of a large extended family, and as such faces multitudinous extra pressures and duties. But that same air of calm and gentleness that drew me to him when I first met him all those years ago has not changed at all.

It is nearing midday by the time we leave Amadou's and the sun is bright as I step out the yard door. Its rays are warm on my skin and I feel the layers of winter peeling away. Outside stands our vehicle: a double-cab four-wheel drive Toyota pick-up. It is battered beyond belief – strapped up and shattered – and I am reminded of the importance of replacing it. Our work would be impossible without a vehicle. In the early days, we made do with public transport and donkey-carts. This was tiring and limiting, however, and turning up at a village or an irrigation scheme in a donkey-cart did not do a lot for Salif's credibility.

Amadou Tall is standing near the Toyota tinkering with one of the non-functioning windows. He is an ex-truck driver: a tougher, more roughened version of his elder brother. I ask him whether he thinks the Toyota will last much longer.

'Of course,' he replies, a little brusquely. I cannot tell if he actually believes this. I have doubts as to whether it will even survive the duration of my visit. As if to confirm this, when we climb in to depart, the vehicle will not start. The

engine cover is lifted, under which Amadou Tall disappears for a while amidst much banging. We get out and push, and it coughs into life.

'The injection pump,' Amadou Tall remarks nonchalantly as we climb back in.

The capital opens up as we make our way into it: a city at first glance of sand and rubbish and people who do not know how to drive. It is as if the desert simply continues here in the town. Vehicles use any part of it that is not actually built on: sidewalks, passageways, markets, people's yards. The larger roads consist of floods of vehicles, which, at intersections, grind violently into each other. So entirely anarchic and un-municipally minded are the ex-desert dwellers behind the wheels of these vehicles, so wholly unable are they to conform to even the most commonsensical rules of the road, that it is not uncommon at a junction to end up in a traffic jam consisting of only three vehicles, all so completely insistent on not giving way that they draw closer and closer to each other until they create a mini gridlock all of their own. At such moments, a little despair comes over me. I look around and I can see only venality: the large, bearded desert man in his tall four-by-four, contempt flashing in his eyes; the rich, fat patron in his new Mercedes, sweating as he leans on his horn; the bad-tempered minibus drivers cruising like predators.

The heat expands, sucking the air out of the streets to be replaced by the black fumes of the tailgating, beaten-up taxi-vans off which people hang like bunches of grapes. The street hawkers and cripples weave in between the jams. Donkey-carts are bullied through. The shops and stalls and markets spill out, covering every inch of the town. There are, they say, three-quarters of a million points of sale in this vastly expanding city of a million and a half or more people.

Our first call of the day is to Amadou – in whose rooms we are staying – to pay our respects, as we have not seen him yet.

He is a first cousin of Salif's.

We find him sitting behind a wide metal desk in a near-empty office at the back of the Department of Water and Hydraulics workshop. Amadou is a large man with a large, shaven head, a pockmarked face and a glint of humor in his eyes. A Moor in neat Western clothes is standing in front of his desk.

'Tell him it cannot be done,' Amadou is saying to the man, speaking French.

'But you know what they are like,' the Moor replies. 'They insist.'

'They can insist as much as they like, but they know it cannot be done,' Amadou answers back.

At this moment he takes note of our entry and gets up to greet us, dismissing the Moor as he does so with a curt: 'Okay?' He reaches across his desk to shake our hands, and, as the man leaves the room, explains: 'They come to me for favors all the time. This time it's an engineer to go over to their new offices and sort out their well pump. They're management, so they are in charge and can ask what they want, even if it's against the rules, which sending engineers to do private work for them is. Because the new offices are not part of the Département. They're just where they run their little "business" from. Even if I wanted to give them an engineer, I could not spare one now.'

Salif gives a wry smile. 'They're your bosses,' he says. 'You shouldn't antagonize them so.' At this, Amadou breaks out into a deep, rumbling laugh, one that has all the various people hanging around his office grinning broadly. 'They're just businesspeople,' he says. 'They cannot do without me and they know it.'

This is true, as it is well known that Amadou is about the only person in the Département in any position of responsibility who does not treat his job simply as a means of personal gain and who actually knows what he is doing.

There is a constant stream of people stopping by to ask his advice on technical matters, to get him to make orders, to book jobs.

In the early days, he had run the family's irrigation project, the one I had helped Salif set up. He was not long back from Russia at the time, where he had studied engineering, and he had nothing else to do. He was exemplary at the technical side of the job, managing to squeeze a rice yield out of the land no-one had ever attained locally before. But he found dealing with the family frustrating.

'They never leave me enough to invest for the next year,' he told me. 'They are like locusts. They eat everything up.'

We do not stay with Amadou long, just long enough to have a glass of tea brewed by the tea 'boy' who resides on the floor in a corner of the office. Then we are off to Monsieur Adrosso, our 'fix-it' man, whose agricultural machinery shop is not far away.

I have known Monsieur Adrosso for a number of years, during which he has provided us with a quantity of water pumps and other such agricultural hardware. An old Africa hand, he came out to West Africa from Italy as a young man in the late 1950s working for an engineering firm and has stayed on ever since. Now over 70 years old, thin as a rake with yellowing skin, he runs an agricultural import company. He greets Salif and me in his showroom as though we were long-lost friends.

'Ah, ah!' he exclaims ecstatically, 'Messieurs Peter and Salif. Why did you not come to see me earlier? When did you arrive? It is good to see you.' He breaks into a bout of serious-sounding coughing. 'God, it's terrible,' he splutters between breaths.

When he has finished, I ask him about his heart, as the last time I was here he was due to go off to Italy to have surgery on it. He is a heavy smoker.

'My heart? It's not a problem,' he says, dismissing the question with a wave of his arm. 'Come, come into my office.'

We leave the showroom, which, like the majority of agricultural and vehicle dealerships in town, is empty, and enter his office. Here, Monsieur Adrosso quickly seats himself behind his desk before opening a drawer and taking out a cigarette. He lights up and is immediately wracked by another bout of coughing. When this is finished, he leans back breathlessly and asks how he can help us.

Dealing with Monsieur Adrosso, I have discovered over the years, is a bit like fishing: there is a certain amount of play involved, and you are never quite sure what you are going to get. On the one hand this can be troublesome; on the other Monsieur Adrosso has provided us over the years with a number of invaluable services.

'Do you know anyone in Customs?' was one of the questions he asked me when Salif first took me to see him. 'No,' he continued, 'but I do. In fact, the Chief of Customs is my great friend. Do you know how good a friend he is?' – Monsieur Adrosso uses the interrogative a lot – 'He is such a good friend I can ring him at any time, like now, see,' he said, picking up the telephone on his desk and dialling a number, 'I am calling him now.' A silence ensued as he waited for the connection, then: 'Ah, Said, it is I, Adrosso. Yes, yes, all well thank you… and you and the family… yes, yes, good… yes, the commission was paid on that last shipment… yes, good. Look, listen Said, I have an English friend here, an Englishman, yes… we will be importing some Lister Pumps… the usual system, eh. Twenty per cent flat, that's right. Good, good. OK, Said, I must go now, OK, bye…' 'There,' Monsieur Adrosso said, replacing the receiver, 'that was him. You heard, didn't you? A flat 20-percent import duty. You could be charged as much as 100 per cent, you know. But we have an understanding. That's how things are done here, you know. Little arrangements, little arrangements.' He chuckled merrily.

In addition to reducing import costs, however, the most invaluable service Monsieur Adrosso provides is simply carrying out his function of importing agricultural machinery: actually producing the goods for us at acceptable prices. All the other importers in town, most of whom we have at one time or another visited, seem as indifferent to our offers of business as are the many vehicle dealerships we have also been to in order to ask about a replacement for our Toyota.

Knowing I can count on Monsieur Adrosso for an opinion on any such matter, and in order to try to clear up my ongoing confusion about why this should be, I now ask him what he thinks about the dealerships' apparent lack of interest in doing any business with us. He looks at me sadly, as though I have a lot to learn.

'What you must understand, Monsieur Peter,' he says, 'is that there is no real agri-industry in this country. There are only peasant farmers and businesspeople. The peasants cannot afford modern machinery and the businesspeople are interested only in quick returns. You will hardly find a single heavy machinery importer here with any stock, agricultural or otherwise. Why is this, you ask? Because the only business they are interested in is the one of making large deals with government or international companies, deals such as supplying 150 water pumps for some state-funded agricultural initiative which they will source from Morocco, getting reconditioned ones made to look new which will break down after a year; or producing two dozen top-of-the range models for a foreign government or corporation wishing to set up a French bean scheme on some newly acquired land that in a few years' time will be abandoned because it is exhausted. You understand,' he continues, 'people here are traders by nature: they want goods in the door one day and out the next. No-one is interested in long-term investment; no-one is interested in developing a genuine agri-industry –

or any other industry for that matter. Why should they be? They are doing quite well as things are.'

This has all been delivered to me in the rapid, highly stylized French unique to Monsieur Adrosso which I can only just follow and which is responsible for the only partial state of comprehension that exists between us. Generally, this does not affect our relationship but, when it comes to more technical matters, it can cause problems. Indeed, so convoluted can our arrangements with him at times become, involving 'proformas', 'bids', 'mid-sea allowances', 'customs rebates', 'forecourt and full set-up differential percentages', that it is not surprising we have occasionally ended up with the wrong piece of equipment. This most recently and most disconcertingly occurred with the purchase of a rice de-husking machine. It is primarily about this that Salif and I have come to see him.

'The rice de-husker...' Salif, who is keen to get down to business, now intercedes.

'Ahhh... yes, yes, yes. The rice de-husker,' Monsieur Adrosso muses for a moment, then continues: 'Monsieur Salif, how many times do I have to tell you? You only have to adjust pressure on the control rack to get the husk out of the reject flue.' He waves his finger at him like a headteacher, then turns to me. 'They never listen,' he says. 'It doesn't matter how many times I tell them, they never listen.'

I glance over to Salif to see whether he is put out by Monsieur Adrosso's patronizing manner, but he is smiling. He knows, as I do, not to take Monsieur Adrosso too seriously. He now takes it on himself to explain the situation again. The fact is that we have had a number of people look at the machine, including Monsieur Adrosso's own mechanic, and it is obvious that we have not received the one we ordered, since this one is specifically adapted to produce little or no chaff, grinding the rice husks to dust instead of leaving them whole for use as livestock feed.

'The husk comes out of the reject flue okay, Monsieur

Adrosso,' Salif says patiently, 'but it is ground to a powder whichever setting you have the rack pressure on. Your mechanic told us himself that it can only be fixed by removing the rack altogether and replacing it with a different one.'

Monsieur Adrosso is waving his hand and shaking his head. 'No, no, no,' he says. Again he turns to me, as if imploring my sympathy. 'They just do not understand machinery,' he says. 'I tell you: there are no more than two or three people in this whole country who understand machines properly, and I'm one of them. But I'll tell you what I'll do, Monsieur Salif,' he says, addressing him again. 'I'll send my mechanic out to you again and make sure this time he knows what to do. OK?' he says, smiling.

The rice de-husker was an expensive piece of machinery that, along with helping farmers make their rice more marketable, was supposed to produce an income to pay some of the running costs of Salif's small development group. It has already been sitting idle for a year and a half. For me, this represents a failure and it is frustrating. 'What about getting a new rack?' I ask.

Monsieur Adrosso grabs a pile of specification manuals nearby and flips pointedly through them. 'See,' he says, 'this rack you talk of doesn't exist. I cannot find it. It doesn't exist.'

I look at Salif to see his reaction. It seems he does not think there is much choice left to him.

'Okay, Adrosso,' he says. 'Send your man.'

We do not stay long after this, just long enough to take a glass of tea. I had wanted to ask Monsieur Adrosso about prices for new Toyotas but Salif has made it clear he would rather I didn't. When it's time to leave, Monsieur Adrosso shakes our hands with enthusiasm and extracts a promise from us that, on our return to the capital to catch my flight out, we will come and have dinner with him. 'I will cook something extra special for you,' he says, smacking his lips. 'King prawns deep fried in batter. And some nice wine. But not for you,' he says, wagging his finger playfully at Salif. 'For you, only orange juice.'

Outside: searing sunlight and heat like a furnace. Amadou Tall is waiting patiently beside the Toyota. I drink deeply from the water bottle that has not left my side all morning. It is March, the end of the 'cool' season, and the temperature must be at least 100 degrees.

We set out on a trail around town looking for an injection pump for the Toyota, which now requires a push each time to start. This involves calling in at a number of spare-part dealers, visiting a couple of sidewalk garages, picking up a mechanic to take with us to another garage where there is a promise of a pump, breaking down, undergoing temporary mid-street repairs, picking up a garage-boy so entirely blackened from head to foot he looks like a Victorian chimneysweep, and finally ending up in an oil-soaked alleyway where 45 minutes of tinkering and hammering by a team of equally blackened men effects the repair we require. Here I dip, a wave of heat-induced feverishness overcoming me. We leave and cruise through town: past a shanty district, a forest of shiny satellite-dish poles rising above it; past the Presidential Palace snuggled closely up to the banks, the ministries and the military barracks; edging our way through the ever-thickening crowds towards the great Cinquième Market where my friend, Mousa Djeng, has a stall. When we can force our way forward no more, we abandon Amadou Tall and make our way by foot.

The Cinquième Market is a test of endurance. Its size and intensity – the heat and smell, the crush of people, the vast array of colors and sights – can easily give rise to a sense of claustrophobia. But I like it. The intensity draws me out of myself. I now no longer feel ill. I move, as though swimming, through the close-packed crowds. Sweat pours down my face. We come to the market, which is indistinguishable at first from the surrounding streets. I have no idea what area it covers, but inside there is an infinity of alleyways and covered passageways, each lined with stalls, each of which is piled high with merchandise: 5,000 plastic sandals; 200 meters of juju items; an alleyway of butchers' tables, their strings of blackened offal alive with flies.

Mousa Djeng's stall is in a wide, uncovered passageway. Down the middle of the passageway sit two rows of vegetable sellers: women in multi-colored dresses behind piles of okra and yams, cabbage and mushed onion balls. Down the sides are small boutiques, the turbaned owners of which hover in doorways with dusters in their hands, flicking stacks of suitcases or piles of shiny kitchen items. And in between each boutique, pressed up against a small patch of wall, are the undergarment sellers. One of these is Mousa Djeng. Like the others, his stall is tiny, consisting of only a small table on which are displayed his wares: underpants, handkerchiefs, vests, bras.

Mousa Djeng is Salif's brother-in-law. He is a farmer from Keniéba, Salif's village, and has sat in this market now for 12 years. Every day, every week, every month for 12 years he has sat in this passageway from early morning till dusk with its press of constantly passing humanity. Never anywhere have I experienced such temperatures as there are in this passageway. Open to the sunlight and closely hemmed in on all sides, the heat is like a hammer blow. I cannot imagine what it must be like in the summer months. And Mousa Djeng has no shade. He sits each day, the direct sunlight bouncing off his forehead. And all this for the most meagre of rewards, as not only does he have to pay rent to the boutique owner whose side wall he uses, but he also must pay both an official market rent and the bribe required by the market authority to allow him to continue occupying his 'illegal' spot. I often wonder just how on earth he survives. He has both a wife and children to support.

It is not these facts, however, that draw me to Mousa Djeng.

What has always made him so special and inspirational to me is simply the look on his face. For Mousa Djeng, whose pale, triangular face is almost oriental in its conformity, has – one can see from the quickest of glances – a compassion and humanity that is exceptional.

He rises from his stool as we approach. 'Monsieur Peter! Salif!' he exclaims, his face lit up. He offers me his seat and pulls another over from a neighboring stallholder for Salif. I see that he does not look well, his face puffy, with a yellowish tinge. Probably jaundice, a common ailment, I reflect. He has not looked well for a number of years.

Most of the other undergarment stallholders in the immediate vicinity are also from Keniéba. This is a little, urban outpost of the village. Mostly, they are young men. Some of them have stalls like Mousa Djeng, others have not graduated to that level of commerce yet and still carry their wares about with them. Everyone looks weary, but there is a palpable sense of camaraderie. Mousa Djeng introduces me to everyone, knowing full well, even though I have met many of them before, that I will not remember their names. He teases them into animation.

'Demba Son... you remember?' he says, a twinkle in his eye. 'You met him in the village fields the year before last... doesn't like to work too hard.' Or, indicating another young man squatting on the ground nearby with a case of wristwatches: 'Ibrahim Tall: a vagabond.' The young man in question smiles mischievously up at us, wagging his finger.

'No, no, no, Djeng,' he says.

I sit with them while Salif goes off in search of someone for whom he has a letter. I ask Mousa Djeng how his business is doing.

'Not so good,' he says, his face momentarily darkening. 'They have put rents up. There is little profit in it now.'

I suggest – half joking, half hopeful he might take up the idea, as it does not look to me as if he can last out here much longer – that perhaps he could go back to the village, take a plot in the irrigation scheme. 'Country life is good for you,' I say.

Mousa Djeng laughs gently. 'It is true. It is true,' is all he says, though.

We sit watching the press of people. As always with marketplaces, I am amazed at how few purchases one actually sees taking place. Now and again, you see someone pick an item up, feel it perhaps, try it against themselves for size, but they never actually seem to clinch a deal.

We are peaceful as we sit, mesmerized by the passing crowds, not feeling the need to converse. Later, when I ask Mousa Djeng whether he has sold anything today, he tells me that he has sold only one vest.

We take our leave when Salif comes back. As we are going, Mousa Djeng presses into my hand three handkerchiefs: a present. I do not want to accept them, especially having just heard that he has only sold one item today, but he will not countenance the slightest objection. 'They are for you… for you,' he repeats with emphasis.

Why is it that, whenever I leave Mousa Djeng, I feel always somehow that I have been blessed?

The sun is low over the town: at its feet the crowds are showing no sign of abating, the traffic at its most chaotic, gridlocking virtually every street. Salif and I pick our way through, stopping off in a street of freezers to see if we can find any reasonable second-hand ones. We do, but they are prohibitively expensive. This is a shame, as I have been wanting to buy a freezer for Salif's wife, Mariam, for a number of years. Electricity finally arrived in Keniéba this year and I know Mariam, who was brought up in a city, finds the summer heat, unrelieved by even as much as a cool drink, difficult.

The traffic and people thin out but we keep walking,

enjoying the soft light and reduced temperature. Later, we stop a taxi and get him to take us back to Amadou's. The serene, quiet district beside the sand dunes where Amadou lives seems a million miles from the madness of the Cinquième.

Evenings at Amadou's can be enlivening or desultory affairs, depending on people's moods. This evening, it seems, will not be enlivening. There are few people around and the inevitable television takes command. Amadou complains of a fever and is quiet most of the time, lying motionless and morose across the carpeted floor, flipping from one anodyne satellite channel to the next. I sit and do various bits of work. Later, we eat fried fish and chips from a large, shared platter, with our left hands. Then I turn in, on my foam mattress in the room that has kindly been put at my disposal.

2 Around Town

An audience with international bankers... The frustrations of the capital... State of the nation... Ramata's story... North Africa's tea ceremony... An Algerian tale

Being Friday, the Muslim holy day, the muezzin down the street is especially keen this morning: the chanting and singing starts at 3.30am and goes on for many hours. By the time I rise at 8.30am, I am exhausted.

We have a rendezvous with an acquaintance of Salif's this morning: Mustapha Demba, who works for one of the large international financial institutions so active and influential in Africa, a man whose brains I want to pick about the development project his organization is funding in the region of the south where we work. When we contacted him yesterday, however, he told us that his office was in the midst of hosting a delegation of the institution's officials who had come to review the project. He could arrange a meeting for us with the head of the delegation, he said.

I have long been aware of this multimillion-dollar project and the massive cynicism directed towards it by anyone who is not directly involved with its implementation and who is not poised to gain financially from it. I want to know if the man with overall responsibility for the project is aware that local people – whether farmers in the target region or ordinary citizens of the capital – regard it as simply another 'gravy train' for those in power. I am fascinated to see whether he is aware of the level of cynicism with which ordinary people in the country regard development projects, especially large, multimillion-dollar ones where the funds and activities are all channelled through local government *départements*.

Mustapha Demba has arranged our meeting for 10.30am, squeezing it into a 10-minute interlude in the visiting delegation's busy schedule.

We find the delegation in a smart hotel in a quiet part of town with which I am not familiar. It is the sort of hotel that can be found anywhere in the world: a building and an atmosphere that seals out any vestiges of the country it is in – five floors of reflective glass and a deep-chilled foyer of marble, clusters of comfy armchairs, piped music and suited businesspeople huddled in corners with well-dressed locals – the club of the élite.

Mustapha Demba meets us out front. He is a friendly, obliging man, always seemingly a little harassed.

'They're running late,' he tells us breathlessly. 'Monsieur Alzane is the program commissioner responsible for the southern development initiative. He will be out soon. It is he who is leading the delegation for whom we are chairing this seminar. I have arranged for you to meet him directly after the round-table fiscal meeting and before he is due to address the delegates in the conference hall. He understands that Salif here is involved in agricultural development in the region and is very keen to meet him. Unfortunately, you will only have a few minutes as we are already behind schedule.'

We take seats in a vacant cluster of armchairs and await developments. The hotel foyer is large and permeated by an air of calm. In town, there may be heat and dust and urban mayhem, but here people drift about as though remote-controlled; whispers of conversations float across the space like flurries of autumn leaves. Salif looks relaxed. Then suddenly there is a hum of commotion at a door beside the expansive reception desk. People are spilling out of a meeting room: a swirl of bobos and suits, animated faces and clasped hands. I see Mustapha Demba, his face shiny, smiling and laughing in a group. Then he is steering the group in our direction: three men, two in suits, one wearing a white bobo almost as immaculate as Salif's. They join us and Monsieur Alzane, a Tunisian, is introduced to us. He is a compact, middle-aged man with an engaging smile. The two other men are introduced as the assistant program commissioner – a tall American – and the regional program facilitator, a smartly dressed Moor who eyes us suspiciously.

The meeting, as promised, is brief. At first there is a little awkwardness, as it is unclear who should take the lead. Eventually Salif is persuaded to do so. He explains the work we are involved in, and then Monsieur Alzane, taking the initiative, questions him closely on many details. The American chips in with a few polite queries. The regional program facilitator remains silent. Time is already nearly out and Monsieur Alzane, now shaking Salif's hand, is tying up with: 'It has been very interesting to meet you. We are here for no other purpose than to help develop agriculture in your region. It is of vital importance that local people are included in this process, and I hope you will make yourself known to the Project Office. Our regional program officer here,' he says, smiling at the Moor, 'will, I'm sure, be happy to meet with you.' The man in question looks anything but enthralled.

I have not yet managed to say much but take the opportunity as the meeting breaks up to address Monsieur Alzane a little to the side. I am not sure how to start and so simply say that people in the south are very skeptical about the ability of the project to deliver any results.

'They do not trust those responsible for implementing the project,' I say.

Monsieur Alzane fixes me with a look of great earnestness. 'That is true,' he says. 'And it is not surprising, as there have been many mistakes in the past. But that is one of the primary objectives of this project: to develop effective delivery systems and restore confidence. What we need is good people, men like your friend here. Send him to us. It is people like him we need.'

I tell him that I will ask him and mention that I have spoken to farmers in the south who say the project benefits are not reaching them.

Monsieur Alzane stays focused. 'It is still early days,' he says. 'Much has changed with us over the last few years and we have introduced new practices. Tell your friend to have confidence in us. It is not easy, but we are doing things differently this time.' Mustapha Demba is at our elbows now, and it is time for Monsieur Alzane to go. With a brief nod of his head, he is off. The assistant program commissioner, the American, politely shakes both my and Salif's hands, but the regional program manager – the 'minder' – is already halfway across the foyer.

Outside, Salif and I decide to walk for a while. We send Amadou Tall ahead to await us at the house of a friend of Salif's whom we wish to visit. The streets here are paved and relatively free of traffic, and, as we walk, we talk. We are strangely inspired by the meeting, perhaps because it brings into focus how simple and effective the work we do is when compared with the Machiavellian complications of doing development work at the level of large international institutions. Salif was impressed by Monsieur Alzane. It was difficult not to be. His charm and natural authority were infectious. I ask Salif if he thinks things might be different this time, but his response is short: 'No.'

'Why not?' I ask

'Because things never change here,' he replies.

'Why not?' I repeat.

'Because it is always the same men in charge. There are too many *interests* for there to be any change. Even the President has little control.'

'But there is much development in Nouakchott,' I say, playing devil's advocate. 'There are buildings going up everywhere. I even heard they are building two new Sheraton Hotels.' And indeed this is true: Nouakchott is on a vast growth spurt, with new districts, shiny banks and market arcades appearing as though overnight. There is money about – of this there is no doubt.

Salif smiles.

'The hotels! Yes, it is true,' he says. 'But it does not mean much. It is all private money. Nothing is done for the city or the poor.'

Again, this is true. There is a free-for-all here, as everyone knows, with the country's resources – fish, iron ore, oil, land – being sold off to the highest bidder by the clan-based Moorish business cartels who, in cahoots with the military, vie with each other for control of the country. A top five per cent garner large sums, some of which they might at least now invest in their own country – not an occurrence that would have taken place only a few years ago. But, as Monsieur Adrosso pointed out the day before, they do not invest in anything as fiddly as industry or other long-term investments, preferring the hothouse of the property market or other such quick-money returns. The city may indeed be booming in one sense – and the vast amounts of vehicles visible and goods for sale indicate at least some sort of trickle-down – but there is almost zero municipal spending, presumably because the few taxes that are collected are not prioritized for such things as drainage systems, roads, sewers or traffic control.

The city, indeed, is a dump: even those areas that might by some stretch of the imagination be termed middle-class,

where hectares of large whitewashed, concrete buildings have sprung up, are surrounded by nothing but a wasteland of sand, refuse, dead animals and, anywhere near the rainy season, fetid pools of water. Indeed, for three weeks during the rainy season last year much of the entire city was under a foot of sewer-filled water. Other than in the fortified compounds of the foreign embassies, there are no parks in the capital; indeed, again, outside the quartiers of the rich and their foreign backers, there is barely a single tree at all. All in the city is private. The poor majority live off the scraps in their vast shanties of squalor: ignored, subjugated, controlled. There are no revolutions taking place here. As Salif said, even the President has little control.

I ask Salif whether he thinks Monsieur Alzane – as implicated as he and his institution assuredly are with the regime that controls the country – is himself personally honest; whether he actually believes that the huge investment his institution is making in the south will not, in the traditional manner, simply be frittered away in a labyrinthine bureaucratic process designed to line the pockets of the élite. Salif is unsure.

'Most people believe in what they are doing,' he says. And it is true. Monsieur Alzane no doubt believes that he and his institution can bring about change here. But the truth is, it is not in the interest of those who are benefiting from this change to look too deeply into the direction in which it is going. In a couple of years' time Monsieur Alzane will be moved on to another job and what goes on here then will no longer be his concern. That is the reality.

We are two cynics, Salif and I: crabby and indignant, perhaps, but also incensed at what we learn and see. It is always like this in the capital: complicated, frustrating. Once we are out in the countryside with the farmers, everything becomes simpler.

Midday, and the sun is directly overhead, all color bleached from our surroundings. By the time we reach the dusty backstreet in the busy, commercial part of town where Salif's friend, Sheik, has his compound, I am gritting my teeth and forcing my feet to carry me forwards. We enter a rusty metal door, and Salif calls out a greeting. In a moment Sheik's wife appears, a tall, slim lady who greets us warmly and directs us across the small compound to the lounge.

The lounge is a simple room, comfortable with gaudy-colored divans lining the walls, purple carpeting and, at the far end, a glass-fronted cabinet, empty save for a few Arabic books and a plastic football trophy. In a corner on a small table is a computer with a cloth draped over it. Although the room feels spacious, it is not particularly large and suffers the disadvantage of having a corrugated-iron roof, the heated metal of which creates furnace-like conditions. Regardless, we collapse into the divans, and shortly Sheik appears.

Sheik is an old colleague of Salif's from the days when they worked for the national mining company in the north. An older man of Moorish extraction, he is tall and thin, with wild grey hair and the air of a disorientated professor. He peers at us over his spectacles and greets us profusely, holding my hands for an extended period, repeating: 'Ah, Peter, Peter... Ah, Peter...' as though he were giving himself time to catch up with the speed of events. He has obviously just woken up.

Sheik teaches economics at a college nearby and is, by his own description, 'a minor intellectual'. He also owns a small copy shop and takes in lodgers in order to supplement an income that is patently inadequate. His passion is politics, and he is a leading figure in one of the many small opposition parties, many of which were banned for years.

Salif and I have been visiting Sheik for a number of years and the first thing that always occurs is the protracted business of providing each of us with a drink. There are choices. Often we go for the easier option of sodas, the bottles of which are fetched from a nearby boutique by any easily locatable local boy or, if they are available, one of his student lodgers. His wife is never implicated in these proceedings. Once the bottles of Coke or Fanta have appeared, glasses must then be found and washed out, a small tray on which to serve them produced, and drinks poured ceremoniously. Sheik conducts all these proceedings with a firm but gracious authority, rolling up his sleeves to do the pouring himself. When he insists we go for the more complex alternative of home-mixed powdered milk or hibiscus drink, however, considerable amounts of time can elapse, because these require many implements and ingredients – water, sugar, blocks of ice, jugs, whisks, glasses and spoons – few of which are ever readily available. However, once all is completed and Sheik has mixed and stirred and tested to his satisfaction, we sit back and relax.

Conversations at Sheik's, not surprisingly, quickly turn political. But this is no man of seething sedition, filled with embittered ideology. Sheik's gradual downward trajectory, from a high point of influence in some earlier government, has been conducted with grace and objectivity. He views the current political situation as no more than farcical and his modest personal circumstances as merely unfortunate. When I mention our recent meeting with Monsieur Alzane and the institution for which he works, he is eloquent.

'That institution has been here for 30 years,' he says. 'Three years ago, they gave $22.5 million for a major municipal infrastructure program. Already, during the planning phase, $14 million, two-thirds of the total, have been *gorged*,' – this last word emphasized with great élan – 'and the remaining $8.5 million are in the process of being massacred. Then, at the beginning of last year, a delegation from the institution came here to see the progress of the project and, in their own words, as reported in the press, went away "well pleased with all they had seen". The whole nation was astounded… a-s-t-o-u-n-d-e-d, I tell you,' he repeats, enunciating the word, his face lit up with the sheer, beautiful incredulity of it.

'This country is in a mess,' he goes on. 'It is like this across much of Africa. The resource boom is producing growth rates in many countries that are impressive – very impressive. And in some countries there may even be some proper development – and by this I mean the development of good governance, of jobs and manufacturing and industry – but for most, and certainly for us here, it means only a short-term feast that puts wealth and power in the hands of people in whose interest it is to subjugate their populations. This sort of development leads only to greater poverty and divide, even to civil war: consequences naturally that are enabled and abetted by those who wish to invest in such places. Not that we have got to that here yet, thanks be to Allah; not that we are incapable of it…' and on he continues for a while, shaking his head and twinkling his eyes long after his French has lost me. But I get the drift. On the subject of state higher education, which comes up a little later, he is equally eloquent.

'The university here is weak – practically non-existent,' he says disapprovingly. 'Those who finish their third year and wish to go on for a masters – and anything less than a masters is worthless here – find it practically impossible without private wealth, as they must go abroad and state grants are very few. And anyway, there are few jobs here for graduates now as the civil service is filled with businesspeople... businesspeople, I ask you. Those who get the very best grades...' he continues, but gets no further as at this moment his wife pops her head in the door and asks if we will partake of the midday meal. We thank her but say that we can't as we promised yesterday that we would take it with Mousa Djeng.

Sheik does not resume his theme when his wife has gone. Instead, he remains staring at the floor for a while, nodding, a seraphic smile spread across his face. Presently, the mood passes and he looks up.

'Tell me of Ramata,' he says to Salif. 'How is Ramata?'

Ramata is Salif's eldest child whom I have known since she was young, the neat, prettily presented child I had seen in the bush taxi all those years ago. Now 25 and living on the outskirts of Paris, she was at one time one of Sheik's student lodgers. Salif looks uncomfortable.

'Ramata is well,' he replies.

'She is married?' Sheik prompts.

'Yes. She is married... to a Senegalese.'

Ramata is a bright, attractive young lady but her story troubles Salif. Salif is a traditional man in as much as he believes in values such as family, respect and filial duty. He has always treated his seven children, and especially the boys, with great – if clearly loving – firmness. These values, however, do not encompass all that is traditional and in many ways Salif is also a modern man. He despises tribalism and all that it does to undermine so much in Africa, he is non-racist, and he is a hands-on father in a way unusual in Africa.

As a result, when it came to Ramata's education, because she showed promise, it did not occur to him for a minute not to spend heavily just because she was a girl. So Ramata, having successfully passed through local primary and secondary schools, came to the capital to attend college.

It took her five years to pass her baccalaureate, or bac, and this was not because she was less academically able in any way, but because, for two years in a row, the results of the exam were so undermined by wealthy parents paying for good results for their offspring that the international baccalaureate board nullified all results in the country. This was a hard time for Ramata as it meant that she had to prepare for and take the exams three years in a row – not that her distress was ever apparent, for she maintained into adulthood the same serene composure that she always had as a child. Each time we came to Sheik's, she would appear, with immaculate manners, looking as serene and well presented as a model on a catwalk.

All this time, of course, Salif was paying not only for her education, which was only partially state-funded, but also for her lodgings and living. And then, when she did finally pass her exams, she had to wait a whole further year for her application for a university grant to be processed, only to hear that, despite having passed the bac in the top 10 per cent, no grant was available for her. With a little help from me, Salif somehow now managed to rustle up enough money not only for a passport, visa and air ticket but also for the fees to study computing at a small university in France. After a year, Ramata was earning enough by working in a fast-food restaurant in the evenings to pay for her own living expenses; after two years, she was covering some of her own tuition fees as well. After her third year, she was only attending college part-time and had a full-time job and resident's permit. She was now financially independent of Salif, and it was only some 12 months ago that she announced she was going to marry a young Senegalese man she had met in France. This came as a shock to Salif and put his 'modernity' to the test, for not only were the young man and his family completely unknown to him, but also his permission for the marriage had not been sought.

For all Salif's disdain of tribalism, the fact is that the Senegalese man is a Wolof, not a Peul, and Salif would prefer that this was not the case. It is virtually unheard of for people of Salif's background to marry outside their ethnic group. Indeed, it is pretty rare for them to marry outside the extended family, but to marry someone from an entirely different people is exceptional. And for it to be done in such a manner, without any consultation or permission being sought... It does test Salif. He does not like it, but the fact is, he has given his blessing for the marriage, and I think perhaps the greatest sadness he and Mariam, his wife, feel is that it almost certainly means Ramata does not intend ever to come back to Mauritania to live.

Sheik smiles sympathetically at Salif's hesitant reply.

'Ramata... Ramata... Yes, she always did know what she wanted,' he muses. 'A girl who knew where she was going.'

Sheik sees us to the door of his compound when we leave. Here he clasps my hand. 'You will come back,' he says. 'Yes, yes, you will come back...' But already I can see that he has moved on; his mind is elsewhere. It cannot be easy, I think, being Sheik.

The Toyota is parked across the alleyway. We make our way across town to the populous Cinquième district where Mousa Djeng, with whom we are to pass the afternoon, lives.

Mousa Djeng's home is in one of the old residential buildings that date from the first major expansion of the city after the colonial era, 40-odd years ago. Constructed of brick, the building is substantial and solid and houses two floors of rooms facing an inner courtyard strung with washing. In each room is a family or a group of students or workmates or any combination of those who can scrape together enough to pay the low rent. There is no running water, sporadic electricity, a squad of ducks living on the roof, and only two toilets for the 70 or 80 residents.

Mousa Djeng lives with his wife and five children in a room on the ground floor. For a number of years this is where I used to stay on my visits. It was not easy, as the building was particularly noisy, with babies crying, music blaring and arguments going on all night. The mosquitoes were bad, the room airless and the toilets unpleasant. But what was lost in physical comfort was surpassed in kindness and welcome. Always, clean sheets would be produced, the room would be fumigated against mosquitoes, and when I looked tired in the evening, the room would be cleared of people, Mousa Djeng and his family sleeping with neighbors.

Mousa Djeng's wife, Salif's sister Fatimata, is a woman with that same blend of strength and tenderness of eye I knew in her, and in Salif's mother, all those years before. She produces a traditional midday meal of white rice, vegetables and fish in a large metal bowl around which we all gather to eat. The food is delicious, a stew of fresh catfish, carrots, okra and aubergine ladled over a bed of rice. Mousa Djeng is attentive, depositing juicy morsels of fish he has pulled from the carcass in front of me like offerings. We eat our fill, then, having washed hands, sit back while tea is made.

There are 10 of us present: me, Salif and the ever-present, but mostly silent Amadou Tall; Mousa Djeng, Fatimata, and two of their children; a couple of young men and a young woman I don't know; and Mustapha, a small, skinny cousin of Salif's who is a military nurse at the main hospital in town and who is inclined to attach himself to me whenever I am in town.

Amadou Tall sets about making the tea, performing the same methodical tea ceremony that is not only being repeated in virtually every room in every house in the city, but also in the majority of houses across the Sahara and West Africa. First, he gathers the required ingredients and implements, most of which are to hand: the tea tin, the  two tiny glasses, the small metal teapot. A bowl for slops is produced; so too are fresh mint, a large mug of water and the sugar. A small aluminium brazier with a few pieces of glowing charcoal is brought in. In tens of millions of rooms the same actions are taking place with only minimal variations, depending on the availability of mint, or using bottled gas instead of charcoal, or sugar coming in lumps rather than loose: rich, poor; urban, rural; Moors, southern tribes; in palaces and desert camps; fuel for busy merchants or stimulant for the addicted. The long hot hours of the afternoon, the long empty days of poverty, pass to the metronomic dance of the tea-maker's hands.

Three times the tea is made from the same tea leaves, added to the heated water, stewed, sweetened, tasted and poured from teapot to glass, glass to glass and back to pot again. Once a good head of froth has been produced, and all implements have been rinsed of any stickiness, the glasses, containing an inch of extremely strong, sweet tea beneath the froth, are handed around on the tray, replenished for each new person who is required to drain his or her glass in a succession of quick, noisy sups. These are the bare bones of the operation, but the art and brilliance, the mesmeric play, is in just how elegantly, how apparently effortlessly and how daringly it is carried out. It is true that for some the operation is simply a function, and in fact most, being modest, would profess it to be little else. But the speed and precision that are applied to the mixing process, pouring the tea into the glasses from ever greater heights at ever greater speeds until the hands and the glass and the teapot are barely more than a blur, belie this. The neat, precise manner in which every part of the operation is performed, from managing the charcoal to handling the often red-hot teapot, to measuring the tea and sugar, tell you there is much more to this than just the quenching of thirst. The best practitioners are those who can drag out the production of the three brews all afternoon or evening. And when the short, sweet explosion of hot liquid does eventually burst in your mouth, it feels good and gives a zest to all those long idle hours.

Mustapha, the military nurse, is sitting uncomfortably close to me. To distract him, I prompt him to tell the story of the time he was in Algeria, where he was sent to train in radiography, a story most of us know well but few tire of hearing.

'There were 22 of us sent there,' he says without hesitation. 'We were sent there for different reasons, although I was in the radiology department. At that time the troubles in the country were still bad and when we arrived we were taken from the airport to the city in buses with blacked-out windows. Sometimes at night we would even hear bombs exploding. We were there for two years and were only allowed to leave the military hospital where we worked once in the last week. Only once in two years,' he goes on, giggling a little now, 'were we allowed to leave. And we went to the cinema. But one of our group... one of our group did not like the film we were going to see, so he... he...' he chokes out, his giggles getting the better of him, 'he stayed... stayed back at the hospital.' Everywhere people are chuckling, as they know what is coming. 'He stayed back at the hospital...' Mustapha goes on, 'because... because... because he didn't like the film.' People are rolling around now, Mousa Djeng holding his stomach as though in pain. 'He... he...' Mustapha just manages to blurt out, 'he thought it would be boring.'

It's too much. People are rolling backwards and forwards with laughter, tears streaming down their faces. 'Boring...' Mustapha repeats again, 'too boring.' All those days and years of boredom, all those hours of hardship are forgotten, as though they never were.

We return to Amadou's as the evening is drawing in. Here there is a scene not dissimilar to the one we have just left: a compressed get-together. Amadou is over his fever of the previous evening and is presiding cross-legged before some tea-making implements. Amadou is a meticulous tea maker and conducts the proceedings with all the precision of his engineer's training.

'You're going tomorrow?' he asks Salif as he pours tea from a great height into a glass, guillotining the steaming thread at just the right moment.

'Insh'Allah,' Salif replies: God willing.

Amadou mixes from glass to glass. 'When will you be back?' he asks.

'In about nine days,' Salif says.

'You saw Adrosso today,' he asks, concentrating on his tea making.

'Yesterday,' Salif replies.

'And his mechanic will fix the de-husker?'

'He's going to send him out again,' Salif says.

Amadou chuckles, shaking his head. 'Adrosso. Ha! A joker – a bandit,' he says.

'Perhaps,' Salif replies a little stiffly, 'but we can only do what we can do.'

Amadou abruptly changes his tone. 'Of course,' he says. 'Of course. Surely you will be able to fix the de-husker.' Salif is older than Amadou. He is also head of the family. The respect in which Amadou holds Salif, and his deference to him, however, stem from much more than just this.

3 Road to the South

The sand-dune sea... Incident in a bush taxi...
Roadblock savvy... Salif's story... The women's
irrigation co-operative... A trip to Casamance...
Plea for a dying town... A US company's land grab...
Survival in a changing climate... Kaédi – routine
disaster zone

We are leaving for Keniéba. This is a journey I have made
many times, and little has changed since the earliest days.
The main difference now is that the tarmac road, instead of
running out as soon as it hits the South, goes all the way to
Kaédi, the main regional town. The route is beautiful. Once
the last tattered remains of the capital have been shaken off,
the road runs true and pure, laid flat like a ribbon over an
endless sea of sand dunes. The sand dunes are ranked into a
succession of huge swells, like those in an ocean, in between
which are long pale valleys. All is golden, the pale gold of the
valleys contrasting with the deep gold of the dunes.

Driving down the open road into one of the wide valleys,
then speeding up the far side towards the crest of the next range
of dunes – with always the added excitement that a vehicle
might appear over the blind summit on the wrong side of the
road at just the wrong moment – is exhilarating. You can lose
yourself and your thoughts far out in the milky sea of sand. The
world here is clean and clear, and always I get the urge to call
a halt to the vehicle, climb out and embrace all that I can see.

The road is constantly under siege from the dunes, with a squad of huge diggers tasked to keep it clear. Scuttling back and forth like crabs on the seashore, the diggers maneuver each dune, helping it, like an old lady, over the road.

Later, after some 300 kilometers, the dunes peter out and the road, which up to now has been running due east, turns south. Now the land is flat and gravelly: a totally unremarkable but still beautiful plain of grey, in between the empty horizons roamed by the goat-, cattle- and camel-herders. Sometimes the concentrations of livestock are greater, sometimes less, depending on the time of year. Earlier in the year, if the rains have been good, the herders will keep further north, but as the pastures are exhausted, or if the rains have failed, they will move southwards where the grasses are fuller. Some are proud desert people with great herds of camels, their odd, pale, cavernous beasts looking prehistoric as they mill about a waterhole. Most are the poorer Black Moors, the Harratin, who, if they are lucky, will have a handful of thin cattle and a herd of sheep and goats. There are tents and camps and small windblown communities. Then, in the South, where the road once again turns east, pretty Peul and Soninke villages start to

appear: close-knit warrens of dung-smoothed houses from which large, brightly colored mosques rear. This is the true Sahel, where cultures, customs and climates meet, merge and clash.

Until we had our own vehicle this journey was always completed in a share-taxi. The downside of this was that the journey could take as much as 15 hours. The upside was the intimacy and camaraderie that can always be found in share-taxis. Each journey is an adventure. Each one never fails to take you to the limit of your endurance. But before any of this, the taxi-park has first to be negotiated.

Each major destination in the country has its own taxi-park in which the share-taxis queue for customers on a first-come, first-served basis. Anything up to 70 of these Peugeots or Mercedes will be ranked in each taxi-park, with a taxi-park chief and a ticket seller in charge.

I remember the start of one particular journey. As usual, Salif and I arrived at the taxi-park early in the hope of catching the first vehicle, but, as usual, we were not early enough. Already the first Peugeot was fully charged and ready to go. In the second, five of its nine places were already sold. Having ourselves taken a further two, this left only two seats. A further hour passed before these were filled, during which time the ranks of young merchandise sellers with their trays of Chinese goods plied their trade, successfully getting money off Salif for first a comb, then a torch and then a pair of sunglasses. Once it was confirmed that all the tickets were sold, the negotiations as to what was going to go onto the roof and how much it would cost began: two goats in a sack; two sacks of grain; four chickens tied by the feet. With each addition, the vehicle sank lower on its axle. The ticket seller was theatrical. One moment laughing, the next shouting, the next sullen or absent, he played the scene to perfection, rebuffing overtures of conciliation from his hierarchical competitor, the taxi-park chief, pulling items already on the roof off in an apparent fury, only finally accepting a compromise when it became apparent that everyone had had enough.

Once this was over, a standoff took place between two passengers over who should sit in the front – it was significant where you sat in the vehicle, the back row being more cramped than the second row, which was not as good as the front. An older man – a rough country farmer type in a skullcap and coarse tunic – had seated himself on the window side of the front passenger seat; an elderly lady already occupied the other half of the seat. There he sat, a look of wooden determination on his face, ignoring the ticket seller. 'Monsieur,' the ticket seller kept repeating, 'you must get up and vacate this place. It has already been reserved.' A businessman with a briefcase and a safari suit stood glowering nearby.

The man in the vehicle continued to stare determinedly ahead of him.

'I said: Monsieur, you must give up this seat,' the ticket seller repeated.

'Why should I give up the seat?' the man snapped.

'Because this Monsieur here reserved it when he bought his ticket.'

'There was nothing reserving the seat when I took it,' the man replied, returning his gaze to the middle distance and ignoring anything more that was said. The ticket seller, a man who knew when he had met his match, closed the door and turned back to the businessman. 'You had better take a place in the back,' he said.

The businessman, however, was incensed. Stepping forward and tapping loudly on the vehicle window, he snapped: 'Vacate your seat, Monsieur. You are holding up the vehicle. What are you? Are you a fool? I reserved the seat. It is not your place.'

The man stared stonily before him, ignoring him.

'Is he a fool? What is he doing?' the businessman, furious

now, complained to those around, then turned back to the ticket seller and demanded to see the taxi-park chief. The chief was nowhere to be found just then, however, so he stalked off to a nearby tea stall where he sat huffily down on a bench.

The rest of the passengers were patient. The situation was absurd, and they discussed it, half laughingly, with each other and with any number of bystanders. Attempts were made to persuade either party to back down. Neither would countenance it, the man in the vehicle mulishly ignoring all suggestions, the businessman too angry now to compromise. It was suggested that the elderly lady in the other half of the seat should be moved to the middle row so that both men could sit in the front, but she was infirm and it had taken some considerable difficulty to get her there in the first place. The impasse continued, then the taxi-park chief appeared.

'Why hasn't this vehicle gone?' he shouted, imposing himself on the scene; then, once he was filled in, continued wildly: 'It should be gone. It's blocking the way. Where's the driver? Get him to move it out of the way.' The driver, however, had gone off with a shrug some time earlier. The chief was angry. He pulled the taxi door open and shouted at the man.

'What are you doing? I will call the police. Get out now.'

He made a half-hearted attempt to pull the man out, which the man fended off like a flustered stork. 'Don't touch me,' he yelped.

'Take his bags off the roof,' the taxi-park chief cried. 'Take them off.' No-one moved to obey him, so he marched off, saying he would fetch the police.

Time was passing, and a crowd had gathered. It was obvious that pride was now at stake. I would not perhaps have remembered this incident were it not for the fact that it was Salif who sorted it out. You could see that the man in the taxi – a country fellow who might never have been to the city before – felt threatened and confused by his surroundings. He did not want to be 'shown up'. Speaking gently, with infinite patience, and addressing him as he would an elder, Salif asked simply that the man take a place in the back so that we could all begin our long journey. This was enough. The deference and respect in Salif's tone was genuine, and it brought the man out of himself. With no more ado he simply climbed out and took his place in the back.

It is Friday, the Muslim holy day, and the city is busy as we head out of town for our destination in the south. There are parliamentary and council elections due shortly in the country and, all along the side of the roads, we pass large billboards advertising parties and their candidates. There are a few women among these, but the majority are men, all wearing dark business suits, and all are of Moorish extraction. Their slogans unanimously trumpet that new, shiny buzzword: transparency.

It is the beginning of the weekend and the *patrons* or bosses are off out of town to their country retreats. These will be well-decked-out tents where dependants and retainers will be waiting with herds of camels specially brought in so that the *patron* and his guests can have fresh camel's milk. They bomb past us in the smartest of overland vehicles. Wheezing lorries struggle up the hills of dunes like old men, billowing out black smoke, colorful tribes of people perched atop their laden backs. Open-backed Toyota Landcruisers – the favored means of transport for true desert folk, with water *guerbas* slung camel-style from their sides and netting holding down the baggage in their backs – stream past, a hunch of turbaned men straining into the wind above their cabs. Occasionally, we pass large articulated trucks coming in the other direction, laden to double their height with hay or wood or sacks of charcoal. These are the true 'ships of the desert', rumbling out across the plains, from country to country, from south to north and east to west, linking ports and markets, bringing the plastic items of the outside world in, transporting 10,000 calabashes.

As we progress, the traffic thins until, after some hours, for much of the time we have the road to ourselves. Amadou Tall drives cautiously: we cannot anyway go very fast. He is adept at managing the many roadblocks where police or military or sometimes customs officers check the legality of vehicles, people or goods, often in competition with each other. Smart vehicles, those obviously owned by *patrons*, simply cruise slowly straight through the blocks, a friendly wave perhaps to the police or customs officers. Amadou Tall, too, likes to try this, only he knows that in our half-wrecked vehicle we are by no means guaranteed success. Each block is a gamble. Slowing down too much as we approach shows a lack of confidence; on the other hand, vehicles are supposed to come to a complete standstill a hundred meters off the roadblock before approaching at walking pace. This means he risks censure if he comes too fast and lack of credibility if he goes too slow. But Amadou Tall was not a truck driver for nothing. He knows how to gauge each block. Sometimes he will pull up and, if requested, we will dutifully present our IDs; at others he cruises right on through. Only occasionally does he get it wrong. Amadou Tall can be tough, though, and negotiates fiercely against any 'fines' the police or soldiers wish to impose. For him, it's all in a day's work.

These days, the only occasion such 'rules' of the road do not apply is when encountering the new militaristic police force, created recently to shore up the regime's control – a disciplined and well-armed cohort of stern-faced young men who can appear suddenly and anywhere. No-one – *patrons*, ordinary people, even the regular police – messes with them, for they do not know the meaning of 'negotiation'.

We drive for four hours, which brings us to Boutilimit, the first and only town we encounter before we reach the South. The place is a hive of commerce spread out in a wide sand

valley and concentrated on the road that passes through its midst. Turbaned men; sharp, desert faces; haggling; piles and mounds of merchandise; donkey-carts struggling under massive loads; laughter, shouts; the smell of dust and spice: we push our way down the road, which has become a market for the crowd of merchants who seemingly need only to move goods from one side of it to the other to make a profit. Here there are many restaurants: open-sided tents with mats on the ground where tea and food is served. We are keen for a stop here, as after four hours we need a break. We stagger into one of the restaurants. Here Salif orders tea and roasted meat. It's sweaty and the sunlight outside the shade of the tent is a blinding white. A few other travellers are flopped down on the grubby mats on which flies are scattered like currants. Nearby, the meat roaster grins under his turban as he stands sweating before his blackened burner. A tea boy is working at a succession of teapots. A large woman with a grubby infant playing in the dust by her side presides over a cauldron of rice, doling ladlefuls onto platters onto which a few pieces of gristle in a sauce are added. People share their platters, insisting that complete strangers join them, as no-one likes to eat alone: it just does not feel right.

It was here in this town at one of these roadside restaurants that, many years ago, Salif first told me something of his background.

He was born in a herders' camp in the bush, not far from Keniéba, he told me. His family was traditionally of the teacher/holy-man caste. In those days, though, he said, life was not as it is now. Even small families had cattle herds 200 strong. Thousand-strong herds were not uncommon. The countryside, he said, was so well forested then that you could travel half a day barely leaving the shade of the trees – now, of course, most of the trees have either died or been cut for firewood. The rains were more dependable then, he said, and people had plenty to eat.

People were proud and strong then, fattened on cow's milk and the couscous they made from their rain-fed millet. Not that life was without difficulty. People had to work hard, but they were proud and had surplus food to take them through the bad years.

Of his six siblings, Salif was the one chosen to be educated. From the age of eight he was sent to Keniéba to attend both primary and Qur'anic schools. This did not excuse him from family chores, however, and every day he would have to walk the 15 kilometers there and back, helping out with the sheep and goats when he got home. It was not easy. At weekends, he said, he would be out with them in the bush. Herding the sheep and goats was the job of the boys. From the earliest of ages, he and his brothers were charged with taking them out for the day to graze. Often, they'd be out from dawn to dusk, the long hot day relieved only by the water container they carried and perhaps a roasted corncob. One day, when he was about six, Salif got lost.

'It was nearing dusk and my brothers and I were heading home when one of the goats became separated from the rest,' he said. 'I went after it, not expecting to have any difficulty in bringing it back. But, for some reason, the animal seemed determined to get itself lost and soon I was fighting my way through an area of thick scrub. I was too far from my brothers to alert them now, and anyway I still thought that at any moment I would catch up with the goat. On I went, always sure I would soon catch the beast, chasing after it as the dusk thickened. Gradually, however, it became harder to see and soon I lost track of the beast altogether. I decided to turn back but was unsure now of the direction and went the wrong way.'

'It was not long before I was lost,' Salif continued. 'When night fell I did not know what to do so I lay down on the sand and slept. The next day at dawn my father found me. They had been looking all night.'

Salif was exceptionally bright and not only did well at primary school, passing the exams to enter the Lycée in Kaédi, but from there he made it on to, first, college in the capital, and then, having passed his baccalaureate with good grades, further education in the south of France. There he studied bookkeeping and accountancy for a placement with the national mining company. He lived and worked in the north of Mauritania at the mining company for 18 years. In that time, five of his surviving six children were born, but during the whole period he was never once put up for promotion. People he had arrived with from college moved on up the hierarchy, some even becoming directors. Many, many others, arriving long after him, also passed on up. Being a Black African from the South, he was effectively barred from promotion. In the end, he'd had enough and he requested early retirement. This was a vital point. If his request was accepted, it meant he would be paid his retirement entitlement, which he could use to set himself up in business back home. If his request was rejected, he would have to resign, meaning he would get nothing. 'For a year and a half my application sat in an in-tray,' Salif said. 'In the end, they gave me nothing. I worked for them for 18 years and I got nothing.'

The noise of the wind and its desiccated, blow-dryer heat coming in through the Toyota's open window is exhausting and it comes almost as something of a relief when, later in the day, we break down: silence; the condensed heat of mid-afternoon; a patch of virgin desert, ours for the while.

It's the starter-motor, of course. The 'new' one is no good. Amadou Tall is unfazed. He tinkers about the engine. We peer in with suggestions. We try the ignition. Nothing. Time passes. At no moment does Salif or Amadou Tall look concerned. I am, though. Even if we manage to get the vehicle going now – and I'm quite sure we will, as when did I ever fail to make it to my destination when travelling in Africa? – we have a lot to accomplish over the next 10 days, and I do not think this vehicle is going to manage for us. The day after tomorrow we have our development consultant arriving to lead the two-day seminar. I do not want to be transporting him on a donkey-cart.

The vehicle coughs into life and we clamber in.

Villages and small towns are more frequent now. Most of them are unprepossessing collections of cement and mud buildings scattered like abandoned bricks on the empty plains. One of these is Danodine, where we stop off as Salif wishes to see a solar-powered irrigation project we have heard about, run by a women's co-operative.

Danodine looks deserted as we approach it over the plain. We find a solitary old man wrapped in his turban against the wind in one of the wide, wind-driven spaces that seem to make up most of the town. We draw up beside him.

'Where is everybody?' we ask, having first greeted him with the ritualistic enquiries after health and well-being of family.

The old man points to the south. 'At the gardens,' he says.

We head on and soon see some movement in the heat haze in a depression beyond the edge of town. The movement turns into a dash of color, which in turn becomes a crowd of women working in an area of fenced-in vegetable plots. Nearby is a bank of eight solar panels and a well.

The women greet us but are busy about their work, carrying water to and from a large cistern. They are playful and smile and giggle at us but do not stop. We ask for the president of the co-operative and before long a tall, shy-looking woman with watery eyes appears. We greet her politely and Salif asks her some questions: how does the system work? Who installed it?

The solar panels, Salif tells me, are connected to a pump 25 meters down in the well, which sends water up a pipe and fills the cistern from which the women are watering their plots. There are 200 women in the co-operative, and they work one hectare in all. The solar panels and pump have been provided and installed by a national agency, paid for, the woman says, by 'foreigners'. Two women have been trained to turn the pump on and off twice a day and to dust the solar panels.

Salif asks the president whether they've had any problems and she points to a group of women on the far side of the co-operative's enclosure, drawing water in the traditional manner from another well. 'They do not want to participate in the solar project,' she says.

'Why not?' I ask.

The woman shrugs. 'They say they were not told about it.'

'Can't they join in now?'

'They say there's never enough water,' she replies.

I can see this is going to take some untangling. Further conversation reveals that the women who come earliest to the gardens tend to use up all the water, leaving nothing for those who come later. This cannot be resolved by leaving the pump on for longer because after four hours the well begins to get low and requires the rest of the day to replenish itself. This is not the main problem, though. The main problem, according to a man who has just appeared beside us and who now politely intercedes, is that the other women do not pay the co-operative stipend.

'All the members must pay a stipend,' the man explains, 'which is used by the co-operative to cover its running costs. Those women refuse as they say they are not benefiting from the solar panels. There is some discord here.'

What interests Salif is seeing whether or not solar-powered irrigation from a well is viable: whether sufficient land can be irrigated for it to be profitable. Of course, if all the equipment is provided for free, it is bound to be economically viable, as the running costs of solar power are almost negligible. But, for a scheme to work properly, it needs to make considerable profits, as the initial investments are high. It certainly does not look as if this is the case here. Working only about half a hectare of vegetables, utilizing no organic farming systems that increase yields and reduce input costs, and with obvious fundamental management and organizational problems, this project is simply helping a limited group of women make some profits in the short term. As soon as there are any serious problems, more than likely it will fold, as is so often the case with projects that are not sufficiently thought through and monitored. I have seen it often enough, as indeed when Salif and I made a research trip to the far south of Senegal in order to visit another solar-powered irrigation project, one that claimed to have set up a dozen such schemes.

This was my and Salif's most ambitious research foray to

date, but one we thought worth making. We travelled south by plane, flying first from Nouakchott to Dakar, capital of Senegal, then south over The Gambia to the southern Senegalese Casamance region.

It was a strange trip. In Casamance, we found ourselves in an entirely different Africa. This was the humid, colorful, tropical south. It could not have been more different from Mauritania. Gone was the formality and bearing of desert or near-desert people. Gone was the clean, stripped scarcity of life. Gone were the glare and the great heat, and gone was the horizon. Here instead were people who slopped around as though made from soft wax; here were scents and spicy smells around every corner; red earth and grass and endless trees. Even the traditional three glasses of tea so common across so much of West Africa were absent here, much to Salif's dismay. 'It's my drug,' he lamented.

The large, friendly director of the local development group in charge of the solar project we had come to see took us in his four-wheel drive on a tour of the forested countryside, becoming increasingly less communicative as it became clear that the projects did not exist: we found only one, which itself was not at that moment functioning.

'We've had problems,' he said. 'There have been funding issues.'

We do not linger long in the vegetable gardens of Danodine. It is excessively hot and the president of the co-operative looks as if she has work to get on with. We are also tempted away by the man who has attached himself to us, who invites us to his home for a rest and some refreshments.

Our new friend introduces himself as Issmou Kah: Salif vaguely knows him. He is tall and bright eyed with a mop of wild hair. He seems excessively pleased to see us. 'Danodine is a good place,' he enthuses as we walk to the Toyota. 'It is where my heart is. I was away for many years working as a teacher in the north, but I have come back. A man cannot deny his roots. He cannot forget his home.'

We rumble over the plain to Issmou's house: a single, sizeable mud-brick building with a tin roof and a veranda. We are installed in a room and provided with a jug of sweetened, powdered milk. Later a platter of rice and fish is produced by his wife, which we eat watched by his many small, wide-eyed children. Issmou is eloquent about the problems of Danodine. He has even produced a full printed and bound report on them, a copy of which he insists I take. The report, which I read then and there, is like a call to arms: an impassioned appeal to the residents of Danodine to reflect on their past, present and future; to mend their differences and strive to save their home from the annihilation he sees coming. For Issmou is very sure about the current state of affairs.

'This town is dying,' he says. 'All the young men are leaving. Only old men and women are left. No-one wants to live here. And why is this? Not just because of the droughts; it is because there is division amongst us. We are Africans,' he laughs, 'and so we argue. No-one can agree on anything. Everybody is arguing. Everybody is jealous of each other. But we can save this town. We can find solutions to our problems. It rests with us. We need only to come together, to drop our differences and work together.'

Issmou's oration is stirring, and I feel that Salif and I are the only audience he has had for some while. I ask him how he earns a living now that he no longer teaches.

'That is a problem,' he says. 'I have some fields, some sheep...' He does not finish.

When we leave, I ask Salif about what Issmou has said, confident that Salif, as always, will know the full story. Salif does not have much sympathy. 'Danodine,' he says wearily. 'has many problems.'

Prime among these, he tells me, is that when the tarmac road to Kaédi was built, some 15 years ago, it was put in the wrong place, bypassing the town.

'During the planning phase,' he says, 'the inhabitants were asked whether they wanted the road to pass directly through their town or not, but the town chief was against this and used his authority to overrule those of the opinion that the road would bring prosperity to the town. The chief was not in disagreement with this, but he argued that it would be much the same if it passed just nearby. What actually happened, though, was that when the road was built, instead of being put right next to the town, as the chief had wanted, it was put where it is now, four kilometers away. This was too far, meaning the town not only failed to profit from being on the road, but whatever trade had come through it on the old road dwindled. Many of the town's people,' Salif says, 'blame this on the chief and are angry with him. This is just one of the problems the town has,' he adds.

Another of them, and the most recent, Salif tells me, relates to a large tract of common land to the north of the town, which is said to have been leased to an American company that wishes to grow wheat there. The area in question extends to some 20,000 hectares, which is vast, and it seems incredible that anyone can be thinking of growing such a moisture-dependent crop in such a dry area when all the water will need to be pumped either from the ground or from a small river some kilometers distant. Nothing is for sure just yet, Salif tells me, and it might be only rumor, but it is said that members of two of the bigger families in Danodine have done a deal with the government agency that has granted the lease to the American company. They claim that traditional ownership of the land in question lies with them as they are the only families to have grown crops on any scale on the land for the last decade. The land, Salif says, is at a high elevation and so rarely used for crops, except by the pastoralists who grow only small patches of millet there, as well as pasturing their livestock.

'It is common land,' Salif says, 'and the town is divided on how to deal with the problem.'

Those who have pastoralist branches, he says, and use the area for grazing livestock are naturally against the sale of the land; those who are affiliated in any way to the two families who are involved in the deal are of the opinion that some benefit will accrue to them. If the land purchase, or land grab, as such opaque deals are increasingly being termed, does take place, in all likelihood all that will happen is that, for the period of the contract, the land will be depleted of nutrients, the rivers and ground sources of water, and the traditional farmers of labor. Then it will fold due to lack of new investment or mismanagement or just general non-viability and everyone will be much worse off than before.

Meagre resources lead to competition, confrontations and power struggles. When I look out of the Toyota window as we pull away from Danodine, I wonder just how anyone manages to survive in such a desiccated and apparently desolate land. By this time of year – the end of the dry, cooler season – there is barely a blade of dried grass left. But there are whole communities down here and survive they do, if only just. This has always been marginal country where there is only a thin line between survival and non-survival. People have evolved coping mechanisms to deal with it. The only trouble is, that line is becoming increasingly thinner as climate change takes an ever stronger grip and drought, flood and mismanagement take their toll.

We arrive at Kaédi, the main regional town of the south, in the late afternoon. Kaédi is an unusual place. By any normal standards it does not have much to recommend it. It is, as one particular traveller's blog I read bluntly put it, 'a shithole in the arse of the world: there is no reason to go there'.

Dating mainly from the colonial era and built originally along traditional French colonial lines, Kaédi might just have been acceptable then, although I suspect anyone posted here would not have been on the fast track to promotion: a couple of wide, tree-lined avenues with a few colonial bungalows set back in spacious compounds; a small, central commercial district and enclosed marketplace; administrative buildings; the post office and European club; outlying districts of mud-brick 'native' dwellings. It sat then, as now, in the grip of a rocky plain of black, shattered hills in one of the hottest places on the globe. Today it is in ruins. Decades of the marginalization of the South have led to such neglect that in places the town seems to have disintegrated. Travelling around it is like being in a disaster zone: smashed buildings, destroyed roads, rotting piles of rubbish with dead livestock thrown in: a dejected, windblown-looking populace.

For such a very dry region, it is surprising how much of this damage is due to rain. Homes built of mud bricks are half washed away, the inhabitants living in the remains. Unpaved roads are so riven by run-off channels that they are no longer passable. Whole districts are cleaved by newly carved dry riverbeds. The complete lack of upkeep or investment in the town has resulted in its becoming a degraded backwater that looks like a rubbish tip. There is no public transport for its hundred thousand inhabitants, nor, until very recently, any taxis either. Electricity supply and telecommunications are sporadic. There are only four doctors in the town, and barely a hotel, restaurant or public space; there are no cinemas and few streetlights: in fact Kaédi lacks just about anything one would normally associate with an urban center. And all the trees have been cut down.

On the other hand, the town, because of its neglect, has not suffered the burgeoning population growth that is typical in West Africa. In a way it is still a very traditional place: a rural focal point more than an urban center. Although its outlying districts appear mostly depopulated, the center is one big marketplace, where nomads leading camels brush shoulders with peasants leading sheep, women carrying baskets of vegetables and the inevitable overladen donkey-carts. Military Landcruisers, in from the desert, shoulder through, a posse of fierce-looking turbaned soldiers clasping rifles in the back. The massive articulated trucks on their way south or north somehow negotiate the close-packed streets. Hardware merchandise spills out of the lines of merchants' boutiques: pick handles, fencing wire, drums of cooking oil, a hundredweight of soap cakes, 10 tons of cement. There is something about the roughened, frontier-like atmosphere of the place that I rather like.

Salif and I have been discussing what to do about our transport problem. We will look for another starter-motor, which Amadou Tall still insists is the problem. I have my doubts, but then I am no mechanic. We drive to the garage, which is the central area of town where transport vehicles congregate. Here the wrecks of abandoned vehicles mingle with the wrecks of still-functioning ones, great trucks gun their engines amid vast plumes of black smoke, men swagger about shouting, ragged beggars beg and touts seek custom for their long-range charges.

We head across the garage to an area behind a row of eating shacks where there is a mechanic's workshop. By now the sun is low and much tinkering takes place under the engine cover. An hour passes and we set off. It is 32 kilometers now to

Keniéba. The vehicle is running, just. We fill it with diesel and make our way to the police post at the exit to town. Unlike the many roadblocks we have passed up to now, perhaps 20 in all, including a couple of the new, feared 'no negotiation' squads, here the police are not interested in our IDs. They are friendly in a condescending way and wave us through. We are now off the tarmac, away from the connection that it gives to the other, more modern and official world and the presence of a foreigner is enough to give us free passage.

At sundown, we stop for prayers. My companions form a line and bow their heads to Allah. I sit on an anthill and smoke a cigarette. Then we are on again, into the night, part of the time following the piste, or built dirt road, part of the time veering off on the myriad tracks that weave, like snakes, through the bush. Then we are there, in Keniéba, Salif's village, an arrival I have experienced so many times, and one that has barely changed in all the years I have been coming: the rushed crowd of children each eager to shake my and Salif's hands; the smiling faces of the adults looming out of the dark; the procession down the thin, sandy ways to Salif's family's compound. Mats are quickly spread out for us as we are surrounded by the uproar of a hundred excited children and the metronomically repeated words of traditional greeting. Later, we are brought a platter of roasted chicken, and tea is made. Later still I am shown to 'my' room, where a mosquito net has been hung over a foam mattress on the floor. Here, as always, I sleep like a log.

4 Keniéba

Rhythms of the morning… Mariam's spirit… The art of rural toiletry… An interview with the Adjutant… The exorbitant cost of free housing… Living with water in a parched land… The irrigation scheme

Morning: I lie under my mosquito net listening to the familiar sounds of early morning life. I have been awake since before dawn. This is mainly due to the cockerels. Keniéba is known as a village because in most respects its life functions like a village. In reality, though, it is a small town of several thousand inhabitants. How many families this breaks down into, I do not know, but each and every family compound, containing perhaps 60 or 70 people, contains at least a couple of cockerels. Across the whole town, this adds up to a lot.

First one crows, then, tentatively, another follows suit. A moment of silence, then a couple more give it a go. Then gradually they all wake up and begin clearing their throats. Before long the cacophony of voices – some tiny and far, some loud and close – fills the air. It is still dark, but soon the thinnest of lights is seeping into the air. In the compounds, shrouded figures are emerging from mosquito nets and rooms, still mute for the moment in the privacy of the pre-dawn world.

I know the routine. I have watched it often enough. Soon the women, their shawls pulled over their heads, will

be working with bent backs and small
hand-held brushes at the patches of sand
outside their rooms, sweeping them in
little clouds of dust of the previous day's
debris. Menfolk, off to the fields, will have
taken a quick breakfast in their rooms and
will be loading a donkey with provisions
or slipping quietly away with a hoe across
their backs. A woman will free a milking
cow from the livestock enclosure and
milk it into a calabash. Then the kids and
lambs will be released and dive excitedly
for their mothers' teats, butting them to
loosen the milk. It is still early and, in the
huts, schoolchildren will be hunched over
bowls of yesterday's leftovers or, if they
are lucky, sticks of coarse bread dipped in
mugs of chicory. Then they are off,
as are the livestock, which weave
their way like commuters to the
plains outside town where a herder will gather them up to
take them out for the day's browsing.

It is now that the women's work begins in earnest: to-
ing and fro-ing like ants to the nearest well, great basins of
water balanced on their heads; tending the infants; washing
clothes; preparing food for the day – an endless litany of
heavy chores. Later they may have to walk many kilometers
to collect firewood, or perhaps they will have duties in the
fields such as bird scaring or winnowing. The rhythmic
thud as they mill grain in the compounds, throwing their
long wooden pestles high in the air before bringing them
down into the wooden mortars, reverberates like a heartbeat
throughout the town.

Since before dawn Amadou Tall has been driving the
piste back to Kaédi where Salif has sent him to see if he can

effect any permanent repairs to the Toyota. We are without a vehicle now.

I emerge from my room to find Salif's wife, Mariam, busying herself about the earthen corridor of the house. She greets me and asks after my wife and children. She is shy and formal, but only briefly. Mariam is a lively, bright, indomitable spirit. She was born and brought up in a city, and most of her married life has been spent in a town. According to her, village life is 'very bad', but this is always said with such provocative good humor, one knows she is not complaining. For Mariam is not the complaining type. She has borne Salif eight children, two of whom died in infancy, and the strain visible on her otherwise bright face tells of the effort she makes in all she does. She is passionate and verbal and no doubt ruffled a few feathers when she first set up home in Salif's family compound. But it is always she, I notice, who raises spirits when people are tired and despondent; it is she who thwacks the children if they are misbehaving, who fusses most when they are ill, who pulls the old folk's legs to get them laughing. But she does not cope well with the heat and is often ill at the hottest times of year. She also has a morbid fear of the rainy season, convinced, she tells me, that the roof of their house is going to fall on her head. She is the antithesis to Salif's cool: lively, passionate and unpredictable.

She shouts out of the doorway to the compound for someone to fetch me the *bidon*, the plastic kettle-shaped container from which people wash hands. She then turns back to me and rattles off a line of Peul, bursting into laughter at my look of incomprehension. 'You don't understand?' she says in her poor French, knowing full well that my Peul is pathetic. She likes to tease me.

The *bidon* is produced and I go out back to wash.

Salif's family compound consists of eight or so oblong buildings enclosing a large yard, one end of which is taken up with livestock pens. Each building houses a different subfamily and is constructed in the traditional manner out of sun-baked mud bricks with a smooth mud and cow-dung finish. The constructions are brown and earthy, the three or four dark rooms inside limited to the breadth of the gnarled tree branches from which the ceiling rafters are made and over which a mud and cow-dung mix is plastered to form the roof. The buildings are considerably cooler than their modern equivalents with tin roofs and concrete block walls but they suffer from rain erosion and need to be rebuilt every 10 or 15 years. Out back of each is the small, open space where ablutions are performed, to where I now head.

There is much that can be written about the peculiarities of the village toiletry experience. I will be brief, mentioning only that this unavoidable necessity is not for the fainthearted and that the 'long-drop' method is fine in principle but in reality has its limitations due to the complete lack of any emptying system and the large number of flies and other insects that like to make their home there. At night, it is a tricky act balancing above the noisome pile while spotlighting the commando raids of cockroaches around your feet. Perhaps it was better in the early days, before Salif's family had dug any of the many, now filled, latrines that surround their living quarters. Then, you simply walked out of town to the surrounding plain to do your thing. The trouble here was, first, that, when required, it was difficult to make a dash, and, second, my 'movements' tended to become a matter of public concern and my trips to the bush were often accompanied by a posse of well-wishers, whose anticipation did nothing for my regularity. And you had to watch very carefully where you trod.

The compound is bright and hot by the time I make my way into it. Salif and a group of men are seated on a raised earthen dais in the shade of a building on the far side. I make my way towards them, shaking hands around the compound as I go. These are people I have known for many years. It is a strange relationship I have had with them, turning up once a year for a couple of weeks. To me, it is like a freeze-frame: the compound and family always look much the same – some people gone, some new faces, a newly rendered building, a new toilet perhaps – but essentially little has changed. Looking back over time, of course, I can see other changes: infants growing into youths, rice replacing couscous as the staple diet, mobile phones becoming common. But those things that really matter have altered very little: the same respect for age is paramount; a devout adherence to a moderate and tolerant interpretation of Islam is universal; deference to the family – putting its needs over those of the individual – is total; and the overriding dilapidation of a poverty born of a disintegrating climate and dysfunctional regime remains the same. For Salif's family, though, my visits must seem quite different. The time between each one constitutes just short of a full year. My appearance amongst them must be like that of a perennial: something noticed but soon forgotten in the whirl of everyday existence; not, as for me, a landmark in the year around which much else is shaped.

I greet Abou, Salif's younger brother, an odd young man with a ready smile but a reluctance to communicate beyond this. In all the years I have known him, we have probably not spoken more than a dozen words at a time. He is married to Uma, a young woman with hands like a blacksmith's and eyes full of mirth. She seems to have had a baby strapped to her back for more years than I can remember and I cannot ever remember seeing her when she was not working.

Mamadou, a first cousin of Salif's, ducks under the low thatch of his veranda to shake my hand. 'Peter…' he exclaims, that familiar, half-shy, half-defensive expression on his face. Mamadou has a reputation – fair or unfair I do not know – for being work shy, although I have seen him often enough in the fields and also working as a carpenter. He is a friendly, if abrasive, character but always makes a point of lending me his radio whenever I am visiting, thoughtfully tuned already to the BBC World Service.

I stoop under the thatch to shake hands with his old mother where she sits on the floor next to their doorway. This remarkable old lady can no longer use her legs and seems content to sit here from morning to night. Indeed, she has sat there for so many years that I cannot remember a time when she did not. In the mornings, when the sun's rays are low, a screen of sackcloth is erected to shade her. Throughout the day, she shells groundnuts, chops vegetables and picks stones from platters of rice. She chats with elderly companions who drop by. Mostly, though, she just sits thumbing her prayer beads, smiling silently to herself.

Harouna, a tall, well-built young man, back for the moment from his *aventures* in Congo Brazzaville, where he works, greets me shyly. He has just got married and is in the middle of constructing a small house for himself, squeezing it in between two others like a shiny new denture in a row of rotten ones. Ismail, a lanky, hard-working farmer with hands like pieces of wood, is more confident in his welcome. He shares a house with his widowed father, who surprised everyone last year by marrying a woman 40 years his junior and promptly siring a baby. The old man always makes a point of coming solemnly up to me on my first night back and delivering a long, official welcome. The last time he did this, Mariam embarrassed him by pointing to his wife and baby nearby, remarking: 'He is old, but look what he has done,' at which the old man's face broke into a wide, sheepish grin.

Many others come up to shake my hand once I have seated myself next to Salif on the dais, some faces I hardly know, some people whose names I should know but don't. There are probably as many as 70 direct family members living in Salif's family's compound at any one time, with a roving population of perhaps the same again. The wider family, of course, is far larger, extending from the closer relations in different compounds in Keniéba itself, to those who reside permanently in the capital or elsewhere. The still-larger circle of the family takes in a vast amount of people dotted throughout this part of Africa, from ancient branches in villages and towns in Mali, to more recent ones in Senegal and throughout southern Mauritania. The largest circle of course encompasses virtually anyone of the same ethnic group with whom, more often than not, some family connection can be found. The extremity of this network goes even beyond this, manifesting itself most clearly amongst newly arrived expatriate Africans in the cities of the world where the simple fact of being black and African is enough to be classed as a 'brother' from whom help can be requested.

For my breakfast, Mariam produces a pot of boiling water with some bananas and dried biscuits – good bland food, for she knows I often have 'difficulties' with my stomach when I visit the village. 'Salif?' she says, holding out her hand.

Salif knows what she is after and digs into his famously bottomless *bobo* chest pocket, producing first a wheel bearing, then a packet of seeds, then two half-cannibalized mobile phones, many scraps of paper with numbers written on them, some letters, three wads of cash and, finally, after a struggle in the deepest recesses, a Lipton's teabag. Mariam sits on the edge of the dais by my feet, dipping the teabag into a glass of the boiling water. A large man approaches.

'Rock,' Salif greets him. Rock is a relation from the compound next door, a giant of a man whom I have known many years and the only person in Keniéba ever to ask me for anything. For years he was after my watch, then some money. He is an educated man and spent many years away from the village and is now bogged down with too many dependants, no money and, according to Salif, a reluctance to work.

'Rock,' Mariam echoes Salif, though with a combative glint in her eye.

Rock grins broadly and greets me. 'You have not been to

visit me!' he exclaims with mock hurt as he shakes my hand.

'How could he come to visit you, you old fool?' Mariam bursts in. 'He only arrived last night.' She laughs, getting up off the dais, and Rock pushes her playfully. Mariam staggers off across the compound laughing loudly. 'Take a seat, Rock,' she says as she goes.

Rock is a little embarrassed by all this, but not unduly so, and sits down to chat with me, telling me how hard life is as a peasant. 'Work, work, work. Toil, toil, toil. That's all it is. We plant crops for the birds and locusts to eat. Ah, but we are strong... we endure,' he says with a strong hint of irony.

I am aware that there is tension between Salif's and Rock's families but I have never got much out of Salif about it.

'You will come to visit me before you go,' Rock demands when he gets up to leave. I tell him, as usual, that I will try to, knowing I probably will not.

Mid-morning, by which time most of the shade in which we are sitting on the dais has been swallowed up. Salif and I decide to relocate ourselves across town to the *Centre*, the building from which our activities take place that Salif's development group constructed some years previously. We have much paperwork to do.

Keniéba is roughly divided into two separate sections: the traditional town inhabited by Black Africans, and the more modern part centered on the main east-west road. The former is a warren of sandy passageways winding behind the half-dissolved walls of the large, interlocking family compounds and ending up in a small commercial center with its covered market and *boutiques*, as the small, basic shops that line every street in Mauritania are known. Moors and their many dozens of trading *boutiques* dominate the newer part of town up by the road, which, alive with commerce and activity, day-by-day eclipses its older, more traditional neighbor.

We make our way through the old town, down the winding

passageways and through the near-deserted commercial area. Here a phalanx of old men, with whom we perform the prolonged ritualistic greetings of hand shaking and enquiries after health and family, sit under a central tree.

The old part of town is placed on the edge of a natural flood plain of baked earth, to the south of which scrub and brush run to the Moshe, a tributary of the Senegal River. To the north, the land rises gently to the road, beyond which is an infinity of gravelly plain. We pass up to the road with its traders' *boutiques*, trucks and roadside restaurants. Beyond is the newest part of the new town, where the transformation of rural existence to urban, of Peul culture to Moor, of the traditional to the modern, takes place before your eyes. At the back, where the plains roll in, giving way to inclines of sand, the newly arrived nomadic Moors, inexorably driven south by the drying of the desert, set up their camps. Only a few hundred meters further in, and there are small, cement box-houses attached to their tents. A little further in, and the boxes are enlarged and have small boutiques included. Further in still, and the houses are larger and there is no sign of tent left at all.

It is here that the *Gendarmerie* is to be found, where the Adjutant, the local military chief, resides. Salif thinks it diplomatic to pay our respects. What with the upcoming elections, and the existent threat al-Qaeda and its affiliates pose in many parts of West Africa, a certain tension prevails that it would be best not to ignore. The recent uprisings in the neighboring country of Mali, partially Islamist in nature, have inspired increased activity among the security forces in Mauritania and there have been instances of terrorism in the country, notably the kidnapping and killing of some foreigners – admittedly some time ago now.

The *Gendarmerie* is a dark, block building of three near-empty rooms, in one of which we find the Adjutant sitting on the floor making tea. He is a well-turned out young man in a starched military uniform: confident and casual, with watchful eyes. He greets us politely and listens to Salif's representations. He nods; gives me an appraising look.

'You have been here before?' he asks.

'Many times,' I reply.

'It is good,' he says. '*Bismillah*' – welcome, in the name of Allah. He turns back to his tea making and Salif and I leave. As we make our way towards the *Centre*, which is nearby, I remark that the Adjutant seems 'okay'. Salif is not in agreement.

'I do not have confidence in that man,' he says darkly.

'What do you mean?' I ask.

'I do not trust him.'

This surprises me. 'Why not?' The man did not seem to me any different from the many military types we come across daily in Mauritania.

Salif's answer is enigmatic: 'Between bandits and those charged with protecting you from them,' he says, 'there is often a relationship.' And, as if to confirm these disturbing thoughts, at that moment Salif's mobile rings. It is the Adjutant.

'He says we are to let him know exactly when and where we are going each time we go into the countryside,' Salif says, even darker now, when he has finished the short conversation.

We discuss the matter further. I feel quite sure Salif is being unnecessarily paranoid. Certainly, in Mauritania the security forces have always used any supposed security threat as an excuse to increase their control of the population as a whole – and, indeed, any enhanced al-Qaeda threat certainly strengthens the regime's hand for more 'support' from the international community – but whether members of the security forces are actually in cahoots with the terrorists, or bandits, as Salif calls them, I do not know. And the few Islamist problems there are in the country are far to the east. There have been no reported issues in this region at all. It is unusual for Salif to be unsettled in this manner. But then the rumor machine in Africa, I know from experience, is deeply pervasive. And Salif no doubt feels a strong sense of responsibility for me. He wants to play it safe and I am happy with that. We agree that we will call the Adjutant but only at the moment we are leaving town, as in this way he will not have time to contact any dodgy associates who might wish to come and waylay me. I try to keep my face straight as we walk, not wishing to undermine the seriousness Salif is attaching to the matter. I suspect the whole melodrama is more to do with the fact that he has taken a dislike to the Adjutant. Both his manner and his role are anathema to Salif.

Shortly, we come to the *Centre*, which is a large, concrete building in a compound surrounded on all sides by a wall. Here we settle down with our papers on the floor of the spacious main room and begin going through the accounts, sweating our way through the figures as Abou, Salif's younger brother, who has appeared, supplies us with a succession of teas. By the time we move on to project reports, it is already afternoon. Still we keep at it, eventually synthesizing all to a number of primary issues: the problems of our nascent well-digging program and the, to me, incomprehensible failure of the community for whom we are digging the well to provide draught donkeys, the only input required of them; the apparent 'drift' of our successful Dohley Women's market garden project from its original aims; and my concern over the tractor-ploughing service Salif and his group provide, which might, I feel, be leading farmers into an unsustainable dependence on a mode of machinery-based agriculture they cannot afford.

Finally, there is the matter of the Toyota. If it fails to materialize, as seems likely, how the hell are we going to manage the two-day seminar that has been arranged for this week? Many months of organization have gone into this meeting, during which the delegates from many ethnic groupings will come together to agree on objectives for the large community project Salif is in the process of developing. Neither of us has met Ibrahim Tandia, the Senegalese development consultant we will be picking up in Kaédi tomorrow who will be leading the seminar, but much rests on him. Mobility will be essential, not just to get him here, but also to bring in many of the seminar delegates who live in remote areas.

The afternoon is well advanced by the time we finish and the heat is shattering, as though the hot season, which is imminent, has already arrived. Temperatures of 40 or even 45 degrees are not uncommon in the hot season, which lasts from April to July, at which time the rains can start.

'Mariam will have food for us,' Salif says encouragingly, noticing the depleted state I am in. We pack up our papers and, indeed, when we arrive back in the family compound, three large platters of food await us, around which we quickly settle down with a crowd of many others. Salif ladles the stew of steaming vegetables and fish onto the platters of rice, and we eat. The small river nearby, the Moshe, kept full throughout the year by dams at either end, produces a remarkable quantity of fish for the population of Keniéba. There are various types, but the best is a member of the large catfish family, whose fleshy meat is deliciously nutty. This, along with freshly cut okra, sweet potato, yam and carrots in a rich tomato and onion sauce, produces a delicious meal, spiced with chili.

There must be 30 or more people hunched around the meal. Salif tells me the family gets through over two 25-kilo sacks of rice per week, plus quantities of millet couscous, vegetables, fish and bread. In theory, the couscous comes from the millet crop the family plants during the rainy season, and the rice comes from the irrigation scheme Salif set up all those years ago, as do the vegetables. In practice, no year works quite like this and differing amounts of these always need to be bought in, along with the quantities of tomato paste, salt and cooking oil used in the cuisine. Sheep and goats are slaughtered only for special occasions. Following the universal law that decrees capacity is always matched by need, even the very best of years never produces enough for all the hungry mouths.

We settle down under a thatch for the rest of the afternoon. By early evening I am up and keen to start out for Mabafé, the family irrigation scheme that we have planned to visit today, eight kilometers to the south. Salif's enthusiasm for the expedition, however, does not match my burning need, despite the heat, to do something active. He turns to Harouna, the young man back from Congo Brazzaville who is preparing the last of the afternoon's three glasses of tea, and asks if he would like to accompany me.

'Of course,' the young man replies without hesitation.

And so it is agreed: Salif will stay back and Harouna will accompany me. We will not call the Adjutant as I will not be going far. Amadou Tall, Salif tells me before we leave, has called. He has left the Toyota with a mechanic who says there is a problem with the radiator. The vehicle will not be serviceable for tomorrow. We shall instead have to take a bush taxi to Kaédi in the morning and look for a vehicle to hire.

We set off for Mabafé out of the rear of the compound. This backs directly onto the flood plain at the edge of town. Nearby is an extensive area of pits where young men labor, digging out the clayey soil that they pack into brick moulds and then lay out in patterns on the ground to bake in the sun. The bricks, Harouna tells me as we make our way around the pits, although cheap individually, end up costing a lot, as even a small house like the one he is building in the compound will consume nearly 6,000 of them. I ask him how much his house will cost to build, and he tells me he will have to outlay the equivalent of $3,000. This is a figure I find astonishing and I

ask him why it will cost this much. Surely, I say, most of the materials are virtually free.

'Nothing is free here,' he says brusquely. I press him further. Surely he and his family can at least provide most of the labor for free.

'Mostly, yes,' he says, 'but I will have to pay for all their food. And there's also the wood for the rafters to be paid for and all the loads of earth and cow dung for the render and mortar, which have to be brought in by donkey-cart, as does all the water to mix with them. There's much to be paid for.' The reality, of course, is that life here, as elsewhere, is not cheap.

We walk on in silence. I must have known Harouna since he was a child, although the truth is I do not remember him. He seems a little ill at ease. I have come across this before from expatriates, those who live away from their villages in the cities of the world. It is not always easy for them when they return to their homes, and it is not made any easier when they find me there. They are unsure of how to react to me, and fear being patronized. I ask him how long he intends on staying now that he is back home.

'A couple of years,' he says.

'It is hard coming back?' I say.

He laughs. 'You have no idea. Working in the fields! It is very difficult when you are no longer used to it. There's nothing to do in the evenings. And you have to be a good man. When you come back to the village you put on your *bobo*, you throw away your cigarettes and you pray five times a day.'

We make our way across the floodplain away from Keniéba and enter an area of scrubby bush through which the sandy track weaves. Small doves flutter off at our approach, and high above, a harrier circles on a thermal.

In the early days of my visits to Keniéba, the countryside around the town looked all much the same to me. Parts of it were sandy, parts hard, baked earth, parts dotted with scrub and stunted trees. But it was all dry and of much the same level. It was only as time went on that I began to understand that this was not the case. Indeed, it was fairly flat country, but not entirely so, and it was these small variations in height, I discovered, sometimes as little as a meter, that made all the difference. This is because of the nature of the rainfall. Coming, as it does, in large downpours after a long dry season when the ground has been baked to a concrete hardness, runoff is extremely rapid, quickly filling the dry riverbeds, or *oueds*, that drain into larger rivers, which in turn flow into the Senegal River. The speed with which this all takes place means flooding is inevitable and indeed, in a normal year, vast areas can be inundated. This is not a problem as the inhabitants of the region have situated their villages in places that are above all but the most exceptional floods and have shaped their agricultural practices around this event.

It is the speed with which the water drains from the land that is so significant. Only tiny variations in elevation can mean the difference between land that drains in an hour, land that holds water for a week, and land that dries up over the period of three months. These, in conjunction with soil types, dictate exactly to what use each part of the land can be put. The higher sandy areas, for example, which drain the fastest, are good only for brief pastures. Land with a higher clay content, say in a slight depression, will hold water for a little longer, allowing sufficient water penetration for a quick crop of sorghum to be grown. Land lower still, where the water takes even longer to drain away, can be planted with millet. And the land with the highest clay content at the lowest elevation, even though perhaps still only a few meters below the highest ground, constitutes the primary agricultural area where millet and maize can be grown in abundance in a good year.

The exact annual precipitation and precise level of the preceding floods are therefore vital. A minor reduction in the rainfall and decrease in the floods can leave huge areas that normally produce crops high and dry. Then again, years that have exceptional rainfall can cause havoc, flooding villages, washing away crops and stranding livestock. If one throws in the fact that the densities of livestock in the south have risen hugely in recent years, due to a general migration from the dryer north – livestock that can cause untold damage to unfenced crops – it becomes clear how very marginal and

vulnerable life is in the region.

Traditionally, the manner in which people survive is to have a mixture of economic practices. Any one family, for example, might have a pastoral branch, where livestock herders are prepared, when necessary, to range far and wide in search of pastures. The families might also have access to tracts of the higher crop-growing land. And the majority of them will probably also have traditional entitlement to parts of the more fertile low-lying areas. In addition, certain family members might be involved in trade or artisanal occupations. This all lends them a flexibility that enables them to deal with the vagaries of what has always been a volatile climate. At least that is how it worked until the parameters of that volatility started to stretch and climate change began to take its toll. Now things are not so simple.

One response people have had to climate change has been to set up irrigation schemes, as Salif's family have done. This, they reason, represents a way forward. Intensive cash crops can be grown using mechanized farming methods that will drag production systems out of the subsistence level at the same time as mitigating the effects of drought. This is the theory upon which the hydrology of the region was altered back in the 1980s, thanks to a vast project that saw large dams built on the Senegal River and its tributaries. Inevitably, this was a controversial project. On the one hand, it did seem a logical response to the devastating droughts of the preceding decade, allowing for a vastly increased amount of irrigated agriculture in the Senegal River Valley, as well as producing hydroelectric power. On the other hand, amongst a score of other controversial issues, the traditional annual flooding of the river valley, upon which large numbers of people depended for their livelihoods, would be affected. The floods, in the receding waters of which people planted their crops, would now occur only in the very wettest of years. Years of poor rain would result in no floods at all.

A small-scale irrigation sector centered on the region around Keniéba has grown up. At best, though, this is a sector that is struggling to survive; at worst, it is simply a means by which a lot of people lose a lot of money. This is because it functions so inefficiently in such unfavorable conditions. The costs of inputs, from pumps, through the fuel for them, to fertilizers and pesticides, continually rise. Rice is inefficiently mono-cropped. Water from huge pumps is flooded in the most wasteful manner onto huge fields of onions, which then fetch low prices at market because a thousand tons of subsidized Dutch ones have just descended upon the markets in Nouakchott. Banks give loans at extortionate rates, often requiring farmers to take machinery of poor quality instead of cash. There are the numerous natural problems to deal with: locusts, bird invasions, floods. And then a pump will break down at just the wrong moment. Or a bag of seed purchased will be of such poor quality that it does not germinate. Or weed management will be sub-standard. Or a cartel of Moorish merchants will have doubled the price of fertilizer. The list of what can and does go wrong is endless and what is remarkable is not that so many of the schemes fold after only a few years, but that many struggle on for so long. One such is Salif's family scheme, Mabafé.

The last of the sun's rays are disappearing as we approach the wire-mesh fence that surrounds Mabafé. Here lie 20 hectares of arable land divided into *planches*, plots of land some 200 meters square. Some 32 families grow crops on these *planches*, paying half their harvest to Salif's family in return for the land, the tractor work used in preparing it each season and the water that irrigates it. Two large pumps are stationed by the Moshe River, which runs adjacent to the scheme, and which, by the use of dams at either end, has a year-round supply of water. This water, once drawn from the river by the pumps, is run onto the land through a network of mud channels and sluices. The main crop is rice, grown during the rainy season, from June to October. Some families will then plant vegetables or some maize, but not many do this.

The creation and development of the scheme has been an ongoing story for many years. It is the result of years of labor and perseverance, often in the face of the most overwhelming difficulties. Years of exceptional rains have led to the inundation of entire crops, meaning the loss of the entire year's harvest and profit. There have been problems with pumps breaking down at key moments and with bird and locust invasions. There always seems to be a problem. And, as with farmers the world over, the costs of the next year's inputs are covered through loans and, when there is no harvest, or a poor harvest, these loans cannot be repaid. But the families persevere, and somehow Salif's family, which owns the scheme, has managed over the years to stay afloat, even investing when they can in new machinery and land. The fence ringing the scheme is the newest of these investments.

It is the quiet season now, the rice having been harvested back in October and the main vegetable crop also being at an end. Many of the *planches*, I see as we arrive, have been ploughed up, on some of which livestock are browsing crop residues. There are only a few people about – those who are growing hot-season vegetables and teams of youths improving water channels in preparation for the following rice crop.

The guardian, a tall, thin man who lives with his wife and children in a camp on the edge of the scheme, greets us. He, Harouna and some others then line up for the sundown prayers. Touching their hands to the earth, they symbolically wash themselves, then stand for the introductory prayers before bowing in homage to Allah three times, pressing their foreheads to the earth. As they rise up, each of them has a small disc of sand imprinted on his head, like a talisman. There is a donkey cart heading back to Keniéba on which we can cadge a lift.

We are a cheerful bunch as we trot along in the evening light: Harouna and I; women with baskets; men with hoes. Each time we come to a place where the ground is rutted, the cart comes almost to a standstill, creaking slowly over the iron-hard earth. Then the driver jigs the donkey up again, and, with a few taps of his stick and a whoop, we are off, the rapidly darkening bush slipping quietly by to the clop of the donkey's hooves. Before we are back it is dark, our surroundings illuminated only by the canopy of stars and that strange luminosity the plains seem to emit at night, as though they were releasing a tiny fraction of the sunlight that has poured on them all day.

Back in the compound, the full swing of the evening has passed. Livestock are shut up. Social groups have split. Salif is waiting for me on the mats and cushions Mariam puts out each evening in front of their house. 'How was Mabafé?' he asks.

'It was good,' I reply. 'But there is not much happening there just now.'

'It's true,' he says, 'but you had a good walk.'

5 To Kaédi

Learning good humor... The old merchant... Salif's sons... The local agronomist... A hometown's lost heyday... Our consultant arrives... Death and Allah's fields... Alisanne's adventures in Europe... The infinite heavens

Salif calls into my room shortly after dawn. One of the elusive bush taxis to Kaédi is about to depart, and he has arranged for it to pass the compound and pick us up. This is the result of an excellent piece of intelligence-gathering on Salif's behalf and is a bit of rare good fortune: transport between Keniéba and Kaédi can be difficult, and you can wait whole days for a bush taxi without success. Despite hastily preparing ourselves for departure, however, the minibus does not turn up for an hour and a half and then, having taken us no more than a kilometer around the edge of town, comes to a stop, steam hissing from under the engine cover.

Salif does not waste any time. Seeing a plume of dust rising on a nearby track, he rushes off to wave another vehicle down. A few minutes later he reappears with a van. We are in luck. It is bound for Kaédi and is departing immediately. Not so fortunately, although it is a large van of the usual bush-taxi variety, it has not been 'converted'. This usually means having holes cut into the sides for windows and a few benches bolted in the back. We will have none of these luxuries but instead must sit in the coffin-like interior on top of a consignment of rice sacks.

Fortunately, there are only a few other passengers. Unfortunately, the driver does not intend to let it remain this way. Only half an hour later, the back is filling up. Every village or camp we pass seems to have two or three people outside waiting for a lift. The driver cannot resist and, by the end, we are crammed to such an extent, our heads pressed against the ceiling, and it is so very hot and airless, that I am angry. I want to get out and remonstrate. This is absurd. It is dangerous. It is horrible. I cannot even imagine what the temperature must be in the back. But I do not. Like all the others, I let a stupor of discomfort and acceptance overcome me. It is a moment, I realize, for gritting teeth and getting through. Like all the others, I do not really have a choice. There may not be any other means of getting to Kaédi today. It comes as a tremendous relief when we get stuck in each of the sandy *oueds*, or dry riverbeds, we meet.

We stagger out the back, a colorful crowd standing incongruously on the pale sand of the *oued*. My anger has evaporated. In the face of the good humor of my fellow passengers, who seem able even now to find things to laugh about, I cannot maintain my *hauteur*. At one of the *oueds* we even have to unload the van's entire consignment of rice sacks in order to lighten the vehicle sufficiently to push it out. How can you take this seriously? How the passengers laugh when they are sprayed with sand from the spinning wheels. How thoughtful they are of each other when we arrange ourselves in the back once more, minimizing their own space in favor of their neighbors. Only one young woman is unhappy, crying for a while before resting her head on the shoulder of her friend or sister, who strokes her forehead as a mother does for a child. I do not know why she is crying, but I do not imagine it is anything to do with our discomfort.

Once in Kaédi we make for the house of Mamadou Kane, a

relation of Salif's whose home we are in the habit of using as a base when in town. It is here that Salif lodged when he was a student attending the Lycée and it is here that two of his sons, also at the Lycée, now lodge.

Mamadou Kane is an old man and one of the biggest merchants in town. Not for him, though, the trappings of wealth. This is a man and a merchant in the traditional mould. His house, dating from colonial times, though large and solidly built, is almost entirely devoid of material possessions. One dilapidated, empty, high-ceilinged room leads to the next, most of life focused on the wide, tiled veranda and central courtyard where chickens peck, pots and pans are scattered and miscellaneous dependants appear and disappear.

Mamadou Kane himself passes his time on a small mat in a distant corner of the veranda. He is tall and bent, with a kindly face and a pair of bottle-top glasses held together with masking tape. Equally ancient friends and business associates pass time with him on mats in his corner, and many hours are devoted to his prayer beads. You do not get the feeling, however, that his business is suffering as a result. The twinkle in the old man's eye speaks of a wily astuteness. His two sons may be off in America, apparently with little intention of returning, but he has obviously built his business with such a sound base that it is secure even in the near-dysfunctional environment of the south. At home, though, it is his wife who rules: a charming and welcoming lady whose casualness belies the strict atmosphere of compassion evident in her home. Mamadou Kane himself has for 15 years grinned at me without the slightest idea what to say next.

'And when are you going to do business with me?' he always asks finally, chuckling at his rhetorical question.

Over the years, I have spent many a night in Mamadou Kane's house. Generally, Salif and I sleep up on the flat roof of one of the buildings, for Kaédi, situated on its rocky plain between low shattered hills, is one of the very hottest places in the region, and hence the world. It also has a fearful mosquito problem and many a sleepless night have I spent there, as Mamadou Kane's house knows no mosquito nets. One night in particular, I was violently ill from something I had eaten. I remember a girl – a house servant – nursing me through the two subsequent, semi-delirious days: a girl with bright eyes, the darkest of black complexions and a voice as soft as down.

Salif's two sons are waiting for us at the door to Mamadou Kane's house. Mohammed and Saidou are two years apart in age, Mohammed 17 and Saidou 15. Saidou, like Salif, is bright and, despite the fact that he is younger than his brother, is in the same year as him at the Lycée. 'He is intelligent,' Salif says of Saidou. 'He passes all his exams with ease. Mohammed,' he says, 'does not like to work.'

Salif's relationship with his sons is, to the outsider, formal in the extreme. He greets them now as though they were mere acquaintances, shaking hands and completing the traditional verbal greetings. He tells them to fetch us some water and, when we settle down on a mat on the veranda, Saidou hands it to us without a word. They do not join us. With me they are also formal, and it was only when they were young that I managed to be more intimate with them. Now, they clearly do not want this. There is a strict code of conduct they are expected to adhere to, a code that requires complete deference to and respect for your elders. This can seem cold but there is nothing cold about Salif's family or their relationships with each other. The bright eyes and cheerful dispositions of the children do not speak of a respect based on fear or intimidation.

Salif is especially attentive to his children's upbringing, and the bonds in his immediate family are particularly strong. But it is not always like this. People often need to think a little before they can tell you how many children they have. They will rarely know their precise ages. When people refer to their 'parents' or 'brothers' and 'sisters', they could just as easily be talking about their cousins or uncles and aunts. In the same way that, in the traditional setting, individualism is transcended by the interests of the family, the dynamic of the wider family eclipses that of the more immediate ones. On the one hand, this creates a large enough unity to withstand significant pressures; on the other, it creates pressures of its own, where individuals and smaller families are unable to take the more spontaneous or autonomous decisions the modern world requires and a leaden inertia can take hold that makes even the simplest of actions difficult to initiate.

For the children, though, the security created by the unity of the larger family is immense. They may be treated with great strictness, frequently thwacked across the ear for misdemeanors and expected to fetch and carry for their elders at any moment, but the love they experience, particularly at a young age, from so many people is evident. The little posses that roam their compounds like renegade bands, playing with whatever bits and pieces they come across, can expect the same care from people in whatever part of the compound they go to. They may be naked, covered in dust and snot, have not a single personal possession to their name; they may be treated often little better than servants, have not a bed between them and be expected simply to sleep wherever they curl up; but they have a world of such loving boundaries that their freedom knows no limits.

Ibrahim Tandia, the development consultant Salif and I are to pick up today, is due to arrive in the afternoon, crossing as planned over the river from Senegal at the official border crossing adjacent to the town. Meanwhile, Amadou Tall, in near-constant mobile communication with Salif, is working on the problem of vehicle hire. We recover a little from our journey in Mamadou Kane's house, then go off to see a colleague.

Monsieur Méline, or Méline, as we know him, has a tiny, cubicle-sized office just around the corner from Mamadou Kane's. It's a long, thin, windowless room leading directly off a dusty street, just wide enough for his desk to span it at the far end. Méline is an agronomist. He has set up business as a consultant and has worked from time to time for a number of government agencies and European Union- or World Bank-funded programs. The walls of his office bear old posters showing the breeding cycle of the locust, or compost-making systems. His metal desk and accompanying filing cabinet spill with reams of paperwork. He has a fan but no computer. Two chairs sit before his desk, one without a back.

Méline rises graciously to greet us as we enter his office.

'Ah, welcome, welcome,' he says, his round, friendly face shiny with sweat. 'So... so... you have come...' He shakes his head, apparently overwhelmed with delight. 'Come, take a seat... please, please, be seated,' he says.

We take our seats and I ask him how business is.

'Ah... ah...' he exclaims, as though he has caught me out making a joke. 'Monsieur Peter...' he laughs. 'What business? You know how it is. Ask Salif. A little bit here; a little bit there. No-one has any money and the agricultural restructuring program people have been working on is in its second evaluation phase. Anyway, there is no work coming from that direction. It is foreign NGOs that give me the best chance of work. I

am just working on a tree-nursery proposal for a community group. It is not much. But what can you do?' he says, an apologetic smile on his face.

Méline has been struggling ever since I have known him. He runs a farmer-training program for us. This he does well, although there are a number of problems. We have also commissioned a few project studies from him, more perhaps than we should have. For the fact is, although Méline clearly knows his stuff agriculturally, he does not know much about project design. What he misses out in the simple details of who is going to do what, for whom and for what benefit, he makes up for in large amounts of irrelevant verbiage and budgetary micro-calculation. His reports are vast and nearly useless, and it is only his great enthusiasm and sincerity that persuaded me, perhaps against my better judgment, to give him such commissions. He is a man you cannot help liking. The fact is, most of the best-qualified development consultants are simply not to be found in towns such as this. They reside on high, internationally funded commissions in the capital, employed in producing the mountains of analyses and reports that consume such a high percentage of project budgets. They avoid rural areas like the plague.

Méline, apparently, does not go for this.

'What are they all doing in the capital?' he asks. 'This is where agronomists should be… in the countryside, where the real work is.' I suspect, not unreasonably, and given half the chance, however, he would not turn down a cushy job in the capital himself.

We have come to see Méline on a difficult matter. The training program he runs for us is going to be consumed by the larger community project we are working on, of which we are not expressly asking him to be a part. We do not mind if he takes a minor role in it, but we have another agronomist who will be in charge. I do not know how the situation stands and am happy to leave it up to Salif. But Salif is close on the matter. I do not know whether this is out of a certain feeling of loyalty to Méline, or because he too is feeling his way forwards.

'Méline can still run some of the training modules,' he told me before.

'And the training is to be structured differently, with more in-field work?' I asked.

'Yes. He could not do that.'

'Why not?'

'He would not want to. He does not have transport.'

'You don't think he would want to carry on with us?'

'He would like to, yes. But he's okay. Don't worry about Méline.'

This has left me little purchase, and I am uncertain what manner to adopt in our meeting with Méline. I leave it in Salif's hands. We chat amiably for a while but nothing as far as I can see is mentioned concerning the 'issue'. It is stiflingly hot, and again I am drooping. Salif tells Méline we have to go and see about hiring a vehicle, and we leave, having promised to pass the afternoon with him.

Amadou Tall has been on the mobile again. He has found a vehicle and driver. We go back to Mamadou Kane's and shortly he appears with two Moors, whom he introduces to us. One is Mustapha, the driver, a large man with a large black beard and the deepest of black eyes. The other is Harana, the vehicle 'boy', a pleasant, fresh-faced young man. Both wear *bobos* and turbans and seat themselves beside us on the mat with little formality. Salif speaks Hassaniya, the form of Arabic spoken by the Moors, and they enter 'discussions', mixing the Hassaniya up with French. These take considerable time, not helped by the fact that we want to pin down the exact details of what we require, when, for how long and how much it will cost, with all contingencies covered. Salif knows as well as I do how things can turn out otherwise.

'And no lifts – no extra passengers,' he says, anticipating

the habit of hire vehicles to double up as public transport when not expressly forbidden from doing so.

'No lifts. No problem,' Mustapha answers.

'And if we need the vehicle for extra days, we pay the same rate.'

'Same rate. No problem,' the Moor replies.

Even though Salif negotiates a price considerably lower than the one initially suggested, the cost is still very high. There is nothing we can do about this, as anything to do with vehicles is expensive in Mauritania. We will not pay mileage but will buy all fuel instead. Once this is concluded, the Moors stand up, shake our hands and depart. I realize we have not even seen the vehicle.

Salif's mobile phone seems to be almost permanently on the go. What with the two-day seminar starting tomorrow, the arrival of Ibrahim Tandia, and any number of issues concerning ongoing projects and his group's agricultural service delivery work, not to mention all sorts of family issues and the job he apparently has to perform as general post deliverer and money transfer agency for all and sundry, he has his work cut out. Often, indeed, I wonder how he manages and I am always pressing him to offload more of his responsibilities. The truth is, though, it is he, not anyone else, with whom people want to deal. The urge to turn his mobile off must be strong, but this he never does. How he managed before the advent of the mobile phone, I cannot remember.

The issue for the moment is just when and exactly where Ibrahim Tandia will arrive. Although he will be coming from Senegal, he is actually based in Germany, where he works for a German organic farming group. His expertise is in working with rural community organizations, and he comes highly recommended. He has travelled from a town in the middle of Senegal to the village of Dohley, on the remote and inaccessible northern border of that country. This is where we run our Dohley Women's Market Garden Project and it is these women who have kindly taken it upon themselves to receive him and dispatch him over the Senegal River to Kaédi. Communication with the Dohley women is not going well, however, their mobile signal being weak.

At around one o'clock we walk to Méline's house to pass the afternoon, as arranged. It seems to me that the hot season has arrived, as it is about as hot as I can remember, the air dense with heat, like a wall. It feels like I am swimming.

Méline inhabits one of the elegant, colonial-era bungalows on an old, wide boulevard. How he comes to be there, and whether he rents it or owns it, I do not know, but it is now in a state of almost total dilapidation, with Méline and his family living in it in a state of gentle penury. He welcomes us at the doorway of the bungalow compound and, seeing the dripping, weary state I am in, immediately suggests I take a bucket bath. This is a wonderful suggestion, and once the bucket has been produced, I disappear behind the tall wall of the toiletry area. Here there is a wooden stool and a plastic basket with a cake of soap and a flannel in it. I have become proficient at maximizing the use of a bucket of water, soaping myself up from head to toe and working down from the top, rinsing it all off again. Always I leave enough water for one final slosh. That moment, no matter how brief, when my head is immersed in the water, is one of the most luxurious I know. For the tiniest of seconds, I am inhaling the humid scent of a grand, tropical waterfall.

Feeling recovered and refreshed, I join Salif and Méline where they are spread out on a mat and cushions in the shade of a wall.

The most notable thing about Méline is the great incongruity between his own personal attributes of warmth and self-effacement and the fact that he has an exceptionally unpleasant son. Perhaps I have been lucky in the fact that I do not remember coming across unpleasant children in Africa before, but this boy, 12 or 13 years old, appears spoilt, rude and highly disrespectful in a way so entirely out of context that it is shocking. Salif and I have often spent time at Méline's and so have come across him before, but I always find it uncomfortable when he slouches over to us on a request from his father to perform some minor service, then argues insolently that he does not want to do it, even refusing sometimes. I feel for Méline then, being humiliated in front of guests, and I am curious always to see what Salif's reaction will be, as this could not be more different from the manner in which his own children behave. He, as expected, does his best to play the situation down, remarking perhaps that children will be children. But I can see that this lessens his respect for Méline. It is not so much that children do not misbehave in Mauritania. Like everywhere, they do. But the sneering insolence of this child towards his father is exceptional. No doubt there is a back-story.

Méline is a Kaédi man, born and bred. For me, the concept of living and existing in Kaédi holds a strange fascination. The town is so very run down and has so very little going for it. It is a rubbish tip with sporadic electricity, subject to the most crushing of heats, a heat that barely lets up the year round. The place feels pointless somehow; as though its creation during the colonial era was a mistake, as though it should never have been here. But here, too, of course, there is a back-story, one with a different perspective to this. I remember one evening Méline and Salif reminiscing about the town, talking of the old tennis courts there used to be out by the old parade ground, of the art-deco cinema, now a shell, and of the now non-existent park where, as students, they would take their books in the afternoons.

'It was something, then, this town,' Méline had said, and I realized then that he was not living in a rubbish tip. He was living in his hometown.

We eat, doze and drink tea. The issue of Méline's

continued employment – or not – is not raised. Perhaps an understanding has already been arrived at. I do not know, and Salif is not telling. When, later on in the afternoon, we leave, however, Méline mentions at the last moment, just as I am shaking his hand, that he is looking forward to the seminar tomorrow. I had not wanted to ask if he would be attending, imagining for some reason that he was not. I am glad that he is.

We are waiting for the call from the Dohley women to tell us that Ibrahim Tandia is on his way across the river. We return to Mamadou Kane's and soon Salif's mobile rings. It is the president of the Dohley Women's Co-operative. Salif can only just make out what she is saying. Ibrahim Tandia is on his way. He calls Mustapha, the driver of the hire vehicle, and tells him to come and pick us up. Shortly an engine can be heard revving outside the compound doorway. It is a handsome vehicle, thankfully in good condition: a more modern version of the same Toyota double-cabin pickup we have. Now commences an hour of confusion as the whereabouts of Ibrahim Tandia and the Dohley woman who is accompanying him – and who is in sporadic phone communication with us – becomes increasingly unclear. We make our way back and forth across town, negotiating dry riverbeds, passing through broken-down compounds and becoming stuck in an absurd 10-vehicle gridlock by the market. By the time we link up with them, all are hot and irritable.

Ibrahim Tandia inspires confidence the moment you meet him. He is sweating but not at all put out by the confusion that has seen him wandering about the hot streets of Kaédi, laughing at the situation and telling us to think nothing of it.

'These things happen,' he says.

He is middle-aged, a little portly, with an open face and engaging charm. He's wearing jeans and an endearingly crumpled safari hat, marking him out, along with me, in a street where everyone else is dressed in traditional clothes.

With Mohammed, Salif's eldest son, who is returning home, and Harana, the vehicle 'boy', in the back of the vehicle, we head out of town for the road back to Keniéba. Mustapha, our driver, now gives us a demonstration of how to go places. The main *piste* to Keniéba, many parts of which are now under construction into a tarmac road – a tarmac road that, a long 15 years in the coming, is now finally picking up speed on its journey to Keniéba – is avoided by most people because its surface is covered in corrugations so deep that it can destroy a vehicle in one journey alone. There is only one way to travel over the corrugations, and that is with speed. If a vehicle is travelling fast enough, its wheels simply skip from the top of one corrugation to the next, leading to a smooth ride. This, however, means that the vehicle's actual contact with the road is dramatically reduced, which leads to a good deal of 'drift'. When combined with the fact that every few kilometers we are required to come to a shuddering halt where a section of the *piste* is under construction or has been dissected by a *oued*, this can lead to an alarming ride. A hundred kilometers an hour seems about the minimum speed at which the road can be taken. Mustapha is in his element. Ibrahim Tandia, sitting up front, is unfazed. Leaning over to us in the back, a grin on his face, he shouts: 'We have a good driver. A true Mauritanian.' Not a flicker passes Mustapha's face. We reach Keniéba in just over an hour: a record.

Early evening: Mariam has laid out the mats and cushions. We settle down, Salif prone, exhausted; Ibrahim Tandia propped easily on an elbow, watching with small, smiling eyes all that takes place around us. The cattle and the goats and sheep are just arriving back from their day's browsing, and the compound for the moment is a farmyard. Two people have appeared. The first is Drémis, as he is called, a first cousin of Salif's, who comes over to greet us and shake our hands.

Drémis is the son of the old woman in the house next door who has lost the use of her legs; the elder brother of 'work-shy' Mamadou. He is a former police officer. When I first met Drémis many years ago, he was a strong man. He was full of brash energy and wont to stomp around the compound ordering people about. No-one minded being ordered about by Drémis because he had a ready humor and was always prepared to back down. Over the years, though, I have seen him change. At first, people did not know what was wrong with him. He became paler and paler until his skin took on a pasty, grey texture. He had problems breathing and eventually went to the hospital in Nouakchott where tests were done and he was told that he had a heart condition, for which he was given medication. Recently, he has developed diabetes. Although still cheerful and robust in manner, today he is a shell of his former self.

'How are you?' I ask, as he shakes my hand.

'I am an old man now,' he says. 'Look at me.' And so he is. He is hunched, moves with a hobble and looks as though a strong gust of wind might blow him away.

Drémis's infirmities, however, I am aware, do not prevent him from remaining highly active in his love life. He has two wives in Keniéba, one at either end of town, and another, I have been told, about which the first two have no idea, in Nouakchott. How he affords these three wives and his many offspring – he himself cannot tell you how many he has – I have no idea, as he only does a small amount of clerical work now for the town mayor. Although it is not unusual for men to have more than one wife in Keniéba, it is not common, and the complexities of Drémis's marital arrangements afford the family a good deal of entertainment. Mariam is merciless. 'You are not old,' she says to him, 'just worn down by all those wives.'

'No, no,' Drémis replies, wagging his finger at her.

There is a dispensary in Keniéba but no other medical

facilities. Drémis is, in some respects, lucky in that he has managed to receive treatment for his condition. Most illnesses go untreated and people simply die. Entirely curable conditions such as jaundice or pneumonia are generally fatal.

Since I have been coming to the village, so many people have died, often the most unexpected ones: young people; those who, when I last saw them, seemed in the best of health. Each year there is a toll. Always it is 'the heart'. There is great sadness always, a sense of loss, and often the women can be heard wailing loudly in the town, as they are highly demonstrative on the death of a close one. But there is also acceptance.

'Life is a field we are set to work by Allah,' an old man once told me. 'Death is another of his fields.' There is little trauma in death.

One of the many who died between my trips – someone who, for some reason, stands out in my mind – is a young student I came to know in the town in the north of the country where Salif worked for the mining company before he returned to the village. I had gone up to stay with Salif in the house he inhabited in the whitewashed, purpose-built complex the mining company had constructed on a salt plain near the sea. This was a strange place but Salif and Mariam had a good life there, eating cheap fish fresh from ocean and forming close friendships with neighbors and colleagues. Their small apartment was something of a focal point for family members and always at night the lounge became a dormitory. Here I met Mohamedou, a tall, bright-eyed young man. He had just recently finished his *bac*, and was looking to further his education. He was full of plans and hopes. We would walk the nearby rubbish-strewn shore where the rusty carcasses of dozens of ships lay decaying, floundering in the shallows like beached whales or creating dark, cancerous shadows further out in the blue. He wanted to go to university: France, Dakar, Russia – anywhere would do. He was young, intelligent, ambitious, and, as we walked, he would tell me how he was waiting – waiting like all the other tens of millions of young Africans hoping for a better life.

'I cannot get a grant,' he said, 'so I am working, carrying fish in the market. I am trying to save money for a visa and a ticket.' He was full of hopes but it did not look to me as if he expected to fulfil many of them. Five years later, Salif told me he had died. He never made it to university, and was still living and working in the north when he became suddenly ill. As for what he died from, Salif could only give me the stock answer: the heart.

Working at the Mayor's office, Drémis, I know, will be busy helping to make arrangements for the elections, which are due shortly after I leave. I ask him how this is going.

'Ah,' he exclaims. 'The elections! Pah, pah, pah. So much to do. There are 74 parties and we have local elections as well. Very complicated.'

I remark on the number of parties, some of which I know have boycotted the elections.

'Each candidate must be very rich,' Drémis says. '*Very* rich,' he emphasizes. 'He will need millions, to provide great feasts for his supporters, and for many other things as well. That is the only way you can win elections here. You must throw a big party and make everyone happy.' Only half the population is eligible for voting, Salif has told me, the government long having been highly exclusive about who can apply for papers: if you've lost yours, or they're damaged, or you've just never got around to applying for them, which is not uncommon in rural areas, you're unlikely to get them, and particularly so if you are of the wrong ethnicity. Mariam has lost hers and has been unable to replace them.

The other person who has appeared in Salif's compound this evening is Alisanne. Alisanne is the younger brother of

Amadou, Salif's cousin in Nouakchott in whose rooms we lodged. It is luck that has brought him to Keniéba the same time I am here, as he lives and works in France and only comes home once every two years. By the same coincidence, I met him last time he was back and he has also visited my home in England. He comes over to greet us where we sit.

Alisanne is bright and friendly, with an easy charm. Stocky, with a shiny, open face, he is younger than me, although no longer the young man who set out for France 12 years previously. He is streetwise and clearly adept at 'working the system'. Where many millions of others wish and talk about making it to Europe, he, apparently, had no difficulty in doing so. And then, once there, in what seemed a very short time, not only had he acquired a council flat in Paris but also, only a short time later, a French passport. These accomplishments he brushes aside.

'Yes, I have a flat. Yes, I have a French passport,' he told me when I last met him. 'There are ways... you know...' It was only when pressed closer about this over the course of a few days that more details emerged. It had by no means been a simple task. He explained: 'Getting there was the most difficult. I went with some companions into the desert. There we paid some Arabs to take us into Algeria. They were not good men. They took our money, but they did not look after us. We did not have enough water, and the vehicle we were in broke down. We had to walk for many days. But we were lucky. I heard of others who were simply taken out into the desert and left to die.'

He made it across Algeria and into France, although he did not furnish details of how he accomplished this. Once in France, he dumped his passport and all means of identification.

'At that time you could get refugee status this way,' he said. 'You read the newspapers and saw where the wars were and told the immigration people you were from that country. To them all black people look the same. They gave you a temporary permit to stay in the country and provided accommodation for you.'

He spent a number of years working the system, gradually improving his official status until, after a sufficient number of years' residency, he was eligible for a French passport. At one period he lived and worked in Belarus. He told me how he would get there. 'It was well known that immigration officials did not bother first-class train passengers if they were asleep,' he said. 'So all you had to do was buy a business suit and a first-class train ticket, and when you came to the border pretend to be asleep.'

Alisanne makes it all sound easy, as that is his way, but I have seen the change that has come over him since he went away and I am aware of the stress and difficulty of being first-generation immigrants into the EU. Life for them is not easy. To those still in Africa, the West may resemble some sort of nirvana where jobs pay well and the standards of living are high. The reality is different. More often than not, first-generation immigrants end up living in the very poorest of housing estates among some of the most socially deprived communities, employed in factories paying the minimum wage, or not even that. The cost of living is exceedingly high; they are isolated; the weather is dreadful; and they have yet to become part of any constituency with sufficient influence to improve their status. On top of this, they must send money home. When Alisanne came to see me in England, I went to pick him up at the house of an acquaintance of his who resided in a housing estate on the edge of a large provincial town not far from where I live. Looking for the right house, I asked a neighbor if he knew the family.

'Fucking blacks,' is all the middle-aged, shaven-headed man replied.

The estate was of the most rundown variety and the flat was almost entirely devoid of furniture or possessions, with no curtains and only a vast television set in the living room. Alisanne's friend – a man from Sierra Leone – was charming and insisted I stay for something to eat. He worked in a nearby factory for the minimum wage, had three young children, and his wife was ill in hospital. When I asked about his rent, I was shocked at how high it was. This man was certainly not living in any sort of nirvana. Even if he had wanted to return to his home in Sierra Leone – and he told me this was his eventual ambition – the likelihood of its happening in the near future was low, as he did not have sufficient money to pay for the flights for all his family and anyway, he told me, there would probably be no work for him when he got there.

Alisanne did not hold a lot of sympathy for his friend, remarking only that he should look for a better job. Alisanne's own job, however, was not much better. Originally, he had worked the streets of Paris and Amsterdam, selling African trinkets and souvenirs. This was a good business for a young man with few responsibilities but, as life became more complicated and he married and found a flat, he moved on to construction sites. This was exceptionally hard work and, although it paid sufficiently, did not produce high rewards for unskilled labor. Years of this exhausted him, and it was during this period I saw the most significant change come over him. The strong young man I had once known became overweight, puffy-faced and stressed. The last time I saw him, he told me he had quit construction.

'I'm at the airport now,' he told me, as ever full of optimism. 'It's good there, although the wages are low.'

He was packing delivery vans for a courier company. Alisanne is bright and intelligent, and it occurred to me that he could get a better job than this. I asked him if he had been to job agencies; if he had looked for jobs in the service industries, for example. I was thinking at the least of a job in one of those many coffee-shop chains up and down the high streets. Surely he could move up from the bottom rung of the employment ladder. But Alisanne was strangely ambivalent about my suggestions.

'No, no. It's difficult,' is all he replied. I wondered how much of the difficulty was practical and how much was to do with a lack of confidence, with a mentality of self-imposed cultural ghettoization. When I probed gently about his life in France it seemed to confirm this. His expectations were low.

'Our life is simple,' he said. 'We work. We eat African foods at home with our wives and children. We go to the mosque to pray. On Sundays we visit our friends. We send money home. That is all. We are Africans,' he laughed, 'we do not need more.'

Alisanne lives in one of the poorest suburbs of Paris, one that a while ago was at the center of some riots. These were known locally as 'The Sons of the Immigrants Riots', as it was not the first-generation immigrants who participated in them but their more culturally liberated offspring. They caused considerable disruption across France. Alisanne was dismissive at the time.

'It's these young people,' he said. 'They do not know how to behave. They want everything without having to work for it.'

Life was not easy for Alisanne, I knew. But he would be the last to admit this. Back in the village he looks happy and relaxed. He greets me warmly, but he does not join us on our mats. 'I have many visits to make,' he says, giving me a wink. I know what those visits mean.

Darkness descends and the mêlée of livestock in the compound clears, the animals making their way to their pens at the far end. The air being a little cooler in the open space of the compound, away from the hot walls of the buildings, Mariam moves us and our mats and cushions further out into it. Here we settle down quietly, awaiting the evening meal. Ibrahim Tandia is clearly familiar with village life. Although he now lives in Germany and, I know, is from an urban background, he is at ease, happy to play with the young children who crawl over him like a giant teddy bear. A little later Mustapha, our driver, and Harana, his young colleague, appear. They, I can see, are a little ill at ease. They are Moors, and this compound in the old part of a Peul town in the heart of the south represents the home-base of Black African culture as much as anywhere. They have no animosity but a whole history of distrust and rivalry between the two communities cannot so easily be swept aside. Salif puts on a show of bonhomie, inviting them to sit down and cracking jokes. The Moors respond cheerfully enough, but their fear of being patronized is apparent.

'You'll eat,' Salif says. The Moors decline politely. 'Yes, surely… you'll stay to eat,' he insists. The Moors mumble their disinclination. 'My wife… she has cooked specially… she will be very angry.' The Moors smile. 'Wait… the food will be here soon.'

Mariam produces a great platter of heavily spiced macaroni to be eaten with bread, one of her specialities. The Moors take

a couple of handfuls each and get up.

'Eat, eat,' Salif insists, but the Moors are up, washing their hands from the *bidon*.

'*Bismillah*. We've eaten,' they say, backing away into the night.

I can see Ibrahim Tandia's eyes gleaming in the darkness.

'Good men,' he says as they depart. 'Good men.'

We lie and stare at the stars, which wink at us multitudinously. In other parts of the compound, groups mumble and stir to the dim glow of an oil lamp or faded beam of a torch. The livestock shift, with the odd explosive passing of air. In between each star are thousands – millions – of others. It is as if there is no blackness at all.

The children have fallen asleep, some curled on the sand, some at our feet, a couple draped over Salif. Mariam is rough with them. The smaller ones she picks up and deposits like sacks of potatoes on the mat by the house door. The others she shakes and pinches to wakefulness: 'Move, move. Wake up. Wake up,' she bullies them. They stagger drunkenly over to the mat where they curl up in a line, their hands pinched between their knees like fetuses.

6 The Seminar

Ethnic complications... A splendid array... Three-way translation... The Moor's protest... A gender lesson... The expert conductor finds an assistant... A memorable journey... A little country banditry... The virtues of compost

It is the first day of the seminar and Ibrahim Tandia is up early. We eat a quick breakfast, then he, Salif and I are off across town to the *Centre*.

Paying for a consultant to come to Mauritania is something of a long-shot. We have never done anything like this before and are eager to see how it will turn out. We were aware only of the importance of the seminar and the necessity of having someone with sufficient experience and authority to lead it.

Salif and I have been wondering for some time how we might create a project that was truly inclusive of the many ethnic and cultural groups in the region. For, in the region near to Keniéba where we conduct our work, there is a large and complex mix, one that has taken me the longest time to untangle. First, there are the Moors, mostly the Black Moors, or Harratin, those descended from freed slaves. Then there are the White 'Arab', or *Bidan* Moors – those more directly descended from the Yemeni Arabs who came south in the 17th century and the Berbers who were already in the region – who are mostly, but not entirely, concentrated further north. Then there are the Bantu Black African peoples, who come mainly from the Peul and Soninke ethnic groups and within whose numbers, as with the Moors, there are further divisions along caste lines. The Peul are a part of the greater Fulani people, traditionally a pastoral, cattle-breeding group, but also a people who, over the centuries, have settled in many towns, gaining reputations for learning, conducting trade and forming powerful states of their own. They are often fairer skinned and more aquiline than other West Africans and some hold a tradition that they originated in southern Egypt. In Mauritania, as elsewhere, the Peul are Muslims, as are their compatriots, the Moors. This, however, has not prevented the history of rivalry and conflict between the two communities that continues to this day.

All these ethnic and social groupings are further divided along occupational lines, such as pastoralists, commercial irrigation farmers, small-scale vegetable growers and traditional farmers. And then there is the gender divide. Across all these groups, the needs of the women differ from those of the men.

Would it be possible to devise a project inclusive of all these diverse groups? If so, it could only help to create some much-needed harmony across the community. It is with this in mind that Salif has spent the last year travelling around the countryside canvassing all the different groups, talking to them about our plans and motivating them to voice their opinions. This has not been easy, as the lack of cross-community collaboration as well as the absence of any cultural precedent for the sort of analytical approach required do not lend themselves to acceptance of a new approach. Of course, there has long been collaboration of sorts between communities, such as the tradition for pastoralists, Moorish or otherwise, to graze their livestock on crop residues, with payment being in the form of the animal manure that then fertilizes the farmers' fields. And for centuries farmers and animal herders have been innovating, adapting their practices to changing climatic or market contexts.

In recent decades, though, the rate of change has been exceptional. The rains are consistently so poor now, for example, that, in order to achieve sufficient water penetration of the soil, many farmers group together to hire tractors to plough their fields; grazing pastures so quickly become exhausted that pastoralists have to travel further and further to find them; and due to the vagaries of markets the world over – markets that are slewed by the neoliberal economic policies and the subsidized efficiencies of the rich world – the prices for cash crops are often so bad that they do not cover costs. Even in the extreme conditions of today, however, there are solutions – solutions we hope Ibrahim Tandia is going to help the farmers discover and develop.

The simple fact of having the seminar is in itself a significant movement in this direction. The desired outcome – consensus on the shape and design of a project – is almost a bonus. The mere fact of having motivated and organized people sufficiently to all come together on one particular day in one particular place for one particular purpose already indicates some degree of success.

So, as Ibrahim Tandia, Salif and I march towards the *Centre*, files and briefcases business-like under our arms, we do so with a sense of confidence and excitement. We are cheerful and optimistic. There will be as many as 150 people present, representing some 35 co-operatives and groups across all sectors of the community. This is the theory.

We reach the door of the compound and, amazingly, not only is there not a single person there, the door is actually locked and Salif does not know where the key is. It is a bad moment. Ibrahim Tandia folds his arms, looking mildly amused. Salif looks embarrassed. I struggle to contain my frustration. Frantic phone calling from Salif ensues. Then he goes off. Ibrahim Tandia and I sit down in the shade of the compound wall.

'They will learn,' Ibrahim Tandia says. 'If they want to modernize, if they want to lift themselves up, they will learn to respect time.'

We sit and wait, and a group of women arrive. Later, some men show up. Later still, Salif reappears with the key, unlocks the metal doors of the *Centre* compound and opens up the main room of the building. People drift in while we arrange chairs, and Ibrahim Tandia sets up a blackboard. We are cheerful again now. Méline is here from Kaédi, as are a number of Keniéba dignitaries. All is coming together, not perhaps as Ibrahim Tandia and I in our efficient, Western way would have liked, but in an African way. It is happening, but slowly. The constituent parts of a complex organizational maneuver are slowly gelling and, before long, there is a great crowd and a loud babble of voices.

The room is large and spacious and chairs have been brought in from all over the town. Everyone is dressed up in their best. All are encouraged to sit, either on mats on the floor or on the chairs. Here, to one side, the women, resplendent in voluminous dresses, are given chairs. In the front row, the town mayor, the local member of parliament and a number of elders look important and impressive in brilliant white *bobos*. Farmers, pastoralists, commercial rice producers: they are all here. Some are bright-eyed and switched-on, some wary, some tall and handsome, some gnarled; many display fine examples of the wide range of bodily ailments so prevalent in rural areas: bald eyes, twisted legs, crazily dysfunctional teeth, severe skin diseases. There are Moors, but only a few, and a great many familiar faces.

Salif starts proceedings by thanking all for coming and calling on the Mayor to speak. The Mayor is a tall, gruff man. He does not stand, but bellows out a traditional speech in which all are thanked for their invaluable participation and Allah is invoked for his blessings.

Next, the local MP rises. Monsieur Tissalou is a large, expansive, white-haired man in the traditional African 'Big Man' mould. Utilizing a well-practised manner, he delivers a long, mesmeric speech that leaves everyone in no doubt as to his magnanimity. He finishes on a useful and valid point.

'We are not all the same. We are not all as one. This is the nature of community: the coming together of peoples of differing castes and tribes and cultures. But does this hinder us? No, it does not. Does it prevent us achieving our aims? No, it does not. Messieurs Salif, Peter and Tandia have come here to assist us. For that, we must thank Allah. All that is done is His work and is done in the light of His benevolence. Allah is our guide and Father. We must all humble ourselves before His great magnificence. And now to end: my part in these proceedings is small and insignificant. I am not here as a participant but only to welcome our guests and give my blessings on your endeavors. But I have one suggestion before I go. Messieurs Peter and Tandia speak French. Already we have translation into Peul. There has been some attempt at translation into Hassaniya for our Arab friends. But I suggest we be more organized about this. I think, Monsieur Salif, for the sake of harmony and equality, translators could be selected and pauses made in all verbal correspondence in order to allow time for every person in the room to understand what is being said. That is all I have to say. My part is done. Soon, indeed, there are elections and I may be an MP no more. But in the meantime, may Allah bless these proceedings with success and harmony.'

Applause commences as Monsieur Tissalou takes his seat, nodding his appreciation about him. A great discussion ensues, resulting in official translators being selected. Everything that is now said is translated three ways: into French, Peul and Hassaniya.

It is now time for Ibrahim Tandia to take the floor. In a more business-like manner, he thanks all for coming and

quickly gets down to explaining the format and objectives of the next two days. Monsieur Tissalou, the MP, cannot restrain himself and every few minutes applauds Ibrahim Tandia and commends him on what he has said, often expanding on this theme for some considerable time. Ibrahim Tandia does not betray the slightest sign of impatience at these interruptions, but calmly continues on from where he left off once free to do so. Presently a question comes from the back.

'Where is the representation from the Moorish community?'

Ibrahim Tandia looks to Salif.

'Uh, we have a number of that community here,' Salif says.

'We are many and there are only two or three here,' the voice calls out. A small, wiry 'White' Moor with an impish face pushes himself forwards.

'I spoke to Ould Barka and Ould Talabaye yesterday,' Salif says, 'and they said they would be here. We also have a number of Harratin present.'

'This is nothing,' the man says, apparently dismissing the

Black Moor Harratin community in one fell swoop. 'What kind of meeting is this that each community is not represented properly? When benefits come to this community, all should get their fair share. Why is this white man here? He is here to help us all. Whatever he has to give us is for all, not just for certain people. It is a disgrace. I say...'

By now such an uproar has broken out in the room that it is difficult to hear what the Moor is saying. People are shouting and arguing. The Moor is putting on a display of great indignation. Ibrahim Tandia is unfazed and just stands there, his arms folded. Salif is trying to reason with people, to no effect. The dignitaries in the front row, including Monsieur Tissalou, who so recently had the crowd eating out of his hand, look impotent.

'We are all represented fairly... everyone was told about the meeting... let the man speak... are they giving out fencing materials?... when's lunch?' people are shouting. One man roars at the Moor: 'They are giving nothing away for free so you can go now.' Another, to great hilarity, shouts: 'The lamb will be here soon. Don't miss the meal.'

The Moor is hopping up and down. He shouts: 'This is nothing. This meeting is nothing.' He stalks to the door. 'It is nothing,' he yells over his shoulder as he departs.

The babble of talk and shouting goes on for some time but gradually subsides as Salif calls all to order. 'Our friend is free to leave if he wishes,' he says when he can finally be heard. 'Let Monsieur Tandia continue.'

Ibrahim Tandia takes up his theme again and, before long, is tying up his introduction. The Mayor and Monsieur Tissalou take this opportunity, along with most of the elders, to depart. Now the seminar can start in earnest. What has passed so far is both an indication of the challenge faced by this disparate, unruly community and of the usefulness of such meetings in creating the space in which steam can be let off. Ibrahim Tandia highlights this at the start of the first seminar session.

'We are here to voice our opinions. Everyone – even those with the strongest opinions,' he says with a smile, 'is welcome to speak out.'

Ibrahim Tandia's first objective, he tells us, is to get people to think about themselves and their communities under the four topic headings of Strengths, Weaknesses, Opportunities and Threats; in other words, to conduct what, in development jargon, is known as a SWOT analysis. This he does unashamedly by splitting the group up along gender lines. He winks at Salif and me as the groups separate.

'You will see what happens,' he says.

The men all crowd outside where, for 45 minutes, a great uproar can be heard. The women stay in the room and settle down, quietly discussing the issues with one of their number elected to record the results. After the allotted time, Ibrahim Tandia calls all back to the room and writes the findings of each group down on the blackboard. It is a joke. The men have managed to record only three bare facts: they need fencing materials; they need wells; and they need seed. The women, on the other hand, have come up with all sorts of details about themselves and the environment in which they live. Strengths consist of sun, good soil, water from the river and available labor. Weaknesses consist of broken equipment, lack of transport, crop pests and poor availability of agricultural inputs such as fertilizer and seed. Opportunities include a ready market for vegetables and the possibility, they hope, for the project to provide them with literacy classes. And the threats consist of desertification and environmental degradation.

'You see,' Ibrahim Tandia says to the gathering, 'the womenfolk do not only have the beauty, they have the brains as well.'

'It is not just for making babies that we are good,' a young pregnant woman shouts out to more laughter.

Ibrahim Tandia is a master at his trade. Throughout the morning I watch him stimulate and then harness the potential of the delegates. How he does this is a mystery, as he never imposes himself or gives opinions. He is like a conductor. At his hands gradually the crowd harmonizes, potential leaders, thinkers and innovators emerging as if by gravity. His technique may involve traditional developmental tools, but it is his charm and presence that produce the results. By the time we break for lunch in the early afternoon, working group leaders have been chosen, and there is an aura of excitement in the air. We are all tired and hot, yes – the temperature in the crowded room must be 45 degrees at least – and in need of some sustenance, but we have a gleam in our eyes. Any doubts I may have had about bringing in Ibrahim Tandia are washed away.

There has been activity in the *Centre* compound all morning preparing a great feast for the seminar delegates. Various members of Salif's family have set up a kitchen there, and large quantities of couscous have been cooked and two sheep slaughtered. Mamadou, Salif's cousin – he with the unsubstantiated reputation for being work-shy – is in charge and, when I popped out earlier in the morning for a breath of air, I found him gleefully up to his arms in sheep's blood, stripping the two hanging carcasses down with an expertise that made it look as if he were undressing them.

'We will feast well today,' he says, grinning happily.

Despite the promise of this, the seminar delegates have sensibly decided that, instead of passing the afternoon in a long drawn-out period of gluttony followed by a single evening seminar session, they will stop only briefly to eat and then crack straight on with proceedings. This will allow them to fit two further sessions in today which, along with two tomorrow morning, will complete the seminar, so giving them plenty of time tomorrow afternoon to regain their homes before nightfall. Everyone is happy with this decision, which, on the one hand, reduces the seminar length by half a day and, on the other, reflects people's enthusiasm for what is taking place, for there is nothing people like better than a long afternoon of eating. That they are giving up what may have been the primary motivation for many of them in coming is a tribute to Ibrahim Tandia's skill.

And so lunch is taken, in the shockingly short time of an hour, just long enough for people to say their prayers, stretch their legs and gather around the great steaming platters of meat and couscous. This is a popular, traditional meal, the couscous being made from the flour of millet, the staple crop, with the meat, consisting seemingly mostly of ribs, stomach lining and internal organs, piled high on top of it. People relish the food, cracking the bones and sucking out the marrow, helping each other twist stubborn joints in two, crunching gristle between their teeth. Tea is being made so that, immediately subsequent to the last mouthful, as tradition dictates, a glass can be had to 'wash the mouth'. And then we are back to work.

The afternoon session is as successful as the morning. A couple of further exercises are carried out, this time with the delegates broken down into more homogenous groups. There is one man who particularly stands out. He is a pastoralist with a wide, bright face and a halo of wild hair. What is most remarkable about him, however, is his intelligence and dynamism. I ask Salif who he is, and he tells me that he is simply a Peul livestock herder from a village a little to the north. Quickly this man emerges as a spokesperson, and it is not long before he is assisting Ibrahim Tandia in almost every facet of the seminar. His grasp of its subtleties is profound, as though he too had gained his doctorate in development studies.

'Monsieur Tandia, do you not think it would be good if you got the groups to mix a little,' he suggests in his good

French at one time. 'Perhaps group leaders could swap places for an exercise.'

At another time, when everyone is looking tired and lethargic, he has us all standing up doing arm-waving exercises. Whether he has come across this technique on some previous training program I do not know, but he has everyone in stitches, which wakes us all up. 'It is good, is it not?' he cries out as he swings his arms, a wild look in his eyes.

We break late in the afternoon, and everybody goes their own way, some to walk back to their villages, most to stay in town. Only a small group of irrigation farmers remains behind. It may already have been a long day, and we are all hot, but Ibrahim Tandia wants to visit their irrigation schemes. Salif, Méline and I are happy to accompany him.

The Moshe River, fed by 52 streams, is the water source for all irrigation in the region. Some 40 kilometers to the east of Keniéba, the river is dammed at a natural convergence of two lines of hills. All but eight of the streams feed into the river upstream of the hills, meaning the dam and its lake capture by far the larger part of the local water resource. The streams that feed the river are seasonal and are dry for most of the year. This is not the case for the Moshe, though, as the dam, along with another at its far end where it joins the Senegal River, guarantees a permanent supply of water. It is this that allows for irrigation farming in what is otherwise such a very dry region.

The Moshe is a small river some 20 to 30 meters across, depending on the season. It wends its way westwards across the Sahelian plain with thorny vegetation hugging its banks. It is where it approaches Keniéba, about halfway down its course, that it is most utilized. Here, much of the land in proximity to it, if not entirely above its flood plain, is of high enough elevation at least to reduce the risk of flooding. In all, there are some 70 private irrigation schemes down the length of the Moshe, covering around 3,000 hectares and benefiting, directly or indirectly, as many as 40,000 people from 50 villages or hamlets. Keniéba takes the lion's share of this, although the reality is that this agricultural sector functions exceptionally badly, with as much as half the land under the schemes either abandoned or exploited so poorly that it produces very little.

We are cheerful in the Toyota as we head out of town to inspect the irrigation schemes, Salif, at the last moment, having made his obligatory phone call to the adjutant. The sun is low, and there is a crowd of people in the back and many more squeezed into the cab. Mustapha, our driver, has a look on his face not unlike that of a camel: dignified and disapproving.

There is only one bridge over the Moshe and it is here at Keniéba. It crosses the river just outside town at a point where the river is at its widest with a long sandy slope running down to its edge. This is a busy spot, as it is to here that livestock herders from far and wide bring their beasts to water. Great herds of sheep, goats and cattle mill about, some just arriving, some held back a little distance until there is more space at the water's edge. The cattle wade in and stand motionless, sucking up draughts of the water. The sheep and goats line the shore, heads bowed. A little further up are a few camels, their long necks bent to their reflections, their nomadic, Moorish owners squatting beside them splashing water up their long, pale arms. A little aside, knots of women work away at large basins of washing, rinsing their materials in the river and joining forces to twist them dry before wending their way like ants back up the path to town, their washing balanced on their heads. Next to the washerwomen, bare-breasted girls soap themselves up whilst a little further out boys gallivant in the water, naked and lithe, like sprites. Despite the heat, I have never seen anyone other than these boys immerse themselves in the river for the sole purpose of cooling off. The only exception to this was one time when Salif, slowly and surprisingly, simply walked fully clothed into a deep part of the river, ducked his head under twice and walked back out. He was dry within half an hour.

We cross the bridge, and the *piste*, or elevated dirt track, runs straight as a die into the distance. For the longest time, my experience of the geography of this region was restricted to the few details I could glean from my large-scale map of Mauritania and whatever parts of it could be reached by donkey-cart, for those were the days before we had a vehicle of our own. Much time was passed rumbling over the plains to the plod of animal traction. Although this allowed me to gain an intimate knowledge of the immediate surroundings of Keniéba, it prevented me from grasping the larger context of a region where even small villages can be 15 kilometers apart. This road, for example, disappearing so enticingly to the distance, had always remained a mystery. I longed to travel down it, to open up the next page in the geographic story; to make it over the next horizon. Always, there seemed some reason preventing me from devoting the time to hitching a lift or taking transport down the road. But then, some years back, a perfect opportunity presented itself. Amadou, Salif's cousin back in Nouakchott, was on a mission to a town 70 kilometers east of Keniéba for his employer, the Department of Water and Hydrology. Returning to Keniéba one evening, we found Amadou installed *en route* for the night with a Toyota, driver and assistant. He was leaving early the next morning, and Salif and I were welcome to join him.

It was the end of the dry season, and the rains had been particularly bad that year. The countryside was burnt and desiccated, and the few cattle we passed as we set out from Keniéba looked emaciated and seemingly ready to drop. Their tall Peul herders, whom we left in our dust, did not look much better. Our driver, Barak, was a jovial man with whom Amadou, sitting up front, kept up an almost continual banter. Amadou himself was in good form. This for him was like a holiday. When I asked him what the mission was, he laughed. 'Just some Prefect up to tricks,' he said.

Barak, the driver, took the road at the requisite corrugation-defying speed, and the 'assistant', Moktar, an older man with a round, cheerful face, chanted what sounded like Qur'anic psalms, but the laughter certain sections created made me suspect were not. Salif was at ease, enjoying being liberated for the moment from any responsibilities.

We headed east and the countryside seemed, if possible, to become dryer, a black, gravelly rubble taking over from the scant pastures. Here, surprisingly, there were a number of tiny villages: desperate-looking collections of shanty-like huts isolated on the windswept plains. A few dazed-looking children stood about; perhaps an old man or woman, but otherwise no-one was visible. I asked Amadou how on earth they survived in such a barren spot.

'They have crops in the *oueds*,' he said. 'A few sheep? Who knows?' He sounded uninterested in these impoverished people but when, a little later, we passed a group of young boys carrying rocks to the side of the road in one of the many places where it had been partially washed away, he told Barak to pull over.

'What are you up to?' he called to the wide-eyed boys.

'We are building up the roadside,' they stammered. 'The road workers give us money for doing it.' At this, Amadou roared with laughter.

'Little bandits,' he said. 'Why should they give you any money? It was probably you who took the rocks away in the first place.'

The boys smiled shyly. 'Bandits,' he laughed again, shaking his head, 'genuine little bandits.' And the boys laughed too, as they could tell Amadou was being friendly. He told Barak to move on but, before we did, he dug his hand into his pocket and pulled out a handful of coins. 'Goodbye, little ones,' he called, scattering the coins on the ground as we pulled away.

Not long after this, I was surprised by a range of considerable hills appearing ahead of us. This was something new to me. Used to the flat monotony of southern Mauritania, I was quite unprepared for this. Soon the road was picking its way through a broken, rocky terrain. The hills looked old: ridges of black, cracked rock protruding like an old man's bones through the surface of the earth. The road was quite incapable of dealing with all this hardness and made no attempt to smooth a passage through the pass up to which we were headed. We were reduced to a crawl as we lurched over the rocks, turning steeply up the final hairpin. And then there before us was a magnificent view, one I had never before been afforded in Mauritania, the view of a distance only height can allow: a gently undulating plain of dry, yellow savannah stretching to such a very finite distance, with not a fence, town, person or any other mark of man visible, that it brought home to me with a sudden jolt a knowledge of the aboriginal heritage of the earth; that all was once unfenced; that the earth was once far bigger than humankind.

We swept down into that land, our spirits high, laughing for no apparent reason, and arrived a surprisingly short time later in the small town of Mbaye, which had been invisible from the pass. If the view from the pass had given rise in me to feelings of the sublime, Mbaye could not have been better constructed to provide the antidote. It was a desperate, forgotten, ignored, end-of-the-earth sort of place where people had left a not very edifying mark. A single, wide street lined with near-empty shops adjoined a shanty of wood and corrugated iron. At one end of town were the police and military posts, the school and the Prefect's residence. At the other, a wide *oued* planted with thin crops and traversed by the long elevation of the *piste*. The population looked threadbare and dejected. There were no vehicles except, amazingly, a single Toyota pickup converted into a Winston Cigarette advert that cruised slowly, as though in a Western, down the empty main street blasting an advert through its loudspeaker. Dust and drifts of plastic blew after it.

We drove through and out the other side to where the pumping station was situated beside the *oued*. Here, in a tangle of palms, a small shack containing the municipal pump was linked to a borehole in the middle of the dry riverbed. Amadou disappeared into the shack, only to reappear a few minutes later. We sped off to the Prefect's residence where he again disappeared. Later I saw him emerge to one side of the building. He was talking to a tall, well-dressed man, evidently the Prefect. The Prefect was animated, gesticulating with his arms. He turned abruptly on his heel and walked off. Amadou came over. He was smiling but remarked only: 'Imbecile.'

We went back to the main street in town and located the only shop that boasted a fridge, beside which we installed ourselves on the floor. The shop was basic, just a rough wooden counter and a single stack of shelves containing a few basic items. The owner was a friendly, intelligent-looking man, fatigue etched onto his face. We drank Fantas and waited.

The problem, apparently, was that the town pump had been reported as not running properly, but, in order to verify this, Amadou needed to replace the water-flow counter with a new one so that he could be sure the readings were correct. He needed the Prefect's permission to do this but the man had argued that this was not necessary. He had told Amadou he would come with him to the pump later. We waited an hour and half, then Amadou went back to the Prefecture, only to be told that the Prefect was in a meeting and could not see him. He returned to the boutique.

'I will put the new counter on anyway,' he said and disappeared with Barak and the Toyota.

'He'll need two hours to get a good reading,' Moktar, Amadou's assistant, remarked. A large woman now joined us on the floor of the shop and started making tea. It was stupefyingly hot, and I was not feeling well, but the lady was jolly and the banter between her, Moktar and the shop owner was lively. When, later, Amadou and Barak returned, they had with them some roasted meat in brown paper, and we set up a veritable picnic in the shade by the road outside the shop. It was dusty, sweaty and unbearably hot, but we were cheerful as we ate the meat with bread, drank new Fantas and washed all of this down with the large woman's teas.

Amadou was entirely unfazed by his standoff with the Prefect. 'He does not want us to install a new meter,' he said, 'because he has been making a profit from the water rates, charging his constituents one rate but having to submit a lower one because the meter is recording lower usage.' And, sure enough, when later we returned to the pumping station, he confirmed that the old counter had either malfunctioned or been tampered with.

'Just a little country banditry,' he remarked dismissively as we left.

The dam on the River Moshe was only a short distance from Mbaye, so, before starting our return journey, we made a detour to see it. It was a tall construction plugging a natural gap where two long lines of hills met. Behind was a vast and astonishing lake. To see so much water in this barren landscape was eerie, and we stood on the dam a little speechless, as none of my companions had seen this sight before either. Dead trees protruded from the surface of the water, indicating that it was not very deep. Looking at the lake reminded me why the storage of water in this way can be so contentious. Already, farmers must pay to take water which once came to them free with the floods after the rains, and whole communities' livelihoods are prey not only to political or economic exploitation, but also, and more likely, to mismanagement. It is not infrequent that whole crops are swept away by surges of water, when co-ordination between upper and lower dams fails.

It was not until some years later that I completed the geographic picture of this region, when I took the road to its conclusion at the far southern tip of Mauritania, near the Malian border. This was a one-way trip, as I was headed for Bamako, the Malian capital, from where I would fly home. Watching the country change from the barrenness of Mauritania to the comparative pastoral softness of Mali was fascinating. In fact, the northerly parts of western Mali that we were travelling through were dry, regarded as semi-desert themselves, but travelling south from Mauritania it did not feel like this. The villages seemed pretty and archetypal of agrarian African life, with round thatched huts, large shady trees and old men sitting peacefully in the shade of lean-tos. The people were colorful and healthy-looking and busy always: in the surrounding village fields, or ferrying mounds of produce to market on donkey-carts, or playing games of football on dusty patches of ground. How very different this was to the sparse existence that clings to the desiccated plains further north in Mauritania! It brought home to me how very difficult life was for people in Mauritania, and how very skilled they were in adapting to it.

'Those fields belong to Daouda Dirana,' Méline shouts from the front of the Toyota where he is squeezed next to Ibrahim Tandia as we cruise slowly up the *piste*. It is late afternoon, the seminar is over for the day and we have come to look at the irrigation schemes.

Méline indicates a large area stretching away to our right. 'He has 150 hectares,' he says, still shouting over the noise of the vehicle as it rumbles over the rough ground. 'But he only grows rice. That is the preferred cash crop because people think it is easy and will always fetch a good price. What they don't factor in is the high cost of diesel for the pumps and the cost of fertilizer.'

'How many hectares does he actually work?' Ibrahim Tandia asks.

'Not more than 30,' Méline replies, and explains how the scheme was part of a southern agricultural regeneration program funded by one of the large financial institutions active in Mauritania. Some $150,000 were spent on the land, he tells us, and Daouda Dirana was supposed to pay back a third of it.

'Why are they working so little land, then?' Ibrahim Tandia asks as we draw to a halt.

'The work that was done on the land was of such poor quality,' Méline says, 'that much of the terrain is not level enough for irrigation. Those responsible for implementing the works took half the money for themselves, meaning a proper job was not done. Meanwhile, Daouda Dirana is an old man and no-one cares whether he repays his share of the loan or not. Once he dies,' Méline says, 'the problem will be gone.'

A little further down the road is another large scheme:

190 hectares this time, with again only a small portion of it actually being worked. The story here though, Méline tells us, is a mixed one: a large amount of money was borrowed from the bank to set up the scheme, which then made a good start with a couple of good harvests. Then three years of disasters – a breakdown, a flooding and an insect invasion – meant they had to borrow more money from the bank.

'Sixty families take plots within this scheme,' Méline says, 'so many will suffer if it collapses. One good year, though, and they will be all right.'

We drive on and enter a gateway. The scheme here – 60 hectares of rice, vegetables and fruit trees – belongs to a family with wealthy connections and was one of the first to be set up in the region. I have been here a number of times and have always found the manager a little difficult. Moktar is tall and gruff, the younger brother of the *patron* who financed the scheme.

'Peasant agriculture… it's nothing,' he said, dismissing my praise of the well-organized scheme the first time I visited it. On another occasion, when I asked about his extensive banana plantation, he only laughed: 'Bananas are difficult. They are like children. They require a lot of time and money, then turn out bad.'

But in truth Moktar is a good farmer and a hard-working one; only, one suspects, a little frustrated at being a farmer rather than a man of wealth and influence like his brother. Ibrahim Tandia has no difficulty in charming him, inspiring him to give us a guided tour of his land. In one area we come across a plantation of fruit trees, next to each of which is a small metal plaque recording its name and variety. Moktar tells us that the trees were planted 10 years ago and are part of a research project the Agricultural Research Office was financed to conduct.

'They've come back to see them just once, though,' he laughs, 'and that was only because they had a film crew with them.'

Over the years I have visited many of the irrigation schemes in the Keniéba region. Generally somewhere between 5 and 25 hectares, these schemes are mostly owned by people who have risked everything to make the necessary investment. Usually, the owners have borrowed money from the banks to pay for the large water pumps and for the initial earthworks. As with the large scheme we saw earlier, the owners then mostly struggle to repay the loans, hampered, like Mabafé, Salif's family's scheme, by any number of problems. This year the issue is birds. From morning until night, people stand in their fields rattling cans to shoo away the huge flocks; some farmers, I've been told, have lost as much as two-thirds of their crops. The courage of these small, commercial farmers never ceases to amaze me. Year after year, they persevere, despite often seeing years' worth of work come to nothing, often going hungry in the process. They have no support and generally very little appropriate agricultural knowledge.

One man I have been visiting for many years has each year a new tale of disaster to relate. Musa is bright and cheerful but, according to Salif, not a particularly good farmer. On 'adventure' somewhere in West Africa as a younger man, as it is known when young men go off abroad in search of work, he returned home to Keniéba, he told me, 'because there was nothing for me there, whereas here we can grow food.' I find him always in the midst of his fields, a smile

of welcome on his face. He is always optimistic, always enthused.

'Not a bad year,' he'll say. 'But next year... next year, God willing, next year will be good.' One year, right in the middle of such a conversation, Musa suddenly hot-footed it away from me across his fields and out of view. A moment later, a vehicle turned up.

'Bank men,' Salif said.

We have time to visit only one further scheme, one we have helped develop so that it can be used as an example of good practice for others to see and copy. Already the sun has set, and the sky is crimson as we make our way to it. An individual for whom Salif obviously has a lot of respect runs the scheme. Mohamedou Samba is a tall, intelligent, gentle man dressed in a plain farmer's tunic. He takes us around his well-tended fields, explaining in good French all the things he has done. Fencing, he tells us, is his main problem, since here, as across much of the Sahel, enclosure of arable land is a big issue. In one part of the scheme we come across a number of compost pits – an innovation we have introduced – and Ibrahim Tandia asks our host what results he has had using the compost.

'I have used it on all my vegetables,' Mohamedou Samba says, 'and the yields are up 30 per cent.' Using controlled test plots, Salif and he have shown that the use of compost can also increase rice yields by 20 per cent. Getting other farmers to follow this example, though, will not be easy. Inspired and financed by certain powerful international institutions and foundations who believe in the concept of an agricultural sector based on the increased use of chemical fertilizers, the government has been handing out sacks of such fertilizer, free for the moment but of course only temporarily so.

We see the promotion of this new 'Green Revolution', as this global movement of new agricultural intensification based on the increased use of external inputs is termed, only putting agricultural production more and more into the hands of the few large transnational corporations that already control so much of the food production chain and which will naturally provide all these inputs. Next it will be genetically modified (GM) seed and all the products that must go with them on which farmers will necessarily become dependent, for each year all seed must be repurchased and each year, due to weakening soil fertility and pest and fungal immunity, more of the linked products will be required. In this manner, before long, if we are not careful, all food production, even at the most basic level, will be balanced on the volatilities and vagaries of a corporate global economic and political system not known for its robustness, sustainability or fairness. This is without even mentioning the vulnerability of such farming systems, with their poor soils and lack of adaptability, to climate change.

All of this Ibrahim Tandia, an internationalist, a wise man and an agronomist, knows well. Digging his hand now into Mohamedou Samba's compost pile, he extracts a handful of the rich, dark earth. Brandishing his fist aloft, his grinning face crimson in the evening light, he cries: 'Brown gold. Behold!'

It is dark by the time we make it back to town. Here the quiet of night quickly envelops us on our mats under the stars. We sit and await our evening meal, which does not appear until nearly midnight. Mariam, it seems, is in no hurry tonight.

7 The Life of the Compound

A moment of triumph... Child's play... Magnificent display... A battle with Polisario... Visions of paradise... Animal attitudes and the need for trees... The Peace Corps volunteer... Is the tractor necessary?... Ibrahim's plan

I wake in the night. All is still. Somewhere far off a donkey brays. Nearer to, a baby cries: not a full-throated wail, but a quieter, weaker whimpering; muffled voices, soothing it. A mosquito drones near my ear, but I am safe in my mosquito net. How I love a mosquito net! It is like a castle, impregnable to all. I can lie, stripped like a corpse, under my tented shroud, safe from all the bugs. Somewhere in the room a cricket starts up, the high pitch of its whine only really noticeable when, a little later, it stops. Later still I go for a pee. Outside, there is a thin, effervescent light. The compound is silent. The night is silent. I step like a thief across the pale sand.

We have a long morning of it at the *Centre*. As agreed, the seminar is to be completed this morning. As expected, there are not as many delegates today as there were yesterday. The night has seen a modest erosion: entirely, it must be said, on the male side. The first session is devoted to an exercise in which groups are asked to perform three tasks: to imagine what life will be like for them 10 years from now; to envisage how they would like it to be 10 years from now; and to think of what they might need to do differently over the next 10 years if they are to achieve what they want. This is a task requiring a sense of projection and aspiration that is less familiar to people who have such a strong belief in fate, for whom the uncertainties of tomorrow are largely left to the care of Allah – 'Insh'Allah', 'God willing', is the standard phrase.

The groups have been selected carefully, though, each with a leader and someone who can write down the conclusions, and Ibrahim Tandia, Salif and Méline go around lending a hand. The conclusions are interesting. Whereas, on the one hand, most people are pessimistic about what they imagine the future holds for them – 'nothing will ever change here,' is the general attitude – they do not, on the other, have an alternative vision beyond the most simple improvements to their lives. They do not, or perhaps cannot, hold any great ambition. Ibrahim Tandia, by now confident in the trust of these people, ties up the morning session with a small lecture.

'Do you know what it is that holds you back?' he asks. 'Do you know what is your greatest threat? Is it the climate? Is it the poor markets? Is it politics? No. Your greatest threat is yourselves. You are strong people. I have seen that these last two days. You are able and courageous. You must believe you can change things for the better. You must believe in yourselves. You have your leaders. Some of you have already formed community groups and co-operatives. You have shown great skill and innovation with your farming techniques. Now is the time to be ambitious. Work with each other. Have a vision of your future and work towards it. I know you can do it. I have seen you, and I know how great you are,' he finishes, bringing to bear all the warmth and passion of his character.

Applause erupts. The women in their chairs to the right are standing, tears in their eyes; the odd person, such as the pastoralist with the wild hair who so stood out yesterday, is cheering, shouting comments back. It is a moment of unity and passion, even for the small 'White Moor' from yesterday – he who stormed out so ferociously – whom I'm now surprised to see tucked in amongst the crowd near the door. He might not be clapping, but he is here, his tantrum apparently forgotten by all.

That the seminar has been a success, we are sure. The next stage will be for Ibrahim Tandia to devise the principal elements of the community project Salif wishes to implement, one that will build on the momentum he has created and engage the communities in meaningful action to combat the many problems that face them. This is what we are hoping for and we are eager to hear what Ibrahim Tandia will propose.

Afternoon; and time to rest. Tomorrow, we are to be away all day, crossing the Senegal River into Senegal and visiting our Dohley Women's Market Garden project. It will be a long day, so we have set aside this afternoon for relaxing. Besides, Ibrahim Tandia needs to do some work, and we have planned a meeting of Salif's development group for the evening.

The sun is strong and mats are spread out in the shade under Mamadou's thatched lean-to in the compound. We lounge on cushions and thin mattresses. Tea is being made and the heat of the afternoon passes in idle chat and casual observation of the passing life of the compound. This is something that never tires me. I have always loved to lounge and watch the little troupes of naked toddlers staggering about as if drunk, by turns cajoled, bullied and cuddled by their elder siblings as they go on their journeys of discovery. Little girls, themselves not long out of toddlerhood, carry infants swaddled to their backs, pretending to be their mothers. Boys trundle around their ingenious trucks and cars constructed from old tin cans and bottle tops, complete with steering wheels and suspension as good as the real thing. Smaller ones might have a nice leaky battery to play with, or a plastic bag. Already you can see the characters emerging: those prone to being bullish; the nervy, bright ones; the bossy girls. Most of them are grubby to the extreme, the older ones dressed in long, stained T-shirts or, for the girls, ragged dresses. Most of the toddlers have green snot coming from their noses; clusters of flies gather at the corners of the smallest ones' eyes. Like children the world over, they squabble and fight, but always with a fierce eye for the adults, whose weight of approbation keeps them from going too far.

One time I saw a boy strike a girl. This brought him the most severe of condemnations and a thwacking from Mamadou that left him sobbing for many hours, to which no-one paid the slightest attention. Another time a boy was chased from the compound, shrieking with terror, escaping over a wall like a thief with shoes and stones thrown after him. I never did discover what he had done. The boys are treated toughly. They stick together in age-group gangs, roaming about warily, as at any moment they might be scolded or, worse, asked to perform a task. They are by no means cowed or dejected, though. Out of the compound, in the town, they have the bright, laughing eyes of mischief: '*Tubab, tubab,*' they will chant after me if they meet me down an alleyway – 'white man, white man'.

Twice a week such boys must visit the Qur'anic school, where for two hours they chant verses of the Qur'an. For the moment, they do not know the meaning of the Arabic words they have copied onto their wooden boards, but the better of them will learn; some, when they are older, might even memorize the entire book, at which time they might attain the title *Marabout*, or Holy One. The sound of their many voices chanting different verses at different pitches creates a melodious harmony that reverberates throughout the town.

The women are busy most of the afternoon and, when not busy, are certainly not idle. They may settle down together for a while on a mat, sipping tea and chatting, but their hands will be occupied, rubbing platters of millet flour into

couscous, picking over bowls of rice to remove tiny, teeth-wrecking stones, or fine-chopping haricot bean leaf. They will also spend many hours working on the intricate hair braids of their sisters or friends.

The women are remarkable always in their appearance. It is as if what life lacks in material and even cultural density – for the region is not of any great musical, artistic or ceremonial note – they make up for in their apparel. It is into clothes as opposed to anything else that the greatest effort is poured. And so the compound can seem at times like a catwalk. A young woman returning with a basin of water on her head is dressed in the most magnificent deep-purple, tie-dyed dress with laced white cuffs, gold gleaming at her ears, ranks of bracelets up her arms and skin oiled to a deep, honeyed brown. Another is lifting a large rock above her head – one that I would have difficulty wielding – and hurling it down onto a large piece of wood in order to break the wood into bits for the cooking fire, and despite the baseness of this lowest of all forms of wood-cutting technology, she is wearing a blue-and-pink checkered confection that would not look out of place in a fashion show. And, given only the thinnest provocation – the visit of an elderly aunt, say, or even just a trip to the market – the women will dress up in veritable ball gowns, their voluminous dresses quite startling in the dusty and dirty dilapidation of the town.

When there is a wedding or baptism, the magnificence of apparel is stunning. On such occasions, a compound will become a sea of mats and beauty. The men will also be resplendent in their brilliant white or sky-blue *bobos*, with gold-embroidered cuffs and collars. A sheep or even a cow will be slaughtered on such occasions. If it is a wedding, throughout the long afternoon people will spontaneously shout out their praise of the marrying couple. They will hold aloft a handful of cash, which will be given to the couple once their marriage has been officially completed on the payment of a dowry by the groom to the girl's father – often in the form of a cow or two – and after an Imam has blessed them; the bride will have been secluded for three weeks prior to this, unable to leave her family's house.

I sit and watch pretty Uma, the wife of Abou, Salif's younger brother, she with the hands of a blacksmith and eyes full of mirth. She is washing her children down, standing them in turn in a basin of water and soaping them up until they are white from head to toe. She squeezes snot from a toddler's nose and flicks it to the ground. She catches my eye as I watch her, and laughs.

There are a number of people about today and the comings and goings in the compound are frequent. A middle-aged cousin of Salif's from Dakar, the capital of Senegal, has shown up. I have met Barou N'Gam a number of times and have even visited him with Salif at his home in Dakar: a shanty in one of the most distant corners of that large city. He is an educated man with a neat black beard and a twinkle in his eyes. He is a pharmacist, but one without a job, as the pharmacy profession in Dakar, he tells me, is riddled with mafia-style cartelism from which he has been ousted. He is in Keniéba for two weeks only, 'on business'. He joins us on our mats under the thatch.

'Dakar is a nightmare now,' he tells me. 'They have dug up all the roads and it takes three hours to get from my house to the center of town.'

'You work in the center of town?' I ask, having forgotten how he earns a living now.

'No, no,' he says, 'there's no work in Senegal.'

'I thought Senegal was doing well,' I say.

'Ah,' he exclaims, 'the place is riddled with corruption. Everything… everything is corruption.' This surprises me, as I have long believed Senegal to be something of a beacon of hope in West Africa. But again, I think to myself, all is relative. What to an outsider may appear an acceptably functioning body politic and economy, to the man on the street who cannot get a job, who is hit for 'taxes' with every step he takes and who lives in a slum, it is a failed state. But I remember now how Barou N'Gam keeps soul and body together: he runs a small Qur'anic school in his house in Dakar and is a serial money borrower. This is probably why he is here now: to borrow money from Salif. He is a pleasant, friendly man, but, like so many, all too willing to rely on the family support network for his survival.

Another who appears this afternoon is a man I have seen before but remember now only when Salif introduces him to me as 'the old combatant'. He is an ex-soldier: a large, angular man dressed in a coarse farmer's tunic.

'You remember him,' Salif says, holding the man playfully by the arm before me as though he were an exhibit. 'He was a prisoner of Polisario in the north during the conflict over

Western Sahara. They kept him in a prison camp for five years.' The man grins cheerfully.

'Five years!' I exclaim, remembering now how very terrible I thought this captivity must have been in the remote wastes of the desert at the hands of a rebel group with probably barely enough resources to sustain itself, let alone prisoners. 'How were you captured?' I ask, Salif translating into Peul, as the ex-soldier cannot speak French.

'There was a battle in the desert,' Salif translates his reply, 'but as soon as the first shots were fired all our soldiers threw their guns down and surrendered. They were all conscripts, black men from the south, and they did not want to fight and be killed.'

The story has drawn people's attention and there is a good deal of hilarity at the part about the soldiers throwing their guns away and surrendering. The man is entirely unfazed, grinning broadly, even joining in the laughter.

'We were no match for Polisario,' he says. 'We did not know how to fight.'

'You certainly knew how to throw your rifles away,' Mariam, who is perched near us, adds. The man chuckles good-humoredly.

Alisanne, Amadou's brother back from France, is amongst us. He comes and sits next to me. This is the first chance we have had to chat, as he has been busy: '…paying visits,' he says a little wearily.

'You have to see everyone?'

'Most,' he says. 'As soon as I get back, all my relations come to see me, then I must visit each of their families and give them a little present.' He smiles.

'How much are you expected to give?'

He laughs at my inquisitiveness. 'There is no going rate. I give what I want: a thousand ouguiya… 5,000, the equivalent of two euros… 10 euros. Not much, but it adds up. These trips home are not cheap.'

For a number of years, Alisanne has been constructing a house on the outskirts of town, bringing money home with him for the next phase each time he returns. I have visited the house a number of times. It is a large, concrete-block building with a flat, cement-sealed roof. Airy and spacious inside, all floors and lower walls are tiled, and there is a bathroom, toilet and kitchen. Windows are barred and more or less permanently shuttered. All in all, the house represents a completely different manner of living to compound life. For a start, all is interior. There is no compound here around which different parts of the family can live. It is designed for a more nuclear group. The heat, glare and dust of the exterior world are cut out, as is the larger family. This is how the new generation wants to be. This is how Salif, I know, if he ever gets enough money together, wants to live.

'But what of the old people? What of the communal life? What of afternoons spent sitting on mats under a shady compound tree,' I have always wanted to ask, disappointed that this should be so. But the reality, I know, is that compound life is hard. The houses fall down with the rains; the children – at least according to Salif – run wild in unruly bands; hygiene is bad and everyone – again according to Salif – minds everyone else's business.

I have often wondered whether Alisanne will in fact ever return to Keniéba to live in his new house once it is finished; for this is clearly the main reason for building it. I ask him how the building is progressing.

'It's slow,' he says, 'but then so is everything here.'

'And when are you going to come back and live in this house?' I ask provocatively.

'Ah!' he exclaims with a grin. 'That only Allah knows.'

It will not be an easy move for him, that I know. And he has children now, who are French: will he abandon them?

It was two years ago that Alisanne visited me at my home

in Britain. For many years he had been on at me to come and see him in France, or for us at least to meet up somewhere. I had never seemed to manage it, and then one day he rang to say he was in England, staying with a friend in a large provincial town near to where I live. He was over to 'check out the employment opportunities', he told me.

He could not have been more charming and polite when he came to stay, instantly engaging my children's interest and affection. He did not remark on any particular aspect of the rural area in which I live or our life there. The only thing he found astonishing was the typical Sunday morning total absence of any signs of humanity in our small local town. Where on earth was everyone? We took him puffing up a mountain and fed him on roast lamb, which he thought 'a bit soft'. Then he went back to France, from where he rang a little later saying that he wanted to 'send' me his nine-year-old daughter. 'How do you mean?' I asked 'You want to bring her over?'

'Perhaps,' he said.

'How would I get her back to you?'

'You can keep her, until she's older,' he replied. I saw that I too was now a part of the 'network'. I declined, of course, which disconcerted Alisanne only slightly, but did not prevent him from insisting I send one of my daughters to him. 'She can stay with us a week... a month... as long as she wants, and she can learn French and see how Africans live,' he said.

Some years previously Salif had also come to stay with my family. Unlike Alisanne, he was overcome by the beauty of the countryside. It was May, and the countryside was indeed looking spectacular. 'Paradise,' was all he could whisper when asked one day what he made of the place. And the lush green fields and forests must indeed have seemed like some sort of agricultural heaven to one used to the wastes of Mauritania. I told him of the cold, black winters of rain; the lack of sunlight; the stresses of modern life. I did not want him to think it was paradise.

Late afternoon; and the light reflected on the wall across the compound grows a deeper shade of gold by the moment. Alisanne, Salif, Mamadou, Barou N'Gam, Abou, young Harouna making tea: we lounge, half asleep, sweaty, idly chatting. Ibrahim Tandia has been shut up in Salif's house all afternoon, working. Mustapha, our driver, and Harana, the vehicle 'boy', have been absent for the day, allowed to return to Kaédi until we next need them.

I watch the compound chickens. I have always found a certain amount of pathos in the activities of chickens. I have come to know these ones well, and their stories are often tragic: the brood of five chicks, one of which has a gammy leg and is always just a fraction too late for the grain of rice or crumb of food – day after day he weakens until his carcass ends up just a part of the compound litter; the not-so-dominant cockerel, bullied relentlessly by the preening 'king' rooster; the scrawny hen, next, you know, for the pot. I find the hens' attitudes to their chicks fascinating. They compete with them for food on an equal basis, shoving them aside and dashing for the crumbs, seeming to be entirely unaware of the maternal instinct. How they all survive is a mystery, as they are never fed, existing only on the most meagre of crumbs to be scratched from the barren compound floor. This does not prevent them, however, from having full social lives. Their relentless jealousies, courtships and couplings form a subliminal, background soap opera to that of the human compound.

The goats also draw my attention. During the day, only the kids are left behind in the compound. They are frisky, independent and eternally curious, constantly besieging kitchen areas and the mats from which people shoo them. They jump onto walls, balancing on their springy hooves before leaping off with an exuberance that is delightful to watch. They and their elders are such a different story from the droopy, silly sheep that plod about, apparently without a thought in their heads.

A ram is tied permanently to a post at the end of the compound. I find a strange fascination watching him repeat over and over again the full repertoire of his existence: circling the post, first one way, then the other, stopping still to bleat loudly at his surroundings; then scratching his nose with a hoof before continuing his eternal circling.

At one end of the compound is the stump of what was once a large, shady neem tree. The tree died some four or five years ago, and the fact that is has not been replaced is something that has nagged at me. What small effort, I have asked myself on many an occasion, would it take to plant a single tree that would benefit so many people? Compounds without trees are bare, glaring places. A tree creates shade, reduces the temperature and generally produces a vastly improved environment in which to live. And it is not just the failure to replace this tree that has perplexed me. Ever since I have been coming here I have been encouraging people to plant trees. Trees can do so much for an environment such as this. They bind soil, create humus and fodder from their leaves, break the wind, humidify the air, produce wood for construction and cooking. Nutritional and medicinal products can be had from their fruits and sap. Crops can be grown under them. And, most importantly, they are an investment in the future. They have the potential to rejuvenate this land. But never – or at least until very recently, as I hope to see tomorrow – have I persuaded a single person to plant a single tree. Even Salif, with the full advantage of the Mabafé family irrigation project, has never planted a single tree. Always there is a reason not to. Always it is next year.

One year, perhaps to satisfy my apparent need for trees, Salif took me to visit what he described as a 'forest', some 40 or so kilometers away. I was a little skeptical, having long been aware that the expression 'forest' generally meant little more than an area with slightly more scrub on it than usual. My shock, then, on Salif ushering me into a 50-hectare plantation of vast, mature trees was considerable. Here were mango trees a hundred foot in height, 50 years old. Eucalyptus, acacia, neem; exotic and native: thousands of trees were interspersed with fruit-tree plantations and even small vegetable plots. And so dense was the foliage, so all-encompassing the plantation, that the outside world – that Mauritania of dust and glare and desert – was completely excluded. This was the humid, green world of the tropics. I was astonished. How could this be? Here? Who had set it up?

The answer was that the plantation had been set up during the colonial era. It was now run by the Agricultural Research Department, the trees irrigated from the nearby Senegal River and overseen by a manager who, in the absence of any salary making it through to him, ran the place on a commercial basis, growing vegetables and selling the fruit from the trees. On closer inspection, as delightful as the place was, I could see that it was in poor condition and that many of the trees were in fact dying. But its existence illustrated to me a fundamental point: with a bit of water, a bit of investment and a bit of organizational ability, this apparently barren, desolate land could be transformed. So speaks the outsider! The question to ask is not simply whether the land can be transformed, but whether it can be transformed sustainably. Will the forest survive? If not, as seems likely, then this is not a path to development. It is an imposition rather than an evolution. As for the neem tree, that it will be replanted is fairly sure, but time is not measured in weeks or months or even years by some; it is measured in generations. When the time is ripe, it will grow once again.

The third and last of Harouna's teas has been taken and it is time for prayers. Salif rises and walks over to the water *bidon* to make his ablutions, washing hands, feet and face. Méline, Alisanne and Barou N'Gam follow suit, and soon they are all standing in a line facing east. Salif leads the prayers, raising his hands as he recites the opening prayers, then kneeling; then bowing three times to the earth. When they have finished, they remain seated on the ground for a while in quiet meditation. I watch them and I feel a twinge of envy. The day may be hot and long, life may be confusing and hard, but five times a day all becomes simple: you are nothing; you have nothing; everything, including your life, belongs to Allah. And in that, and in the routines of the five daily prayers, is a discipline that can only be beneficial in somewhere so very trying as the south of Mauritania.

It is time for a promenade. Salif suggests we pay a visit to the Keniéba Peace Corps volunteer.

The American Peace Corps is a phenomenon. Set up in the 1960s at the height of the Cold War, it was seen as a way of promoting US influence and creating understanding between Americans and others. Today, it has many thousands of volunteers who are sent with the minimum of support to some of the remotest villages in the world. Here, for two years, they do a little teaching or help with minor projects. Its personnel are young, generally well educated and middle class. I have come across them throughout Africa and without exception they have been friendly, idealistic and delighted in their postings. Life can be extremely tough for them, though, and they often suffer from illness and loneliness. They embed themselves deeply amongst the people with whom they are living, becoming a part of a family whose name they temporarily take. They have little contact with the outside world and are allowed home to see their families only once during the two years of their posting. I have always been fascinated by the almost filial relationship these Peace Corps Volunteers have with their hosts, as well as the paternalistic attitude their hosts take towards them.

Keniéba is on the Peace Corps map. It has had volunteers for many years and I can always be sure there is one around. We find Clare, or Aliou Demba, as is her local name, in the compound of a large family down a long passageway in a distant part of the town. We greet the inhabitants of the compound and they call for Aliou, who shortly appears from a hut. She is young – perhaps 22 – thin and pretty, wearing a typical African wrap-around dress, with a twist of material in her hair. She greets us formally, delicately shaking our hands and going through the full, traditional greeting repertoire of the locals, then asks whether we would prefer to talk in the compound or her hut. We decide on her hut and she leads us in, offering us cushions on her mat on the floor. I can see she is a little nervous, perhaps unsure of the purpose of our visit, perhaps just unused to seeing a fellow Westerner.

'Shall I make some tea?' she asks, then goes about gathering all the implements for a traditional tea. 'You've had the local tea. I've been learning to make it, but I'm still not very good at it,' she laughs. We chat and she tells us about her life here.

'I'm just coming up to the end of my first year,' she says, 'with one year to go. I think I am just now getting into it. At first, it was hard to understand what was going on, especially as my grasp of the language was so poor. I speak it more or less fluently now and am really starting to enjoy myself. These people are incredible,' she says, suddenly passionate. 'Binta, here,' and she indicates a young woman who was already in the hut when we came in and is sitting with us on the mat, 'can you believe that she is only 15 and was married last month.' She speaks some Peul to the girl who shakes her head embarrassedly. 'I asked if 15 was young to get married. They take on a lot of responsibility at such a young age,' she says. 'They are grown up by the time they are 15, often already with a child. Binta is from a village quite far from here and has come to live with her husband's family. It must be very hard for young girls like her. She comes to my room often and we are great friends now.' She leans over and, with a tenderness that is touching, takes Binta's hand in her own. 'We are friends, aren't we?' she says in English, smiling at the girl. 'I've been teaching her some English,' she explains. Binta dissolves into giggles.

I ask Clare how she finds compound life, aware as I am that it can be claustrophobic for a Westerner. Again, she laughs. 'Oh, it has its moments,' she says. 'The family like me to always eat with them, not anywhere else. They are very jealous of me, but we have an arrangement now that once a week I am allowed to eat with the local health nurse, with whom I do some work. That was a great concession on their part.'

There is something fresh and charming about Clare, although I can see she also has a steely determination. She has been ill, she tells us, and was for a long time quite lonely, but she has grown up considerably, she says, since she has been here. 'I will never forget my time in this village,' she remarks. 'It will stay with me always.' And I think how strange it is that soon the lives of Clare and her host family will part for ever, each to take on such different trajectories: she, no doubt, soon forgotten in the mill of everyday existence; they, always a distant and treasured memory, a souvenir of her young self. I ask Clare what she thinks her family will get from her stay and she looks at me curiously.

'I don't know,' she says, then laughs: 'Something, I hope.'

Dusk is already creeping over the town as we leave Clare's hut. We have arranged a meeting of Salif's development group. Arriving back at the compound, we find already congregated there the treasurer – a quiet, shy man who rarely speaks – and Demba Samba, Salif's main assistant. Demba Samba first reports on the problems they have been having trying to organize the many small-time farmers who want to hire the development group's tractor.

'There are too many of them,' he says in his forthright manner. 'They all want our tractor at the same time. They come to me all day; even in the middle of the night.' They have serviced nearly 22 different farmers groups this year, he tells us, representing some 300 farmers. 'It is very hard to co-ordinate,' he says.

Are we encouraging an unsustainable form of agriculture through the use of the development group's tractor for ploughing? That is the question I wish to look into. On the one hand, of course it is desirable that even small-scale African agriculture is increasingly incorporating more modern farming methods; on the other, though, much of the land being used in regions such as this is extremely marginal, with soils vulnerable to leaching from rain or displacement by wind. And, as always in remote places, there are problems with spare parts and maintenance, meaning tractors are not always reliable. Plus, the cost of fuel is so volatile that it amazes me that farmers and the tractor owners can find such an activity economical.

'The tractor must be expensive to hire,' I say. 'How can these farmers afford it? Surely, working their land by hand is more economical.'

'No. It is better for them to hire the tractor,' Demba Samba succinctly corrects me. 'A tractor can do in a couple of hours what by hand takes a week. And, because of the deepness of the plough, you get much better water penetration, leading to better crops and so better profits.'

'But surely the labor for hand work is free, done by family members,' I say.

'That is right,' Demba Samba replies. 'The weeding is done by family members either way, but there are not enough young men available nowadays for the first dig, as so many of them must go away on *aventure* to look for money. And to hire people in to do it is just not economical.'

I am still not clear about this but decide to drop it for

the moment. Ibrahim Tandia, who has been following our conversation, now joins in.

'People want to use tractors,' he says calmly, 'and rightly so. Agriculture in Africa must develop. But there are many different forms of development, each one suited to its own context. For example,' he goes on, 'there is much land being bought up in Africa at the moment for industrial farming: the so-called Land Grabs. Many see this as the way forward for African agriculture: farming on a large scale, with the most modern methods producing the largest yields. And in some circumstances this might indeed be sustainable. But even when it is, these big projects, as some of us know only too well, are not as easy to operate as many seem to think. They rely on stable governments, stable market prices and a stable climate, none of which are currently very available. And of course the fact is that the people whose lands are used for these schemes – the local people – are often those who fare worst, meaning that the very people improved agriculture should be helping – the poor – are in fact those who benefit the least.' Ibrahim Tandia pauses.

'But there is another way forward,' he says, 'one that favors local people.' This is what we have been waiting for: his take on the situation; his proposal.

'It is a way,' he goes on, 'that local people are in many respects already implementing, if not very efficiently; a way that is particularly suited to this region, which is very underdeveloped.'

Development, Ibrahim Tandia tells us, especially in regions like this, is not just about food or health or housing issues. It is about empowerment – empowering people to be able to make their own choices. It is about using what is available locally and about building up some resilience to the uncertainties of the volatile world that surrounds us. This means, he says, listening to people: hearing their concerns and ideas. And it means, most importantly, letting local people claim ownership of the available resources, whether these be land, water or even the availability of labor. And the best way of doing this is for local people to use those resources effectively, and to unite themselves into viable economic forces that can stand up to the outside interests that wish to take over their land.

'What we are talking about,' he says, 'is simply improved farming methods, better organization and, most importantly – and this is what I tried to impress on people this morning in my closing speech at the seminar – confidence. Farming methods must be better adapted to current market and climatic circumstances; people must learn to co-operate with one another and organize themselves into effective groupings; and they must have the confidence to step out of old ways, believe in and make the most of themselves.'

'What we will have then,' he says, a gleam now discernible in his eye, 'is a project that incorporates all of these. There will be many elements: integration of livestock with agriculture; organizational and management training; rice intensification and diversification; an animal health program; instruction in new planting methods, in rain-catchment, in compost making. These and other activities will be conducted in different locations with farmers across all the various agricultural sectors. Other farmers will come to see them with their own eyes. Seeing Is Believing. That will be our motto. The project will be of five years' duration, with learning seminars at mid- and end-point, and during its course much will be learnt about unity and co-operation.'

'Much of this,' he finishes, 'is of course what you and the farmers have in some ways been doing for a long time already. But I hope I can add a little impetus and a little structure to your work.'

We are amateurs, Salif and I. It is a pleasure to hear someone as experienced as Ibrahim Tandia.

Demba Samba speaks up. 'It's good,' he says.'Very good.

But how are we going to do it?'

'Through hard work, of course,' Ibrahim Tandia laughs. 'Plus the project plan I will provide you with.'

As I climb under my mosquito net that night I feel a confidence I have not had for a while: we did the right thing in bringing Ibrahim Tandia here.

8 Across the Senegal River

The socialist survivor... Does foreign aid undermine self-help?... The monster pump... Why large, centralized schemes fail... Crossing the river by dugout... The women's co-op and their organic bounty... A grand gift... Africans in America

Mustapha, our driver, and Harana, the vehicle 'boy', are back with the Toyota. They are waiting for us first thing in the morning. We are going to visit our Dohley Women's Market Garden Project just over the Senegal River: nine hectares of vegetables farmed by the 312 members of the Dohley Women's Co-operative. We will travel there via Kaédi in order to pick up Monsieur Po, the project agronomist and manager. We will not be crossing into Senegal at the official border post there, however, slipping instead quietly and bureaucracy-free by dugout canoe across the Senegal River further upstream.

We cruise with disorientating ease back up the *piste* to Kaédi in the Toyota. Monsieur Po we find in his house in a suburb of town that looks as though it has been struck by an earthquake: low, brown buildings are everywhere tumbled down, their earthen bricks dissolving back into the brown earth from which they came. Children and families with washing lines and goats inhabit parts of compounds still in use, and here and there the odd fully functioning homestead with shiny tin roofs and a large satellite dish survives. It is in one of these that we find Monsieur Po.

Monsieur Po appeared on the scene some years ago: a small, wiry man with a sharp look in his eyes. I did not take to him at first. He was wearing a 'Mao' safari suit – a buttoned-up, collarless garment in utilitarian blue – and seemed fastidious and a little irritable. He was an administrator in a near-defunct government agricultural research agency and I thought him one of those types devoted to efficiency and the detail of procedure: the sort whose kingdom the world over is the minutiae of bureaucracy. But Monsieur Po grew on me and in time I came to see that his creed was not authoritarianism but socialism. He sprang from that now-extinct period when a number of African countries experimented with Marxism, promoting nationhood over tribalism, even going to the lengths in some places of moving people off their lands and forming soviet-style farm collectives. It was not successful. Economies collapsed, undermined by inefficiency, politics and corruption; riots and coups d'état ensued. But it did breed many educated, idealistic young people for whom the post-independence belief that Black Africa could be reborn on the back of hard work and diligence still rang true.

Some years ago there were still many of these people around. I used to come across them on my travels: teachers in far-distant villages sticking diligently to their curriculum despite the fact that they had not been paid for a year-and-a-half and must take their classes under a tree; or administrators in government departments that had been stripped by their directors of all resources but continued to do the best they could in the circumstances: people who believed in the possibility of a modern Black Africa where nationhood was greater than tribehood and Africans had as much ability as anyone else. Monsieur Po is a remnant of such people and we have been lucky to get our hands on him, as he is a man of both commitment and ability.

'Monsieur Peter, Salif,' he greets us in his compound, eyes bright. Ibrahim Tandia has gone off on an errand in the Toyota. There are a number of people about: wife – wives? – offspring, others; we greet them only briefly as Monsieur Po has never made any effort to introduce his family to us. In a corner of the compound sits the shell of a car against which is leant the small motorbike we have provided Monsieur Po with. We go into his room in one of the buildings surrounding the compound, which is overflowing with files and paperwork. In the corner is a television set with a cloth draped over it, and an open laptop lies in the middle of the carpeted floor.

'You will take some tea and eat?' Monsieur Po asks, then barks an order out the door. We exchange a few pleasantries but before long we are delving into the paperwork side of the project.

The Dohley Women's Market Garden Project is in the third of its four funded years and, so far, it has been a success, inspiring people over a large region and even featuring on local radio. This is mainly due to the hard work of the members of the Dohley Women's Co-operative, but is also in no small part a result of the meticulous care employed during the planning phase.

It was some five years ago that the President of the Co-operative, one Madame Diop, approached Salif, asking him whether his development group could help them resurrect their currently defunct market-gardening activities. They had a large nine-hectare site near to the Senegal River but no way of irrigating it. Previously they had had a pump, but this had grown old and had broken down, and they did not have the money to replace it. Madame Diop, the President, produced a formal dossier of request.

From the start the project looked as though it had potential, although there were a few issues that I felt needed sorting out before we made any commitment. The primary of these revolved around the number of newly built, modern houses I had noticed on my first visit, which surrounded the otherwise impoverished traditional center of the village. These new houses were clearly the property of expatriates, those from the area now living in the cities of West Africa or elsewhere. One of them, I noticed, even had a Mercedes parked outside its door. There was money here. What on earth, then, were these people doing asking Salif and me for funds? They should be raising them from within their own community. I asked Salif about this. I asked Monsieur Po. I asked Madame Diop. But it took some considerable time before I got an answer I could understand.

The issue seemed important to me, as it brought into focus a fundamental question: were foreign development agencies deemed a 'soft touch' and, as such, no matter how good their intentions, undermining the more natural dynamic of self-help?

There was money around: indeed, there is generally money around when there are investment opportunities. Banks lend money, entrepreneurs invest it; it can be winkled out of family members. But this money is only readily available if the investment opportunity is indeed genuine. No-one is happy about producing funds for schemes that have little chance of giving a return. And so it is quite possible to have a community where some members – probably non-resident ones – have some money while the rest exist in a state of poverty. Those with funds will certainly fulfil their duty and send money home, money that will fend off total destitution – and even this amount, as any expatriate will tell you, tends to be considerable – but they will be reluctant to go beyond this and invest, for example, in local agricultural enterprises if they see that the local economy is dysfunctional. They know only too well where that will end; there are certainly plenty of examples in the irrigation sector, on some of which they may have already burnt their fingers. It is better to spend any hard-earned, surplus money in the solid bricks and mortar of a building than to throw it away on some hopeless business venture. The result of this is that people and regions can slip further and further into poverty despite the fact that, in theory at least, money is available. What was needed here, then, it seemed clear, was the development of a farming model that, even in the difficult local context, could be seen to turn a genuine profit, one that would encourage local investment. We would work with the Dohley Women's Co-operative and try to develop with them such a model; we would inspire local people to invest in it; and we would use the results of the project as an example to others. It would not be rocket science, but would be based on the simple business principle of keeping input costs down while increasing outputs like yields and produce value.

The plan Monsieur Po and the members of the Dohley Women's Co-operative came up with was based on the use of a small diesel pump drawing water from the Senegal River involving a large, camel-proof fence, bands of windbreak, forestry and fruit trees, a piped water distribution system and organic farming practices that reduced input costs while increasing yields. A hierarchy of responsibility was devised, with the highly capable and quietly indomitable Madame Diop at the top, and co-operative financial management was put on a more sustainable basis, with stipends due strictly on a monthly basis, and reinvestment in the scheme compulsory.

From the start, the enthusiasm with which the women conducted the project was remarkable and, within only a few weeks of our commitment to it, 300 compost piles had been created. Now, only four years on, the full nine hectares are being exploited, each of the 312 women having a minimum of two *planches* of land, each *planche* measuring 200 square meters. Water management and use is so efficient that the entire scheme is capable of being irrigated by the

comparatively tiny one-cylinder water pump stationed at the Senegal River a few hundred meters away. And, because of the high compost use and the water retention qualities it gives to the soil, growing periods are extended, meaning that each year the women can squeeze in three successive vegetable seasons, the produce of which, again because of the compost, always finds a ready market as it looks, tastes and conserves better. At the last project evaluation, local families reported incomes up by 30 per cent. Not that there haven't been 'issues' along the way, one of which crops up as Monsieur Po and I now go through the year's project reports on the floor of his room.

'Yes, the expatriates have fully paid for the second pump and it was delivered in the middle of the year,' Monsieur Po says, referring to the project element that required the local people to pay for a standby pump. 'In fact,' he goes on, 'it has already proved useful as the one-cylinder pump was out of action for some weeks, having been submerged in the rising waters of the river. It is mounted on a floating platform,' he continues, 'which will protect it from the river and also make it easier to maneuver, as, being a three-cylinder pump, it is very heavy.'

'Did you say three cylinders?' I ask.

'Yes, it's a three-cylinder pump,' Monsieur Po repeats.

This is a massive pump and alarm bells are ringing in my head. One of the main purposes of the project is to minimize water usage and so reduce costs, not something likely to be achieved by a pump that can produce up to 10 times the volume of water of our small pump.

'Why have they bought such a large pump?' I ask.

'They got it for a good price,' Monsieur Po says. 'It is some years old.'

I am not happy. No longer can we demonstrate, it seems to me, that nine hectares can be irrigated with a small capacity of water. Even the flood-irrigation people don't have three cylinder pumps.

'It's too big,' I say. 'Surely, it will be impossible for the Co-operative now to restrict its water usage, and their diesel costs are going to go right up.'

Monsieur Po considers for a moment. 'It's true,' he says, 'it is too large, but that's what they bought: what can we do?'

'It won't change anything,' Salif adds. 'It's only the standby pump. They won't use it all the time.'

'The temptation will always be there,' I say. 'One flick of the switch and they can have their entire week's worth of water in a day.'

'They won't do that,' Salif replies. 'The water channels couldn't take it for long, anyway.'

I've noticed in the Co-operative's annual finances, which are open in front of us, that a not-inconsequential sum of money has been used this year to purchase a quantity of the 25-centimeter piping needed for large pumps. 'They've invested in large-diameter piping, I see,' I say. 'Presumably that's to use with the pump.'

'Yes, that's right,' Salif replies.

'Then it seems to me they intend on using the large pump at least to some significant degree,' I say.

'No, not necessarily,' Salif replies with a certain finality in his voice. I am still not happy.

'I think you don't need to worry yourself too much,' Monsieur Po intervenes. 'It won't change a thing.' I decide to drop the subject. When we get to Dohley, things might look different, as they so often do.

There are a number of other more minor points that need ironing out about the project, but on the whole I can see that things are going well, and I am keen to get out there and see it all with my own eyes.

'Do the women know we are coming?' I ask tentatively, as I prefer to arrive in Dohley unannounced. The 312 women of the Co-operative, as well as probably double that number in younger sisters and other female non-members, have a tendency to use any excuse for a party, and my and Salif's arrival can sometimes descend into a mêlée of such intensity that clear thinking, or indeed mental survival at all, is nearly impossible. Salif smiles. 'They don't know which day we are coming,' he says, 'but they know you are here and that we are coming this week.'

Monsieur Po laughs. 'They've got something planned, I can tell you that. You're not going to get away with a quiet visit this time.'

Later Ibrahim Tandia appears with Mustapha and Harana in the Toyota. Although it is still barely midday, a cloth is spread on Monsieur Po's floor and a meal of rice and fish produced. Mustapha is a changed man here in Kaédi. Gone is his shyness. Although perhaps not yet what could be called forthcoming, he digs into the food with relish, scooping up

vast quantities in his large hand, and sits back afterwards with a contented look on his face. Harana, younger and more cheerful by disposition, laughs at my messy eating technique.

'Here, like this,' he says using his few words of French and showing me how to squeeze the rice into a neat, mouth-sized ball.

Our meal finished, we set off for Dohley, crossing the top of a small dam where the Moshe joins its larger brother, the Senegal River.

The Senegal River, which here acts as the border between Mauritania and Senegal, is a slowly surging body of sandy-colored water around 600 meters wide. In the dry season, flat 'beach' areas, where patches of maize are grown and the odd dugout is pulled up, hem its length. There is no great profusion of vegetation hugging its banks; instead, it passes nakedly through the parched savannahs of the Sahel like the great drainage ditch it really is. It traverses sparsely populated lands and only a few fisherfolk ply its waters. Villages are rare on its banks. This is because in the rainy season the river transforms itself. From being a brown, sleepy snake, it becomes with frightening speed an uncontrollable

monster. It will rise seven or eight meters in a day, flooding many millions of hectares of river valley until there is a vast glinting inland sea stretching from horizon to horizon.

Many fisherfolk stand down by the water's edge where we cross the dam, poised like herons, ready to spin their nets out over the churning patch where the Moshe and Senegal rivers merge. Here, we find a police post. This is a border area, and so a certain tension prevails, especially since the Islamist troubles in neighboring Mali.

'Where are you going?' demands the police officer who walks over to us after snapping us a smart salute. We tell him we are going up country to visit a village. He eyes us suspiciously. Salif has reported the same by phone to the adjutant.

'Papers,' he says.

We hand him our various IDs and he takes them off into his hut. Time passes. Might we be prohibited from proceeding? Shortly, he is back.

'Have a good day,' he says, handing our papers back through the vehicle window. I feel guilty. It is a little naughty of me, I know, to be crossing the border in this way. But then Dohley is so easily accessible from where we are going to cross, directly on the opposite bank; we will be there only a few hours; and crossing at the official post in Kaédi might not only be problematic as the status of the border's openness is not always clear, but it would also leave us in quite the wrong place without any transport. Emphatically, I'm afraid, this is far easier.

We skirt a large area of rice paddies. This is one of the huge, government-run irrigation schemes that were set up at the same time as the dams were built on the Moshe and Senegal rivers, altering the hydrology of the region. It is surrounded by a tall bund protecting it from floods and covers some 2,000 hectares. A few peasants with straw hats work in the plots they hire from the centrally managed scheme in exchange for a percentage of their harvests. Canals of water dissect the plain, with sluices and ditches servicing different areas. It looks impressive, but Salif is dismissive of it. For him, it demonstrates exactly why it is that large, centrally managed schemes do not work.

'The directors treat the scheme as a source of private income,' he says. 'The yields here are some of the lowest in the region. Water supply is inconsistent and the soils have become salty.' People, he says, are charged such a high price for the inputs that it is very hard for them to make any profit and much of the land is in fact left uncultivated.

We traverse after this a wild, scrubby country a little inland from the river. This is a route Monsieur Po knows only too well, as three days every month he must take it to visit Dohley.

'You should have seen it last year,' he says. 'I could only come on bicycle as there were floods everywhere. Even then I had to wade through areas of water carrying my bike.' I try to imagine Monsieur Po in such a posture, but somehow cannot.

In one place we pass the remains of a village. This is a poignant spot that draws disapproving clicks of the tongue from those in the vehicle, for this is one of the many villages whose inhabitants were thrown over the border during the period of ethnic troubles in the country. A few broken huts stand about on the bare earth; the shards of a shattered water jar; the stump of a tree.

Finally we ease our way over broken ground towards a tall tree that turns out to be at the top of the bank overlooking the Senegal River. Far on the other side can be seen a straggle of low, brown buildings: Dohley.

The pirogue owner paddles slowly across the river, working diagonally upstream against the current in order to keep us on target. Halfway across, Ibrahim Tandia grabs a spare paddle in the bottom of the boat and rolls up his sleeves to lend a hand.

'This is the life!' he shouts, his face lit and happy, making us all laugh. As soon as we reach Dohley he will leave us, starting his long journey back through Senegal to Dakar, then on to Europe. Having Ibrahim Tandia with us has been a privilege and an inspiration. Both Salif and I have learned much from him. It certainly seems like he has enjoyed his trip.

By the time we reach the far side, a crowd has gathered: as Monsieur Po predicted, we are not going to get away with a quiet visit this time. An uproar of welcome ensues as soon

as we step ashore and hands in the dozens are thrust at us to shake. Women are singing and doing little impromptu dances, ululating. Children whirl around like tops. We are propelled with the throng up the slope and towards a large, thatched communal area. Here Madame Diop, the Co-operative President, and members of the management committee are waiting to meet us.

Madame Diop is a woman of deceptive qualities. She has eyes full of compassion and a quiet, even shy, manner, but she also has a tangible strength and is well respected. She ushers us over to where a large spread of mats has been prepared. Here we are regally sat down. Not all the 312 members of the Co-operative are present, but by the looks of things a great many of them are, seated now in all their finery in a great press around us: noisy, unruly and laughing with a certain mischievousness in their eyes. I do not feel comfortable but I know only good will is intended. The women want to make known their great appreciation for being given the chance to create the irrigation scheme. They want to impress on Salif, Monsieur Po and me their gratitude. We have little choice in the matter.

Madame Diop sits beside us, as do a couple of women from the management committee whom I know well: one, a woman carrying the young infant she has had since I last saw her, has the dark, flashing eyes of an Amazon; the other is fair, pretty and sophisticated-looking. Both speak French, which is unusual among village women, and indicates probably that they are not Dohley-born but have ended up here through marriage, perhaps from the capital or some other large town.

'How has the year been?' I half shout to them amid the noise.

'Aiee,' the one with the flashing eyes replies, 'you should have seen the floods. They came right up to here where we are sitting. It was very frightening.'

The other smiles with astonishing gentleness. 'We've had a

good year,' she says softly. 'The project has given us much to do, and for this we are happy.'

A group of men appear and step their way self-consciously through the crowd to shake our hands. The menfolk of Dohley are as proud of the irrigation scheme as the women. They are proud of the part they have played in it, for it was their physical labor that constructed the fence and did much of the initial groundwork. And they are proud of what the women have achieved. Time and again I have heard this repeated: how proud the menfolk are of what the women have achieved. Here, at least, the conflict between the sexes that so occupies much of the development world is not so apparent.

The men, having shaken our hands, look about for places on the mats. Madame Diop is one of the first to stand up and accommodate them, as space is at a premium. This is done with graciousness, though, and the men are appreciative. Any deference implied, one can clearly see, is purely formal.

Soon another group of men can be seen approaching the back of the crowd. These are the old men, the village elders, and Salif quickly rises to go over and greet them. I too rise and put my shoes back on to go over and shake their hands. Once this is completed, Salif and I retake our places, and Madame Diop stands to make a short speech, Salif translating, as she does not speak French. We are thanked for coming, Allah is thanked for bringing us here and various other themes along similar lines are introduced, but I can see that Madame Diop is at pains to restrict herself, as the main event, I am aware, is reserved for later in the afternoon. There is some clapping from the assembled women when she finishes and an elderly lady also rises to give a speech, which, when it appears to be taking on too much momentum, Madame Diop politely interrupts, explaining that the plan is for us to visit the co-operative fields before it gets too late. A group of 10 or 15 of us now extract ourselves from the crowd – Monsieur Po, Salif and I; Madame Diop and a number of other women;

and a couple of the men – and we make our way out into the brilliant white glare of the mid-afternoon.

The co-operative fields are a kilometer outside the village over a naked plain. They stand only some 200 meters from the bank of the Senegal River, surrounded by a tall wire-mesh fence. When the project first started, the nine hectares consisted of the same baked plain that surrounds them: an expanse of apparently barren desert, as hard and bald as concrete. Now, only three years into development, the land is transformed. Along one side stands a windbreak of eucalyptus trees, along the near side of which runs a 10-meter strip of forestry, consisting of species that have medicinal or other benefits such as gum Arabic, neem and acacia. At one end of the scheme is a small banana plantation and an area planted with mango and citrus trees in between whose rows, and in the shade of which, certain crops are grown. The rest of the land is divided up into two separate sets of plots that the women work individually.

The nearer of the two sets was the first to be developed and has already produced three harvests; the further one is just now coming into development. Pipes run from the irrigation pump down by the river up into the scheme from where open channels take the water to the plots. One large water basin and a number of smaller ones are dotted about. These are unused and will probably remain so, as the initial plan for women to draw water by bucket from the smaller basins did not work out. For a start, there was not enough water pressure to carry sufficient water from the larger tank to the smaller ones. Then it was found that the women who appeared earliest in the day to irrigate their plots quickly used up what water there was, leaving none for those who came later.

Indeed, there have been many 'evolutions' during the course of the project. For example, it was found that many of the women were less than conscientious when it came to caring for those parts of the scheme that were owned collectively, with profits paid into the Co-operative's exchequer, as opposed to those from which the profits were kept individually. These first included all the trees, as well as certain crops, and poor attention to irrigation schedules had resulted in considerable losses. This led to a change to the Co-operative constitution allowing for fines to be brought against any such culprits. In another example, initially one small area of the scheme was to employ drip irrigation, a system that uses only the bare minimum of water, but it was decided that this should be dropped as it required a level of management the women might be unable to maintain. There have been many other changes during the course of the project, some of which have cost money, some of which haven't. But from the start, the objective was for the project to evolve, experiment and discover, and if this was to lead to some losses, so be it.

It is satisfying to see the land green and in production; to hear the enthusiasm of the women; and to know that people travel from far and wide to come and see the 'marvel' of the Dohley Women's Market Garden. This local fame of the project, I am aware, is not so much to do with any successes it might have achieved – although certainly people are also interested in these – as to do with the fact that it has happened at all. Such is the cynicism directed at development projects in the region that people were astonished to see something beyond words and rhetoric actually manifest itself.

We make our way across the plain towards the co-operative fields. A tall, lugubrious man with a goatee beard keeps pace with me. This is Abou Mody, leader of the village youth league and self-appointed village 'overseer' of the women's market garden scheme. It was the young men of the village, under this older man's supervision, who constructed the fence and did much of the initial land and canal work for the scheme, and of this Abou Mody is immensely proud. He

maintains a proprietorial interest in the project.

'We were very lucky this year,' he announces as we walk. 'Even though the floods were exceptional, they did not reach the scheme.'

'Are the co-operative lands ever flooded?' I ask. 'They are very close to the river.'

'Never – they're on high ground and never flood… never,' he adds with an emphasis that is then undermined by his next statement: 'They only flooded a little this year.'

Monsieur Po, who is walking beside us, intervenes: 'The water caught just one corner of the land, but nothing was lost. One minute there is no water in this land,' he adds, 'and the next you are up to your neck in it.'

We come to the large metal signboard announcing in proud, spidery writing the details of the market garden: who funded it, who owns it and how many hectares it covers. I take a photograph of Monsieur Po and Salif standing beside it.

Down by the river we find the water pump, or rather

pumps. The small one-cylinder one we have provided, which has been shown to be capable of irrigating the full nine hectares despite its small size, is on one side, currently unused. In the water on a floating metal platform sits the huge three-cylinder pump the community bought as a standby. It is connected to a system of large pipes running up and over the bank towards the scheme. We follow the pipes and spend the next half hour wandering about the market-garden fields. It is the end of the cool, dry season, the main vegetable-growing period, and everywhere the women's plots are in production. Cabbages, carrots, onions, tomatoes, lettuce, mint, sweet potatoes, turnip and marrow: the list of varieties is long and in places there are even some crops left over from the previous hot season, such as hibiscus, aubergine, chili and manioc. These, Monsieur Po tells me, should not be here, as they are by now yielding very little and are taking up valuable space that should have been planted with the cool-season vegetables.

'But I cannot get the women to uproot crops that are still in production, no matter how poor that production,' he says. 'They do not like doing it and fail to understand the importance of respecting the correct seasons. The result is that many of them are only getting one or two seasons on much of their land, when they could be getting three. This affects the profitability of the whole scheme.'

The women who have accompanied us to the fields, and the few who are already there, are unconcerned with such quibbles, however. They delight in showing me their crops and produce and soon set up a great merriment of dancing and singing. When I take my camera out for some photographs, they pose magnificently, insisting that Monsieur Po, for whom they clearly have an affection, join them.

We do not linger long at the scheme as the afternoon heat is like a sledgehammer, battering the tops of our heads, and there is still much to be got through back in the village.

Once we have inspected the forestry and fruit trees and walked along the windbreak – I am astonished to see that the eucalyptuses have now grown six meters since they were planted as seedlings three years ago – we make our way back.

We are installed on the balcony of Madame Diop's house. This is next to the central thatched area where the majority of the women are still gathered. Here we are served a meal of rice and fish with plenty of vegetables followed by a Lipton's tea for me, the production of which becomes something of a performance as the entire village needs to be scoured before the requisite glass and teaspoon can be found. Once all is accomplished, and Salif, Monsieur Po and myself are relaxed and comfortable on our cushions on our mat at the end of the balcony, the Co-operative's committee members gather before us for a meeting.

The whole scene strikes me as somewhat unfortunate: the men positioned regally on their 'dais'; the women deferential and subjugated before them. It is not how it should be; not that anyone else has a problem with this, and the meeting goes ahead with full, non-deferential participation. The issues of the pump, the lack of crop rotation and a problem concerning management of the irrigation system – which the women seem disinclined to take responsibility for – are thoroughly discussed with the following conclusions: the large three-cylinder pump – which the women insist they dislike using anyway because it is very hard to get going and uses up so much fuel – will be taken off its floating platform and replaced with the smaller pump until a new platform can be bought for that, thereby re-establishing the primary project objective of showing that high input costs are not required to run such schemes; the crop-rotation issue will be sorted out by dedicating a certain area

to the use of only the hot-season vegetables – meaning the women's natural abhorrence for cutting still-yielding plants can be accommodated, as the crops can remain there all year if necessary; and the issue concerning the women's disinclination to manage the water-distribution system will be resolved by the simple expedient of hiring a man to do the job. Minutiae these may all be, but they are important issues for which intelligent, pragmatic solutions are ably delivered.

Speech making: we are gathered outside, back on the mats. The crowd has swelled and there is a certain tension, or sense of anticipation, that I cannot quite fathom. Salif, Monsieur Po and I face the crowd, with Madame Diop and various committee members to our left. Abou Mody and a couple of other men stand nearby. The speech making goes on for a long time. Salif begins briefly enough, thanking all for their participation in the project and outlining its accomplishments. I am then asked to say a few words and I make efforts to produce a speech that at least half lives up to the expectations of people for whom the oral tradition is something of an art form.

Then Madame Diop rises and demonstrates a full and elaborate example of that art. Salif attempts interpretation, although I can tell by the brevity of his statements that much of what Madame Diop is saying goes untranslated. This does not matter. Nor does it matter that the speech seems to take on a circular structure, coming back periodically to where it began. What comes across is passion, humility, gratitude and courage. Madame Diop stabs the air to make her points; draws to long, poignant pauses. She speaks softly, at times almost inaudibly; then her voice rises: loud, strong and full of determination. Salif, Monsieur Po and I come in for much praise, as do the co-operative women who also, though, undergo a period of significant finger wagging. Allah features largely. The women listen, clap and murmur agreement. Each time Madame Diop draws to a pause, I think: 'surely now she has finished'. But each time she sets off once more. Her voice becomes all: mesmeric, enrapturing. We all sway and murmur to its rhythms. Then suddenly, almost before I am aware of it, she has stopped and another has taken her place.

A series of speakers now take the floor, ending with the old woman who had been interrupted earlier on, before we went to the fields. She is a tall woman wrapped in a sky-blue shawl, with a face as smoothly wrinkled as a prune. She speaks for a long time, sometimes to the apparent hilarity of her audience. She speaks of many things, some quite unconnected to the project, and, as she does so, it occurs to me how very democratic is the oral tradition. Each can have his or her say, no matter how apparently irrelevant the content.

It is evening now and the light is soft, and suddenly there is a shift in the atmosphere. A small commotion takes place at the back of the crowd; then someone is making their way towards the front carrying a package. A buzz of excitement fills the air and I am aware that everyone is looking at me. I click. There's to be a presentation. This is what the sense of anticipation was about. The person arrives at the front and hands the package to Madame Diop, who, in turn, passes it on to me, grinning hugely. In my hands is a parcel – a present – wrapped in gold, shiny wrapping paper. I am amazed. Never before in rural Africa have I come across the concept of wrapping paper and wrapped presents. This is like a Christmas gift. I know only too well the amount of thought and effort that must have gone into its production. Everyone is waiting.

'Open it,' Monsieur Po says. 'It is their present for you.'

I cannot tear the paper off as I would at home as it seems here a criminal waste, so I carefully part the sticky tape with which it is held together and reveal a set of magnificent traditional men's clothes: a beautiful sky blue *bobo* hemmed with gold stitching and starched to an immaculate crispness;

and a pair of short, baggy trousers of the same material. I have no choice, of course. I must put the *bobo* on, and, as I pull it over my head, the whole crowd bursts into uproarious laughter. I am moved.

As if this were a signal, suddenly now the formal part of the evening is over. The crowd rises and erupts. Singing, dancing, shouting and laughing, the women and huge quantities of near-hysterical children and youths create a great mêlée of commotion. Amidst this, a smart-looking youngish lady with a round, friendly face suddenly appears beside me and delicately offers me her hand to shake. She introduces herself and tells me she is from Dohley but lives in Paris, from where she has just today arrived. She wants me to know how very appreciative she and all the women of Dohley are of the market garden: how very proud of it they are. She is earnest and sincere, and I find these words from someone having so recently come from the comparative opulence of western Europe highly moving. Her words remind me that it is not so much the financial input we have provided that is important – as presumably this would not so impress someone from Paris – but the motivational and organizational contributions that have made such a difference.

Next, two men appear whom I have also not seen before.

'Howdyado,' one of them reels out in English spoken in a strong American accent. 'How d'ya like it here?' I am a little taken aback.

'Hi,' I stutter, in English. 'Where are you from?'

'Louisiana,' is the reply.

For some reason I have the urge to laugh. Here I am, wearing a sky-blue *bobo*, standing in a throng of 300 over-excited people in the pink evening light, exhausted, dirty and a little dizzy, and someone is speaking to me in the broad drawl of the American south.

'What are you doing here?' I ask, half shouting because of the noise. A child falls against me. A woman is clapping by my ear.

'We're back for a holiday. This is our home,' the man shouts back. 'We work in Louisiana.'

'How is it in Louisiana?' I ask, unable to think of anything else to say.

'It's okay,' is the simple response. An idea occurs to me.

'And when you're there,' I shout, 'do you live as Africans or Americans?' It's a strange question, I know, and I ask it half jestingly, but then, because I am actually quite interested in the response, I add: 'For example, do you eat African food from a single platter, like here, or use a knife and fork?'

The man is unfazed. 'We live as Africans. Of course,' he says.

Our conversation does not proceed beyond this point, because at this moment Monsieur Po appears and tells me it is time to go: we are to make our way down to the river's edge where a pirogue is waiting to take us back to Mauritania. I have just time to shake the hands of the two 'Americans', and then we are off, the crowd following close behind.

Down at the water's edge, the splendor of deep evening is in full swing: the river, a strip of mercury; the sky, hemmed in mauve. The women are surpassing themselves and the uproar is all-encompassing. I struggle through to where the pirogue is pulled up in the water and leap onto its pointed prow. Monsieur Po and Salif clamber in behind me. Hands are thrust at us to shake: Madame Diop, Abou Mody, members of the committee, giggling boys, many women. And then the boat is pushing out into the current. There are shouts and cries of farewell as we paddle slowly away from the shore. Slowly, gradually, the din recedes.

For a long time we can see and hear the crowd still laughing and singing on the shore, but soon it is the peace and smooth ripple of the river that holds us in its grasp. Now I can see how near night it is: Dohley disintegrating into the darkness of the shore, the sky mostly black. We are silent as we pass the halfway mark, inhaling the clear, musky moistness of the river, only the slurp and gurgle of the paddle audible as it churns rhythmically at the dark water. On the far bank, on the Mauritanian side, I can see the silhouette of the Toyota beside the tree. When we reach the shore, we come to a halt with a lurch and walk slowly up to the vehicle. Here is Amadou Tall. We are back to our old vehicle, which has been mended. He shakes our hands with the enthusiasm of long parting.

'I have been waiting,' he says, grinning. 'The Toyota is fixed.' And, indeed, the vehicle fires on first attempt and we are off, following the beams of our headlights across the dark countryside.

In Kaédi we stop briefly at Monsieur Po's, to drop him off and to meet up with Mustapha, our old driver, whom we need to pay. Mustapha is smiling and cheerful and gives me such a very warm and impassioned thank you that I see, contrary to impressions, we have indeed made an impact on him.

The journey back to Keniéba feels long and it is with tremendous relief that I eventually collapse into bed in my hut.

9 Among the Pastoralists

An encounter with the police... The True Peul... In defense of tractors... Why teenage boys must work... Siting future wells... The sacrilege of selling cattle... Artistic herders... Heroic well-diggers... A dispute over donkeys... A lost herd

We are going out to Bokel Djouli today, a pastoralists' encampment a little to the north where we are in the process of digging a well. We will pass the night there. This is a favored spot of mine. I especially like to be amongst the pastoralists on their empty plains, and Bokel Djouli is the home of a particular friend. But we had a long day of it yesterday and will not head out until later on. So, for the larger part of the morning, I lounge about my room, going through a few papers with Salif, dozing and shooing away flies. We eat an early meal at midday and drink a quick succession of teas; then we are off.

It is early afternoon and the hottest time of day. The town is quiet, people sheltering from the fierce sunlight like mariners from a storm. We pass up over the road following a sandy track northwards through a scattering of Moorish encampments. To my surprise, just as we are leaving the last of these behind, we pass a police post and are called to a halt. This is unusual, as there are not normally such posts in this area.

The two police officers at the post look surly and one of them heads over to us. He asks for my passport and takes it over to his companion, who studies it closely. Soon they are back at the vehicle. What am I doing here? Where is my *mission*, my signed document stating my purpose and employment? Whose vehicle are we travelling in? They are aggressive and seem suspicious of me. Salif tells them that the Adjutant is aware of our movements, as he has just called him, but this does not seem to impress the men. They are police, not gendarmes.

I do not have a *mission*, as I always travel to Mauritania on a tourist visa. I have long been aware that, were I to seek official status in the country by registering with the relevant ministry to conduct development activities, this might well undermine the work Salif and I do. We would then most likely find it hard to avoid working in conjunction with some government agency not of our choice, which could then claim ownership of at least a part of the work we do, leaving us prey to exploitation. Only last year, we narrowly avoided something like this happening. A government agency for water and hydraulics got wind of the fact that Salif was involved in well digging at our project in Bokel Djouli, which at that time was still at the planning stage. The director of the agency, a Moor of some influence in the region, got a message through to Salif saying that he could not go ahead with the well digging without his permission and without the involvement of his agency. This, Salif knew well, was shorthand for saying that, if the director did not get a cut of the action, he would prevent the work from going ahead. Salif had no choice but to take the matter to the regional Prefect, hoping he would find in Salif's, rather than the agency director's, favor. To give him his credit, this is what the man duly did, saying the director's permission was not required, and we were able to go ahead with the well without interference. But it was a close-run thing and illustrated clearly the benefits – at least in the current state of affairs in southern

Mauritania – of keeping our heads below the parapet.

Having received my somewhat vague replies to their questions about my lack of *mission*, the two soldiers go off again, still in possession of my passport. A long period ensues. Has my long period of anonymity finally come to an end in southern Mauritania? We sit patiently, stewing in the heat. Then one of the soldiers finally emerges, saunters slowly over to where we are parked, and, with a nod, hands me back my passport. They were probably just bored.

There are three predominant types of terrain in the region of southern Mauritania in which we work. There are the lower-lying flood plains of the Moshe and Senegal rivers, where the majority of the agriculture takes place and where the towns of Keniéba and Kaédi, as well as many villages, are to be found. To the south are sandy, more elevated lands, also containing many villages, some parts of which are still well forested, the tall, thorny trees creating a canopy that in places is almost complete. To the north, meanwhile, is the land of the pastoralists. Here there is the same, more elevated sandy terrain, but the trees are gone and the vast stretches of open country – in some places rising to plateaus of black, gravelly rubble; in others falling to wide expanses of soft sand – run unheeded to a horizon not far beyond which is the true desert.

This is a land of bleached straw-grass, barren plains, mud-hut and thorn-stick villages that are little more than herders' encampments, and a sky that at times is a dome of blue, and at others an unglimpsable sheet of fire. So inhospitable can this country be that those who live in it are either there because over the centuries they have become highly adapted to its conditions, or because they are poor and marginalized and this barren area is all that is left to them. Those from this last group come mostly from the Harratin community: the Black Moors, descended from freed slaves, many of whom occupy the position of the lowest status and privilege in the country. The first group, those who have long been in the region and are highly adapted to living in it, constitute the core of Peul society: the *Vrai Peul*, or True Peul, as Salif calls them. Traditionally, these cattle-breeding livestock herders would have been semi-nomadic: affiliated to 'home' villages where the Qur'anic schools, markets and the larger family were to be found, but for most of the year following the rains and pastures with their herds. When on the move they would have lived in camps in the countryside, some only temporary structures for groups of young men on the move, others more substantial villages where families would remain on a semi-permanent basis.

Today, this pattern has changed, for it was these people who were most affected by the great droughts of the 1970s and early 1980s, with most of their livestock perishing. Many went to the towns, never to return, and those who remain have greatly reduced herds and these days rely more on the seasonal crops they plant and the extra animals they tend for the 'town' families. This has resulted in their lifestyles becoming more settled and their camps more permanent. Young men will still travel far with their livestock, when necessary going south even into Mali to find pastures, but life is harder now. The pools upon which they water their animals – left in riverbeds after the rains – now dry up much quicker, or never form at all; pastures are thinner and are more rapidly exhausted; crops are harder to cultivate; and the cost of living has gone up, meaning the herders get relatively less money now for their animals. But the Vrai Peul are indomitable, proud people, and I have always found their dignity and independence of spirit inspiring. They are tall, fair-skinned and fine-boned, and they step across the wide expanses of their country in the wake of their white, scimitar-horned cattle as though the rest of the world did not exist.

Amadou Tall is in his element as we head north into this

land of sand and scrub: he drives much better off-road than on. We traverse a few deep *oueds* of soft sand despite the fact that we are still in two-wheel drive mode, the engagement of four-wheel drive being reserved, in traditional manner, for only once one has already become stuck. To me, it seems like we drive with randomness, ranging widely across the difficult country, swivelling frequently through 90 or even 180 degrees in order to find a route. But this is highly familiar territory to Amadou Tall and Salif, my companions, who themselves come originally from a Vrai Peul family. Before long we have made our way to an expansive area of arable fields. These are the traditional rain-fed fields of a number of semi-pastoral families who, during the rainy season, set up small camps nearby. People are working the land, breaking it up with hoes in preparation for the rains and the planting of the millet crop. In one area, Salif's development group's tractor is at work, ploughing. This is what we have come to see and we walk over to where the owner of the land is standing.

The farmer is a stocky man in a white tunic, a turban loosely piled on top of his head. In his hands is a hoe, as he has been working at some soil lumps left behind by the tractor. He is sweating profusely and straightens up to greet us. Salif asks him how the work is going.

'It's good,' he says in surprisingly proficient French. 'The tractor is very good.'

'How much does it help you?' I ask him. I still have to answer that vexing question of whether or not we are encouraging an unsustainable form of agriculture by providing access to our tractor for ploughing.

'The tractor,' the man replies, enunciating the words carefully now, as though he knows what is in my mind, 'is six times more economical than working the land by hand.'

'That is a lot,' I say. I ask him to explain how this comes about.

'We get much better yields,' the man says. 'Last year, for

example, I only managed to plough half my land with the tractor, and the half I did by hand produced nothing... nothing, I tell you. The rains were weak last year and so the water did not lie on the ground long enough for it to penetrate the soil. But on the land worked by the tractor,' he continues proudly, 'the ground is so well broken that the water penetrates deeply and we get good crops. Tractors,' he finishes, 'are very good.' I suspect it might not only be because he speaks good French that Salif has brought me to this man.

We walk over to where people are digging the land with hoes: these are the fields for which there is not sufficient money to hire the tractor. It is tough work, as the ground is baked hard. Most of those working are boys and young men, as it is for this category of males, between the ages of about 10 and 18, that the lion's share of the hardest manual labor is reserved. According to Mamadou, Salif's cousin back in the compound, this is because they are 'closer to the ground' and so do not have to bend so far. I have always found it interesting how, in contrast to the developed world, where a man's physical working prime is reckoned to be somewhere in his mid to late twenties, here it is early youth that represents the physical resource of most value. From around the age of 20, a young man might be free to go off 'on adventure', or to seek local employment that will allow him to start raising the money he will need to get married. But before that, his vitality and durability are fully exploited: he is expected to work. And surely it does help that, at the beginning at least, he is 'closer to the ground'.

The speed and efficiency with which the tractor shears through the hard soil, when compared with the laborious, meter-by-meter task of working it by hand, speaks volumes on the subject of modernization versus traditional farming methods. Of course, there are all sorts of issues involved in mechanization, including the problems of soil run-off and nutrient depletion, but, watching the boys break the soil for crops that may well simply wilt or become prey to birds, locusts or the ever-threatening camels – and anyway will at best not produce a yield sufficient to support families – I cannot help sympathizing with the desire to move beyond subsistence farming. As Ibrahim Tandia said: African agriculture must develop.

We range widely over the countryside in search of four villages that have been selected as possible locations for further wells. The digging of wells is a new area for Salif and me, and reflects perhaps our natural liking for these pastoral peoples who, along with their poorer Harratin neighbors, have always seemed to me the most marginalized of communities. They demand little and so get little. They have little or no representation, even at local level. Governments and authorities have long seen pastoralists as little more than a nuisance, as, by the nature of their mobile lifestyles and independence of mind, they are harder to control. But in marginal lands such as these, the ability to move about and mix agriculture with animal husbandry is perhaps the best way forward.

The main problem the people from this region have is

simply a lack of access to clean drinking water. Often, they will have to travel 10 kilometers to their nearest permanent source of water, which is likely to be of poor quality. Periodically, a government agency that has won a grant or been allocated some funds will show up and dig a well or sink half a dozen boreholes. But these projects are generally conducted with such an eye to what monies can be creamed off into the pockets of their managers and directors that the work is done poorly and the wells and boreholes do not function properly. So we decided we would help to dig some wells, starting with the one at Bokel Djouli, which is already under way. Meanwhile, Salif has been busy canvassing other communities and commissioning hydrological surveys, because, at 40 or 50 meters, the water table is deep, and we want to be sure of finding water.

The four villages consist of collections of well-established Peul herder camps, 500-600 people strong, although a couple have adjoining camps of Harratin as well. Peul herder camps are different from other villages. For starters, as opposed to the rectangular, mud-brick style of construction typical across much of Mauritania, they favor the cooler, round, thatched hut, the wooden frame of which is plastered in a smooth render of cow dung and mud: textured and attractive. Here and there they are painted in simple geometric patterns, and, instead of being huddled all together in tight, interlocking networks, as in the other villages, they stand a little apart from each other, giving a sense of space and openness.

We do not stay long in each village: just long enough to locate the village chief, have a brief look about and confirm details such as the number of inhabitants and the distance to current water sources, these being some of the criteria upon which each village was selected. One of the villages has a borehole where a number of women are working at a treadle pump, pumping the foot pedal up and down, two at a time. It is hard work and produces only a thin stream of water.

Perhaps inevitably, there are problems with the pump, which needs a new part, but this is only obtainable in Nouakchott, many hundreds of kilometers away. The women work the pump continuously all day long and well into the night in order to fulfil the village's domestic water needs. I have a go at the pump myself, much to the amusement of the women. It is hard work pushing it down, and I can see why they do it two at a time.

We are seated on a spread of mats in the shade of a hut: Salif, myself, an old village chief and a number of other men. Around us are dotted further round huts, beyond which stretch the golden plains. The men are dressed in *bobos* and turbans, their sandals scattered around the edges of the mats, their roughened hands and feet, idle for the moment, poised and sculptural. There is a question I want to ask, although I am aware it might cause some controversy. Salif translates for me.

'You number here some 500 people, split between four camps,' I say. There is a murmur of agreement. 'You have 150 cows and 280 sheep and goats.' Heads shake in agreement. 'Your nearest source of permanent water is the Mabafe, six kilometers away.'

I pause a moment, then ask: 'What is the current value of a reasonable-quality bullock?'

A discussion ensues, resulting in a figure Salif relates to me that is roughly the equivalent of $400. This is a lot, as I expected.

'You have told me you need veterinary medicines,' I continue, 'and that your borehole needs fixing; you would like to have a well.' I pause. 'Why don't you sell some of your cattle to pay for some of these things? Only one or two head would do. Over time, you could even probably pay for the construction of a well.'

Salif is smiling. The men look at each other, unsure how to

take this; some also smiling.

'It is a good question,' one of them says in French.

There is a well-known Peul saying to the effect that 'the Peul never sell their cattle'. I quote this to them now, asking if this is the reason, and they laugh, as they can see now that I am not a complete idiot; that I am not making a 'serious' proposition: how could I be? Should a man be expected to sell his inheritance; dispose of his heirlooms? For this, more than anything else, is what the cattle herds represent to the Peul.

But of course it *was* a serious question. They will not go against this deeply embedded instinct to preserve their herds, an instinct that will prohibit them from parting with any significant part of them to alleviate even life-or-death situations. But perhaps, if Ibrahim Tandia's plan comes to fruition, we can sow the tiniest seed of such an idea. Because, if they want to survive, they, like everyone else, are going to have to adapt the way they think and operate. That is the new reality.

We pass a number of Harratin villages and I ask Amadou Tall to pull up at one of them. Ever since my earliest days in Mauritania, wandering in the desert amongst the Moors, I have had a soft spot for the Harratin, the Black Moors. Being descended from slaves captured by the White Moors centuries ago – and also freed long ago – they are a community with the lowest 'caste' status in Mauritania. Not all are poor or powerless, and they constitute the majority of the country's urban population. Even one or two government ministers come of Harratin stock. But of all the marginalized, dispossessed peoples in the country, it is the rural-dwelling, small-scale animal-herding, Harratin families who stand out the most.

These people have long ago been abandoned by White Moorish society with its strong families, clans and regional affiliations. They have long lost any connection to the original

Bantu Black peoples from which they came, with their all-encompassing cultural traditions and wide networks of connections and loyalties. They wander the barren fringes of the desert with only the weakest ties to the land, with little history or tradition, and with only a handful of livestock. They have no *patron* families or 'home' villages or tribal support networks.

Those I came across in my wanderings lived under scraps of tents, tending threadbare patches of crops when the rains allowed, only surviving with the greatest difficulty. When I came to them, they would invite me to stay the night. I would be given hospitality and companionship, despite their great shyness of me. Their children – weak, naked and begrimed – would cry at the sight of me. Their exhausted wives, worn down by toil by the age of 20, went trancelike through the motions of accommodating me. And the menfolk were monosyllabic. But always I felt behind this their great desire to give to me, to share with me, as this – to give and share – was about all they had left.

We pull up beside the scrappy collection of mud buildings. The place looks windblown and deeply impoverished. A few numb-looking children stare at us. Then, an old man in the rags of a *bobo* appears. His face is a ravage of pockmarks and destroyed teeth. Soon other men appear. They look a desperate sight: ragged, disfigured, coughing deep chesty coughs. I am a little shocked at the pitiful state of the place, especially when compared with the neighboring Peul villages that always maintain, despite their poverty, a neat, cared-for aspect.

Salif greets the men in Hassaniya, the Moorish language. He asks them a few friendly questions, but then reverts to ritualistic greetings, as I have not mentioned any particular reason as to why I wanted to stop here. I am not quite sure myself. The old man with the pockmarked face offers me a greeting. I reply rather weakly with the query: '*Ça va? Ça*

va?' – Okay?

'*Ça va pas,*' the old man immediately retorts back in French. '*Je n'ai pas du manger, ni d'argent, ni de vêtements. Bien sûr, ça va pas*' – I do not have any food, nor any money, nor any clothes. Of course I am not okay.

I do not know how to respond to this, but the old man is speaking to Salif now. 'He says can we dig them a well,' Salif says. The old man speaks some more. 'He says that if we do this, Allah will smile on us always.' The old man speaks again. 'With a well, he says, they will live like princes.'

'Has this village been considered as one of the possible sites for a well?' I ask.

'Yes, it was considered,' Salif replies, 'but it was not chosen.'

'Why not?'

'Because the people are too disorganized,' he says. 'They would not be able to form a committee and they could not decide what contribution they would give the well-digging team.' These are two of the further criteria a village needs to fulfil in order to be chosen: that they show the ability to participate in the well digging and that they form a group to manage the hygienic use of the well afterwards. Apparently, this community is not up to this. The old man grins at me toothlessly. The others stare implacably.

We do not remain in the village long after this. There is little we can do here. I feel impotent as we drive away; frustrated that, for the moment at least, there is nothing we can offer these people.

A dry riverbed: men drawing water from temporary wells dug into its surface. These are the inhabitants of Bokel Djouli, which is nearby, and, at this time of the year when the countryside is at its driest, this is where they get their water. The wells, perhaps a dozen in all, consist of pits three to five meters deep. Men stripped to the waist stand at the top of a number of them with long poles over their shoulders. At the end of each pole hangs a water container made from a car tire's inner tube. A man will let the inner tube drop into a pit where another submerges it in the small pool of water that has accumulated there. Using the weight of the other end of the pole as a counter lever, the first man then swings the inner tube up and, with a series of practiced movements, pours its contents into a number of plastic water containers waiting to be loaded onto donkeys for the journey home.

The first person to greet us is my friend Moussa, a tall man with an afro and eyes of the deepest black. His naked torso is streaming with sweat from his exertions at the wells and he greets us with the warm, wry smile and glint of humor in his eye by which I always remember him. His French is excellent.

'You are to spend the night. That is good,' he says. 'We have already selected a goat for you' – this, in reference to the animal that will be slaughtered in my honor despite my annual insistence that this is not necessary. 'We have chosen a good fat one,' he smiles.

Every day at this time of year, Moussa and his companions come here, digging the wells ever deeper and drawing off the water that has accumulated in them since their last visit. It is backbreaking work but Moussa seems always to go at it with relish. I have never heard him complain, even though each year when the rains come, the wells collapse and need to be dug all over again. The water that comes from them is also of poor quality, as livestock pollute it, and dirt and scraps continually fall into them. Indeed, Moussa himself only last year was the victim of such a bad waterborne infection that, had it not been for his quick thinking and Salif's prompt actions, he would have certainly died. Severe vomiting at night was the first indication that something was wrong. By morning, he was delirious, with extreme stomach cramps. Knowing that this was not one of the ordinary stomach complaints with which he and his family were only too familiar, he managed to call Salif on his mobile phone. Salif immediately sent the Toyota to fetch him and, when he arrived in Keniéba, decided to send him straight on to Nouakchott, as it was well known that the hospital in Kaédi was badly understaffed and people sometimes had to wait days there before being seen. It must have been a desperate journey to Nouakchott, Moussa deteriorating in the back seat through all those long hours. But eventually they arrived and found a doctor, who said that Moussa's infection and its resulting complications were so bad that he would certainly have died had he not received such prompt attention.

Moussa is to remain at the wells and meet us at Bokel Djouli later on. We drive on and arrive at the village, which consists of four Peul herder camps. Each camp is separated from its neighbor by several hundred meters, and each is encircled by a wide band of dried cattle dung, for it is around each collection of huts that the livestock gather at night: close and intimate. The camps themselves are surrounded by simple stick fences inside which the earth is scraped clean and in places plastered in the same smooth render as the huts. These last, and especially those of Salim's camp, are the most comfortable and pretty constructions I have ever seen in Mauritania where, on the whole, styles of accommodation rarely aspire beyond the utilitarian.

Here, the render of the huts is worked in such a fashion as to give them a beautifully finished, 'earthenware' look, with rounded doorways, tiny, triangular windows and 'hems' as seamlessly attached to the smoothed earth upon which they stand as anthills. It is the insides of the huts which most impress, though. Here, again, the neatness and attention to detail goes well beyond the purely utilitarian. Geometric patterns are painted on the walls, and possessions – some packed in trunks, some hanging from pegs, some displayed on long shelves – are arranged with the care of a shrine. The center of each hut is taken up by a large wooden dais covered in mats and cushions and on the walls are pinned photographs of friends and relations, poignant reminders of people from far away and long ago: smart young men, full of hope in some distant city; highly dressed women with the fear of the camera in their eyes; almost completely faded ancients. It is the sense of pride and care inherent in these huts and camps that strikes one. The people may have little, but they still believe in themselves; they are unbroken.

Moussa has two wives, both friendly, pretty and hard working; each with a hut of her own. He has five daughters and, to his relief I imagine, an infant son. The relief would not be because Moussa in any way regrets his many daughters – he patently adores them – but simply because women do not tend livestock and, if he does not want the entire burden of this falling on his shoulders as he gets older, he must have some sons.

We are greeted at the camp and mats are spread for us in the shade of one of the huts. Before we settle down, however, we make our way towards one of the neighboring camps, near to which is the well we are digging.

The digging of this well has been long and painful. This is partly because it is the first one we have dug and so there has been a steep learning curve. It is also to do with the fact that we have encountered a band of hard rock, reducing the rate of progress at times to a meter a fortnight. For five months already, from the end of the last rainy season, all through the dry season and now into the beginning of the hot season, the well-digger and his team have been hard at it. Another reason why the work has been so problematic, however, is because we decided to follow the route of an old, defunct well, reasoning that at least then we would be sure of striking water. As this well, though, had originally been poorly constructed, failing even to be sunk at a true perpendicular and having large cavities in its sidewalls, this has proved difficult, in essence requiring the meter-by-meter deconstruction of the existing well, all concrete and steel reinforcing rods included. And all this has been accomplished without the use of power tools; all has been done with hammer and chisel. This is not how it should be and lessons have been learned.

In my opinion, the well-digger – who is a local professional – and his team are nothing short of heroic. Salif tells me that few people would stick it out with the conditions they have had to put up with: over-long exposure to extreme heat and isolation; an inadequacy of tools; and a vastly overrun schedule. It is Salif's gift that he is able to pick out such people.

Ahmedou Soro, the well-digger, is a softly spoken, middle-aged man with the demeanor of a hermit or monk. Back and forth from the well he leads the donkey, which draws the bucket of rubble up 40 meters on the end of a long piece of rope. The well is beautifully constructed, a meter and a half wide, straight as a die and smoothly lined with steel-reinforced concrete. There is a call from the bottom, and with the next run of the donkey a young man, half-naked and grey with dust, appears swinging from the rope, one foot

in the bucket. His shift in the confined patch at the bottom of the well is over, and he switches with the young man who has been ferrying the rubble away in a wheelbarrow. Under a lean-to nearby, the third member of Ahmedou Soro's team is occupied bending steel-reinforcing rods on a vice. It is physical work, all of it: gruelling and relentless.

Ahmedou Soro cannot leave his donkey, so the next time he comes to a stop at the top of the well I go over to greet him. He is cheerful and polite and I peer into the black depths of the well.

'It's a long way down,' I say. 'How deep do you think you will you have to go?'

'Forty-five meters, possibly more,' he says.

'How long will that take you?'

He thinks a moment. 'It depends on the rock,' he says. 'It could take a further month.' This is a long time and I am just thinking how clearly we cannot continue in this fashion when Ahmedou Soro prompts: 'What we need is a pneumatic drill. With a pneumatic drill the job will go much faster.' I assure him that we will look into it and that if we dig any further wells, we will certainly not do so in the manner we have done this one.

There is another issue I want to ask Ahmedou Soro about, the one concerning the supply of donkeys by the local community. Donkeys are used not only for pulling the rubble out of the well, but also each morning for emptying the water that collects in it overnight. The Bokel Djouli community were supposed to supply these but, amazingly, as comparatively small as this contribution towards the digging of their well is, they have failed to do this consistently and Salif has even had to bring in donkeys from Keniéba. This is doubly incomprehensible considering that herder villages such as these are always well endowed with donkeys, and in fact generally have far more of them than they need. I find this whole issue highly dispiriting. Can these people really be so cavalier about their future that they will not even contribute the small amount that has been asked of them in order to secure something as important to their survival as a permanent supply of water? Am I missing something here? Are Salif and I being taken for a ride? I ask Ahmedou Soro for his view on the matter.

'They are poor people,' he says. 'Perhaps they do not have the donkeys to spare.' This is not good enough for me, I think angrily. They should make sure they have the donkeys to spare. We agreed on this before we started.

We go back to Moussa's camp, where there is now a gathering of people, as Salif has called a meeting of the well committee to see if we can get to the bottom of the matter. Deep down, I suspect there will be a logical answer, as indeed there usually is. But for the moment I am filled with chagrin.

It is evening by now; the light is soft and the shadows long. Moussa has turned up with a couple of other men, and we all settle down on a large spread of mats. Salif does the talking. Yes, it is confirmed that there have indeed been problems supplying donkeys to the well-diggers. Yes, it is understood that the supply of such donkeys was a requirement of the community. A prolonged discussion ensues. The committee consists of six men and two women: a friendly and jolly bunch who I can see are making an effort to lend the issue the importance I am obviously attaching to it. The problem, it emerges at the end of the discussion, is to do with the fact that there was not sufficient pasture near to the village this year as a result of the poor rains, meaning the donkeys had to be sent off and so were not available to the well-diggers. This is still not good enough for me.

'But that is their concern,' I say to Salif. 'They agreed that they would provide the donkeys and so they should have found a way to do this. They could have brought fodder to them here, for example.' Salif translates this and the committee members again plunge into voluble discussion.

'It is true,' one of them eventually says, 'we failed to provide the donkeys. We would have brought fodder to them here, but by then we had no fodder left.' Perhaps, I think to myself, this is it: these people simply do not have the resources to contribute even the small amount of help we have asked for. Perhaps we should not have even asked for it in the first place, even though it is important that communities show commitment to their well by contributing to its construction, as it is through such a commitment that they demonstrate their ability to run and maintain a well for the benefit of the larger community. I am just starting to think that this must be the explanation, or one that is going to have to be good enough anyway, when Moussa, who all along has been sitting a little apart petting a young daughter curled, feline-like, in his lap, interjects: 'If I may say something?'

'Of course,' Salif replies.

'I think the main problem here is one of misunderstanding,'

he says, speaking to me in French, which most present do not understand.

'The people here do not understand about charities and aid agencies,' he goes on. 'They think anyone involved in aid or development is part of the government and will therefore naturally be defrauding any project they are involved with. Many of them,' he says with a smile, 'even think Salif here is making money out of this well. Why should they contribute towards the well, then, they think to themselves, if it is only helping to enrich others?'

'And what about those who do not think this?' I ask.

'It is difficult,' he says. 'It is difficult to get people to provide donkeys when some refuse.'

'Hmm,' I reply, not entirely satisfied with this answer either.

'Do not think that there have not been any donkeys supplied,' Salif chips in now. 'It is just that there were not enough and the ones we had got tired. The committee assures me this will not happen again.'

And so we leave it at that. Somewhere in the gulf between the expectations and requirements of the Western funder and the on-the-ground reality for the African receiver – an inherently undesirable and, in fact, I believe, quite misunderstood relationship – lies the truth. It is a meeting point that will never satisfy either but, for the moment, in such situations, is better than nothing.

A sun flattening on the horizon: in a moment it is gone and soon fingers of dusk are creeping over the land. The livestock arrive home shortly before dark – great herds of sheep and goats rustling softly over the ground like a thousand leaves. Kids and lambs are released and for a while their and their mothers' cries drown out all else as they hunt for each other amongst the milling herds. The cattle arrive last, like long-range explorers, plodding their slow, inexorable pace along paths worn onto the

dry earth. They make their way to the camp where in a mass they stand chewing the cud or settle their large carcasses down like boulders. Moussa, now finished with the meeting, which has broken up, wanders amongst them with a small stool under his arm and a bowl in his hand. The cattle shake their wide, scimitar horns, flick a tail; scratch a white flank with a hoof. They are peaceful, unhurried; majestic. Moussa steps amongst them like a heron amongst the rocks on the seashore. He finds the ones he is looking for, quickly hobbles them and squats down on his stool for a brief milking.

Watching darkness come over this pastoral land, and watching the herds of livestock settle down for the night, is deeply soothing. It is as if the world were sighing, letting out a deep breath: the sound and smell of animals all around; the greying distances; the pretty mud huts perched on their scraped patches of earth, here and there the glint of a cooking fire now visible; the naked children still playing in the last of the light; the women clanking pots as they prepare the evening meal. There is something about the pastoral life, linked as it is to the rhythms and pace of its livestock, enacted under the great arch of the heavens, that draws me in. If there were one place on the globe I would call the home and hearth of humanity, it would be here: somewhere where life is closest to being uncluttered and elemental.

We are to eat a goat but the preparation of it, I notice, has not yet even started. Indeed, it has not yet even been killed but is bleating pathetically at a peg nearby, awaiting its fate. This Moussa seals once he has finished with the livestock. To the light of torches, the beast is held down, its head facing east to Mecca, while its throat is swiftly cut and its blood and life drained away. Now it is hung from a post for Moussa expertly to strip down and butcher. The women receive the cuts into pots already boiling. Choice bits will be roasted. We are to have a feast, and I am glad to see there are quite a number present, as my stomach, which is always troublesome, will not put up with much. The evening is long and dark. Those around me are in cheerful moods, and the conversation is lively. I lie back listening to the babble of conversation, watching the stars. Dish after dish of the goat comes: roasted, boiled, on a bed of couscous, with some salad even.

Later, in the darkness that falls like a cloak all around us, Moussa tells a story. It is for my benefit, clearly, as he speaks in French.

'We used to have great herds here,' he says. 'So vast we could not count them. But when the big droughts came our lives changed forever.'

'I was a boy at that time,' he goes on. 'The droughts lasted many years and it was hard for us. We sent animals east and west in search of pastures. My father even knew of places to the north where grasses could be found in the driest years, and at that time there were also many more trees whose seeds we could feed to the animals. But it was hard.'

We are silent as we sit under the stars listening, even those – the majority – who cannot understand French.

'For a long time, though, we lost only the weakest of our beasts. This was because my father was a good herder and understood about livestock health. Then, one year towards the end, the drought gripped even tighter and it was at this moment that my father decided to send the cattle south into Mali. We had not yet sent the cattle south, as that was where everyone was heading and there was much competition over the few pastures there were there. But by now we were losing beasts at a fast rate, and to have any hope of saving those that remained my father saw that he had no choice. There was nothing left in Mauritania.'

'My brother at that time,' Moussa continues, 'was a young man of 17 or 18 and my father decided that it would be he who would take the cattle south. He himself did not want to leave the family, as we were all suffering at that time, and he knew we needed his support. So my brother, Mohamed, took the beasts south with the aid of two young cousins. They went into Mali, where we heard from someone that they had found some grazing. Then all went silent. Six months passed, and we heard nothing. Eight months passed, and my father set out with his brother to see if he could find them. They too were gone a long time.

'I was about 12 then, and it was up to me to look after the family while my father was away, as my brother and I were his only sons. We were living in Keniéba at that time, as there was nothing for us in the countryside. All our livestock were dead except one bull and a handful of sheep and goats, which we had somehow managed to keep alive. It was at this time I started going to school.

'My father came home after two months and told us that Mohamed and our two cousins who had gone with him were dead. We could not believe it and we were deeply grieved.

They had been killed, my father said, in a skirmish with some villagers.

'My father had not gone to the village where they had been killed,' Moussa continues, his voice low now but still clear in the darkness of the night, 'as he was warned that, if he did so, the villagers might grow angry with him and do him some harm. Their bodies, he was told, had been burned.

'Apparently, the villagers claimed that it was they who had first been attacked. The villagers, my father was told, had gone to complain to my brother and some other herders who were with him at that time that they had not paid the price they had agreed upon for some fields of millet stalks the villagers were allowing their cattle to graze. My brother and the other herders, it was said, had refused to give up the goats that had been agreed as the price and had attacked them with knives. The deaths occurred when the villagers retaliated and a battle ensued.

'But later on my father heard a different version of this story from one of the herders who had been with my brother but had escaped. According to this boy, although a price of some goats had indeed been agreed upon for the grazing, the villagers increased this price every day, eventually refusing my brother and the herders access to the village wells unless they gave over half their cattle in payment. When my brother and the other herders refused this, the villagers came to them in the fields in numbers, armed with machetes and even some old guns, and it was then that the battle ensued which resulted in the deaths. The cattle, the boy said, were stolen and sold.

'The matter was looked into by the authorities, but at that time there was such turmoil and destitution in the Sahel, with people dying of hunger every day, that the case was never cleared up. Mohamed was my elder brother and so from that time on, with the exception of my father, I was the eldest male in the family. And that,' Moussa says, that glint of humor I know him by so well now again visible in his eye, 'as everyone knows, means lots of responsibility.'

I sleep that night on a mat under the stars. Salif and Amadou Tall opt for the inside of a hut and so, once everyone else has gone to bed, I am alone. I wrap a sheet about myself and for a long time I just lie, listening to the silence. Somewhere far off on the plain a pack of dogs is howling. Later, a donkey brays, loud and painful. I wake many times that night, and at each waking wonder for a moment where I am; then, as I see the stars overhead, remembrance washes over me like a cool breeze.

10 A Day of Wind

The redundancy of dogs… The value of a fence… Culture and money… Donkey ploughs and microcredit… The selflessness of Salif and Mariam… An audience with the Mayor… Classroom floors and blackboards… The ancient hunter

First thing in the morning, Moussa is out amongst his herds. He wanders through the sheep and goats, slowly circling after the kids and lambs, for whose hind legs he makes sudden lunges. Soon he has a handful of each dangling from his hands like fruits. Meanwhile, a rampant donkey is attempting to mount its not-very-willing mate. Hooves flash like gunshots and long, yellow teeth are bared. A billy goat is pursuing one of its vast harem, groaning in the throes of pheromonal ecstasy. The cattle, earliest of risers, are long gone.

I am always pleased to see the dogs, which slink about the edges of the camp. They are always of the same sleek, long-legged, hunting-dog model, as though this is the final mongrel conclusion. Their heads are small and their white, shorthaired coats are splattered with brown, and, it seems to me, there is always a smile on their faces. This is surprising, as they do not have very good lives. In fact, I have never quite understood why they exist at all. Their role as protectors is more or less redundant, as livestock raiders here are pretty much a thing of the past, and all wild animals of any size have long been wiped out in Mauritania. And yet every herder camp has any number of dogs dashing territorially about, and they can also be found in villages and towns throughout the country. No-one, as far as I can see, feeds them, except perhaps periodically throwing them a bone or some leftovers. They are emaciated, flea-ridden and frequently disabled from fights. Never have I seen a human touch one or in fact pay the slightest attention to them beyond hurling the odd stone. And yet still they smile, confident deep down, one feels, that they remain 'man's best friend'.

Today will be a day of wind. By early morning, gusts of stinging dust are swirling around and the sky is grey, as though overcast. We take our leave of Moussa and his family promptly. We leave them standing in a family group inside the little fence that surrounds their camp: tall Moussa with a child in his arms; two or three young, pretty girls smiling confidently; his two wives, waving.

Salif and Amadou Tall are in a cheerful mood as we head out, inspired perhaps by the the plains of the Vrai Peul calling to their pastoralist heritage.

'It is a good day,' Amadou Tall shouts over the noise of the wind, despite evidence to the contrary.

'We will go to the south,' Salif replies. 'It will not take us long. We will finish by midday.' His face is lit and happy and unusually carefree.

Today is my last day before we return to Nouakchott and we still have a number of tasks to accomplish with some farmers with whom we are working in the south.

In a couple of hours we are in different country. Here we are amongst trees; tall thorny trees that in places almost meet overhead. In the old days a lot of the region was like this, and it's said you could travel to Kaédi from many parts of it without once having to leave the shade of the trees. What it is that has protected these trees where elsewhere they have disappeared, I am not sure. Perhaps the communities here are more organized and have been able to prevent the villagers and commercial charcoal burners from cutting them down. Perhaps the authorities have been more resolute in applying the anti-deforestation laws. Or perhaps the lie of the land is such that the trees were more able to tap a water table that had not fallen too deep. Whichever is the case, it is a pleasure to be amongst trees again.

I ask Amadou Tall whether there are any wild animals left here.

'Many,' he replies with a confidence of which I am doubtful. 'There are baboons, which eat the villagers' maize. And hyena. Many others.'

'Have you seen them?' I ask.

'No, no, I haven't seen them, but it is said a hyena took some lambs near Djente village this year.'

'When we were children we saw baboons often,' Salif says diplomatically, 'and there were antelope everywhere. Now, though...' He does not go on and I can understand why. There are no large animals left now. Those not killed by the droughts have either been hunted out or simply shot by communities for whom the bigger species of wildlife represent only a threat. Indeed, the only time I did see a sizable animal anywhere near here, a baboon crossing a road in northern Senegal, the driver of the vehicle in which I was travelling instantly screeched to a halt, grabbed a pistol from under his seat and wildly let fire at it through the window, deafening us both in the process.

Of the smaller examples of wildlife, there is still a certain amount remaining. Now and again on our long drives across even the driest country, I have seen desert hares, with their large, veined ears that act as cooling systems. I have seen pale desert foxes, squirrels and rodents of many types. There are partridge and quail and other small birds whose names I do not know. And often, circling on the thermals far above, are harriers. But the larger animals, I suspect, are the stuff now only of story and rumor.

It is in this forested area that, some years ago, the marginality of the whole region was brought home to me. It was December, the cool, dry season, and, almost without precedent for that time of year, it rained. It was not a large amount of rain, but neither was it a shower: perhaps 300 millimeters over a couple of days. What was remarkable about this was how it affected both people and livestock. Already the cool season, the rain made it even cooler, temperatures dropping to five degrees, which, along with the dampness, caused widespread deaths among herds of sheep unable to cope with exposure to even such mildly adverse conditions. I came across them in the woods: groups of otherwise quite healthy-looking beasts lying dead on the sand. Even some people died from exposure, their bodies unable to cope with the unfamiliar cold. Truly, I realized, this was a region where the line between survival and death is very thin.

The villages in the area we have come to are more substantial than elsewhere. They have proper mosques painted in bright colors, marketplaces, even the odd shop. Now and again a vehicle passes through. They are like smaller versions of Keniéba: networks of sandy passageways and compounds. Fields of millet lie about them, and herds of sheep and goats drift over the surrounding countryside like cloud shadows. To the north is a long depression where, for 15 kilometers, millet is planted as the rainy season floodwaters recede. This is the primary agricultural land for the region and we have been involved in helping to put up a fence to protect some of it from livestock. We drive now to this fence, which does not look particularly remarkable but, Salif assures me, makes a huge difference to the villagers' lives, concentrations of livestock in the south, which is comparatively humid, having increased so much. Salif tells me that last year, before the fence was started, only 2,000 of the 10,000 hectares it will eventually enclose were planted. This year, even though the fence is not yet completed, 4,000 hectares have been sown. This, I think to myself, must be one of the most painless and cost-effective forms of assistance we have given to date. I am even assured by Salif, who has conducted a consultation with the communities involved, that the pastoralists will also benefit from it, as large areas of pasture within the fencing will be protected from over-grazing.

'But what of the Harratin and White Moor animal herders?' I ask, for they too both bring livestock into the area and will probably be less welcome within the fenced area. Salif gives me a weary look.

'It is not a problem,' he says. 'There are ways for them to get through. It is their camels that cause much of the problem.'

I am straying into difficult territory here, I know, as it is this issue – the conflict of interests between the Black African farmers and semi-nomadic Moorish livestock herders – that is and always has been one of the main points of contention between the two communities. The Moors, a confident, bright, opportunistic desert people, descend south as the

pastures wither further north and graze their animals on the high-ground pastures where grazing rights are free to all. They also negotiate with the villagers for access to fields of crop residues where the dung of their animals adds to the soil fertility. But of course it does not always work as smoothly as this and progressively, as the Moors descend south in larger numbers, often settling there for good, the grounds for contention between the two communities grow, with crops being damaged by badly supervised livestock, communal pastures being stripped too early on in the season and land-tenure issues arising.

We proceed to a village where we are proposing to work with a women's co-operative on a small vegetable-growing scheme. Although similar in some ways to the Dohley Women's Market Garden Project in that organic farming methods will be employed, this is on a different scale, with water being drawn by hand from a well as opposed to the mechanized irrigation system of Dohley. The co-operative land is a little outside the village in a clearing in the woods: one hectare of vegetable plots surrounded by a fence. There are only a few women about, as it is the end of the main vegetable-growing season and most of the plots have been harvested. I am told that the co-operative consists of 200 women and that they want to increase their land to two hectares. They also need to re-dig their well, for which they are asking us for funding, as in the cool season it runs dry. We wander about looking at a few compost heaps the women have already made under Salif's instructions, and I ask Salif what the costs of the project will be.

'Re-digging the well and extending the fence are the main costs,' he says; then, after making a calculation on his mobile phone, comes up with a figure that is the equivalent of around $1,500. It is my turn to make a calculation. The 200 women of the co-operative come from probably about a hundred different families. This works out at about $15 a

family – say $20 if one includes various other costs such as seeds and implements. This is hardly a large amount, and again I am confronted by that same question: why is finance being sought from us when it appears quite within the ability of the villagers to pay for the changes themselves?

'If they organized themselves, these women could quite easily pay for this,' I say to Salif, quoting him my figures. The president of the women's co-operative is with us: a tall, tough-looking woman. Salif puts the question to her.

'It could not be done,' she says simply, Salif translating.

'Why not?' I ask.

'They would not pay,' she says.

I look at Salif. 'Why would they not pay? It is not a large amount.'

'They don't have the money,' he says. 'They do not have the cash available. And even if some families did, they would not all, and certainly not all at the same time. Some would pay and some would not, and then there would be problems.'

I understand. It is the same issue as always, one that I seem to be having the greatest difficulty in getting into my head. The problem is not financial but organizational, even hierarchical, or perhaps even more to the point, it is cultural.

There simply is not the hierarchical structure or precedent for the gathering of a communal fund for agricultural use. Certainly, communal funds do exist, for example for the construction and upkeep of mosques. But this is a time-honored practice for a non-profit-making activity. To gather money for what would be a profit-making activity across all the many different families of an entire community has never been done before and would, as everyone knew, be highly problematic. How to co-ordinate the fundraising? Under what or whose authority? What penalties would there be for non-payment? How would profits be split? And the fact is, in the context of the financial pressures all families constantly live under, the money required from each of them is indeed significant. A women's co-operative would never be prioritized to receive such surplus cash – at least not until such schemes could be shown to be worthwhile financially.

In another village, we inspect a donkey plough. Animal traction for working the land is unused here and it was Monsieur Po whose idea it was to produce this plough for farmers to experiment with. The results, I am told, are spectacular. The farmers have found it to be far more economical than working the land in either the traditional manner, by hand, or by tractor, and there is now a great demand for it. Our hope is that farming in this manner might catch on.

We stop at some fields where we are working with farmers on rainwater harvesting, helping them dig small, foot-high barriers across the contours in their fields. A gnarled old farmer points to one side of one of these simple barriers, where the stalks of an already harvested millet crop are small and threadbare, and compares it to the other side of the barrier, where the water was prevented from running away and the stalk density is at least double.

And we go to a village where we have started a small

microcredit program. Microcredit is a proven development tool. Small pots of money are lent to groups of women who then set up and run their own loan schemes, lending small sums to their members for income-generating activities such as vegetable growing, material dyeing or even simply a bit of commerce. The repayment rates are generally exceptionally high and the schemes are seen as a way of stimulating economic activity and helping women who traditionally have poor access to income-generating opportunities. Our scheme has only just got under way, with $3,000 being lent so far to 10 different groups. The main challenge, Salif tells me, is to get the women to engage with the idea: doing business, even at this level, requires a degree of ambition that many of them simply do not have.

The wind is coming and going; hot on the hand like a blow heater and laden with throat-tickling dust. It gusts violently across the landscape, twirling dust devils to life. Next moment there is a lull and all seems calm.

We head back to Keniéba and arrive around midday. I

am feeling exhausted. We install ourselves in Salif's lounge, as outside all is dust and wind. I do not feel well and doze. Later, a platter of food is produced. It is *mafé*, the Senegalese peanut-stew speciality, although when I mention the dish's provenance, Mariam will have none of it.

'Those Wolof know nothing of cuisine,' she says, referring to the predominant Senegalese ethnic group. 'This is a Peul dish.'

'Certainly the Peul make it very well, and differently,' I hastily backtrack. Mamadou is with us.

'This is what we eat during Ramadan,' he says. 'After we have fasted all day, it is nourishing, as it is full of vitamins.'

The food is helping me feel recovered already. I ask Mamadou whether he also gives up drinking water during Ramadan, as is the requirement between sunrise and sunset.

'Mamadou does not even give up food,' Mariam interrupts.

'Ha!' Mamadou exclaims indignantly. 'What are you talking about? I give up food, except when I am working in the fields. A man cannot work physically without sustenance.'

Mariam laughs. 'Salif drinks nothing in Ramadan,' she says to me.

'That must be hard,' I say.

Salif shakes his head. 'It is hard,' he says, 'especially when Ramadan falls in the hot season.'

'But still you do it,' I say.

'Mostly,' he replies.

'And is ill by the end,' Mariam adds indignantly.

Salif looks tired. He is under almost continuous siege from his mobile phone, his family, villagers, farmers and, for the moment of course, me. At times I see the deep weariness on his face, as he is not a natural leader. He is a quiet man, who one feels would prefer a quiet life.

I am wondering about Salif and Mariam. For the last couple of years, on my departure from Mauritania, I have given Salif some money to pay for the making of bricks for the new house I know he wants to build, the first step towards which is to accumulate sufficient of the concrete blocks modern houses are constructed from to make a start. I know for a fact that he has not used this money for bricks, allowing it instead to be absorbed into the ever-pressing financial needs of the larger family. How can you make bricks when someone needs an eye operation? Or when another's roof has caved in? Others manage, but not Salif. Mariam is still waiting for the fridge she has been talking about for a decade, the one I know she so badly wants, as she finds the hot season unbearable and craves the ability to have a cool drink. But Salif and Mariam, I know, are people who do not expect more than that which comes to them. Never have I heard them voice discontent.

Late afternoon: we have a few last tasks to accomplish. We must go to see the town mayor and pay a visit to a primary school that we have been helping. The wind seems to have settled, although the air is still dusty.

We find Demba Mody, the Mayor, in the *Mairie*, in the new part of town. Demba Mody has a difficult job. His responsibilities are heavy and broad, ranging from all matters municipal, to agricultural issues, issues of a traditional nature, all social and inter-community problems and, most importantly, to acting as the link between the lay town community and the military authorities, represented here by the Adjutant. And all this has to be done without the clout of any real power or any of the significant finances that go with it, since both these, as everyone knows, reside firmly in the hands of the military.

Demba Mody is a tall, gruff man with a shaggy head and bloodshot eyes, and he is unashamedly autocratic in wielding what authority he has. This is an effective approach, considering the many conflicting demands of his role, and the fact that he has been repeatedly re-elected as Mayor for more years than I can remember reflects this. I always make a point of paying him a visit when I am in town. This is both because I sympathize with the difficulties he has to face and because, as weak as his real authority is, it would not be wise to ignore him. He is still a man of some personality.

Any number of people can always be found lurking about the dilapidated building that acts as the *Mairie*. Mostly they are petitioners: farmers with complaints about neighbors or seed suppliers; townspeople whose local well has been fouled; householders who need help on any number of issues. A Moorish merchant might be there seeking a signature allowing him to build a whole new row of merchandise stores that the Mayor knows would be illegal due to their obstruction of a thoroughfare but is powerless to stop because the Adjutant has given the enterprise the nod. A group of landowners might be trying to negotiate with the Prefecture a land title but need an affidavit from the Mayor affirming the land in question has been in constant use by them for more than 10 years. Demba Mody is a realist and deals with everything with little preamble. He will listen to the petitions, then make his decisions and move on to the next.

We are greeted at the door to the *Mairie* by Drémis, Salif's cousin from the compound who does a small amount of clerical work for the Mayor, he with the heart condition and complicated love life.

'Ah, Peter, Salif, you are here. The Mayor will be delighted to see you,' he greets us in his trademark booming voice. 'We are very busy with this election, but the Mayor will see you in a moment. Please, sit down. You will only have to wait a few minutes.'

He smiles, his thin, once-round face strained with the effort of remaining the jolly person he is despite the collapse of his body. There are only two chairs in the porch area that acts as foyer to the Mayor's office, and both are taken. Noticing this, Drémis glares at the two farmer-types occupying them and they both graciously get up, offering their places. I at first decline, but Drémis, who insists, is not one to be defeated, so I sit myself down.

'There is a French mission in town,' Drémis says by way of making conversation. 'Have you seen them? French youths… delinquents… fools.'

'What French people?' Salif asks. Neither of us has any idea what he is talking about.

'Ah… the French,' Drémis replies, as though this were enough explanation, but then adds: 'they have come to build a youth center for our young people. It will be very good and have solar panels to run a DVD player or some music. They are young criminals, mad.'

'What do you mean?' Salif says.

'You know,' Drémis replies. 'They are simple.' He taps his head. 'There are others to look after them, and they have come to build the youth center.' No doubt this is some French social rehabilitation scheme.

'What have you been doing today?' I ask Drémis, to change the subject.

'Pah, pah, pah,' he exclaims, 'there is too much to do. The Mayor is standing for re-election. There is much to organize.' At this moment the door to the Mayor's office opens and the Mayor appears, leading a large Moor by the hand. They are finishing their conversation, and take leave of each other with overly loud bonhomie, business completed. Demba Mody sees us.

'Monsieur Peter, Salif – greetings. Come into my office,' he says with little formality. We are jumping the queue, I know, but I do not feel mentioning this will strike a chord. Demba Mody throws himself behind his large metal desk, and we take a seat on the two chairs across from it that are about the only other things in the room. He does not say anything; just stares at us musingly, as if his mind were elsewhere. Salif tells him why we are here: to pay our respects, to have a chat. Still the Mayor seems distracted, stroking his chin.

'Hmm, yes, very good, very good,' he says. Then suddenly

he comes to himself. Perhaps he was contemplating his last interview, no doubt some tricky matter… a favor perhaps… perhaps a deal of some sort. Or maybe he is wondering how to respond to the question he knows we are going to ask about some match-funding the Mayor's office was supposed to produce for the primary school.

'We've had a difficult year,' he says, shaking his head, 'very difficult. The poor rains… the birds. The farmers are desperate and there have been budget cuts in all government departments, meaning less money for helping them. A very difficult year.' We discuss such matters for a bit.

'The seminar was very good,' he says at length, the beginning of which he witnessed. 'Excellent. You are working with all members of the community. This is very good. It is good that you show that this is what you are doing. People must realize that this work is not only for Salif's family. You know how these people are. They can be very jealous, very suspicious.'

'Of course. Our work is for the community as a whole,' Salif replies.

Has Demba Mody had complaints, I wonder, or is he just making his own point? I decide it is time to bring up the matter of the match-funding. We are buying books for the school and building a room to put them in, and the deal was that the Mayor's office would pay half the costs. This it has so far failed to do. I ask Demba Mody when the money might be available.

'Ah, this is a problem,' he exclaims. 'This is not good. We need to help the schools. The headteacher has been in here a number of times asking for things. He has even given me a letter. Alas, what with the government budget cuts, the Mayor's office has not received the finance we expected. We are hoping to get more. But for the moment we simply do not have any funds.' And, according to Salif, they never will, as Demba Mody, despite his initial commitment to the project, is not one to put education high on his agenda. I look at the Mayor and know Salif is right. This is a man of diplomacy, and there will always be bigger fish than headteachers; or ourselves, for that matter.

It is stiflingly hot in the Mayor's office and I am happy when, shortly after, we leave it. Demba Mody comes with us out to the front of the building.

'We appreciate the work Salif and you do in our community,' he says looking me directly in the eye. 'This is the work of Allah, and it is taken note of.' He is a man, I believe, who means well.

The primary school, to where we go next, had 700 pupils when I first visited it a few years ago, and only nine members of staff and seven classrooms. The teaching materials consisted of only a handful of exercise books – which the higher-grade children shared – a few blackboards and 10 teaching manuals. The headteacher, Sidi Khan, a quiet, committed man, devoted his life to doing the best he could for his students. He presided over the few decrepit buildings of the school from his small office, and in the evenings did the rounds of the family compounds, making sure his charges were doing their homework, helping them and relaying the few exercise books. We financed the provision of extra books and the construction of a number of desks, as in most classrooms the children had to sit on the floor. Then things improved. A change in government brought in a boost to the education budget. Were these the first signs of better things to come, of a governmental renaissance? Perhaps. A second primary school was even constructed, although Sidi Khan was sent off to some distant posting and I have not seen him for a number of years. Now, however, I am happy to hear from Salif that he is back and has been put in charge of this new school.

We pull up at the door to the school compound and go in.

The place is new and tidy, with two low, freshly painted rows of classrooms facing each other across an expanse of sand. Sidi Khan sees us from a classroom where he is teaching and comes out to greet us. Although polite and formal, he is warm and takes us over to his office where we talk of how the school is faring. They still lack resources and there are problems with the classroom floors, he says. The contractors who built the school, probably with the connivance of the managers who controlled the budget, so reduced the cement content of the concrete floors that they have already broken up and, if there is any wind, the rooms fill with dust.

'I took the Mayor a letter,' Sidi Khan says, 'stating this and listing all our other requirements. This was so it could not be denied that we have made our representations.' I do not know quite what he means by this but Sidi Khan is an intelligent man and I imagine that this is the next step in the game of chess that all who want something in Mauritania must play.

A little later, Sidi Khan leads us up the row of classrooms where, at our appearance in each doorway, 50 small faces stare at us in astonishment before their teacher orders them to stand. Two or three to a desk all jammed together on what is now a sand and dust floor, they immediately leap to their feet and chant out in unison: '*Bonjour, Monsieur le Directeur.*' The teachers look sweaty and overworked and Sidi Khan nods his head to each one as though he were a general inspecting his officers. The school is clearly strictly run under his authority. Teaching methods may definitely be of the 'old school' variety, the knuckle-wrapping ruler still very much in evidence and most learning done by rote, but, in his last year at the last school, Salif tells me, Sidi Khan managed an 80-per-cent leavers' pass rate, a remarkable feat in the circumstances.

Having decided we will devote the remaining school budget to fixing up the classroom floors and reblackening the already-faded blackboards, we take our leave of Sidi Khan. We have two further visits to make. The first of these is to a small shop in the marketplace. This is the workplace of Abou Tidane, a tailor, whom we find sitting at his sewing machine, pushing the foot pedal up and down as he feeds his material through. Abou Tidane is a compact, cheerful man with the hands of a farmer and, at our appearance, his face creases into the biggest of smiles.

'Allah... welcome,' he exclaims getting immediately from his seat to shake our hands. He is an immensely likable and friendly man and I have come to give him a photograph I took of him and his family on my last trip. Although Abou Tidiane works in Keniéba, his home is a tent some five kilometers out of town, where he lives with his wife and their three disabled children. Having three severely disabled children is a massive disadvantage in somewhere as difficult as southern Mauritania, and how Abou Tidiane and his wife manage I have no idea. But the extent to which they love their three children is evidenced by his request that I photograph them and by the tender manner in which he lays his hands on their shoulders in the pose.

'Ah, truly, we look like Africans,' he laughs, when I give him the photograph.

Our final visit is to Salif's great uncle, an ancient of a hundred years according to Salif. Whether or not the old man has in fact achieved this milestone I do not know, and I doubt if anyone actually does, but he certainly has the look of one who harks from a different era. He is in a room at the back of a large, neat compound that is home to Salif's paternal aunt. The room is dark and empty except for the old man, who sits, like an idol, in the dim light on a mat on the earthen floor with his prayer beads. Once, he would have been a tall, strong man, but his long limbs and body are now rendered to little more than bone and sinew. He wears nothing but a loincloth wrapped about his middle, his head is bare and his brown leathery body glows softly in the golden light.

We enter the room and squat down. As Salif takes the old man's hand and goes through the formulaic greetings, the old man slowly looks up. His eyes are blue from cataracts and the paper-thin skin of his forehead is creased with strain. He mumbles the greetings, then rallies and reaches out to take my and Salif's hands. Now he mumbles a blessing, coughing periodically as he does so, a deep rattle in his thin chest. In a corner of the room, leant up against the wall is an ancient, flintlock musket, for the old man, Salif tells me, was once a hunter.

I think of the Africa he must have known: one connected to its long history; one little changed over millennia; one steeped in its own traditions and societal norms – hunters, *griots* or storytellers, crops in the fields, a passing *marabout*, migrations, early, easy deaths, ancient mud-built towns, the weekly market, rains, stories, endless herds; one that is now rapidly disappearing. It would have been a hard life, as there was little ease or physical comfort then, but it would have been one with certainties that now no longer exist. The old man lets go of our hands; pulls his own down his face in the motion of washing himself. We are blessed. We get up to leave. A woman enters.

'Old Father,' she calls to the old man. 'It is Salif and his Nasrani.' The old man nods his head.

'Salif... Oumar Boubou's grandson,' she says.

'Yes, yes,' the old man croaks.

'He does not remember much,' the woman says. 'But he is strong.'

I lie in my hut that night and think of the old man. I think of the peace and humility that was in his face and hope that when my time comes to end my journey on this earth, I too will have found such peace and humility.

11 Away

**The journey north... How would Westerners cope?...
The Saudi problem... Businesspeople in charge...
Fish-market beach... Adrosso and Amadou again...
Doorway to another world**

Dawn: cockerels crowing; shrouded figures outside their rooms, sweeping the sand of yesterday's debris. Salif calls me early and we take a quick tea with Amadou Tall in the lounge. Mariam is up. She offers me her goodbyes.

'Give my blessings to all your family,' she says. 'When will your girls come to see us?' I think of all the cockroaches; the spiders. I'm not sure. 'Some day, I hope,' I say.

Amadou Tall shoulders my rucksack and carries it out back to where the Toyota is waiting. We are in. Mamadou is by the window and I shake his hand. Then we are off.

The return journey to Nouakchott is like a river draining into the sea: there is a gravitational pull and inevitability about it. We stop briefly in Kaédi, to refuel. As early as it is, already the town is busy, already the dust is up: the donkey-carts, the peasants with their produce, the merchants, the gunning vehicles, the beggars and madmen, all preparing for another day of toil. As dysfunctional and hard as life is here – with the powerful easily rising, as in any jungle, above the vulnerable, and poverty clawing at the very fabric of society

– I cannot help wondering just how we in the West would cope in similar circumstances. I fear we would not come out of it so well. I fear a breakdown of economy and reasonable authority would result in an orgy of self-preservation that would make this place look positively cozy.

We traverse the south; then turn north. It is roasting, and better to have the Toyota window at least partially closed, as the wind is so hot and desiccating. We pass the tented camps, the herders, the nomads with their prehistoric camels on the empty plains that are home to them. They pass and are gone. We make good progress despite the many roadblocks, which do not hold us up too much. At one of them an old man is disputing with a soldier.

'Your ID is out of date,' the soldier keeps repeating.

'So what?' the old man replies, 'so am I.'

Soon, the south, Keniéba, the farmers and their fields are in the past. Now we are in the surreal landscape of the dune seas. If we turned right, I think to myself, and drove a true bee-line to the northeast, we could go 2,000 or 3,000 kilometers before we came to another road: what a great chunk of untrammelled world. Of course, there would be people. As we ploughed our way across dune sea and plain, we would meet up with nomads and their herds on unexpected pastures only they knew were there, or traversing the empty wastes on journeys of necessity. We would stop and greet them and share a tea; then move on.

The hours elapse, and we are silent. I seem finally to have run out of questions for Salif. We stop for a break in the town of merchants on the road. They have not ceased their trading; they do not notice our passing. A child stands begging with an empty tin where we take our tea and eat some biscuits. As we leave, Salif gives the boy the remainder of the biscuit packet and immediately three others with tins descend on him, squabbling over the spoils. The tea shack owner shoos them off like pigeons. Their tins denote them

as the students of a Qur'anic school, required to beg for their meals: beggar scholars.

Amadou Tall seems unaffected by the drowsiness that nods my and Salif's heads. He sits up, eyes fixed on the mirage-shimmering distances into which the Toyota moves like an ant. Then finally the electricity pylons appear, looping off into the desert where they power the great pumps that suck up the fossil waters that service the capital from whence they have come. We are still an hour-and-a-half outside Nouakchott, but soon the traffic is thickening; shacks and half-built buildings appear beside the road. Suddenly, I notice a change in the atmosphere. It is no longer dry. My skin is sticky. It is humid: the sea.

The city accumulates; then we are in a traffic jam. There is still desert around, but also buildings and a dual carriageway of green minibuses: fuming, stationary, people hanging off them. It's all very sudden. We negotiate our way to the center

of town, then out again south to Amadou's district. It is
1.30pm. We have made excellent time. We install ourselves
in Amadou's rooms where only Fama, his wife, is present,
curled up asleep with her infant on the floor.

Amadou: large, shaven head; pockmarked face; sensitive
eyes. He appears, as he has some hours off from work. He
settles down on the carpeted floor of the lounge to make tea
but is uncommunicative until I address him.

'We need to buy a pneumatic drill for our wells project,'
I say to him. 'Do you know anything about the drill-to-
compressor power ratio?' This is technical stuff, at which I
am hopeless. How big a drill should we buy for work at the
bottom of a well; and so how big does the compressor then
need to be? This is what I need to ask. I have some paperwork
that I brought with me describing various well-digging
methods. I have it out in front of me. Amadou looks over
from his tea making.

'How deep will you be drilling?'

'Up to 50 meters,' I say.

'Hmm,' he muses. The tea is hot in his pot. He lifts it off the
burner and starts pouring it into the tea glasses, mixing it back
and forth from glass to pot and pot to glass, concentrating.

'There are some details of compressors here,' I say. 'But I
cannot make sense of the specifications.' He puts the teapot
down and gets up to come over.

'This is no good,' he says, looking at the papers. 'These
compressors are under-rated for your use.'

'Do you think we could buy a powerful enough second-
hand compressor here?' I ask.

'Maybe.' He sits down again and resumes his mixing. 'I'll
email you some specifications. Maybe you should look for
one in England and send it over.' He busies himself with the
glasses. Shortly, he looks up: 'And these Islamists,' he says.
'What about these Islamists?'

'What about them?' I say.

'Ah…' he chuckles; then: 'Bin Laden… he was the first of them. He was a clever man, but a fool as well. He hurt the Americans. The first to do so. People respected him for that, even if they did not like him. He was a fool, though, because he thought America was the problem.'

'What is the problem?' I ask. He is tasting the tea now, daintily holding the small glass, half filled with froth, between his fingers. He flips open the top of the teapot, pours the rest back in and returns the pot to the burner.

'The problem is the Saudis,' he says. 'They're the real capitalists. It is they who manipulate the price of oil, upon which the whole of the capitalist system rests. And as long as everyone expects their cars to be filled each day with fuel, they will have governments who will deal with such people, or anyone else for that matter. Bin Laden himself was a Saudi. He came from one of the richest Saudi families. Do you know the Saudis are even here in Mauritania, buying up land?'

'Are they?' More Land Grabs.

'And we will sell it. Always the African is ready to sell what is not his.'

'Should they not sell these lands?'

'Tens of thousands of hectares they want. Who does it belong to, this land? They're clever. Of course, it belongs to the businesspeople who are selling it. At least they are the ones with the title papers. That's how it is. That's how things work here.' He returns his attention to his teapot, lifting it off the burner with a piece of paper to protect his fingers from the hot handle. He says: 'There is a well-known Senegalese journalist who said: "The African thinks only of his stomach. When it is empty, he looks to fill it. When it is full, he sits back and does nothing."' He chuckles again, deep and rumbling. 'It's true, is it not?' I cannot tell whether the question is rhetorical or not.

'There are improvements,' I say. 'At least people know what good governance is now; at least they have heard of it.' I am thinking of that word, transparency, so prominent now in politic-speak.

Amadou's tea is ready. He pours a thin stream from a great height into the two glasses where they sit on their metal platter. The froth froths and he cuts the stream short with a twitch of his wrist. He reaches the platter over for me to take a glass; he shakes Salif by the shoulder where, tired after our trip, he is dozing on a divan and offers one to him. We drain our glasses in quick sups and toss them back, rolling them across the floor.

'You know, when I was in Russia,' he continues, 'the people used to say: "we are happy because we are not dead". That was when the winter froze everything and there were power cuts and everyone was cold. They'd say it after a few drinks, as the Russians like to drink. In Africa it is the same. We are happy, even as our governments rob us. You see the people: they are smiling, laughing, aren't they?' This time the question definitely is rhetorical.

'They say governments are getting better,' he continues. 'I too have heard this. Maybe somewhere it is true. But what difference does it make? The poor will always get poorer. It is always the same businesspeople in charge.'

'It takes a long time for real change to filter through,' I say. I want to say: there is a different, more modern Africa out there, now. There's a new generation that is dynamic and worldly wise. One by one, they will oust the old regimes; they will secure the change that is happening for the better. But do I believe this? What about all those natural resources for which foreign governments will increasingly compete, willing, on the insistence of their consumers, to make deals with the type of people who do not have the common interest in mind, the type with a vested interest in protecting the status quo? What about the ideological battles – the 'war on terror' – and the realities of climate change and the pressures these will bring to bear? But against this there is always the majority who are not greedy, or corrupt, or stupid – those like so many of the farmers I have met, the sheer weight of whose courage, inventiveness and resilience will surely, one hopes, like water, wear down even the hardest of adversaries.

Amadou shakes his head, musing: 'Perhaps,' he says, 'God willing.'

At this moment Fama appears with a cloth. She does not speak, and we watch as she spreads the cloth on the floor. Shortly she is back with a platter of fish and rice and we gather around to eat, big Amadou cradling his tiny infant in his lap, feeding tiny morsels of rice into its mouth like a bird feeding its chick.

4.00pm: we have some shopping to do. I also want to visit the fish-market beach, the color and salty confusion of which somehow seem always an appropriate conclusion to each trip. And we have not forgotten our rendezvous with Monsieur Adrosso.

Salif needs a new mobile phone, as his current one is old and does not work properly. We go to the corner in the center of town where the phones are bartered on the sidewalk. Nearby are a number of stationery shops. I persuade Salif to accept some files, a calculator and a briefcase. He says he does not need them, but I have seen the piles of papers in his room. Then we head north, past the hospital and out across what used to be the empty salt plain that separated the fish-market beach from the rest of town, an area no-one thought would be of any use as it was just too salty, inhospitable and liable to flooding. Now it is entirely built up: a whole district of whitewashed condominiums and mini-palaces all already starting to dissolve back into the salt plain from which they sprung – all, Salif tells me, under water during last year's floods. And all, he says, built with bank money, whatever that means.

The beach in Mauritania is around 600 kilometers long: an unchanging slope of sand stretching almost the entire length of the coast. It is unmarked, unused and undistinguished in any way. Then, as though making up for this, it becomes all of a sudden for two kilometers a dash of intense color. Here are 2,000 traditional fishing vessels pulled up high on its slope; an infinitely diminishing perspective of tall, pointed prows; flags fluttering in the breeze; crowds, wandering and congregating; nets, stacks of pots and wooden shacks: a whole small world of fisherfolk and fish-based commerce.

Out to sea, more of the long, brightly painted fishing boats ride the swell, some anchored, some preparing for a two-or three-day expedition out over the horizon, some readying themselves for the dash over the breakers to the shore. Here, the moment these last touch ground, a crowd descends on them like crabs, their catch stored in a large wooden box to be quickly distributed: in mounds on donkey-carts for the bigger merchants, or relayed in fish boxes to the ice-packing warehouse, or carried off in basins on women's heads for the city markets of tomorrow. Sitting on one end of the boats while the other unweighted end is swivelled around, a dozen oilskinned crewmembers gradually sidle the boats up the steep incline of the beach, eventually slotting them into their places with the other vessels, some of which are so huge you wonder how on earth they could ever be so maneuvered.

Salif and I wander. We remove our shoes and let the sea wash over our feet. This is such a contrast to the interior, to the somehow orderly, meticulous life of the farmer. It feels carefree: luxurious. We wander beyond the last of the fishing vessels, past the rusting wrecks of three large trawlers embedded in the sand. This sea, this coast, is one of the richest fishing grounds in the world, and unfortunately, the world has realized it and is plundering it accordingly. Japanese, Chinese, European, Korean: they are all here, dredging the fish, allegedly running down the local fishing boats when they get in the way, paying large 'licence' fees to government ministers who talk a lot about how they will use the money. Meanwhile fish stocks decline and what was once the primary source of protein for one of the poorest countries in the world is now a dwindling resource to which locals are only allowed restricted access. It is a familiar story, one that illustrates all too clearly the difficulty of co-ordinating poverty alleviation with a moral basis across all the different governing institutions of a rapacious global economy, even when there is the will to do so. It is another in the endless list of exploitation stories that litter Africa and the world – a story, however, that, for now at least, is not mine.

We used to walk up the beach all the way to the port, some ten kilometers off, but we no longer do this: those were earlier, perhaps more carefree days. Instead, we turn back, shortly coming to a boat that has just come in off the sea, which we watch. There is a crowd milling about it, and the catch is being distributed. But here it is the fisherfolk themselves who are doing the ferrying, and in the strangest of fashions. They are stuffing as many of the fish as they can down their baggy oilskin trousers, having first tied the bottoms with bits of string. They are stuffing them in frantically, crazily: large dogfish, dozens of smaller ones; then they dash up the beach to deposit them in some unseen destination before returning for more. Fish are everywhere, spilling out of their trousers, slipping and tumbling onto the sand where scrabbles of small boys dive for them. Salif is giggling uncontrollably at the sight.

'Look, see,' he says, as one of the young men trundles past, fish protruding from even his shirt. 'The owner of the boat has failed to pay the crew. Ah, truly, they are taking matters into their own hands.' Tears of pure, light-hearted joy are streaming down his face.

Later, we sit and watch the sun slide into the sea as the market packs up for the day; then we are off to Monsieur Adrosso's. I do not know what to expect at Monsieur Adrosso's, as I have never been to his house before. I am disappointed. The old man greets us at the door to his comfortable villa with genuine warmth and enthusiasm – 'Monsieur Peter, Salif, so good to see you. How was your trip? I have a very special dinner for you' – and the dinner is indeed delicious – langoustine deep-fried in batter taken at the glass dining table in his modern lounge. But the manner in which he treats the servant who waits for us, clicking his fingers at him irritably when he gets things wrong, barking at him in a manner so very alien to the culture in which I have been submerged for the last eleven days, not to mention the derogatory way in which his taciturn son talks of 'the Blacks', mean that both Salif and I are relieved when we return to the cozier, more egalitarian world of Amadou's rooms.

Here, a full evening is in swing: Amadou, as usual, presiding over the tea; Isa, Salif's pretty other daughter who is in minor disgrace having had a child out of wedlock – a child Salif inevitably dotes on; Mustapha, the military nurse who told the story of his time in Algeria; any number of cousins, students and other hangers-on. Few of them may have jobs; fewer still any money in their pockets. For most of them the long hours of each day might represent a struggle of Herculean proportions, but they have in each other and in their culture of gentleness, discipline and acceptance, a security that is solid; one that, it is true, might breed a certain complacency, but also one that all of us, including the modern Africa that is coming, might learn from.

1.00am: my alarm. I have a three o'clock flight. I wake Salif where he is asleep in the lounge.

'Leave Amadou Tall,' he says.

'Isn't he driving?' I ask.

'No, Amadou is.' The other Amadou, he means: our host. This is strange. He has work tomorrow.

'Why is Amadou taking us?' I ask.

'I don't know,' Salif replies. 'He said that he wanted to.' That's all.

Salif wakes Amadou. We clamber into his vehicle. We are silent: tired and half asleep. The city is empty. We rumble over uneven sand; then bump up onto the tarmac. The long, neon-lit avenues lead us towards the airport. We come to a roundabout. Here there are a couple of soldiers standing beside the road. They wave at us to stop: a checkpoint. Then Amadou does something odd, reckless – something I have not seen anyone do in Africa before. He aims the vehicle at the soldier most prominently in the road and drives straight at him. The man just has time to leap out of the way. I gasp. Salif exclaims loudly. But we are past.

Amadou's gaze is fixed on the road: fierce. No-one speaks. We arrive at the airport and pull into the parking lot, Amadou's ancient, wheezing vehicle coming to a standstill like an old man taking his last breath. Amadou climbs out and hands me my rucksack. His face is stony: defiant.

'Okay?' I ask.

'Of course,' he replies brusquely; then suddenly his face clears and the warm, kindly look I know him so well by comes back. 'Don't worry about those soldiers,' he smiles. 'They are nothing.'

'But they can be dangerous,' I say.

Amadou laughs.

'Not so dangerous,' he replies. 'Not so dangerous.'

I part from Salif by the airport terminal beside which a cordon of soldiers with batons stands, preventing anyone without a ticket from entering. We embrace. I will not see him for a year. Then I turn, show my ticket, and am swallowed up in the doorway to another world.

TIMBER PRESS
POCKET GUIDE TO
Shade
Perennials

TIMBER PRESS
POCKET GUIDE TO
Shade
Perennials

W. GEORGE SCHMID

TIMBER PRESS
Portland ◆ Cambridge

Frontispiece: *Farfugium reniforme* with *Hosta rupifraga* (lower right)

Published in 2005 by

Timber Press, Inc.
The Haseltine Building
133 S.W. Second Avenue, Suite 450
Portland, Oregon 97204-3527, U.S.A.

Timber Press
2 Station Road
Swavesey
Cambridge CB4 5QJ, U.K.

www.timberpress.com

Printed through Colorcraft Ltd., Hong Kong

Library of Congress Cataloging-in-Publication Data

Schmid, Wolfram George.
  Timber Press pocket guide to shade perennials / W. George Schmid.
    p. cm. -- (Timber Press pocket guides)
  Includes bibliographical references (p.   ) and index.
  ISBN 0-88192-709-0 (flexibind)
  1. Perennials. 2. Shade-tolerant plants. I. Title: Shade perennials.
II. Title. III. Series.
  SB434.S2973 2005
  635.9'543--dc22
                              2004013926

A catalog record for this book is also available from the British Library.

All photographs are by the author unless otherwise noted.

Dedication

To Hildegarde, my wife, friend, and supporter for over half a century. Her love and encouragement made this book possible.

Acknowledgments

Thanks again to all those people and places mentioned in An Encyclopedia of Shade Perennials, on which this pocket guide is based. Special thanks to Allan Armitage, Tony Avent (Plant Delights Nursery), Hans Hansen (Shady Oaks Nursery), Lynne Harrison, Don Jacobs (Eco Gardens), Darrell R. Probst (Garden Vision), and Barry Yinger (Asiatica). My thanks to the good folks at Timber Press, who work so diligently to make a book out of a jumble of words and pictures. Sigi Schmid, my youngest son, has accompanied me on many rewarding hikes through the Appalachians; his support, companionship, and keen eyes have helped me discover the many small wonders along the way.

About This Book

The entries in this pocket guide are arranged in alphabetical order by scientific name. If a genus or species name appears to be missing from this alphabetical listing, it may be because the name has been changed by taxonomists. To find the current name, look up the "missing" name in the index, which provides a page reference to the correct name. Cultivar names are enclosed in single quotation marks. Synonyms for cultivars, if any, are listed after the current name, in parentheses, or are mentioned in the descriptions. Each plant description is followed by cultivation notes, beginning with hardiness zone numbers (based on the United States Department of Agriculture map), indicating the zone(s) in which the plant can be successfully cultivated. Also included are recommended soil conditions and a range of shade gradients, as described in the introduction and abbreviated as follows:

FS = full shade
MS = medium shade
WS = woodland shade
LS = light shade

CONTENTS

Opposite: *Peltoboykinia watanabei* with *Saxifraga stolonifera* (left)
and *Aspidistra elatior* 'Variegata' (background)

PREFACE

Aside from playing in the dirt at home, one of my most cherished pursuits is visiting the shady, natural gardens of the Appalachian Mountains. Several times each spring, summer, and fall, family and I visit different remote spots there to hike and photograph the natural wonders of this exalting area. To call such places "gardens" may be irrational, because a garden in the strict sense of the word has always meant an enclosed space set aside by man for the cultivation of plants. Nevertheless, the inspiration of such a natural, shady garden is boundless and provides a model for what many refer to by the oxymoron "natural garden." Frankly, I think it should be called the "new American garden." Most older gardens have tree cover and as our newer American gardens age, the trees we planted become shade-giving trees making our gardens shady places. There, shade perennials have become key players in creating the restful, comforting gardens inspired by the visits to our mountain Shangri-la. For me, gardening is a labor of love, and those mountain visits restore my gardening ambitions. I return ready to dream, plan, and work to prepare things for the next season. Photographs taken in the natural forest go a long way in providing new ideas and the stimulus to incorporate them into my garden design. The great American woodlands are a paradigm for our own shady gardens. It is true that as a gardener I tend to add my own personal touch, mix native and exotic plants, and combine natural and synthesized designs. Nature's composition, however, dictates a blending of soft colors and textures. Its supple contours look relaxed; there are no straight lines that have to be maintained. Even weeds, the nemesis of classic gardens, have a hard time getting a foothold. While no garden is maintenance-free, following nature's example reduces a gardener's workload and provides more time for relaxation and enjoyment.

The bones of the garden—trees, shrubs, vines, and other woody perennials—are a given for a shady environment. It is the perennials, both herbaceous and evergreen, that make a shade garden complete. Without them there would be shade, but no garden. This book is a guide to the very best of the available shade perennials. It includes the "classics" we have used for many years and many of the new introductions coming from Asia as well as our own shores. Make your shady garden complete!

Opposite: *Tradescantia virginiana* with *Hosta kikutii*

INTRODUCTION

Where there is light, there must be shadow. As long as the sun shines, anything that moves—man, animal, or machine—is trailed by its own shadow. In days gone by, shade was considered bad. Majestic shade trees and tall shrubs were ruthlessly eliminated, sacrificed to the idea that gardens, parks, and lawns must be open to the sun. But to consider shade a detriment to gardening is incorrect. Many informed gardeners now make the most of shade. Before they can do so, however, they must define shade.

Defining shade is more an art than a science: it is impossible to establish a permanent value for a given spot in the garden. Light levels vary, from morning to sunset, for sunny and cloudy days, and with the passing of the seasons. Theoretically, full shade is where direct rays of sunlight never reach. The best place to look for full shade is on the north side of a structure where direct sunlight never reaches.

Anything less than full shade is more difficult to define. In nature, trees as the prime shade givers produce most shade. Their height, shape, and leaf cover also modify shade. In the mornings, almost full sun reaches under the loblolly pines. Later in the day the long-needled, open tree branches provide dappled shade. A Canadian hemlock casts a much denser shade; and a willow oak allows almost full sun to reach under its leafless branches in midwinter, while in summer the tree crown casts dense shade. Thus, different trees give various shade patterns throughout the year, changing with each season.

Keeping records of where, when, and to what extent shade exists during different seasons is essential to defining shade in the garden and is an important task for gardeners. In gardening, homework always pays. Happily, most so-called shade plants are content with some sun exposure. No flowering garden plant succeeds in con-stant full shade. It is important to remember that too much sun can burn a plant and too much shade may cause it to stop flowering or to fade away altogether.

Shade Defined

Here are what I consider popular definitions of shade, sometimes in conjunction with the degree of sun exposure, rated from zero to 100. Zero denotes total absence of direct exposure to sun, 50 indicates half direct sun and half shade (with full sun occurring usually mornings and afternoons, and shade prevailing while the sun is high in the sky), and 100 represents full-sun conditions from sunrise until sunset.

1. Total and perpetual shade exists where the direct rays of the sun never reach and where reflected light is absent. Sun exposure and reflected light are practically zero. Few plants, if any, grow under these conditions.

2. Full shade (FS) occurs under wide- and low-branching deciduous tall shrubs and trees or evergreen trees with tight branching structure and dense foliage that cast deep shadows during most daylight hours in the main growing season in spring and summer. During winter, however, under deciduous trees, sun exposure can be near 100. At low sun angles some sun exposure may occur at sunrise and sunset for short periods of time, full shade conditions prevail for most daylight hours. Effective average sun exposure is less than 10 (perhaps one or two hours of direct sun exist at low angles).

3. Medium shade (MS), also called filtered shade or dappled shade, exists under high-branching deciduous trees, evergreens, and

Opposite:*Blechnum spicant* backed by *Hosta kikutii* f. *leuconota*

conifers that have an open structure. Sun exposure is between 30 and 50, with direct sun exposure occurring for two or three hours after sunrise and before sunset for trees in the open. Obviously, morning sun is much more beneficial for shade garden plants than hot afternoon sun.

4. Woodland shade (WS) is complex, something between medium and light shade. In densely forested areas, it might approach full shade for part of the day; in lightly wooded areas, medium shade may prevail most of the time. Open woodland is lighter and brighter; shade is dappled, and sunlight dances across the forest floor. Our garden "woodlands" are frequently open, with the trees of neighbors contributing to the shading.

5. Light shade (LS), also called open shade or traveling shade, exists where shade occurs for only part of the day, with full sun exposure, possibly exceeding two-thirds of daylight hours, for the remainder of the day. The shade may be filtered through singular, small trees or may be a dense shadow cast by a man-made structure or a tree with a concentrated leaf mass. Sun exposure under these conditions exceeds 60. Areas that receive some midday shade will see considerable direct sun during morning and afternoon. Even during times of shading, the open exposure allows considerable reflected light to reach the shaded area, and bright light conditions exist.

Bones of the Shady Garden

In nature as well as in gardens, shade is never a constant: it depends on a fluctuating framework of trees and shrubs—the bones of the garden. This shade-giving framework changes steadily and thus alters the location, timing, and intensity of the shade it provides. In time, gardeners may have too much shade. The remedies are simple. The most obvious and frequent solution is to cut down trees or tall shrubs or to resort to "limb-

ing up" the offending trees. Some trees and most tall shrubs need periodic pruning for best performance anyway, so this pruning can be performed with ultimate shade requisites in mind. As trees and shrubs grow older, eventually they die and must be removed or storms topple them. Gardeners should be aware that their shade might disappear in spots. With the passing of time, all gardens change.

Shade Without Trees

For gardens without shade-giving trees, shade may be created by erecting shade houses or vine-covered pergolas. These can be rudimentary structures or they can take on a more architectural tone. As decorative, functional, and useful as they may be, these structures can never replace the living beauty of shade-giving trees and shrubs in a woodland garden.

The Garden's Floor

The wild woodland floor is made up of the by-products of tree growth and organic life in the woods. Such woodland soil is to die for but rarely, if ever, is such "gardener's gold" available. In many residential areas, the suburban landscape is so thoroughly disturbed that gardeners must "create" their own soil.

To take available soil and improve it to attain good physical structure and openness (a condition sometimes referred to as good tilth) is time-consuming, labor-intensive, and often expensive. Adding organic matter to natural clay or sandy soils is essential. Among the types of organic matter suitable for gardens are ground bark, coarse sphagnum peat, or ground natural waste, such as peanut hulls or corncobs. Ground tree clippings can be obtained cheaply and are sometimes free for the taking. Gardeners can collect pine needles, leaves, or other natural waste; once composted, these materials make fine soil amendments. There is nothing better than adding humus from a gardener's compost pile.

Knowing the soil is essential to making a garden. Many county extension offices of the United

States Department of Agriculture (USDA) provide a soil analysis service either free or for a nominal charge. Soils can be acid, alkaline, or neutral, which level is indicated by the pH number. Neutral soil is represented by pH 7. Readings above 7 indicate increasingly alkaline conditions, and those below 7 indicate increasingly acid conditions. Inexpensive pH meters are available at nurseries, so gardeners can do their own pH testing.

Many shade perennials with large leaves require considerable available and constant amounts of water in the soil. These conditions can be accomplished by adding organic matter to the soil. Some soils can hold too much water. Slow-draining clay soil, for example, must be "opened up," also by adding organic matter. Few shade perennials survive in stagnant soils. Soils must be able to breathe. Good garden soils have a high percentage of open space, called pore space, usually occupied by air and water—the best have around 50 percent solid matter and 50 percent pore space. In fine clay soils the pore spaces become very small, but surface tension increases, so the soil can hold large amounts of water. Clay soils have poor percolation and thus are usually sticky and wet. Again, adding liberal amounts of coarse, organic matter improves the soil.

Agricultural topsoil is composed of 90 percent mineral and 10 percent organic matter. Old, undisturbed woodland soil, by contrast, can have as much as 50 percent organic matter. A high volume of organic matter is preferred in soil for the shady natural garden. Although organic content is important, some mineral content should be included for balance by mixing in natural, mineral-rich topsoil.

Many cultivated shade perennials, except some wildflowers, are relatively heavy feeders. The best fertilizers are slow-release types like Osmocote Plus. The 18–6–12 formula, with six months' time release, is ideal for shade gardens. Chemical fertilizers, such as ammonium nitrate or superphosphate, are not recommended.

Making soil does not mean replacing existing topsoil but adding organic matter to the culti-

Arisaema ringens with hostas

Hostas with ferns in the woodland

vated surface layer of soil. It is important to get the soil analyzed to determine the amount of organic matter required. It is not enough to "make" or improve soil, but it must be maintained in good tilth. From time to time it will be essential to "smell" and "feel" the soil and to have it retested. The soil of shady gardens under pines and oaks can become more acid in time, and it is prudent to test the acidity now and then.

Trouble in the Garden

Trees are usually the shade-giving "roof" of a garden, but they can bring trouble—namely, damage to the underlying plants. Physical damage is common: trees bombard the garden below with large cones, nuts, pine needles, and other cast-offs. Tree droppings, such as the resinous droplets that descend from many pines or the sticky nectar exuded by some flowering trees, turn black in short order by way of fungal action.

Shade trees stretch their feeder roots over large areas. They feed greedily on the splendidly friable, fertile soil provided in the planting areas and can eventually stunt the shade perennials grown there. Check for invading tree roots at regular dividing time. If root invasion has occurred, remove the roots, screen the soil, and replant everything. This is a good time to divide plants for increase. Landscape fabric in the bottom of the beds sometimes delays the inevitable bed restoration.

Gardeners' Enemies

Viruses that mottle the blossoms of tulips are considered beneficial. Others, however, cause chlorosis (yellowing of the leaves), "bad" mottling or mosaicism (white or yellowish spots), blotching (whitened areas larger than spots), wilting and collapse of plant tissue, leaf curl, mosaic and ring spots, general reduction in vigor, and stunting. Viruses are spread by cutting or sucking insects that carry cell sap from one plant to another, as do gardeners who use the same garden tools first on infected and then on healthy plants. Usually, a visit to the county USDA extension office or a univer-

sity's plant pathology department can help identify viral diseases and seek countermeasures.

Bad bacteria and fungi generally enter plant tissue that is cut, torn, or abraded, and once inside the plant tissue, multiply rapidly. They can cause decay, contribute to secondary infections, and may kill the plant. Treatment comes often too late, because bacterial and fungal diseases, such as crown rot, start hidden in late autumn and the destructive action continues below ground until spring. By the time the plants are expected to produce their spring flush of leaves, the rootstock may have turned to mush.

Early detection of symptoms is essential. That is why good gardeners spend a lot of time in their personal landscape visiting the plantings and checking everything: they try to detect problems before they become disasters. Some gardeners exclude all plants and any other materials brought in from outside in a "quarantine area."

During the growing season, bacterial and fungal diseases are easily spotted and gardeners should become familiar with their symptoms. Examples of these maladies are leaf spot, anthracnose, crown gall, mildews, rusts, smut, cankers, black spot, and some blights. A visit to a county USDA extension office is particularly valuable, because some pathogens concentrate in certain regions of the country, and these offices are aware of such infections and can recommend countermeasures. Whatever treatment options are used, they should respect our environment.

Nematodes are very small, unsegmented roundworms. Root gall nematodes are cyst-forming and invade the root structures, leading to stunted growth or loss of vigor. Some granular nematicides are available and can be tried, but the environmental consequences must be considered. Good cultural practices can overcome some of the damage.

Foliar nematodes invade the aboveground portions of plants, particularly the leaves, disfiguring them. The damage does not show up until early in summer. Total eradication is possible only with extremely dangerous chemicals and is not advised.

Gardeners may have to be practical and learn to live with these pests. The best way to keep populations down is to remove any disfigured leaves as soon as they show up, thus preventing the eggs from escaping into the ground when the leaves disintegrate in fall.

Bugs and other critters are among the gardener's enemies. When gardeners see a wonderful rose blossom chewed to bits by Japanese beetles or a perfect hosta leaf cut to ribbons by armyworms, they instinctively reach for the big insecticidal artillery. Of late, conscientious gardeners have replaced chemical insecticides with beneficial predatory insects, which take over the role of biological insect control in gardens. Still, a huge number of "bad" insect species make life miserable for gardeners. Insects have only two goals in life: to eat as much as possible and to procreate as much as possible. They do both as quickly as possible.

Biological controls are the best ways to protect against bugs: ladybugs control aphids, mealybugs, and other soft-scale insects; predatory mites fight thrips and spider mites; predatory wasps are used against whiteflies. Beneficial nematodes are very effective against any pest that lives just below the ground or crawls upon it, like the grubs and adults of weevils, borers, Japanese beetles, wireworms, armyworms, root maggots, and a host of others. Green lacewings predate on aphids, scales, and whitefly; tiny parasitic wasps combat insects both as larvae and adults. The product Bt (strains of the bacteria *Bacillus thuringiensis*, available in powder form) paralyzes those ravenous caterpillars. Most important, encouraging songbirds to visit the garden is a very effective control of all insect pests. Several mail-order houses specialize in providing such environmentally friendly solutions for bug control.

Exclusion methods may be as simple as setting a trap to catch Japanese beetles or hanging up flypaper, one of the oldest exclusionary devices known. A number of other trapping devices are available.

Slugs and snails have horny, rasplike teeth that can cut through even the most substantive perennial leaf or sprout. Adults can devour an entire shoot or a complete leaf. When the slug eggs hatch in late winter to early spring, the application of a molluskicide is most effective. A thorough cleanup to remove all hiding places, as early as possible in spring (or even begun in late fall), another absolute must.

Highly effective products that contain a selective, mollusk-specific attractant and a poison are available; a small, beadlike amount suffices, so the environmental impact is minuscule. Poisoned bran products attract pets, birds, and other wildlife and should not be used. A dish sunk into the ground and filled with beer is a famous exclusion device for slugs; slugs absolutely love that beverage and promptly drown themselves in it.

Oxalis regnellii purple form

Biological controls include toads, birds, shrews, chipmunks, and turtles, and these should be encouraged.

Weevils, or snout beetles, specialize on specific plants and have become a significant pest for azaleas, rhododendrons, and many shade perennials, such as hostas. Visual damage consists of irregular notches eaten out of leaf margins. Even more destructive are the cream-colored, orange-headed beetle larvae, which feed on the roots. The beneficial nematode *Heterorhabditis heliothidis* is an effective biological control when applied as directed.

Butterfly and moth larvae. Butterflies are beautiful, but during their larval stage, many species cause great damage to ornamentals. Only chemical methods work fast enough to control overnight infestation and are the only choice in difficult, but usually localized situations. Slow-acting biological controls include predatory wasps and insect-eating birds and mammals. Repeated, early applications of Bt (*Bacillus thuringiensis*) kill the larvae. Timing is of the essence with this biological control. The neem tree is the source of a spray reputed to be effective against caterpillars and other insect pests. Beneficial nematodes have proven highly effective and long lasting, but their application must be timed in concert with the appearance of caterpillars. Organics include dormant oil sprays and biodegradable soap solutions.

Mammals. Deer and rabbits are among the worst offenders when it comes to wildlife feeding on garden plants. Rabbits are easily fenced out, but deer are another matter: fences with a minimum height of 8 ft. (2.5 m) topped with barbed and electric wire are recommended.

Plant roots are not immune from animal attack. Voles use abandoned chipmunk tunnels to get to the roots and rhizomes of garden plants.

Tree squirrels are a nuisance, and terrestrial squirrels, like chipmunks, eat insects and slugs, but their extensive burrows can damage root systems, as do gophers and moles. Ask your county extension office for permissible controls in your area.

Contained in the Shade

Container gardening is popular, because potted plants can be moved around easily. Even very large, heavy containers are made transportable with the aid of casters or rollers. Almost any plant can be grown just about anywhere in a pot, provided the gardener knows the plant's cultural needs. Potting is a superb way to give importance to exceptional plants even when placed among ground plantings. Another very obvious benefit is the ability to store dormant plants over the winter. Many tender and subtropical perennials go dormant when cold weather arrives and can subsequently be moved to frost-free locations like a heated garage or basement.

Garden design and plant layout can be fine-tuned by using potted plants in experimental locations. If a plant looks out of place, simply lift it out of the ground and move it to a more appropriate location. When the final position is found, the plastic container is removed and the plant claims its permanent spot in the earth. Unfortunately, regular watering of container subjects is vital and can be a burden.

SHADE PERENNIALS
FOR SPECIFIC PURPOSES AND LOCATIONS

The lists that follow are representative only and do not include every shade perennial described in this guide. Gardeners are encouraged to be creative in their use of shade perennials in the landscape.

Fast-Growing Plants

The following plants can grow aggressively, even invasively, particularly in enriched garden soil. Some spread by runners (aboveground stolons or underground rhizomes), others by producing prodigious amounts of viable seed. These plants are widely planted but they must be watched. Remove runners or deadhead flowers before seeds are produced.

Aegopodium podagraria
Ajuga spp.
Anemone spp.
Aquilegia spp.
Begonia grandis
Corydalis lutea
Eomecon chionantha
Lamium spp.
Lobelia cardinalis
Lysimachia spp.
Petasites spp.
Phlox divaricata
Polygonum spp.
Viola spp.

Groundcover

The best groundcover is evergreen: it maintains leaf cover throughout the year. This trait is particularly important in areas without snow cover. Fast-growing herbaceous plants can be used where out-of-season leaf cover is not required. Groundcover is selected from plants that usually spread by rhizomes or stolons, thus requiring fewer plants to cover a given area. Clumping species can also be used but require mass planting of many individual plants to obtain full coverage.

Evergreen Groundcover

Acorus gramineus 'Minimus Aureus'
Ajuga reptans
Asarum arifolium
Asarum europaeum
Asarum shuttleworthii
Asarum splendens
Bergenia cordifolia
Epimedium spp.
Galax urceolata
Helleborus orientalis
Liriope spp.
Mitchella repens
Ophiopogon spp.
Pachysandra spp.
Pulmonaria officinalis
Pulmonaria saccharata
Saxifraga stolonifera
Saxifraga veitchiana
Tiarella spp.
Vinca minor

Herbaceous Groundcover

Achlys triphylla
Aegopodium podagraria 'Variegatum'
Arisarum proboscideum
Asarum canadense
Aster divaricatus
Astilbe ×arendsii
Astilbe japonica
Begonia grandis
Brunnera macrophylla
Carex siderosticha 'Variegata'
Chrysogonum virginianum (evergreen in zone 7)
Claytonia spp.
Convallaria majalis

Opposite: *Disporopsis fusca-picta* with *Hosta* 'Great Expectations' (background)

Cornus canadensis
Disporum sessile
Galium odoratum
Hakonechloa macra
Heuchera spp.
Hosta spp.
Iris cristata
Lamium spp.
Lysimachia spp.
Maianthemum spp.
Mazus reptans
Omphalodes verna
Petasites spp.
Podophyllum peltatum
Pulmonaria longifolia
Sanguinaria canadensis
Selaginella spp.
Vancouveria hexandra
Waldsteinia fragarioides
Wasabia japonica

Plants for Wet Soils

Many shade perennials require moist, but well-drained soil conditions. The following are suited for constantly wet soils.

Acorus spp.
Brunnera macrophylla
Diphylleia cymosa
Erythronium spp.
Hydrophyllum virginianum
Ligularia spp.
Lobelia cardinalis
Lobelia syphilitica
Matteucia struthiopteris
Mertensia virginica
Osmunda regalis
Polygonum spp.
Primula spp.
Rodgersia spp.

Plants for Dry Shade

Most shade perennials require moist soil to perform well in gardens. A few are quite tolerant of dry soil in the shade.

Ajuga reptans
Asarum spp.
Aspidistra spp.
Epimedium spp.
Helleborus spp.
Hepatica transsilvanica
Heuchera americana
Geranium maculatum
Gillenia trifoliate
Liriope spp.
Mitchella repens
Pachysandra terminalis
Polystichum acrostichoides
Saruma henryi

Plants with Foliage Interest

An important factor in the shady garden is the inclusion of plants with large showy and/or variegated leaves that are long-lasting or evergreen. Most medium to large ferns and grasses can be used for this purpose but are not individually listed here.

Acanthus spp.
Achlys triphylla
Amorphophallus spp.
Arisaema spp.
Arum spp.
Asarum spp. (larger-leaved)
Begonia grandis
Bergenia cordifolia
Brunnera macrophylla
Darmera peltata
Diphylleia cymosa
Farfugium japonicum
Farfugium reniforme
Helleborus spp.
Heuchera spp.
Hosta larger spp.
Peltoboykinia tellimoides
Peltoboykinia watanabei
Petasites spp.
Podophyllum spp.
Pulmonaria spp.
Syneilesis spp.
Tiarella spp.
Wasabia japonica

Plants for Winter Interest

Unfortunately, few plants are showy in gardens throughout the year. Most ornamental grasses and sedges give part-time winter interest. Evergreen plants and ferns contribute to gardens year-round.

Ajuga reptans
Asarum arifolium
Asarum europaeum
Asarum shuttleworthii
Asarum splendens
Bergenia cordifolia
Dryopteris erythrosora
Dryopteris marginalis
Epimedium spp.
Galax urceolata
Helleborus spp. (evergreen)
Hepatica maxima
Liriope spp.
Mitchella repens
Ophiopogon spp.
Pachysandra spp.
Polystichum acrostichoides
Pulmonaria officinalis
Pulmonaria saccharata
Saxifraga stolonifera
Saxifraga veitchiana
Tiarella spp.
Vinca minor

Leaf Color

Long-lasting leaf color is very important in the shady garden. Aside from innumerable shades of green, leaves may be bright yellow, maroon, purple, blackish green, and even black. Still others are variegated with several colors in each leaf. Some plants have a fleeting color spurt, but turn green later on. Only plants with leaf color or variegation that lasts more or less all season are included. See plant descriptions for specific details of color and variegation.

Yellow Leaves

Acanthus mollis 'Hollard's Lemon'
Acorus gramineus 'Oborozuki'
Acorus gramineus 'Ogon'
Acorus gramineus 'Minimus Aureus'
Carex elata 'Aurea'
Carex elata 'Bowles' Golden'
Carex siderosticha 'Lemon Zest'
Dicentra spectabilis 'Gold Heart'
Hosta (many yellow cultivars)
Lysimachia nummularia 'Aurea'
Milium effusum 'Aureum'
Selaginella kraussiana 'Aurea'
Thalictrum aquilegiifolium 'Amy Jan'
Tradescantia 'Sweet Kate'
Tricyrtis formosana 'Gates of Heaven'
Uvularia sessilifolia 'Cobblewood Gold'

Blackish Leaves

Ophiopogon planiscapus 'Nigrescens'

Bluish or Blue-gray Leaves

Hosta (many cultivars)
Selaginella uncinata

Whitish Leaves

Hosta (many cultivars)

Variegated Leaves

Acorus gramineus 'Albovariegatus'
Aegopodium podagraria 'Variegatum'
Ajuga reptans 'Arctic Fox'
Ajuga reptans 'Silver Beauty'
Ajuga reptans 'Variegata'
Arachniodes simplicior
Arisaema serratum 'Silver Pattern'
Arisaema sikokianum 'Variegata'
Arum italicum (many cultivars)
Hosta (many cultivars)
Asarum spp. (many)
Athyrium niponicum var. pictum
Bletilla striata 'Albostriata'
Bletilla striata 'First Kiss'
Brunnera macrophylla (many variegated cultivars)
Carex (many variegated cultivars)
Convallaria majalis 'Albostriata'
Convallaria majalis 'Aureovariegata'
Disporum cantoniense 'Aureovariegatum'
Disporum (many cultivars)
Farfugium japonicum (many cultivars)
Hakonechloa macra 'Alboaurea'

Hakonechloa macra 'Albovariegata'
Hakonechloa macra 'Aureola'
Helleborus argutifolius 'Janet Starnes'
Heuchera (many cultivars)
Hosta (many cultivars)
Iris foetidissima 'Variegata'
Iris tectorum 'Variegata'
Lamium (many cultivars)
Liriope (many cultivars)
Lysimachia congestiflora 'Outback Sunset'
Lysimachia punctata 'Alexander'
Milium effusum 'Variegatum'
Ophiopogon (many cultivars)
Pachysandra terminalis 'Silveredge'
Pachysandra terminalis 'Variegata'
Persicaria (many cultivars)
Petasites japonicus 'Variegatus'
Pinellia cordata
Pinellia tripartita 'Gold Dragon'
Pinellia tripartita 'Silver Dragon'
Plantago major 'Variegata'
Podophyllum difforme 'Kaleidoscope'
Polemonium caeruleum 'Brise d'Anjou'
Polygonatum (many cultivars)
Pulmonaria (many cultivars)
Rohdea japonica (many cultivars)
Saxifraga stolonifera
Selaginella kraussiana 'Variegata'
Smilacina japonica 'Angel Wings'
Smilacina japonica 'Halo'
Tiarella (many cultivars)
Tricyrtis (many cultivars)
Vinca minor 'Alba Variegata'
Vinca minor 'Argenteovariegata'
Viola variegata

Architectural Plants

The following plants have tall flowering spikes or imposing leaf structures. In either case, they are good plants for accent.

Acanthus spp.
Amorphophallus spp.
Arisaema (some species)
Aruncus dioicus

Aspidistra elatior
Astilbe biternata
Astilbe grandis
Astilboides tabularis
Cimicifuga racemosa
Cimicifuga simplex
Disporum cantoniense
Farfugium reniforme
Ligularia dentate
Ligularia stenocephala
Lilium martagon
Lilium superbum
Lobelia cardinalis
Osmunda cinnamomea
Osmunda regalis
Peltoboykinia watanabei
Petasites spp.
Polygonatum cirrhifolium
Polygonatum verticillatum
Pteridium aquilinium
Rheum palmatum
Rodgersia spp.
Tricyrtis hirta 'Togen'
Veratrum spp.

Plants for Full Shade

Some plants may have reduced flowering or may not flower at all in full shade, but they will nevertheless provide a foliage display. Most fern species fall into this category.

Acanthus spp.
Ajuga reptans
Asarum spp.
Aspidistra spp.
Danaë racemosa
Carex fraseri
Iris foetidissima
Ophiopogon japonicus
Pachysandra spp.
Polypodium spp.
Rohdea spp.
Vancouveria hexandra
Waldsteinia

Opposite: *Disporum cantoniense* in bloom

Acanthus mollis
Bear's breeches

Mediterranean. Flowers pinkish white, hooded-tubular, purplish bracts; flowerstalks 3–7 ft. (0.9–2 m) tall; May–July; clumping, to 4 ft. (1.2 m) wide and high; leaves to 36 in. (90 cm) long and 18 in. (45 cm) wide, glossy dark green, arching, cut and dissected. Zones 6–8. Morning sun, LS to WS. Neutral, well-drained soil. This is a great accent plant with an imposing flower spike. Surround it with groups of smaller hostas and ferns.

'Hollard's Lemon', leaves greenish yellow.

Latifolius Group, leaves larger, more shallowly lobed, glossy dark green to 4 ft. (1.2 m) long.

'Niger', leaves very dark green, glossy.

'Oak Leaf', leaves shaped like a red oak leaf, dark green, shiny.

'Rue Ledan', the white hooded flower makes for a bright appearance.

Acanthus spinosus
Spiny bear's breeches

Mediterranean. Flowers pinkish white, purple bracts; flowerstalks to 40 in. (1 m); May–July; clumping, to 4 ft. (1.2 m) wide and 36 in. (90 cm)

Acanthus mollis

Acanthus spinosus flower spikes

high; leaves to 12 in. (30 cm) long and 10 in. (25 cm) wide, glossy dark green, deeply cut and dissected to the midrib, with soft spines in the margins. Zone 6. Morning sun, LS to WS. Neutral, well-drained soil. This species is a bit more cold hardy than *Acanthus mollis* and gardeners in zone 5 report success.

'Spinosissimus', leaves narrow, margin deeply incised and heavily bristled.

'Summer Beauty', white flowers with spiny, purple bracts on tall stems to 6 ft. (1.8 m). Garden origin.

Achlys triphylla
Vanilla leaf

Western North America, eastern Asia. Flowers white, many, in 2-in. (5-cm) clusters; flowerstalks 12–20 in. (30–50 cm); May–July; clumping, rhizomatous; leaves green, to 6 in. (15 cm) across, with toothed lobes. Zone 7a. MS to FS. Soil acid, well-drained, rich, cool. Best for northern or western gardens. The overlapping leaves have three large, jagged-toothed lobes. Makes a solid groundcover.

Aconitum ×cammarum

Sterile hybrids (*Aconitum variegatum × A. napellus*) as listed below; June–August; flowers in branching clusters; clumping; to 4 ft. (1.2 m) tall; leaves large, mostly glossy sometimes dull, medium to dark green, divided into lobes. Zones 3–7. WS to MS. Soil slightly acid, moist, but free-draining and cool. Strong-growing plants with tall stems.

Achlys triphylla (Lynne Harrison)

Aconitum ×cammarum 'Bicolor' (Allan Armitage)

'Bicolor', flowers blue and white.

'Coeruleum' ('Caeruleum'), flowers dark blue.

'Francis Marc', flowers large, very dark blue.

'Nachthimmel' ('Night Sky'), flowers large, dark violet.

'Spark's Variety' ('Spark'), flowers dark blue on stalks 5 ft. (1.5 m) tall.

Aconitum carmichaelii
Azure monkshood

Asia. Flowers blue to blue-violet in dense, branched clusters to 6 ft. (1.8 m) tall; September–October; clumping; to 40 in. (1 m) tall and 18 in. (45 cm) wide; leaves large, glossy dark green, leathery, divided into lobes. Zones 3–7. Sun to LS. Soil slightly acid, cool, moist, and fertile. Taller stems may need staking. Best for northern gardens.

'Arendsii', plant to 4 ft. (1.2 m) tall and 12 in. (30 cm) wide, flowers deep blue.

'Barker', flowers pure violet.

'Kelmscott', flowers light blue-violet.

Var. *wilsonii*, plant more elongated and open than the type, flowers violet.

Aconitum napellus
Common monkshood

Europe, Alps. Flowers deep blue in straight, branched clusters; June–August; clumping; to 4 ft. (1.2 m) tall and 14 in. (35 cm) wide; leaves glossy, dark green, divided into lobes that are deeply incised. Zones 3–7. Sun to LS. Soil slightly acid, cool, moist, and fertile. Taller stems may need staking. Best for northern gardens.

'Album' ('Albidum'), flowers off-white.

Aconitum carmichaelii 'Arendsii' (Allan Armitage)

Aconitum napellus 'Newry Blue' (Allan Armitage)

'Bressingham Spire', flowers dark violet-blue; requires no staking.

'Carneum' ('Roseum', 'Rubellum'), flowers rose-pink.

'Gletschereis' ('Glacier Ice'), flowers white, early and long-lasting.

'Newry Blue', flowers dark navy blue; plant to 5 ft. (1.5 m) tall; erect.

Acorus calamus
Sweet flag

Northern Hemisphere. Flowers greenish yellow in a dense spadix, protruding from a spathe; May–July; rhizomatous, evergreen; leaves sword-shaped, green with distinct midrib, to 4 ft. (1.2 m) tall in water, shorter when growing in garden soil, to 14 in. (35 cm). Zones 4–11. Sun to LS. Moist to wet soils or grows in shallow water.

'Variegatus'. Variegated sweet flag. Leaves striped with creamy white.

Acorus gramineus

China, Japan. Flowers in a spadix to 3 in. (8 cm) long on a short spathe; rhizomatous, tufted; leaves grasslike, 6–12 in. (15–30 cm) long, in dwarf forms 2–4 in. (5–10 cm) long. Zones 6–9. Sun to LS. Moist to wet soils.

'Albovariegatus' ('Argenteostriatus'), leaves white-striped, dwarf.

'Minimus Aureus', leaves yellow, short, 2–3 in. (5–7.5 cm). Looks like a small, golden tuft of grass. Adds bright spots in shady corners (see photo on page 195).

'Oborozuki', leaves bright yellow.

'Ogon' ('Wogon'), leaves yellow with creamy yellow variegation.

Acorus gramineus 'Albovariegatus' backed by *A. gramineus* 'Minimus Aureus'

Acorus gramineus 'Ogon'

'Pusillus', compact clump of green leaves to 3 in. (8 cm).

'Yodo-no-Yuki', leaves green with whitish green variegation.

Actaea alba
White baneberry
Eastern North America. Flowers white, small, grouped in ball-shaped cluster, to 2.5 in. (6 cm) long on flowerstalks 3–4 ft. (90–120 cm) tall; April–July; clumping; to 30 in. (75 cm) tall and wide; leaves dark green to 20 in. (50 cm) long, divided into toothed leaflets to 2 in. (5 cm) long; berries white. Zones 4–7. LS to MS. Acid, well-drained, fertile soil.

Forma *pachycarpa*, fruit red.

Actaea alba flower

Actaea rubra
Red baneberry
Eastern North America. Flowers white, small, many in egg-shaped cluster, 2.5 in. (6 cm) long; flowerstalks green, to 32 in. (80 cm); April–July; clumping; to 24 in. (60 cm) tall and 30 in. (75 cm) wide with dark green leaves, to 14 in. (35 cm) long, divided into toothed leaflets to 2 in. (5 cm) long; berries red. Zones 4–7. LS to MS. Acid, well-drained, fertile soil. White flowers in spring and bright red berries in fall add color to the shady garden.

Subsp. *arguta*, leaves much smaller than those of the type; plant grows to 18 in. (45 cm) tall and wide.

Forma *neglecta* ('Neglecta'), fruit white.

Actaea spicata
Herb Christopher
Europe. Flowers white, sometimes with a bluish hue, many in a small, egg-shaped cluster; flowerstalks green, to 24 in. (60 cm); June–August; clumping; to 20 in. (50 cm) tall and 18 in. (45 cm) wide; leaves 14 in. (35 cm) long, divided into many lance-shaped, dark green, toothed leaflets and sub-leaflets, to 2 in. (5 cm) long; berries black. Zones 4–7. LS to MS. Acid, well-drained, fertile soil.

Adiantum capillus-veneris
Southern maidenhair
Southern Europe, North America. Fronds on slender, unbranched, shiny blackish stalks; composed of light green, lobed leaflets to 16 in. (40 cm) tall and 8 in. (20 cm) wide; creeping rhizomes. Zones 7–9. LS to WS. Moist and fertile soil. The plant's delicate appearance adds grace and beauty to the woodland garden. It shudders in the slightest breeze and animates its spot (see photo on page 42). A few more cold-tolerant cultivars are available.

'Banksianum', vigorous grower, more upright stalks. Comes true from spores. Zone 6 with protection.

'Fimbriatum', the lobes are fingerlike and extended.

Adiantum capillus-veneris with *Polygonatum odoratum* 'Variegatum'

'Imbricatum', a dwarfed form with deeply cut lobes.

'Mairisii', the fronds are broadly triangular with leaflets elongated triangular; an older cold-resistant hybrid.

'Scintilla', twisted leaflets, deeply cut, almost skeletonized.

Adiantum pedatum
Northern maidenhair, American maidenhair

North America, eastern Asia. Fronds to 30 in. (75 cm) tall and 10 in. (25 cm) wide on strong, shiny blackish, erect stalks, equally forked at the top, each fork bears several curving, light green leaflets to form a flat, horseshoe-shaped frond. Zones 3–11. LS to FS. Acid, moist, and fertile soil. This is a native maidenhair fern every gardener in North America can grow. Unique with its horse-shoelike fronds, it is long-lived and suitable for full shade (see photo on page 200).

Subsp. *aleuticum* is slightly smaller than the type. When young, the new fronds are pinkish, and the leaflets are bluish green and more trian-gular. This subspecies has two dwarf forms: 'Compactum' and 'Nanum'.

'Asiaticum' has drooping fronds.

'Imbricatum' makes a tight, upright clump with small, glaucous bluish green leaflets.

'Japonicum' is closely related to *Adiantum pedatum* subsp. *aleuticum* and has young pink-ish to reddish bronze fronds that later turn darker green.

'Laceratum' has deeply cut leaflets.

'Miss Sharples' has yellowish fronds.

'Montanum' makes a very compact clump.

Subsp. *subpumilum*. Dwarf maidenhair fern. Small fronds to 4 in. (10 cm) with bluish green leaflets. This cute dwarf fern, which grows to 6 in. (15 cm) tall and 10 in. (25 cm) wide, should be placed up close to garner attention; it is offered as 'Minor' and 'Minus'.

Aegopodium podagraria 'Variegatum'
Bishop's weed

Eurasia. Flowers tiny, creamy white, gathered in a flat-topped inflorescence to 3 in. (8 cm) across,

Adiantum pedatum with *Polygonatum biflorum*

stems to 14 in. (35 cm); June–August; rhizomatous, spreading; leaves divided into toothed leaflets, dark green with a creamy white margin and occasional white splashes in the leaf. Zones 4–9. LS to FS. Any soil. Good groundcover but aggressively spreading and it will take over in cultivated areas. Deadhead before seed sets. It will grow where nothing else will, like under dense trees where darkness reigns and tree root competition sucks the soil dry.

Ajuga reptans
Carpet bugleweed
Eurasia. Flowers blue, small, in whorls on a spike, 4–6 in. (10–15 cm) tall; April–June; rhizomatous, evergreen; with leafy stolons 4–12 in. (10–30 cm) long, rooting at the points where the leaves are attached; lower leaves, dark green, in a rosette, to 2 in. (5 cm) long and 1 in. (2.5 cm) wide. Zones 3–8 and evergreen to 15°F (?10°C). Any moist soil. This popular species is an excellent and colorful groundcover. A rapid spreader, it can invade adjacent border areas or lawns. Many cultivars are available.

'Alba', flowers white.

'Arctic Fox', silvery gray leaves and a narrow, dark green margin.

'Atropurpurea', easily the most popular and widely available form. It has coppery leaves with a purple tinge and bright blue flowers on fairly tall stems.

'Bronze Beauty', brilliant, deep bronze, metallic leaves.

'Brownherz', coppery, very dark purple-brown leaves.

'Burgundy Glow', leaves with silvery green centers, suffused with pink and cream toward the margins. Pink bracts and light blue flowers.

'Catlin's Giant', the largest bugle available, runs as fast as the species. Leaves are very large, purple, and nicely fluted.

'Cristata', leaves all twisted out of shape, the entire mound is distorted. For those who like grotesque plants, this one will satisfy.

'Jungle Beauty', indigo-blue flowers, crinkled bronze-green leaves.

'Multicolor', every leaf on the plant has different colors.

Aegopodium podagraria 'Variegatum' as a groundcover

Ajuga reptans 'Atropurpurea' in the landscape with *Hosta* 'August Moon'

Ajuga reptans 'Jungle Beauty'

'Pink Beauty', flowers deep pink, smaller than 'Rosea'.

'Pink Delight', flowers bright pink, leaves crinkled green.

'Pink Elf', flowers pink, smaller than 'Rosea'.

'Pink Spire', flowers pink on taller pink stems, to 7 in. (18 cm).

'Rosea', flowers rose-pink.

'Silver Beauty', leaves green overlaid with gray and white-margined.

'Silver Carpet', leaves overlaid with silvery gray.

'Tottenham', flowers with pinkish shading to lilac.

'Valfredda', flowers bright to dark blue, leaves small, brown-tinted.

'Variegata', leaves flecked with creamy white.

Amianthium muscitoxicum
Fly poison

Eastern North America. Flowers tiny, white turning greenish, in a dense cluster, 2–4 in. (5–10 cm) long on tall flowerstalks to 36 in. (90 cm); May–June; clumping; basal leaves straplike, green, smooth, to 14 in. (35 cm) long and 0.8 in. (2 cm) wide, blunt-tipped. Zones 4–8. LS to WS. Moist, acidic soil. An elegant native for the wildflower garden. The flowering spike and raceme remain on the plant and make a modest, but interesting early autumn display.

Amorphophallus bulbifer

Northeast India. Inflorescence to 18 in. (45 cm) tall; spathe to 4 in. (10 cm) wide, hooded, pink inside, outside green with pink; spadix pink; leaf 4 ft. (1.2 m) tall, petiole dark olive-green, spotted silvery green; 3-parted, to 36 in. (90 cm) wide, leaflets dark green; bulblets form at the apex junction of the petiole and at major leaf divisions. Zone 7a. LS to WS. Moist but well-drained soil a must. This smaller snake palm has a slight but not pungent odor. It makes bulblets on top of the leaf; these can be removed and planted for increase.

Amianthium muscitoxicum flower spikes (Don Jacobs)

Amorphophallus bulbifer inflorescence

Amorphophallus konjac
Devil's tongue

Indonesia to Sumatra. Inflorescence to 6 ft. (1.8 m) tall; spathe funnel-shaped with collarlike limb, dark purple; spadix purple, tapering toward the top, to 36 in. (90 cm) long and 2 in. (5 cm) wide, supported by white-spotted flowerstalk; leaf on thick petiole 5 ft. (1.5 m) tall, tapering, dark green, speckled silvery; leaf solitary, 3-parted, to 36 in. (90 cm) wide, dark. Zone 5b. LS to WS. Moist but well-drained soil a must. This species is one of the hardiest and most prolific in the genus. It also has a huge, colorful flower structure that attracts attention in spring. Mature tubers form stolons bearing small tubers. The foul odor of the flower lasts but a very short time.

Amorphophallus paeoniifolius

India, New Guinea. Inflorescence to 12 in. (30 cm) tall; spathe cup-shaped, with upper margin incurved, very wavy, wide, purple in the throat; spadix cone-shaped, with many folds, honey-colored; leaf on thick petiole to 8 ft. (2.5 m) tall, light green marbled silvery; leaf solitary, 3-parted, to 7 ft. (2 m) wide, leaflets light green. Zone 7b. LS to WS. Moist but well-drained soil a must. This snake palm is very large and its tuber takes on huge proportions. The inflorescence is so outlandish only a picture can come close to describe it. The leaf is its glory and adds to the garden from spring until late summer.

Anemone ×hybrida
Japanese anemone

Hybrid (*Anemone hupehensis* var. *japonica* × *A. vitifolia*). Flowers semi-double light pink to 4 in. (10 cm) across, in loose groups on flowerstalks, erect, 3–5 ft. (90 cm–1.5 m); August–October; spreading rapidly; leaves basal, medium green, 3-lobed and deeply toothed, divided into several leaflets, 4–8 in. (10–20 cm) long. Zones 4–8. Some sun to WS. Moist, fertile soil. These hybrids are the mainstay of autumn-flowering anemones. The flowerstalks are very tall but strong; notwith-

Amorphophallus konjac inflorescence

Amorphophallus paeoniifolius inflorescence (Tony Avent)

standing, stake them in unprotected areas before they are bowed by autumn winds.

'**Alba**', to 36 in. (90 cm), flowers single, white, to 3 in. (8 cm).

'**Alice**', to 32 in. (80 cm), flowers semi-double, pink, to 2.5 in. (6 cm).

'**Elegantissima**', 5 ft. (1.5 m), flowers semi-double, pink.

'**Géante des Blanches**' ('White Giant', 'White Queen'), to 36 in. (90 cm), flowers semi-double, to 3 in. (8 cm), broad, clean white. Spreads rapidly.

'**Honorine Jobert**', a white sport first described in 1858. Remains the most popular single-flowered garden anemone.

'**Königin Charlotte**' ('Queen Charlotte', 'Reine Charlotte'), to 5 ft; (1.5 m) tall, flowers large, semi-double pink, to 4 in. (10 cm).

'**Kriemhilde**', flowers semi-double, pale purple-pink, darker outside.

'**Luise Uhink**', to 4 ft. (1.2 m), flowers to 5 in. (13 cm).

Anemone ×*hybrida* 'Kriemhilde'

Anemone ×*hybrida* 'Honorine Jobert'

'Pamina', to 36 in. (90 cm), flowers double, rosy red, to 4 in. (10 cm).

'Profusion', flowers rosy pink, to 4 in. (10 cm).

'Rosenschale', to 32 in. (80 cm), flowers, dark pink, to 4 in. (10 cm).

'Whirlwind', to 4 ft. (1.2 m), flowers semi-double, pure white, to 4 in. (10 cm). Very hardy.

Anemonella thalictroides
Rue anemone

Eastern North America. Flowers single, white, cup-shaped to 0.8 in. (2 cm) in loose groups, flower-stalks thin, erect, 3–10 in. (8–25 cm); March–May; spreading; leaves basal, divided into several oval, bluish green leaflets, 4–6 in. (10–15 cm) long. Zones 4–7. LS to WS. Moist, but not wet, well-drained, fertile soil. A lovely native with long-lasting flowers for the woodland or shady border. Rue anemones are long-lived when given a position sheltered from strong winds. They resent being moved or other-

wise disturbed. In warmer zones with hot and dry summers supplemental watering is required.

'Alba Plena', flowers white, fully double.

'Cameo', flowers pink, double.

'Green Hurricane', flowers small, lime-green, button type.

'Oscar Schoaf' ('Flore Pleno', 'Schoaf's Double', 'Schoaf's Pink'), flowers rosy pink, double.

'Rosea', flowers rosy pink.

'Rosea Plena', flowers long-lasting, rosy pink, double.

'Rubra', flowers rosy red.

'Semidouble White', flowers white, semi-double.

Anemonopsis macrophylla

Japan. Flowers pink to pale violet, 2–5 in groups, nodding, cup-shaped to 1.5 in. (4 cm); flower-stalks upright, purple, 24–32 in. (60–80 cm); August–September; clumping; leaves 2- or 3-lobed on long petioles, toothed, shiny dark green,

Anemonella thalictroides (Allan Armitage)

leaflets, 3–6 in. (8–15 cm) long. Zones 5–6. LS to WS. Cool, moist, acidic soil. A valuable shade garden plant in northern climates and where the summers are cool. It is a good companion in the moist woodland border when planted with hostas, ferns, astilbes, and native wildflowers.

Aquilegia caerulea
Rocky Mountain columbine

Western North America. Flowers many, purple and white, with long, knobbed spurs, upright on leafy, unbranched inflorescence; flowerstalks 20–30 in. (50–75 cm); May–July; clumping; leaves basal, divided, lobed gray-green leaflets, to 1.5 in. (4 cm) long. Zones 3–8. Some sun, LS to WS. Moist, acidic soil. This native columbine is not as robust as some other species, but it is longer lasting when compared to the hybrids. Easily raised seedlings can continually rejuvenate the planting. This is an excellent species for woodland shade, and several plants should be planted to form a colony.

'Albiflora', flowers yellowish white.

'Candidissima', flowers large, pure white.

'Citrina', flowers lemon-yellow.

'Crimson Star', flowers bicolored, red and white or creamy white.

'Cuprea', flowers red with metallic, coppery glow.

'Haylodgensis', flowers bright blue; hybrid origin.

'Helenae', flowers bright blue; hybrid origin.

'Himmelblau' ('Heavenly Blue'), flowers deep blue, long spurs.

'Koralle' ('Coral'), flowers salmon-pink, coral; hybrid origin.

'Maxistar', flowers large, bright yellow, very long spurs.

'Olympia', flowers red and yellow.

'Rotstern' ('Red Star'), flowers red and white.

Aquilegia caerulea backed by *Polygonatum odoratum* 'Variegatum' (Allan Armitage)

Aquilegia canadensis (Allan Armitage)

Aquilegia canadensis
Canada columbine

Eastern North America. Flowers red and yellow with bright red spurs, many, nodding, on leafy unbranched inflorescence; flowerstalks 20–30 in. (50–75 cm); April–July; clumping; leaves fernlike, 4–6 in. (10–15 cm) long, divided into light green, lobed leaflets. Zones 3–8. Some sun, LS to WS. Moist, acidic soil. Great woodlander with flowers that go on five to six weeks. Good for northern and southern gardens. This columbine is one of the best available. Its brilliant flowers last up to six weeks and carry on into early summer. Combine with August-flowering hostas and autumn-flowering anemones for color during most of the summer. Use several plants to form a colony.

'Corbett' has yellow flowers.

'Nana' is a smaller version of the type to 12 in. (30 cm).

Arachniodes simplicior
Variegated shield fern

Japan, China. Fronds to 4 ft. (1.2 m), on slender, leaning, green stalks emerging in rosettes; leaves shiny dark green with a yellow band along the midrib, to 16 in. (40 cm) long and 10 in. (25 cm) wide, tapering at the tip. Zone 7a. LS to WS. Soil acid, moist, and fertile. A superb variegated fern for southern gardens. Incorrectly sold as Arachniodes aristata 'Variegata'. This colorful fern's shiny leaves provide highlights anywhere in the garden. Best grown in a sheltered, shady, moist position.

Arisaema angustatum

Korea. To 18 in. (45 cm) tall; spathe hooded, green with narrow white stripes, light green, striped pinkish white outside, lighter inside; May–July; to 40 in. (1 m) tall; leaf solitary, green

Arachniodes simplicior

Arisaema candidissimum summer leaves with Adiantum capillus-veneris

Arisaema angustatum var. peninsulae spathe

with some grayish marbling in the leaflets. Culture similar to Arisaema candidissimum.

Var. peninsulae is taller than the type, to 4 ft. (1.2 m). The bright red fruit held up high is eye-catching.

Var. peninsulae f. variegata is similar but has beautiful, irregular silver markings running along the midrib of the leaflets.

Arisaema candidissimum

Western China. To 18 in. (45 cm) tall; spathe hooded, pinkish-white and white-striped outside, hood whitish; June–July; leaf solitary, with three shiny green leaflets, broadly ovate, to 8 in. (20 cm) long. Zones 5–9. LS to WS. Moist but well-drained soil a must. A superb, slightly fragrant jack. Plant up close along a shaded path. Different colored clones are available in commerce, some almost white and others with a light to deep pink spathe.

Arisaema consanguineum

Himalaya to western China, Taiwan. To 40 in. (1.0 m); spathe hooded, light green or white-striped purple, flaring, green hood; spadix darker green; May–June; leaf solitary, with 11–22 radiating, narrow, green to yellowish green leaflets to 14 in. (35 cm) long with drooping extensions; berries red. Zones 5–9. LS to WS. Moist but well-drained soil a must. Spathe colors vary, some are green and others are purple with white stripes. In commerce the latter, more desirable jack is offered.

'Himalayan Form', a wild clone with green spathes.

Arisaema candidissimum inflorescence

Arisaema consanguineum inflorescence

'Red Form', a wild clone with white-striped, purple spathes. More desirable than 'Himalayan Form'.

Arisaema dracontium
Green dragon

Eastern North America. To 36 in. (90 cm); spathe green, open on the spadix side, flaring hood upright, bending; spadix whitish at base; May–June; leaf solitary, with 5–15 dull green oval leaflets, to 8 in. (20 cm) long; berries red. Zones 4–8. LS to WS. Moist, fertile soil. This native jack is a graceful addition to the shady woodland where it can get attention rising above smaller companions. Plant as in nature where it quickly forms a small colony.

Arisaema fargesii

Western China. To 32 in. (80 cm); spathe purple with white stripes continuing into down-curved hood; spadix extension bent forward; June–July; leaf solitary, with three shiny, light green leaflets, broadly ovate, to 15 in. (38 cm) long. Zones 6–9. LS

Arisaema dracontium inflorescence

Arisaema fargesii inflorescence

Arisaema flavum inflorescence

Arisaema ringens inflorescence

to WS. Moist but well-drained soil a must. In leaf similar to *Arisaema ringens*, this jack is an imposing accent in the woodland. It needs plenty of space.

Arisaema flavum
Yellow-flowered cobra lily
Himalaya to western China. To 20 in. (50 cm); spathe tube globelike, pale yellow, in the upper part brownish; hood yellowish green, purple inside; June–early July; leaves 2, with 5–11 radiating, green leaflets, oblong lance-shaped, to 5 in. (13 cm) long. Zones 7–9. LS to WS. Moist but well-drained soil a must. A cute jack with a midget yellow flower. Give it a place up front so the cute inflorescence cannot be missed. The leaves are not small and carry on until late summer.

Arisaema ringens
Ringent cobra lily
China, Taiwan, Korea, Japan. To 48 in. (1.2 m); spathe purple with light green stripes, sometimes uniform pale green, hood sitting helmet-shaped atop wide with deep purple, curled, earlike appendages; spadix yellow, not visible; May–June; leaves two, with three large leaflets, glossy medium green, broadly ovate, 18–36 in. (45–90 cm) long; berries red. Zones 6a–9. LS to WS. Moist but well-drained soil a must. This is one of the most impressive and showy arisaemas for the open garden. Easy of culture and one of the best for long-lasting display value. Its leaves are among the largest and thickest, coming through hot, dry summers with aplomb given supplemental water (see photo on page 13).

Arisaema saxatile
Rock-dwelling cobra lily
Japan. To 16 in. (40 cm); spathe narrow tube, pure white outside, long hood upright to slightly oblique; spadix green, tapering and extending beyond the spathe tip; June–July; leaves two, with three leaflets, narrow, lance-shaped, green, with sharp, tapering tip; berries red. Zones 6–9. LS to WS. Moist but well-drained soil a must. A lovely

Arisaema saxatile inflorescence

small jack. The outstanding flowers brighten up shady corners with their glowing white spathes. Plant up close for the lemony scent.

Arisaema serratum
Japanese cobra lily

China, Korea, Japan. To 60 in. (1.5 m); spathe split at top, to 5 in. (13 cm) long, cylindrical, with flaring hood, pale green with white stripes, or dark purple; spadix green, short, with short tail; May–June; leaves 2, each with 7–19 lance-shaped, green, radiating leaflets, wavy, narrowly to 10 in. (25 cm) long. Zones 5–9. LS to MS. Moist but well-drained soil a must. A fabulous tall jack planted as a small group popping out of plantings of woodland ferns and hostas. Very cold hardy and suited for northern gardens.

'Silver Pattern', with attractive silver markings in the leaf centers. The best form available.

Arisaema sikokianum
Shikoku cobra lily

Japan. To 30 in. (75 cm); spathe pinched at the center, flaring hood erect, interior white, base

Arisaema serratum 'Silver Pattern'

purple, exterior dark purple or deep reddish brown; hood pinched at the base then widening, erect purple inside green striped, purple outside; spadix white, enlarged, knoblike top; May–June; leaves two, unequal in height, the lower with three leaflets, the upper with five leaflets, ovate, dark green, 6 in. (15 cm) long; berries red. Zones 5–9. LS to WS. Moist but well-drained soil a must. This is the cobra lily everyone wants. Its inflorescence is unlike any other and gives it that "wow" impact. Good for northern and southern gardens.

'Variegata'. A selection with silvery gray markings along the leaf midrib.

Arisaema speciosum
Showy cobra lily

Himalaya to western China. To 24 in. (60 cm); spathe to very dark purple, white striped, white inside with purple margins; hood very long, purple inside and out; spadix greenish, bending, with long reddish purple appendage; early May–June; leaf solitary, with three large, green leaflets, broadly ovate, to 18 in. (45 cm) long.

Arisaema sikokianum inflorescence

Arisaema speciosum leaves

Arisaema speciosum inflorescence

Berries red. Zones 7–9. LS to WS. Moist but well-drained soil a must. Attractive, crinkly, large leaves last well into autumn. A large, fascinating flower with an outlandish, long spadix tail makes this an interesting jack. It comes up early so protection from late freezes is in order.

Arisaema tortuosum
Tortuous cobra lily

Himalaya to western China. To 6 ft. (1.8 m); spathe green, rarely purple; hood whitish inside, green outside, bending; spadix extension long, green or purple, thick, projecting from the tube first erect, then outward in an S-curve; May–June; leaves 2, each with 5–17 leaflets, lance-shaped, green, to 12 in. (30 cm) long; berries bright scarlet. Zones 5–9. LS to WS. Moist but well-drained soil a must. The king among jacks, easily overtopping a tall man. The spathe projects a purple spadix tail high above the leaves so becomes a focal point. The berry cluster's bright scarlet color becomes a beacon in the late summer garden. Popping up between tall, blue and gray hostas and large clumps of reddish autumn fern brings out the best in this jack. Also offered under its synonym *Arisaema helleborifolium*.

Arisaema tortuosum inflorescence

Arisaema triphyllum
Jack-in-the-pulpit

Eastern North America. To 48 in. (1.2 m); spathe green or reddish purple; bending forward up or down; spadix appendage green or purple; April–June; leaves two, with three ovate, green leaflets, 3–8 in. (8–20 cm) long; berries red. Its distinct forms vary in color and size. Zones 3–8. LS to WS. Moist, well-drained soil. This native jack is of easy culture and should be in every garden. It pops up year after year with minimum care and increases its colony by seeding around and by way of underground offsets.

'Atrorubens'. Purple jack, ruby jack. The most desired form with its fine reddish purple spathe; spathe hood folded down; the leaves are sometimes grayish green underneath or with a gray bloom all over.

Arisaema triphyllum 'Atrorubens'

Arisaema triphyllum 'Gosan Giant' with *Dicentra canadensis*

'Gosan Giant'. From northern Georgia. Similar to the type, green spathe with hood remaining upright; to 5 ft. (1.5 m) tall.

Subsp. *pusillum*; similar to the type but flowering two to three weeks later; with three or five leaflets.

Subsp. *stewardsonii*. Indian turnip. A northern form. Has prominent light-colored ridges on the spathe hood with a spathe that is blackish inside.

Arisarum proboscideum
Mouse plant

Italy, Spain. Spathe tube reddish brown, base white; hood red, tip whiplike; spadix hidden; April–May; rhizomatous; leaves glossy green, arrow-shaped to 6 in. (15 cm), emerging in crowded bundles. Zones 5–9. LS to WS. Moist, fertile soil. The mouse plant is cute but small so plant along paths. It fits well in a deeply shaded corner with other small companion plants, such as small hostas, ferns, and dwarf astilbes. The tufts of shiny leaves add to foliage diversity.

Arisarum proboscideum inflorescence

Arum italicum
Italian arum

Mediterranean Europe. To 18 in. (45 cm); spathe tube and hood greenish white; May–July; tuberous; leaves arrow-shaped, glossy shades of green with silvery markings, triangular, to 16 in. (40 cm) long; showy orange berries. Zones 6–9. Some sun to LS. Moist, fertile soil. This arum fits well in a protected corner that receives some morning sum. Combine it with hostas, heucheras, and other bold-leaved plants, which can fill in voids during summer dormancy. Great for winter color where there is little or no snow cover.

'**Chamaeleon**', leaves broad, marbled yellowish green and greenish gray.

'**Immaculatum**' (sometimes assigned to *Arum maculatum*), leaves unmarked, plain green.

'**Marmoratum**', leaves large, marbled in yellowish white.

'**Pictum**', leaves smaller, marbled silvery gray and cream. Not to be confused with *Arum pictum* (sold as *A. nigrum*), which has glossy green leaves with a purple cast in spring and which produces a blackish purple spathe, hood, and spadix in fall.

'**Tiny**', leaves small, no more than 4 in. (10 cm) long, triangular, arrow-shaped, and beautifully marbled with yellowish white.

'**White Winter**', leaves narrow, marbled with pure white; plant small.

Arum italicum 'Pictum'

Aruncus aethusifolius
Dwarf goatsbeard

Korea, Japan. Flowers tiny, whitish, on an erect, open, branched inflorescence to 6 in. (15 cm) long, above the leaves; to 15 in. (38 cm) high and wide, with leaves, to 10 in. (25 cm) long, divided into small, ovate, green leaflets, deeply incised. Zones 4–8. LS to FS. Cool, acid, moist soil. A wonderful addition to small gardens that cannot accommodate the larger goatsbeards. Its leaves turn bright yellow in autumn, brightening the garden together with hostas, which also turn color about the same time.

Aruncus aethusifolius

Aruncus dioicus

Aruncus dioicus
Goatsbeard

Europe to eastern Siberia, North America. Flowers tiny, creamy to greenish white, carried on a large inflorescence. Spikelike clusters of densely arranged flowers branch off a tall, central stalk reaching 7 ft. (2 m) in the wild but in gardens more often 4–6 ft. (1.2–1.8 m); bushy, 4–5 ft. (1.2–1.5 m) tall and 4 ft. (1.2 m) wide. Large green leaves to 15 in. (38 cm) long, divided into leaflets to 5 in. (13 cm) long, smooth, medium green, with deeply toothed margins. Zones 4–6. Some sun to LS. Cool, acid, moist soil. Best for northern gardens. This very large goatsbeard needs plenty of space and its huge flower clusters and clumps of ferny leaves cannot be missed in any garden. An imposing plant (see photo on page 71).

Var. *kamtschaticus* from Kamchatka Peninsula is similar to 'Kneiffii', with the leaf mound to 24 in. (60 cm) tall. Unlike the species, this small variety does well in hot southern gardens as long as the soil is kept moist.

'Kneiffii' is considerably smaller than the species, 3.5–4 ft. (1–1.2 m), with whitish flowers and a more ferny appearance in leaf. Possibly a selection of var. *kamtschaticus*.

'Southern White', a hybrid (*Aruncus aethusifolius* × *A. dioicus*) with multibranched, slender spikes of white flowers that resemble those of *A. aethusifolius* but are much more dense and numerous; vigorous and suited for hot-summer areas in zones 7 and 8; size is intermediate between the parents.

Asarum arifolium
Arrowhead ginger, little brown jugs

Eastern North America. Flowers brown, shaped like jugs, hidden; April–May; evergreen, clumping, 6 in. (15 cm) tall and to 18 in. (45 cm) wide; leaves mostly arrow-shaped with rounded lobes, to 5 in. (13 cm) long, dark green with gray-green patterns. Zones 4–7. WS to FS. Any acid to neutral soil. A native ginger available with a profusion of different leaf forms and variegation patterns. This is a great garden plant, deep rooted, and very

Asarum arifolium

drought resistant. It stands up to heat and forms large, attractive clumps of evergreen leaves.

Asarum canadense
Canadian ginger

Eastern North America. Flowers greenish brown, tub-shaped, emerging between leafstalks; April–May; deciduous, rhizomatous, to 12 in. (30 cm) tall; leaves paired, to 6 in. (15 cm) long, kidney-shaped, hairy, plain green. Zones 3–7. WS to MS. Any acid to neutral, somewhat dry soil. A widely grown, excellent garden plant. Very cold hardy for northern gardens and good in southern gardens, where it stands up to heat and drought and faithfully returns year after year with a luxurious, fast-growing, ground-covering, green car-

Asarum canadense

Asarum europaeum

Asarum hirsutipetalum

pet of large leaves. It does not like overly wet soils (see photo on page 177).

Asarum europaeum
European ginger

Europe east to the Caucasus. Flowers brown, bell-shaped; April–May; evergreen, rhizomatous, prostrate, to 4 in. (10 cm) tall and 12 in. (30 cm) wide; leaves to 2 in. (5 cm) long, kidney-shaped, glossy, plain. Zones 4–7. MS to FS. Acid, moist soil. An excellent wild ginger with prostrate growing habit, forming glossy, evergreen mats. It is one of the hardiest asarums and best in areas of cool summers.

Asarum hirsutipetalum

Japan. Flowers yellowish, inflated, tub-shaped, purple-veined; April; evergreen, clumping, 12 in. (30 cm) tall and to 18 in. (45 cm) wide; leaves heart-shaped, 7 in. (18 cm) long and 6 in. (15 cm) wide, shiny light green in spring, later dark green with the veins outlined in light green. Zones 7–9. MS to FS. Acid, moist soil. The leaves are usually rich green and not variegated but they are very large and a mature clump stands out in the garden or in a container. Great when planted with ferns and lacy foliage wildflowers. The flowers are stunning albeit somewhat hidden in the foliage. Different leaf patterns such as white, silvery gray, or yellow mottling are occasionally available.

'Kinkonkan' ("golden crown") has yellow variegation.

Asarum kumageanum

Japan. Flowers purple, inflated, tub-shaped, yellowish margins; April; evergreen, clumping, 10 in. (25 cm) tall, and to 16 in. (40 cm) wide; leaves to 6 in. (15 cm) long, triangular, shiny dark green mottled with yellowish green. Zones 7–9. MS to FS. Acid, moist soil. A beautiful species for southern gardens. The leaves have a shiny, rich dark green base color with the leaf interior mottled with large patches of a yellowish green, almost golden looking mottling. Several forms are in commerce, some with silver markings. Expect considerable differences.

Asarum hirsutipetalum flowers

Asarum kumageanum

Asarum shuttleworthii
Shuttleworth's ginger

Eastern North America. Flowers brown, hidden; April–May; evergreen, rhizomatous, to 6 in. (15 cm) tall and to 18 in. (45 cm) wide; leaves to 3 in. (8 cm) long, round with overlapping lobes, green with silvery markings. Zones 5–8. MS to FS. Acid, moist soil. A wild ginger with prostrate growing

Asarum shuttleworthii

Asarum splendens with ferns

habit, forming mats of leaves which hide the "little brown jug" flowers in spring. Vigorous cultivars are available.

'Callaway', a selection of var. *harperi*, has leaves to 2 in. (5 cm), with mottling; vigorous habit.

'Gosan Valley' has leaves to 2.5 in. (6 cm) long and 2 in. (5 cm) wide, with very pronounced mottling of silvery white on dark green.

Var. *harperi* has smaller (compared to the species), rounded leaves to 1 in. (2.5 cm). Zone 6.

Asarum speciosum

Eastern North America. Flowers purple with white "sunburst" inside; April–May; evergreen, clumping, to 8 in. (20 cm) tall and wide; leaves to 6 in. (15 cm) long and 3 in. (8 cm) wide, arrow-shaped, unmarked green. Zones 5–8. MS to FS. Acid, moist soil. Most forms have an erect growing habit showing the gorgeous flowers in spring. The leaves are plain green but large and the long-lasting flowering display is one of the best of the native North American wild gingers.

'Buxom Beauty' is a distinctly marked and rounder-leaved selection.

Asarum splendens
Chinese wild ginger

China. Flowers dark purple, urn-shaped; evergreen, rhizomatous, to 10 in. (25 cm) tall and to 18 in. (45 cm) wide; leaves to 6 in. (15 cm) long, triangular, dark green with outstanding, cloudy silver markings. Zones 5–8. MS to FS. Acid, moist soil. This is the most vigorous wild ginger anywhere and is one of the easiest to grow and propagate. The gorgeous leaves will withstand winters to zone 6b. Herbaceous in colder regions. Incorrectly sold as *Asarum magnificum*.

Aspidistra elatior
Cast-iron plant

China, Japan. Flowers like "corn cobs," hidden; clumping, to 4 ft. (1.2 m) high; leaves erect or leaning, oblong-elliptic, dark glossy green, arising directly from the rhizome, to 36 in. (90 cm) long and 3–5 in. (8–13 cm) wide. Zones 6–9. MS to FS. Moist, well-drained soil. This is the ubiquitous cast-iron plant. Its beautiful, glossy, dark green leaves grow in tight, upright bundles that even high winds will not flatten. Many variegated forms are in commerce. A great accent plant for

Aspidistra elatior as a mass planting

deep shade when planted among ferns and hostas (see photo on page 6).

'**Akebono**' ("dawn of day"), has a white stripe in the leaf center.

'**Asahi**' ("morning sun") has progressive whitening and streaking toward the leaf tip, becoming almost all white at the tip.

'**Hoshi Zaro**' ("starry sky") is white-speckled all over.

'**Milky Way**' ('Minor') is white-speckled and similar to 'Hoshi Zaro' but smaller.

'**Okame**' has white blotches throughout the leaf.

'**Variegata**' has irregular (wide and narrow) white stripes throughout the leaf.

'**Variegata Ashei**' has leaves with a pale center and irregularly white striped more or less equally throughout.

'**Variegata Exotica**' has bold, wider irregular white stripes throughout.

Aspidistra cultivars
Cast-iron plant

'**China Moon**' has leaves spotted with creamy yellow.

'**China Star**', leaves spattered with yellow specks.

'**China Sun**' has leaves that are speckled with light yellow dots.

'**Irish Mist**', a selection of *Aspidistra lurida*. Grows to 18 in. (45 cm), yellow speckles and markings appear all over its mature leaves. Zones 8–9.

'**Leopard**', a selection of *Aspidistra linearifolia*. Evergreen, clumping, to 30 in. (75 cm) high; leaves elongated straplike, dark shiny green, speckled with yellow spots to 20 in. (50 cm). Zones 7–9.

Asplenium platyneuron
Ebony spleenwort

North America. Fertile fronds in rosettes, to 20 in. (50 cm) tall, erect, dark green, sterile fronds to 10

Aspidistra elatior 'Variegata' with hostas and ferns

Aspidistra linearifolia 'Leopard'

in. (25 cm), bending down. Zones 3–9. Some sun. LS to WS. Dry, slightly acid, neutral, or alkaline soil. This is a small, rugged fern for dry places and soils not permanently wet. Abundant in the wild and prevalent in suburbia where it pops up everywhere. In gardens its small size and charming looks are appreciated as is its habit of spreading itself around.

Asplenium scolopendrium
Hart's tongue fern

Eurasia, eastern North America. Evergreen fronds simple, produced as single leaves to 15 in. (38 cm) long, 2 in. (5 cm) wide; leaves in crowns, strap-shaped, with wavy edges, leathery, glossy light green above and duller below. Zones 5–8. WS to FS. Ever-moist, alkaline to neutral soil. A variable and attractive species of which many lobed, incised, forked, and crested garden forms have been named. It is suitable for deep shade and prefers high humidity so benefits from misting or overhead watering during dry periods (see photo on page 95).

'Crispum', fronds to 20 in. (50 cm) long, evenly wavy, deeply folded and ruffled margin (see photo on page 95). Often confused with 'Undulatum'.

'Crispum Golden Queen', fronds greenish yellow, to 20 in. (50 cm) long, evenly wavy, margin ruffled.

'Cristatum', fronds to 14 in. (35 cm) long with crest divided many times, each division with a spreading, crested tip.

'Digitatum', fronds to 20 in. (50 cm) long, many-branched, each ending in a flat crest.

'Fimbriatum', fronds to 30 in. (75 cm) long, heavily fringed.

'Laceratum Kaye', broad fronds to 14 in. (35 cm) long, deeply and unevenly divided, shredded, with crested tip.

'Marginatum', narrow fronds to 18 in. (45 cm) long, deeply lobed margins.

'Ramosum', fronds to 14 in. (35 cm) long, divided into two branches, forming two blades.

'Speciosum', fronds to 30 in. (75 cm) long, deeply folded and pleated.

'Undulatum', fronds to 18 in. (45 cm) long, darker green than 'Crispum', with wavy, less wavy margins.

Asplenium platyneuron

Asplenium scolopendrium

Asplenium scolopendrium 'Crispum'

Asplenium trichomanes
Maidenhair spleenwort

North America, Eurasia. Evergreen fronds produced in rosettes, fertile fronds 4–7 in. (10–18 cm) tall, erect, tapering at top and bottom, dark green, sterile fronds flat on the ground. Zones 5–8. LS to FS. Dry alkaline soil. This dainty, pretty fern requires an elevated position in the shady rock garden near a path. It does not like soggy or wet soils.

'Cristatum', leaflets with the capitate frond tip only crested.

'Incisum', leaflets triangular and deeply incised.

'Incisum Moulei' ('Moulei'), leaflets linear and deeply incised.

'Ramocristatum', leaflets branched with frond tip on branches crested.

'Trogyense', leaflets triangular and deeply incised.

Aster divaricatus
White wood aster

Eastern North America. Flowers white, rayed, to 1 in. (2.5 cm) across; in flat-topped clusters on flowerstalks 20–36 in. (50–90 cm); July–October; deciduous; leaves dark green, elongated heart-shaped, toothed, 3–6 in. (8–16 cm) long. Zones 4–8. LS to FS. Any soil in dry or moist shade. Good late summer color and foliage for the woodland garden. Spreads prolifically by seed so do not plant near areas of delicate wildflowers that might be overwhelmed.

Astilbe ×arendsii

Garden hybrids. Similar in habit to *Astilbe japonica*. Zones 5–8; LS to FS. Permanently moist, fertile, acidic soil. Beware of ordering duplicate plants under both the original German cultivar name and its English translation. Blooming seasons are early (May–June), midseason (June–July), and late (July–August).

'Bergkristall' ('Mountain Crystal'), white flowers, midseason; 40 in. (1 m) tall.

'Bressingham Beauty', light pink flowers, midseason, bronze-tinted leaves; 36 in. (90 cm) tall and 24 in. (60 cm) wide.

Aster divaricatus

Astilbe ×arendsii 'Cattleya'

'Cattleya', lilac flowers, late; 4 ft. (1.2 m) tall and 36 in. (90 cm) wide.

'Fanal', dark crimson flowers, early; leaves dark; 32 in. (80 cm) tall and 18 in. (45 cm) wide.

'Granat' ('Garnet'), crimson-red flowers; 32 in. (80 cm) tall and 24 in. (60 cm) wide.

'Irrlicht' ('Jack o' Lantern', 'Will-o'-the-Wisp'), white flowers, early to midseason; 18 in. (45 cm) tall.

'Rotlicht' ('Red Light'), bright red flowers, bronze-tinted leaves, midseason; 36 in. (90 cm) tall and 24 in. (60 cm) wide.

'Weisse Gloria' ('White Glory'), white flowers, late; 36 in. (90 cm) tall and 18 in. (45 cm) wide.

Astilbe biternata
False goatsbeard

North America. Flowers tiny white to light yellow on a tall, branched drooping inflorescence to 4 ft. (1.2 m) tall and 36 in. (90 cm) wide; June–July; leaves large, dark green, divided into many leaflets with sharply toothed edges. Zones 5–8; LS to FS. Permanently moist, fertile, acidic soil. This handsome and imposing native astilbe should be grown more in gardens. After flowering, the shrublike leaf mound provides fine foliage in the garden.

Astilbe chinensis
Chinese astilbe

Siberia, China, Korea, Japan. Flowers pinkish on a slender, branched inflorescence 24 in. (60 cm) high and wide; July–August; leaves divided into many leaflets, dark green, serrate edges, hairy. Zones 4–8. Sun, LS to FS. Permanently moist, fertile, acidic soil. An attractive, vigorous garden plant with a creeping rootstock. Available cultivars are all hardy to zone 4.

Var. *davidii* has pink flowers; 6 ft. (1.8 m) tall and 36 in. (90 cm) wide; larger than the species, needs water and some sun, spectacular.

'Finale', bright pink flowers, leaves dark; 20 in. (50 cm) tall and 18 in. (45 cm) wide.

Astilbe ×arendsii 'Irrlicht'

Astilbe biternata

Astilbe chinensis 'Superba' with hostas

Astilbe japonica 'Bonn'

Var. *pumila* ('Pumila'). Dwarf Chinese astilbe. Has lilac flowers; 10 in. (25 cm) tall and 9 in. (23 cm) wide; leaves small, dark green with red tint; small, sun-tolerant, creeping. It is a late-flowerer and good for covering small patches of ground.

'Purpurlanze' ('Purple Lance') also has darker, more vivid flowers than the type. Another excellent, drought-tolerant cultivar.

'Superba', intense magenta flowers on a tall, conical, branched inflorescence held by strong, brownish stems, late; 4 ft. (1.2 m) tall and 36 in. (90 cm) wide; leaves small, dark green with bronze tint. Outstanding.

Var. *taquetii* ('Taquetii') has reddish purple flowers; is smaller, 4 ft. (1.2 m) tall and 24 in. (60 cm) wide, with bronze-tinged leaves.

'Visions' has dark raspberry-pink flowers tightly clustered on flowerstalks to 14 in. (35 cm). Suited for dry regions with periods of drought.

Astilbe japonica
Japanese astilbe
Japan. Flowers white, on an open, slender, branched inflorescence; 30 in. (75 cm) high and 24 in. (60 cm) wide; May–June; leaves narrow, with glossy dark green leaflets, margins toothed. Zones 5–9. Some sun, LS to MS. Moist, fertile, acidic soil. Hybrids involving this species were bred mostly in Germany; all have medium green foliage.

'Bonn', carmine-red flowers, early; 28 in. (70 cm) tall.

'Deutschland' ('Germany'), white flowers, early; 18 in. (45 cm) tall and 12 in. (30 cm) wide.

'Möwe' ('Seagull'), salmon-pink flowers, early; 28 in. (70 cm) tall.

'Peach Blossom' ('Drayton Glory'), peachy pink flowers, early; 24 in. (60 cm) tall and 18 in. (45 cm) wide.

'Red Sentinel', deep crimson flowers, loosely arranged, early; 24 in. (60 cm) tall and 18 in. (45 cm) wide.

Astilboides tabularis
Shield-leaf Rodger's flower
Eastern China, North Korea. Flowers tiny, white flowers carried on stems to 6 ft. (1.8 m); June–August; to 36 in. (90 cm) tall and 5 ft. (1.5 m) wide; leaves shieldlike, to 36 in. (90 cm) long, light green, with hairy cover, rounded in outline but with large, toothlike lobes, often deeply incised. Zones 5–7. Sun, LS. Moist, fertile, acidic soil. A great accent plant near a water feature or in open woodlands. It anchors plantings of hostas and ferns, and during flowering it is absolutely spectacular.

Athyrium filix-femina
Lady fern
Cosmopolitan. Fronds deciduous, to 36 in. (90 cm) tall and 12 in. (30 cm) wide, in rosettes, leaning with age; leaves divided into many pairs of light green thin leaflets, wedge-shaped, subleaflets deeply cut and toothed, mostly blunt. Zones 4–8. LS to FS. Moist, fertile, acidic soil. This is the ubiquitous lady fern found in many gardens. Its best features is that fronds are produced continually during the growing season, so wind or rain damage to fronds is quickly replaced by new growth. Many different forms exist in the wild and a large number of cultivars are available.

Astilboides tabularis flower

Athyrium filix-femina var. *asplenioides*

'Acroladon', fronds repeatedly branching, resulting in an unusual, ball-shaped clump; to 12 in. (30 cm).

Var. *asplenioides* is the commonly occurring and widely available southern form.

'Fieldii' ('Fieldiae'), tall and strong-growing with paired leaflets forming a cross pattern; to 30 in. (75 cm).

'Frizelliae'. Tatting fern. Fronds with very short leaflets shaped into rounded lobes resembling tatting; to 20 in. (50 cm).

'Frizelliae Cristatum', similar to 'Frizelliae' but with the main frond forked into a 3-tipped top; to 20 in. (50 cm).

'Ghost', a tall form with narrow, paired leaflets of a ghostly gray on reddish brown stems. Makes an elegant and unusual statement in the garden.

'Minutissimum'. Dwarf lady fern, small lady fern. Makes a dense rosette; to 12 in. (30 cm).

'Setigerum' has very slender leaflets; to 20 in. (50 cm).

'Victoriae', narrow, paired leaflets forming a checked pattern; to 40 in. (1 m). Distinctive.

Athyrium niponicum
Japanese lady fern

East Asia. Fronds to 14 in. (35 cm), in rosette-shaped clumps, 18 in. (45 cm), either green or greenish brown, darker near the base, grooved, arching; leaves divided, leaflets green wedge-shaped, narrow, to 5 in. (13 cm) long; subleaflets deeply cut and toothed. Zones 4–8. LS to FS. Moist, fertile, acidic soil. The Japanese form of lady fern. Despite its delicate appearance, it is one of the best ferns for the garden. The species and its variety spread vigorously by spores. Although the type is rare, a variegated form, the colorful Japanese painted fern, is most acclaimed and widely available everywhere. Its physical size is about the same as the typical species, but it is slightly smaller in some forms.

'Apple Court', a crested form.

Athyrium filix-femina 'Minutissimum'

Athyrium niponicum var. *pictum*

Athyrium otophorum showing colorful young frond with more mature ones

Begonia grandis volunteers surrounding a bench in the garden; in the pot is the tender, cane-stemmed *Begonia* 'Angel Wings'

'Burgundy Lace', new fronds purple with silver stripes.

'Pewter Lace', fronds in shades of gray pewter.

Var. *pictum* ('Pictum', 'Metalicum', 'Metalicum Pictum'). Japanese painted fern. Possibly the most popular lady fern around. Wine-red stems, adjacent leaflets are suffused with reddish to bluish hues, changing to a lighter, metallic gray toward the tips—a distinct bar effect. Very hardy in northern gardens; not bothered by heat in southern gardens (see photo on page 153).

Athyrium otophorum

China, Korea, Japan. Fronds to 30 in. (75 cm), in clumps; leaves divided into green to greenish gray leaflets, to 3 in. (8 cm) long and 1 in. (2.5 cm) wide. Zones 5–8. LS to FS. Moist, fertile, acidic soil. This species shows good color in new fronds but fades later. Most commercial offerings have beautiful wine-red stalks with greenish gray leaflets.

Begonia grandis
Hardy begonia

Southeastern Asia. Flowers lightly fragrant, soft pink, hanging down; August to frost; stems upright, to 36 in. (90 cm), branched, yellowish green; leaves to 8 in. (20 cm) long and 5 in. (13 cm) wide, heart-shaped, green above, ruby red below; fruit 3-winged. Zones 7–9. LS to FS. Moist, fertile, acidic soil. This hardy begonia multiplies prolifically. Somewhat variable, especially in leaf color, and it comes in both pink- and white-flowered forms.

'Alba' has flowers that are almost white, with a hint of pink.

'Claret Jug' is similar to the type with the flowers a deeper pink.

'Simsii', flowers larger than the type, with the same pink color.

Belamcanda chinensis flowers

Belamcanda flabellata 'Hello Yellow' with *Hosta montana* flowers

Belamcanda chinensis
Blackberry lily

Himalaya, Eastern Asia. Flowers orange-red, spotted with maroon or yellow, 1.5 in. (4 cm) across; July–September; clumping; leaves on the stem, to 12 in. (30 cm) long and 1 in. (2.5 cm) wide, sword-shaped, medium green; shiny black berries. Zones 7–9. Sun to WS. Moist, well-drained soil. Adaptable to some shade but the gardener must determine how much shade can still produce flowers. Variable in flower color. Most of the plants offered in commerce are orange with dark red or maroon spots. Cultivars are offered and come true from seed if isolated.

'Freckle Face' has yellow flowers spotted with maroon specks.

Belamcanda flabellata
Blackberry lily

China, Japan. Flowers light yellow, to 2 in. (5 cm) across, July–September; clumping; leaves basal and placed on the stem, to 8 in. (20 cm) long and 0.8 in. (2 cm) wide, sword-shaped, medium green; shiny black berries. Zones 7–9. Sun, LS to WS. Moist, well-drained soil. Smaller than *Belamcanda chinensis* but with slightly larger flowers.

'Hello Yellow', pure yellow, unspotted flowers, tolerates shade.

Bergenia cordifolia
Pigsqueak

Caucasus to Siberia. Flowers small, many, pale red to dark pink in clusters on red flowerstalks to

Bergenia cordifolia backed by blooming *Aruncus dioicus*

18 in. (45 cm) tall; March–May; clumping, to 24 in. (60 cm) wide and 18 in. (45 cm) high; evergreen basal leaves, deep to mid-green, with purple or bronze coloration in some cultivars, to 12 in. (30 cm) long, rounded, heart-shaped, often puckered. Zones 3–8. Morning sun, LS to MS. Moist, fertile, well-drained soil. Strong sun exposure and lack of moisture will brown the leaves.

'**Abendglocken**' ('Evening Bells'), leaves dark purplish green.

'**Bressingham White**', flowers pure white.

'**Purpurea**', flowers magenta-purple; leaves reddish bronze.

'**Rotblum**', flowers ruby red and taller stalks.

Blechnum spicant
Deer fern

Western North America, Eurasia. Fronds in rosettes; stalks, erect; dark green sterile leaves to 20 in. (50 cm), evergreen; fertile leaves taller to 28 in. (70 cm). Zones 5–8. Sun, LS to WS. Moist, well-drained acidic soil. Forms a neat, compact clump and is useful in many places of the garden. Remove the old fronds to enjoy the beauty of fresh growth (see photo on page 10).

'**Cristatum**', tips of the leaflets branched.

'**Serratum**', with deeply serrated leaflets that are densely arranged.

Bletilla ochracea

Eastern China, Japan. Flowers fragrant, light yellow, dark yellow or lavender lip; May–June; clumping; stems 18 in. (45 cm); leaves basal and placed on the stem, to 12 in. (30 cm) long and 1 in. (2.5 cm) wide, lance-shaped, green, heavily pleated, striate. Zones 5–8. LS to WS. Moist, well-drained soil. The best forms have light yellow flowers with a dark yellow lip. Other forms available have a lavender coloration in the lip but commercial sources do not differentiate. Also available under the incorrect name *Bletilla striata* 'Ochracea'.

Blechnum spicant

Bletilla ochracea flowers (Tony Avent)

Bletilla striata

Eastern China, Japan. Flowers fragrant, rose-purple, pleated magenta lip; May–June; clumping; stems 24 in. (60 cm); leaves basal and placed on stem to 15 in. (38 cm) long and 1 in. (2.5 cm) wide, lance-shaped, green, heavily pleated, striate. Zones 5–8. LS to WS. Moist, well-drained soil. Flower color varies; most plants in commerce have magenta to rose-purple flowers with a typical orchid shape. The lip is covered with wavy pleat.

'**Alba**' (f. *alba*) has white flowers with a faint flush of purple on the lip.

'**Albostriata**' ('Albomarginata') has a thin, white margin on the leaves.

'**First Kiss**' combines the flowers of 'Alba' with the leaves of 'Albostriata'.

Botrychium virginianum
Rattlesnake fern

Eastern North America, Eurasia. MS to FS. Fertile and sterile fronds on common stem; sterile frond singular, deciduous, triangular, to 10 in. (25 cm) long and 12 in. (30 cm) wide, divided into light green leaflets; fertile frond is a spore cluster. Zones 3–8. WS to FS. Moist, well-drained soil. Larger than the other grape ferns, it comes up early in spring. A small group makes a wonderful, lacy display in the fern glen or among wildflowers

Var. *intermedium*, subleaflets wider and almost touching.

Brunnera macrophylla
Siberian bugloss

Caucasus to western Siberia. Flowers small, many, bright blue or white, on a branched inflorescence to 8 in. (20 cm) long; April–June; clumping, to 24 in. (60 cm) wide and 18 in. (45 cm) high; basal leaves, green, to 8 in. (20 cm) long, rounded, with a pointed tip. Zones 3–6. Morning sun, LS to MS. Moist, fertile, well-drained soil. Best for northern gardens. Lack of moisture will brown the leaves. Several cultivars are in commerce. Those with variegated leaves should not be exposed to direct sun because even a short exposure may brown the light colored leaf areas.

'**Dawson's White**' ('Variegata'), creamy white margins; flowers blue.

Bletilla striata flower

Botrychium virginianum var. *intermedium* (left) and the type (center right) with *Polygonatum geminiflorum* (right margin)

Brunnera macrophylla 'Dawson's White' (Hans Hansen)

Brunnera macrophylla 'Silver Wings' (Hans Hansen)

Calanthe discolor 'Eco Rose' (left) and 'Eco White' (Don Jacobs)

'**Hadspen Cream**', leaves have narrower, irregular, creamy to yellowish white margins, sometimes also spotted creamy white; flowers blue.

'**Silver Wings**', leaves are large and irregularly spotted with many large silvery white spots; flowers blue. A large and vigorous cultivar.

Calanthe discolor

Japan, Korea, eastern China. Flowers to 20 per stem, to 1.5 in. (4 cm) across, greenish brown to green, lip light lavender to pink or white; April–June; semi-evergreen, clumping; stems to 20 in. (50 cm); leaves basal, lance-shaped, green, 12 in. (30 cm) long and 1–1.5 in. (2.5–4 cm) wide. Zones 7–9. LS to MS. Moist, fertile, coarse, well-drained soil. Orchids offered in commerce have variable flower color, with brown-pink seen more than others. Now available is the very similar, but hardier (zone 6) *Calanthe tricarinata* with yellow flowers and red lips. Several hardy cultivars are in commerce.

'**Eco Rose**', rose-tinged flowers with rosy white lips; a vigorous multiplier.

'**Eco White**', yellowish white flowers with white lips, mature flowers very white; a floriferous clone, easy to cultivate.

'**Kozu**' ('Kozu Spice'), a natural hybrid (*Calanthe discolor* × *C. izu-insularis*), has mixed flower colors. More robust than its parents and easy to grow.

'**Takane**', a group of hybrids with or possibly selections of var. *sieboldii* with mixed flower colors. Most have bright yellow flowers with white lips.

Campanula poscharskyana
Dalmatian bellflower

Croatia. Flowers many, deep purple outside, tubular bell-shaped; August to frost; stems upright, leafy, to 7 in. (18 cm); leaves 2 in. (5 cm) long, basal, rounded kidney-shaped, medium green, margins toothed; plant clump-forming, spreading by rhizomes.

Zones 4–6. Some sun to LS. Moist, fertile, well-drained soil. Best for gardens from zone 6 north. In zone 7 and given shade this species will flowers sparingly but is very useful forming a tight, low-growing groundcover.

Campanula takesimana
Korean bellflower

Korea. Flowers many, unusually colored creamy yellow flushed with purple outside and spotted red inside, tubular bell-shaped, 0.8 in. (2 cm) long; August to frost; stems upright, leafy, to 15 in. (38 cm); leaves basal, heart-shaped, medium green, margins toothed; clumping. Zones 5–7. Some sun, LS. Moist, fertile soil. The nodding flowers with cream-colored bells blend well into a shaded garden. Best in cool summer areas. In zone 7, grow it in a position where it gets quite a bit of morning sun and shade during the hot summer afternoons. Usually sold under a cultivar name.

'Beautiful Trust' has pure white flowers.
'Elizabeth' is as described for the species.

Campanula poscharskyana used as groundcover

Campanula takesimana 'Elizabeth'

Carex comans
Hair sedge

New Zealand. Flowers spikelike, inconspicuous; leaves evergreen, almost hairlike, arching, to 18 in. (45 cm) long, yellowish to whitish green; clumping, tufted. Zones 7–9. Some sun, LS to WS. Moist, fertile soil. This "hairy" sedge can get untidy and needs "combing out" frequently to clean debris from the clump.

'Bronze Mound', bronzy brown leaves.

'Frosty Curls', leaves whitish with white, sometimes curly tips.

Carex elata
Tufted sedge

Eastern Europe. Flowers brown, overtopping leaves; clumping, densely tufted, leaves evergreen, sword-shaped, 24 in. (60 cm) long, to 0.5 in. (1 cm) wide, pleated. Zones 7–9. Some sun, LS to WS. Constantly moist, fertile soil. The typical species is rarely offered. In spring, the yellow-leaved forms start out a bright yellow and turn into a yellowish green by mid-summer. All forms require some direct exposure to sun.

'Aurea' has yellow-margined leaves.

'Bowles' Golden' is widely available and has bright yellow leaves, thinly margined with light green to green.

Carex fraseri
Fraser's sedge

Eastern North America. Flowers on solitary stalk, to 6 in. (15 cm) tall, showy, creamy white to greenish white, looking like an upturned brush to 0.5 in. (1 cm) across; rhizomatous; evergreen leaves broad, to 2 in. (5 cm) wide and 10–24 in. (25–60 cm) long, strap-shaped, leathery, grooved lengthwise but lacking a prominent midrib, wavy. Zones 5–9. LS to FS. Moist, fertile soil. The most

Carex comans 'Frosty Curls'

Carex fraseri

Carex grayi

shade-tolerant sedge available and easily the most attractive during flowering. This uncommon sedge makes a great addition to the wildflower border in company with small ferns, galax, and dwarf Solomon's seals.

Carex grayi
Morning star sedge

Eastern North America. Flowers shaped like a spiked club, 1 in. (2.5 cm) across the spikes, first greenish then brown; clumping, tufted; leaves deciduous, sword-shaped, 12–24 in. (30–60 cm) long, green, keeled along center rib. Zones 6–9. Some sun, LS to WS. Moist, fertile soil. An outstanding sedge. Its bright green leaves and un-

usual star-shaped seed pods beg attention in the garden. It propagates by seed and makes a wonderful give-away plant.

Carex morrowii
Japanese sedge

Japan. Flowers brown, inconspicuous; clumping, tufted evergreen leaves sword-shaped, 18–24 in. (45–60 cm) long, arching, narrow, keeled along center rib. Zones 7–9. Some sun, LS to WS. Moist, fertile soil. The typical species is rarely offered. Variegated cultivars are common and the variegation holds best in some shade. All do best in constantly moist soil. Considerable shade is tolerated.

Carex morrowii 'Aureovariegata' with uvularias and ferns

'Aureovariegata' ('Evergold') with broad, whitish yellow center with dark green, narrow margins.

'Goldband' ('Fisher', 'Fisher's Form', Fisher's Gilt', 'Gilt') has creamy center banding in the leaves.

'Silk Tassel' has very narrow white-margined leaves; silky clump.

'Silver Scepter', white-edged; rhizomatous, expanding.

'Variegata' is a common green form with thin white margins.

Carex phyllocephala
Japanese palm sedge

Japan. Flowers inconspicuous; rhizomatous, forming dense clumps; leaves sword-shaped, 7–10 in. (18–25 cm) long, green, keeled along the midrib, striated lengthwise; leafstalks to 12 in. (30 cm), with leaves emerging along the length, becoming more closely spaced toward top, finally tufted and whorled at the top, palmlike. Zones 7–9. Some sun, LS to WS. Moist, fertile soil. Evergreen in zone 7. An outstanding and unusual garden sedge.

Carex phyllocephala 'Sparkler'

'Sparkler' has irregular white stripes in the leaves. Tolerates considerable shade. Seeds produce plain green plants.

Carex plantaginea
Evergreen broadleaf sedge

Eastern North America. Flowers inconspicuous; rhizomatous, forming dense, tufts of basal leaves; leaves evergreen, lance- or sword-shaped, 7–9 in. (18–23 cm) long, dark green, keeled along the midrib, striated and pleated lengthwise. Zones 5–9. Some sun, LS to WS. Moist, fertile soil. This native is a great evergreen sedge where less-hardy Japanese sedges cannot be grown. A wonderful companion plant in the shady woodland garden, grouped with small ferns and small to medium hostas. In tight groups it makes an excellent groundcover. It will naturalize, coming up here and there. Good in both northern and southern gardens.

Carex siderosticha
Creeping broadleaf sedge

Japan. Flowers blackish brown, inconspicuous; rhizomatous, forming dense clumps; leaves sword-shaped, 7–10 in. (18–25 cm) long, dark

Carex plantaginea

Carex siderosticha
'Variegata'

green, keeled and pleated along the midrib and striated. Zones 7–9. Some sun, LS to WS. Moist, fertile soil. The typical species is rare. Best for a solid groundcover in light to woodland shade. The attractive, grasslike plants juxtapose well with ferns and hostas in the shady woodland garden. Moist conditions are required for a rapid spread.

'**Island Brocade**', yellow edges with occasional irregular, narrow, yellow stripes in the leaves.

'**Lemon Zest**', bright lemon-yellow leaves.

'**Variegata**' has creamy white, narrow margins with occasional irregular, thin, white stripes in the leaves.

Caulophyllum thalictroides
Blue cohosh
Eastern North America. Flowers small, yellowish green, clustered on a branched flower spike; April–June; clumping, rhizomatous; leaves divided into many dark green leaflets 1–3 in. (2.5–8 cm) long, 3-lobed. Zones 3–8. WS to FS. Moist, fertile soil. This very hardy eastern wildflower is still rarely grown. The flowers are rather ordinary, but the leaf mound and bright blue berries add considerable texture and color to the garden. Should be planted more frequently.

Chamaelirium luteum
Fairy wand
Eastern North America. Flowers tiny, many; female and male flowers on separate plants; flowers in flower spikes on leafy spike, to 40 in. (1.2 m); male flowers more showy, on elongated, cylindrical, branched inflorescence to 8 in. (20 cm), erect, but with bending top; male plant shorter; May–June; herbaceous, clumping; leaves in a rosette, spoon-shaped, green, smooth, 3–8 in. (8–20 cm) long and 0.8–1.5 in. (2–4 cm) wide. Zones 3–8. WS to FS. Moist, fertile, acidic soil. This beautiful and easily cultivated native is best as a group of three to five with small ferns, wild gingers, small hostas, and other wildflowers.

Caulophyllum thalictroides

Chelone glabra
White turtlehead

Eastern North America. Flowers white, tinged lavender near tips, beard white, snapdragon-like, 1–1.5 in.
(2.5–4 cm) long, tubular, in clusters on erect flowerstalks to 36 in. (90 cm); July–September; herbaceous,
clumping; leaves opposite, green, lance-shaped,
toothed, 3–6 in. (8–15 cm) long. Zones 4–9. Some
sun to LS. Any moist soil. This species needs some
sun and does best in constantly moist soil to provide
a long blooming period in late summer.

Var. *elatior* has a deeper purple coloration in
the throat.

Chelone lyonii
Red turtlehead

Eastern North America. Similar in habit and cultivation to *Chelone glabra*, except the flowers are
purple to red; flowerstalks to 40 in. (1 m); leaves
smaller 2–6 in. (5–15 cm).

'Hot Lips' has bright pink flowers and purplish
bronze new leaves, turning dark green.

Chamaelirium luteum, emergent leafy scape of
female plant (left) and mature flower spikes of
male plant (right) (Don Jacobs)

Chelone lyonii

Chrysogonum virginianum
Green and gold

Eastern North America. Flowers solitary, yellow. 1–1.5 in. (2.5–4 cm) across; April–October; stoloniferous, creeping, evergreen south, deciduous north; leaves opposite, heart-shaped, hairy, green 1–4 in. (2.5–10 cm) long. Zones 5–8. Some sun to WS. Moist, well-drained soil. A quite variable species with differences in the flowers and the leaves are either smooth or have toothed margins. The southern form is stoloniferous and produces many runners. The northern typical species has a more erect, taller habit and is less suitable for groundcover applications but makes a nice companion plant in the open woodland border. Inquire before ordering. A number of cultivars have been named.

'Allen Bush', a dwarf form with leafy stolons; flowers smaller, yellow.

'Eco Lacquered Spider', long, purple stolons and purple into the leaf bases and the leaf.

'Graystone Gold', overlapping yellow petals and almost round leaves.

'Pierre', softer green leaves and long bloom duration.

Cimicifuga racemosa
Black cohosh

Eastern North America. Flowers white, small, with unpleasant odor, many in elongated clusters on leafy flowerstalks 3–8 ft. (0.9–2.5 m); July–September; basal leaves twice divided into heart-shaped, lobed, toothed, dark green, leaflets rounded, 1–3 in. (2.5–8 cm) long. Zones 4–8. LS to WS. Moist, acidic soil. The best bugbane for the garden. Its tall, majestic flowering stems bloom before any of the other species and take four to five weeks to finish flowering.

Cimicifuga simplex
Autumn snakeroot

Eastern Asia. Flowers white, fragrant, small, many in dense, elongated clusters to 12 in. (30 cm) on flowerstalks to 4 ft. (1.2 m); August–September; leaves basal, divided into toothed, dark green leaflets. Zones 3–8. LS to WS. Moist, acidic

Chrysogonum virginianum

Cimicifuga racemosa

soil. Characterized by attractive, cylindrical racemes of dense, white flowers, this species has a very long, late summer blooming period. Good in both northern and southern gardens.

'**Atropurpurea**', white flowers; leaves deep purple in spring, greening up later but remaining dark throughout the season.

'**Braunlaub**' ('Brownleaf') has very dark, brownish green leaves.

'**Brunette**', lavender-tinted white flowers, fragrant; dark reddish purple leaves fading to brownish dark green in autumn.

'**Elstead**' ('Elstead's Variety'), buds dark pink to purple, opening to white flowers in loose, feathery flower spikes on purplish stems to 5 ft. (1.5 m); green leaves. A selection of var. *matsumurae*.

'**Hillside Black Beauty**', white flowers; blackish purple leaves fading to very dark brownish green in autumn.

Var. *matsumurae* is a later-blooming Japanese form.

'**Prichard's Giant**', white flowers very fragrant; heat-tolerant.

Claytonia caroliniana
Spring beauty

Eastern North America. Flowers white to pink, with red veining; March–May; clumping; leaves two, on long leaf stalk, oval, opposite, dark green, to 2 in. (5 cm) long. Zones 5–8. Sun to LS. Moist, gritty acidic soil. This charming, early blooming ephemeral should be planted with later-rising permanent groundcovers, like small ferns and small hostas to cover the areas left open by it.

Claytonia virginica
Virginia spring beauty

Eastern North America. Similar in habit and culture to *Claytonia caroliniana*, except leaves narrowly lance-shaped, with no leafstalk.

'**Lutea**' has orange-red flowers with dark red veining.

Cimicifuga simplex 'Brunette' autumn leaf color

'Robusta' is a clone larger than the type, with larger flowers.

Clintonia borealis
Bluebead lily

Eastern North America. Flowers small, greenish yellow, drooping bell-shaped on flowerstalk, 6–15 in. (15–38 cm) tall; May–August; herbaceous, rhizomatous; leaves 2–6, basal, broadly oval, keeled, shiny dark green, 5–8 in. (13–20 cm) long and 1.5–2.5 in. (4–6 cm) wide; shiny blue berries. Zones 4–7. LS to FS. Moist, leafy soil. The ubiquitous yellow clintonia is unfortunately not adapted well to southern gardensand may not flower if given too much shade to keep it cool. Try it anyway. The striking leaves last all through the season. The blue berry clusters are showy in summer. Clones with white berries are known.

Claytonia virginica

Clintonia borealis as leaf cover

Clintonia umbellata inflorescence

Clintonia umbellata
Speckled wood lily

Eastern North America. Similar in habit and culture to *Clintonia borealis*, except flowers smaller, white, spotted with green and purple, erect, star-shaped; black berries.

Convallaria majalis
Lily-of-the-valley

Eurasia. Flowers strongly fragrant, small, waxy white, drooping, bell-shaped on arching flower-stalk, 6–12 in. (15–30 cm) tall; May–June; herbaceous, rhizomatous, spreading; leaves 2–3, basal, broadly elliptic, keeled, shiny dark green, veined, 2–10 in. (4–25 cm) long and 1–3 in. (2.5–8 cm) wide; shiny red to red-orange berries. Zones 4–7. LS to FS. Moist, well-drained, fertile, acidic soil. This is the widespread lily-of-the-valley grown in gardens the world over. Many variants are known and have been named.

'Albostriata' ('Albistriata'), leaves striped along the veins with white.

'Aureovariegata' ('Lineata', 'Striata', 'Variegata'), leaves narrowly striped yellow along the veins. Another form has leaves with yellow margins; another, leaves that are spotted with yellowish white. Read catalog descriptions carefully.

'Flore Pleno' ('Plena') has white double flowers.

'Fortin's Giant' ('Fortin's', 'Fortune', 'Fortune's Giant'), a robust selection with wider leaves.

'Hardwick Hall', broad, dark green leaves with pale greenish yellow margins.

Forma *picta* has filaments spotted purple at the base.

'Rosea' has pink flowers.

'Rosea Plena' has pink double flowers.

Var. *transcaucasica*, of uncertain origin, is similar to the type.

'Vic Pawlowski's Gold', leaves closely striped with white or clear yellow.

Cornus canadensis
Bunchberry

Northern temperate zone. Flowers with peripheral white bracts, to 1.5 in. (4 cm), in a ball-shaped, yellow cluster; May–July; herbaceous, rhizomatous, spreading; 4–8 in. (10–20 cm) high;

Convallaria majalis 'Albostriata' with hostas

Cornus canadensis

leaves 4, broadly ovate, green, whorled at the top of the stem, 1.5–3 in. (4–8 cm) long; berries red. Zones 2–6. LS to WS. Moist, fertile, acidic soil. An extremely hardy attractive groundcover for northern gardens. Difficult in zone 7 and south.

Corydalis lutea

Europe. Flowers golden yellow, with blunt spurs, small, many in branched clusters; April–September; herbaceous, mounding; to 16 in. (40 cm) tall; leaves fernlike, divided into dull green, wedge-shaped, lobed leaflets; seeds prolific.

Zones 5–7. LS to WS. Moist soil. Best for northern gardens but will succeed in southern gardens in moist, cool shade.

Cypripedium calceolus
Yellow lady slipper

North America. Flowers purple-brown, twisted top petals, with a yellow lip, petal pouchlike to 2 in. (5 cm) long, on tall stalks to 24 in. (60 cm); April–August; clumping; leaves 3–5, on the stem, elliptic, pleated, green, distinctly hairy, 2–8 in. (5–20 cm) long. Zones 4–7. LS to WS. Moist, fer-

Corydalis lutea
backed by
Stylophorum
diphyllum

tile, acidic soil. Available from propagated stock, this is the most widely grown yellow lady slipper that succeeds in gardens. Never dig in the wild nor accept plants collected in the wild.

Var. *parviflorum* is smaller in all respects.

Var. *pubescens* is larger than the type and sometimes available from rescued stock.

Cyrtomium falcatum
Japanese holly fern

Southern Japan and China to India. Evergreen fronds in rosettes on slender stalks shiny green, arching; leaves to 36 in. (90 cm) long and 10 in. (25 cm) wide, divided into very shiny dark green, leathery, hollylike leaflets 6 in. (15 cm) long. Zones 6–9. WS to FS. Moist, acidic soil. This fern is striking in its habit and its shiny, bright green leaf mound highlights its position in the garden. Best from zone 6 south, it should be grown in a sheltered, shady, moist position. In northern gardens, use containers for overwintering.

'**Butterfieldii**', leaflets have toothed margins and long, drawn-out tips.

'**Compactum**', a dwarf form.

Cypripedium calceolus
var. *pubescens*

'Cristatum' ('Cristata', 'Mayi'), leaflets have crests; fronds are forked and have terminal crests.

'Mandaianum', leaflets are triangular with fringed margins.

'Rochfordianum', leaflets glossy, dark green with coarsely toothed or slightly lobed margins; a vigorous form.

Cyrtomium fortunei

Southern Japan and China, Korea. Evergreen fronds in rosettes on purplish stalks, bending down, arching; leaves to 24 in. (60 cm) long and 8 in. (20 cm) wide, divided into grayish green, leathery, sickle-shaped leaflets 4 in. (10 cm) long and to 1.5 in. (4 cm) wide. Zones 7–9. WS to FS. Moist, acidic soil. Noticeable purple-colored stems and midribs on the leaflets highlight the mound. Evergreen in zone 7.

Cyrtomium macrophyllum
Large-leaved holly fern

Southern Japan and China, Korea. Evergreen fronds in rosettes on green stalks, arching; leaves to 18 in. (45 cm) long and 7 in. (18 cm) wide; divided into grayish green, leathery, sickle-shaped leaflets, 3.5 in. (9 cm) long and to 2 in. (5 cm) wide. Zones 7–9. WS to FS. Moist, acidic soil. This outstanding fern is similar to *Cyrtomium fortunei* but has much larger, broader, bold leaflets unlike many of the finely divided ferns commonly seen. Best for southern gardens but a good patio container plant in northern gardens.

Danaë racemosa
Alexandrian laurel

Turkey, Iran. Flowers small, greenish yellow, inconspicuous, on stems to 4 ft. (1.2 m) tall; May–August; clumping, rhizomatous; true leaves

Cyrtomium falcatum 'Rochfordianum'

Cyrtomium fortunei with *Dryopteris sieboldii*

Cyrtomium macrophyllum frond (center) surrounded by *Cyrtomium fortunei*, *Asplenium scolopendrium* (top left) and its cultivar 'Crispum' (bottom left)

Danaë racemosa

on the stem, early and deciduous, evergreen, leaflike branches, glossy green, 1.5 in. (4 cm) long and 1 in. (2.5 cm) wide; berries orange. Zones 6–9. Morning sun, LS to WS. Moist, well-drained soil. A great new architectural plant for winter gardens with evergreen "leaves" and bright berries. No garden should be without it.

Darmera peltata

Western North America. Flowers small, pink, in clusters on bare red stems, 3–4 ft. (0.9–1.2 m) tall; April–May; Rhizomatous, spreading; leaves umbrella-like, to 24 in. (60 cm) across, green, lobed; leaf stems stout, upright. Zones 6–9. Morning sun, LS to WS. Moist, boggy soils. A great accent plant near a water feature or as a background grouping in open woodlands. Very

large. It flowers very early before the leaves arise and late freezes may spoil the display. Still offered as *Peltiphyllum peltatum*.

'**Nana**', a dwarf form to 24 in. (60 cm) in height, has much smaller leaves, 9–12 in. (23–30 cm) across, with flowers smaller accordingly. Excellent for adding bold leaf texture to smaller gardens.

Dennstaedtia punctilobula
Hayscented fern

Eastern North America. Fronds to 30 in. (75 cm), produced singly or in groups directly from the rhizome; deciduous, rhizomatous; leaves green, to 16 in. (40 cm) long and 8 in. (20 cm) wide, divided into shiny yellowish wedge-shaped, opposite leaflets; subleaflets numerous. Zones 3–9. LS to FS. Moist, acidic soil. This fern has a fresh,

Darmera peltata 'Nana'

Dennstaedtia punctilobula

Dicentra canadensis

shiny yellowish green color that brightens the woodland garden. It grows and spreads fast in the border so must be watched.

Dicentra canadensis
Squirrel corn

North America. Flowers fragrant, white, petals heart-shaped, inflated spurs, on leafless stalk to 12 in. (30 cm) tall; April–May; rhizomatous; leaves basal, triangular, divided into bluish green, elliptic, lobed leaflets. Zones 4–7. LS to FS. Moist, acidic soil. This ephemeral, summer-dormant species nevertheless makes a wonderful spring display. Plant with more lasting companions (see photo on page 50).

Dicentra chrysantha
Golden eardrops

California. Similar in habit to *Dicentra canadensis*, except flowers many, to 75, yellow, with pungent odor; July–September; much larger, to 5 ft. (1.5 m). Zones 7–8. LS to MS. Moist, acidic soil. Late, yellow flowers for southern and western gardens only.

Dicentra cucullaria
Dutchman's breeches

North America. Similar in habit and culture to *Dicentra canadensis*, except flowers not fragrant, white, resembling "inverted Dutchman's breeches" on stalks to 16 in. (40 cm) tall; April–May; rootstock a cluster of pink oval tubers; leaves basal, pale bluish green, divided into elliptic, deeply lobed, incised leaflets. Referred to as Dutchman's breeches for the shape of the beautiful and unusual white flower. Larger than *D. canadensis*, it also becomes summer-dormant.

Dicentra eximia
Turkey corn

Eastern North America. Flowers 4–40, deep pink, not fragrant, with heart-shaped inflated spurs, inner ones tipped red (the "blood drop"), hanging from arching stalks to 24 in. (60 cm); April–May; clumping, rhizomatous; leaves basal, to 10, triangular, divided into grayish green beneath, elliptic leaflets. Zones 4–7. LS to FS. Moist, acidic soil. A native and the best bleeding heart, this species closely resembles the popular Asian

Dicentra eximia

Dicentra spectabilis. This eastern native is best for the shady garden because it does not go summer dormant like the other natives and provides intermittent late flowering. It is good in northern and southern gardens. *Dicentra formosa* (western bleeding heart) is the western counterpart of this eastern species but is not as heat tolerant. They look alike so make inquiries as to origin before purchasing.

'**Adrian Bloom**', a darker-flowered (almost ruby-red) seedling of 'Bountiful' with a longer bloom period; red-tinted stems; medium green leaves; clumping.

'**Alba**', creamy white flowers with light green leaves.

'**Aurora**', flowers white, larger than the type; grayish green leaves; spreading, rhizomatous.

'**Bacchanal**', crimson-red flowers, larger than the species.

'**Bountiful**', purplish pink flowers, much larger than the species, flowering spring and later in summer; red-tinted stems; medium green leaves; clump-forming.

'**Coldham**', burgundy flowers; fernlike bluish leaves.

'**Luxuriant**', flowers red, much larger than the species; medium green leaves; spreading, rhizomatous.

'**Margery Fish**', pure white flowers, much larger than the species; finely divided bluish gray-green leaves.

'**Pearl Drops**' ('Langtrees'), flowers white tinted pink, much larger than the species; silvery gray-green leaves; vigorously spreading, rhizomatous. A choice cultivar.

'**Silversmith**', very light creamy white flowers flushed pink; leaves bluish green; clump-forming. Considered an improved 'Alba'.

'**Snowflakes**', flowers very white.

'**Spring Morning**', deep pink flowers, late-flowering; leaves medium to dark green; clump-forming.

'**Stewart Boothman**' ('Boothman's Variety'), deep pink flowers; vigorous, spreading.

'**Sweetheart**', snow-white flowers.

'**Zestful**', long-lasting deep rose flowers; grayish green leaves.

Dicentra scandens

Himalaya to western China. Flowers many, hanging on leafless, arching stalks, yellow or white; April–October; veining, climbing; terminal leaves with tendrils. Zones 6–8. Some sun, LS to WS. Moist, acidic soil. The only climbing bleeding heart in commerce, it is a most floriferous species and blooms from spring until autumn. A vigorous plant and quite tolerant of hot summers.

'**Athens Yellow**' offers hundreds of yellow flowers in everblooming succession; it is a climbing plant for the fence row or trellis.

Dicentra spectabilis
Bleeding heart

Northern East Asia. Flowers and leaves as in *Dicentra eximia*, except to 4 ft. (1.2 m) tall. Zones 3–7. Some sun, LS to WS. Moist, acidic soil. The flowers are larger than those of most native species. It forms a sizable clump of fernlike grayish green leaves but is also summer-dormant. Holds up better in northern gardens.

'**Alba**', white flowers.

'**Gold Heart**', yellow leaves and pink flowers.

'**Pantaloons**', more vigorous than the type.

'**Rosea**', deep pink flowers.

Diphylleia cymosa
Umbrella leaf

Eastern North America. Flowers small, white, in dense clusters above the leaves; May–June; clumping; leafstalks, red, 24–38 in. (60–95 cm) tall; leaves umbrella-like, to 24 in. (60 cm) across, green, deeply cleft along the centerline, lobed; berries

Dicentra scandens 'Athens Yellow'

Dicentra spectabilis

Dicentra spectabilis 'Gold Heart'

Diphylleia cymosa

Disporopsis arisanensis

large, blue. Zones 7–8. Some sun, LS to WS. Moist, acidic soil. A great accent plant near a water feature or as a background grouping in open woodlands. It requires deep shade and lots of moisture and grows well with moisture-loving ferns.

Var. *grayi*, from Japan, is very similar but smaller.

Disporopsis arisanensis

Taiwan. Flowers white, lobe tips purplish, bell-shaped, 0.5 in. (1 cm) long, in the leaf axils; May–June; rhizomatous, spreading; stems arching, to 8 in. (20 cm) tall; leaves shiny green, alternate, to 2 in. (5 cm) long, elliptic; berries dark blue. Zones 7–8. Some sun, LS to WS. Moist, fertile, acidic soil. An elegant, evergreen woodlander for southern gardens. Evergreen during mild winters in zone 7a and so a valuable plant in the garden.

Disporopsis fusca-picta

China. Similar in habit and culture to *Disporopsis arisanensis*, except much larger; stem height of 18 in. (45 cm), leaves to 4 in. (10 cm) long. A striking addition to a shady garden that will make a tight groundcover in time. Sometimes sold as

Disporopsis pernyi

D. arisanensis. Evergreen during mild winters but removal of the old stems will allow observation of the bright, new shoots (see photo on page 18).

Disporopsis pernyi

China. Flowers white, fragrant, 0.8 in. (2 cm) long, bell-shaped, in the leaf axils; May–July; rhizomatous, spreading; stems arching, to 18 in. (45 cm) tall, leaves evergreen, alternate, shiny dark green, 4–6 in. (10–15 cm) long, lance-shaped; berries dark blue. Zones 6–8. Some sun, LS to WS. Moist, fertile, acidic soil. A Chinese species long known to gardeners. Its glossy, evergreen leaves make it an outstanding garden plant and it contributes well to a multitextured garden scene.

Disporum cantoniense
Thai fairy bell

Southeastern Asia. Flowers variable, white, pink, red, or purple, 0.5–1 in. (1–2.5 cm) long, bell-shaped, in groups of three to seven, in the leaf axils; May–July; rhizomatous, spreading; stems erect varying heights, to 6 ft. (1.8 m), many-branched; leaves lance-shaped, glossy green, to 5 in. (13 cm) long; berries bluish black, sometimes red. Zones 7–8. Some sun, LS to MS. Moist, fertile, acidic soil. These differing Asian fairy bells are becoming great garden plants. Several subspecies have been imported and are evergreen in zone 7, but become herbaceous in colder regions. The many-branched, taller forms clothed with glossy, green leaves confer great architectural garden value (see photo on page 23).

'Aureovariegatum' has glossy, yellow-streaked leaves on sturdy stems to 36 in. (90 cm), and white flowers.

Var. *cantoniense*, collected in northern Thailand, has deep rose-red flowers and makes a great addition to gardens.

'Green Giant' has huge stems to 10 ft. (3 m).

'Night Heron' has purplish leaves.

Disporum flavens
Korean fairy bells

Korea. Similar in habit and culture to *Disporum cantoniense*, except flowers yellow and stems to 36 in. (90 cm) tall; berries black. Hardier, to zone 6.

Disporum cantoniense with purple blooms

Disporum flavens

Disporum languinosum
Yellow mandarin

Eastern North America. Flowers yellow, to 0.5 in. (1 cm) long, tubular, in groups of three or four; May–June; rhizomatous, spreading; stems erect but leaning, downy, to 24 in. (60 cm), branched, with ovate, green leaves to 5 in. (13 cm) long, shiny above and downy beneath; red berries. Zones 5–8. LS to MS. Moist, fertile, acidic soil. A favorite native species that has been planted in gardens for a long time. Its attractive yellow, spidery flower petals followed by red-orange, oblong fruit makes it a good garden plant. Use in groups for best effect.

Disporum sessile
Japanese fairy bells

Japan. Flowers green-tipped white, 1 in. (2.5 cm) long, bell-shaped, in umbels of 1 to 3; May–June; rhizomatous, vigorously spreading; stems erect, branched, to 24 in. (60 cm) tall; leaves lance-shaped, matte dark green, to 4 in. (10 cm) long; berries black. Zones 5–8. LS to MS. Moist, fertile, acidic soil. The typical all-green species is rarely seen. Its white-variegated sport has found world-wide acceptance in gardens. The variegation is quite changeable and the plants spread aggressively via underground rhizomes. Due to this plant's great garden value, a little straying afield is welcome in most gardens. Occasionally offered as a selection of *Disporum pullum*.

'Chigger', a dwarf form to 3 in. (8 cm) tall, with central yellow stripe.

'Cricket', leaves white-centered.

Subsp. *flavens*, with yellow flowers.

Var. *inobeanum*, a dwarf form.

Var. *stenophyllum*, yellow and white variegated forms are available.

'Variegatum'. Variegated fairy bell. A white-margined sport of the type. Offered in narrow- and wide-leaved forms.

Disporum smilacinum

Japan, Korea, China. Flowers white, 0.5 in. (1 cm) long, expanded bell-shaped, starry, solitary, rarely 2; May–June; rhizomatous, spreading; stems erect, branched, 6–10 in. (15–25 cm) tall; leaves elliptic, shiny dark green, small; berries bluish

Disporum languinosum

Disporum sessile 'Variegatum'

black. Zones 5–8. LS to MS. Moist, fertile, acidic soil. The typical all-green form has wide-ranging rhizomes which expand slowly to make a dense groundcover. Its fairly large, white flowers contribute to its garden value. Many variegated forms are known.

'Aureovariegatum' has glossy leaves with dazzling yellow stripes and a yellow tip in spring; later in the season the variegation becomes creamy white. Long used in Japanese gardens, it makes a lovely groundcover or accent group.

'Dai Setsurei' ("large snow mountain") has green leaves with white stripes.

'Ginga' ("milky way") has whitish leaves with green flecks and spotting.

'Kinkaku' ("golden pavillion") has yellow leaves streaked green.

'Ki-no-Tsukasa' ("yellow chief") has a yellow margin and yellow streaks growing from the tip into a green leaf.

'Kinsho' ("golden wing") has yellow leaves with delicate green stripes.

'Seiki-no-Homare' ("pride of the century") is similar to 'Kinkaku' but with more yellow in the leaf.

Dracunculus vulgaris
Dragon arum
Asia Minor. Spathe large, 24–36 in. (60–90 cm) long, pale green outside, purple inside, spadix erect, long, shiny black, foul-smelling; June–July; tuberous; leaves fan-shaped, segmented, 6–8 in. (15–20 cm) long, dark green, with whitish markings, flowerstalk to 5 ft. (1.5 m). Zones 7–8. LS to MS. Moist, fertile, well-drained soil, dry in summer. A conversation plant and while in bloom not for those with sensitive noses. It nevertheless fills the craving for weird plants some shade gardeners have and its large, unusual leaves provide color and texture until midsummer.

Dryopteris clintoniana
Clinton's wood fern
Eastern North America. Fronds to 38 in. (95 cm) tall and 8 in. (20 cm) wide, with long tapering tips; in bundles on slender blackish stalks, erect, slightly leaning; leaves evergreen, composed of 10 to 15 pairs of lance-shaped, light green leaflets, 3–5 in. (8–13 cm) long; subleaflets deeply cut and lobed. Zones 4–6. LS to FS. Moist, fertile, soil. A vigorous evergreen fern that requires moisture during dry periods. Best for northern gardens. It needs a sheltered spot that protects the tall fronds from being laid flat by winds.

Dryopteris dilatata
Broad buckler fern
North America, Eurasia, South Africa. Fronds deciduous to 12 to 38 in. (30–95 cm) long and 4–15 in. (10–38 cm) wide, in rosettes on slender, brown stalks, erect, slightly leaning; leaves composed of 10 to 15 pairs of lance-shaped, dark green leaflets, 3–5 in. (8–13 cm) long; subleaflets deeply cut, lobed, and toothed. Zones 4–6. LS to FS. Moist, fertile, soil. A large, vigorous, but deciduous garden fern. Many cultivars with crested and forked fronds are available.

'Crispa Whiteside' ('Crispa'), crisped fronds; to 16 in. (40 cm).

'Grandiceps', fronds with large, terminal crests; to 20 in. (50 cm).

'Lepidota', leaflets with very thin segments giving lacy appearance.

'Lepidota Cristata', leaflets crested, appearing forked.

'Standishii', leaflets very narrow, open appearance; to 16 in. (40 cm).

Dryopteris erythrosora
Autumn fern
Eastern Asia. Fronds evergreen, coppery red when young, turning dark green, to 38 in. (95 cm) tall and 12 in. (30 cm) wide, in vase-shaped bundles on slender, glossy, reddish brown stalks; erect, leaning; leaves composed of 8 to 20 pairs of lance-shaped, shiny dark green leaflets to 3–8 in. (8–20 cm) long; subleaflets deeply cut, lobed, and toothed. Zones 5–9. LS to FS. Moist, fertile, soil. A most outstanding, slow-growing, but robust, evergreen fern that can withstand all kinds of weather, including long periods of heat and drought. Placement in medium to full shade is helpful in hot summer areas. More hardy than originally thought, it

Disporum smilacinum 'Aureovariegatum' late in the season

Dracunculus vulgaris

Dryopteris dilatata

Dryopteris erythrosora

has been seen in zone 5 gardens and is indispensable for northern and southern gardens (see photo on page 141).

'Gracilis' is a highly decorative selection of the species.

'Purpurascens' offers very red to purple coloration.

Dryopteris filix-mas
Male fern

Cosmopolitan in northern temperate region. Fronds deciduous, 3–5 ft. (0.9–1.5 m) tall and to 20 in. (50 cm) wide; in vase-shaped bundles on slender brown stalks, erect, slightly leaning; leaves composed of 16 to 30 lance-shaped pairs of leaflets, usually dark green above, lighter green beneath, to 3 to 8 in. (8–20 cm) long; subleaflets lobed and toothed. Zones 2–8. LS to FS. Moist, fertile, soil. One of the most common ferns seen and an extremely variable species with many named cultivars. The fronds are deciduous, but in southern climates turn to bright yellow

Dryopteris filix-mas

color as late autumn approaches so contribute to autumn gardens. One of the most cold hardy ferns. Many cultivars with crested and forked fronds are available.

'Barnesii', tall with very narrow fronds, the leaflets tilted forward with the subleaflets overlapped, giving a crisped appearance; to 40 in. (1 m) long and 6 in. (15 cm) wide.

'Crispa', crisped fronds of overlapping leaflets and subleaflets.

'Crispa Cristata', fronds crisped and crested; 12–20 in. (30–50 cm).

'Crispa Jackson', a tall large-crested form; to 32 in. (80 cm).

'Crispa Martindale', a small-crested form with curving leaflets.

'Cristata'. English crested male fern, king of the male fern. The original crested male fern, with crests on the tips of the leaflets only. Now surpassed by cultivars that are more crested and branched.

'Furcans', like the typical species but with leaflets divided at the tip.

'Grandiceps Willis', multibranched with tasseled terminal crests.

'Incisa', a huge, vigorous selection of the type, to 5 ft. (1.5 m), with fronds to 16 in. (40 cm) wide and narrow leaflets to 1.5 in. (4 cm) wide with long, narrowing tips, incised and cleft.

'Linearis', very narrow, crisped, with finely divided leaflets.

'Lux-lunea', terminal crests and variegated leaflets; to 20 in. (50 cm).

Dryopteris goldiana
Goldie's fern

Eastern North America. Fronds deciduous, to 4 ft. (1.2 m) tall and 12 in. (30 cm) wide, in bundles on slender tan stalks, erect, slightly leaning; leaves, composed of 12 to 16 pairs of lance-shaped, shiny dark green, later bronze-tinted, leathery leaflets, 4–6 in. (10–15 cm) long, backwards tilting; subleaflets deeply cut and toothed. Zones 3–8. LS to FS. Moist, fertile, soil. This vigorous species is the giant of the native North American wood ferns. It is evergreen and large and can be easily recognized by its backward-tiling leaflets. In southern gardens it requires supplemental moisture during dry periods, but once established it is a long-lasting garden fern for the background and in a shrub border. Very cold hardy.

Dryopteris ludoviciana
Southern wood fern

Southeastern North America. Fronds evergreen, to 4 ft. (1.2 m) tall and 10 in. (25 cm) wide, in a row on slender beige stalks erect, slightly leaning; leaves composed of 10 to 15 pairs of shiny dark green leathery, leaflets, fertile in the upper half of the frond with the subleaflets longer, sterile in the lower half with subleaflets shorter, wider. Zones 7–8. LS to FS. Moist, fertile, soil. A good fern for southern gardens as long as soil moisture is available.

Dryopteris marginalis
Marginal wood fern

North America. Fronds evergreen to 36 in. (90 cm) tall and 10 in. (25 cm) wide, in rosettes on stalk, light green, leaning, very scaly at base; leaves composed of 14 to 22 pairs of opposite, lance-shaped, shiny bluish green above and lighter green beneath, leathery leaflets, fertile in the upper half, sterile below, 2–6 in. (5–15 cm) long; subleaflets deeply cut; spore cases at the margin. Zones 3–8. LS to FS. Moist, fertile, soil, but very adaptable to acid or alkaline, light or even heavy soils. One of the best garden ferns, it is a vigorous evergreen with a large, knobby, aboveground crown of tightly rolled-up fronds. Its bluish green color and leathery substance make it an ideal, long-lived, evergreen fern. Not bothered by hot and dry summers, it is good in northern and southern gardens.

Dryopteris marginalis with hostas

Dryopteris sieboldii

Eomecon chionantha

Dryopteris sieboldii
Siebold's fern

Southern Japan. Fronds evergreen to 30 in. (75 cm) long and 20 in. (50 cm) wide, bending down in a row on slender stalks; evergreen leaves composed of three to five pairs of entire, sickle-shaped in outline, lobed, leathery, lance-shaped leaflets, fertile in the upper half of the frond, sterile lower, 6–10 in. (15–25 cm) long, dark verdigris-green above, lighter beneath, covered with felty hair. Zones 6–8. LS to FS. Moist, fertile, soil. This unusual fern fools some people into believing it is not a fern due to its leathery leaves with their smooth margins. Place along a path where all can comers can view it and where it is guaranteed to be a conversation plant (see photo on page 95).

Eomecon chionantha
Snow poppy

Eastern China. Flowers white, shallowly bell-shaped, to 2 in. (5 cm), yellow centers, in small groups on branched flowerstalk to 16 in. (40 cm) tall; May–June; rhizomatous, quickly spreading; leaf stems green, upright, 10–12 in. (25–30 cm) tall; leaves leathery, grayish green, kidney-shaped, to 6 in. (15 cm) long; sap orange-red, pungent. Zones 7–9. Sun to WS. Moist, fertile, well-drained soil. A charming runner, this poppy can be potentially very invasive. In a large container placed on the patio or out in the garden it shows off its beautiful blooms for weeks in early spring. The crown of gray-green leaves adds to the summer display. Not recommend in the ground for small gardens.

Epimedium franchetii

EPIMEDIUM

Cultivation for all species and cultivars is similar. Zones 5–9. Some sun to WS. Moist, fertile, well-drained soil. Rhizomatous, slowly spreading unless clumping is indicated. Cut old leaves in late winter, before flowers and new leaves emerge.

Epimedium franchetii

China. Flowers to 1.5 in. (4 cm), bicolored red to brownish red with yellow; with spurs; leaves divided into lance-shaped, evergreen leaflets, emerging bronze, later turning medium to dark green; 12–18 in. (30–45 cm) tall, clumping. This floriferous species has up to 20 flowers per stem, held above the leaves.

Epimedium grandiflorum
Bishop's hat

China, Korea, Japan. Flowers 2–3 in. (5–8 cm), with long spurs to 1 in. (2.5 cm) long, bicolored rose-colored with white; leaves divided into deciduous leaflets, reddish coppery when young, later light green, spiny; to 12 in. (30 cm) tall. One

of the best-known epimediums and outstanding for its large flowers with very long spurs. Many cultivars in the *Epimedium grandiflorum* complex produce a second flush of taller leaves after flowering. Consult catalogs for the latest listings.

Subsp. *coelestre* is a large form with light to greenish yellow flowers produced above the leaves. Zone 3.

'**Crimson Beauty**', dark red flowers with white-tipped spurs, leaves tinted dark bronze in spring.

'**Elfenkönigin**' ('Queen of Elfs'), large white flowers with long, white spurs, to 2 in. (5 cm); vigorous.

'**Harold Epstein**', a selection of subsp. *koreanum*, has very large bright yellow flowers and forms a large clump.

Subsp. *higoense* is usually small, even diminutive, with much smaller white flowers above the leaves. The leaflets are neatly margined with dark green on a light field in spring.

'**Koji**', dwarf with deep lavender flowers.

Subsp. *koreanum* is among the largest garden epimediums and has many selections, with

Epimedium ×perralchicum 'Frohnleiten'

yellow or greenish yellow flowers on a mound with bright green leaves.

'**La Rocaille**', a selection of subsp. *koreanum*, has very large yellow flowers and arrow-shaped leaves; it spreads vigorously and is tall, to 16 in. (40 cm).

'**Lilafee**' ('Lilac Fairy'), dark lilac flowers, purple-tinted leaves in spring.

'**Nanum**', dwarf with white flowers.

'**Queen Esta**', dark lavender flowers, purple-tinted leaves in spring.

'**Red Queen**', vivid rose-red flowers, large, to 14 in. (35 cm).

'**Rose Dwarf**', dark rose-pink flowers, lance-shaped leaflets.

'**Saxton Purple**', purplish red flowers; leaves tinted bronze in spring.

'**Silver Queen**', silvery white flowers with long spurs.

'**Sirius**', rose-pink flowers above bright, light green leaflets.

'**Violaceum**', dark violet flowers with white-tipped spurs, leaves tinted dark bronze in spring.

'**White Queen**', very large white flowers with long, white spurs, to 2 in. (5 cm), leaves tinted dark bronze in spring.

'**Yubae**' ('Rose Queen'), dark rose-pink flowers with white-tipped spurs, leaves tinted dark bronze in spring.

Epimedium ×perralchicum

Garden hybrid (*Epimedium perralderianum* × *E. pinnatum* subsp. *colchicum*). Flowers to 1 in. (2.5 cm), bright yellow on short stems; leaves evergreen, divided; to 16 in. (40 cm) tall.

'**Frohnleiten**', flowers to 2.5 in. (6 cm), bright lemon-yellow, held on 16-in. (40-cm) stems, leaves divided into evergreen, heart-shaped, lobed leaflets, mottled reddish pink when young, later dark, glossy green, spiny along wavy margin; to 12 in. (30 cm) tall. Outstanding garden plant.

'**Wisley**', huge flowers to 3 in. (8 cm) across, bright yellow, spurs tinged reddish or brownish, held on stems to 16 in. (40 cm) tall. Luxurious foliage.

Epimedium pubigerum

Eastern Balkans, northern Turkey, southern Caucasus. Flowers to 1.5 in. (4 cm), creamy white to pale yellow; above the leaves; leaves divided into ovate, heart-shaped medium green, shiny leaflets, evergreen, leathery; to 10 in. (25 cm) tall. Drought-resistant; floriferous, to 30 flowers per stem.

Epimedium ×versicolor

Garden hybrid (*Epimedium grandiflorum* × *E. pinnatum* subsp. *colchicum*). Flowers to 0.8 in. (2 cm), bicolored bright red to orange with yellow, with spurs; leaves divided into heart-shaped, ovate, evergreen leaflets, flushed with bronze in spring, later medium green, spiny; to 12 in. (30 cm) tall. LS to MS.

'Cupreum', coppery red flowers.

'Neosulphureum', bright yellow flowers.

'Sulphureum', larger, vigorous, darker yellow flowers, longer spurs, leaflets speckled brown. Also sold under the name *Epimedium macranthum* var. *sulphureum*.

'Versicolor', reddish orange flowers fading to a very pale salmon; leaflets green blotched red in spring, green later; vigorous.

Epimedium ×youngianum

Garden hybrid (*Epimedium diphyllum* × *E. grandiflorum*). Flowers to 0.75 in. (2 cm), with or without spurs, from white to rose, some to purple; leaves divided into narrowly ovate deciduous leaflets, flushed with reddish pink in spring, later medium green, toothed, wavy margins; to 20 in. (50 cm) tall.

'Azusa', larger, flowers white with long spurs; silvery on top of leaves.

'Beni Kuyaku', flowers rose-red.

'John Gallagher', flowers pale rose.

'Merlin', flowers purple, held above foliage.

'Milky Way', flowers pure white, with long spurs; leaves silvery on top.

'Niveum' flowers pure white, sometimes spurred; purple-tinted leaves in spring. Also sold under the name *Epimedium macranthum* var. *niveum*.

'Pink Blush', flowers whitish, distinctly flushed rose-pink; a dainty plant, not more than 6 in. (15 cm) in height.

'Roseum', flowers pale violet to very pale purple.

'Yenomoto' has the largest white flowers; the inner sepals and spurs are very long.

Epimedium pubigerum

Epimedium ×versicolor 'Sulphureum' as a groundcover

Epimedium ×youngianum 'Milky Way'

Erythronium americanum showing fully recurved sepals and petals

Farfugium japonicum 'Crispata'

Erythronium americanum
Yellow trout lily

Eastern North America. Flowers 1.5 in. (4 cm), solitary, bright sulfur-yellow inside, brownish purple outside on stem 4–10 in. (10–25 cm) tall; February–May; summer-dormant; leaves elliptic, basal, erect, shiny dark green mottled brownish red, 3–8 in. (8–20 cm). Zones 3–7. Some sun, LS. Constantly moist soil a must. Best for northern gardens. Used as annuals in southern gardens.

Farfugium japonicum
Leopard plant

Eastern Asia. Flowers daisylike, light yellow, 1.5–2 in. (4–5 cm) across; 6–14 in clusters on multibranched flowerstalks, green with white woolly coating, 18–28 in. (45–70 cm) tall; September–November; clumping, to 24 in. (60 cm) wide and 18 in. (45 cm) high; leaves basal, large, 8–12 in. (20–30 cm), rounded, kidney-shaped, dark green to grayish green, glossy, atop erect, green leaf stems, coated with a white, woolly covering. Zones 7–8. LS to MS. Moist, fertile, well-drained soil. The green, typical species should be grown more widely as it makes a handsome groundcover or accent plant. It looks great among ferns and astilbes and its other uses are similar to those of hostas. Evergreen during mild winters in zone 7.

'Argentea' ('Albovariegata', 'Variegata', 'White Wonder'), white-variegated in a more pie-shaped than mottled or marginal pattern; each leaf is different.

'Aureomaculata' ('Kimon'). Leopard ligularia, leopard plant. The classic yellow-spotted leopard plant. The spots are randomly placed and variously sized. Seedlings raised from this cultivar are occasionally variegated, but many revert to the all green type.

'Crispata' ('Cristata', 'Chirimen'). Parsley ligularia. A particularly interesting green form that has ruffled and crisped margins, reminiscent of fancy parsley. Also sold as 'Shishi' ("lion").

'Green Dragon'. Dragon ligularia. Leaves grotesquely deformed—what the Japanese consider a dragon (*ryu*) form.

'Izumo Chirimen' has irregular patches or sectors of cream and white.

'Kagami Jishi', leaves variegated like 'Aureomaculata' and margined like 'Crispata' but deeply lobed.

'Kimon Chirimen', a hybrid between 'Aureomaculata' and 'Crispata', showing characteristics of both.

'Kinkan' ("corona"), leaves with a thin, uniform yellow margin; described as a gold-ring type.

'Ryuto' ("dragon's head"), leaves grotesquely deformed.

'Yaezaki', leaves green, flowers double.

'Yaezaki Hoshifu', leaves like 'Aureomaculata', flowers double.

Farfugium japonicum 'Argentea'

Farfugium japonicum 'Aureomaculata' (left) and typical species (right)

Farfugium japonicum 'Green Dragon'

Farfugium reniforme

Galax urceolata in bloom

Farfugium reniforme

Southeast Asia. Habit and culture similar to *Farfugium japonicum*, except the leaves are large, thick, and glossy dark green, to 18 in. (45 cm) in diameter, kidney-shaped, smooth-margined. This large and attractive species tolerates some sun. It grows larger than *F. japonicum* and makes a bold, tropical-looking accent plant (see photo on page 2).

Galax urceolata
Beetleweed

Eastern North America. Flowers many, tiny, white, in a spikelike cluster on a green, leafless, upright flowerstalk to 32 in. (80 cm); May–June; rhizomatous; evergreen leaves are basal, large, 2–4 in. (5–10 cm), rounded, heart- or kidney-shaped, dark green, glossy, toothed margin. Zones 5–8. LS to MS. Moist, fertile, well-drained, acidic soil. A superb native groundcover with lovely, long-lasting flower spikes. Flowering increases in locations with some sun exposure, but the species flowers reliably in medium shade. Moisture is imperative during spring when the flower stem elongates; any drying during this time may abort flowering. After setting seed, the species is very drought tolerant and survives long, dry late summer periods.

Galium odoratum
Sweet woodruff

Eurasia to Siberia. Flowers many, tiny, white, fragrant, star-shaped in clusters; June–July; rhizomatous, vigorously spreading; to 18 in. (45 cm) high; leaves emerald-green, arranged in whorls, 1.5 in. (4 cm) long, 0.5 in. (1 cm) wide. Zones 5–8. LS to MS. Any moist, well-drained soil. A nice creeping groundcover with many clusters of white, star-shaped flowers and a dense, green cover of equally star-shaped leaves. Best for cool summer areas, but given lots of moisture and shade it can succeed in southern gardens.

Gentiana andrewsii
Closed gentian

Eastern North America. Flowers in tight clusters, bottlelike, closed, dark blue, sometimes white, 1–1.5 in. (2.5–4 cm) long, on erect stems 12–24

Galium odoratum

Gentiana andrewsii

in. (30–60 cm) tall; August–October; herbaceous, clumping; basal leaves in a rosette, stem leaves in opposite pairs and in a whorl at the top, 2–4 in. (5–10 cm) long, dark green, lance-shaped to oblong, stalkless. Zones 4–7. LS to WS. Always moist soil. This native gentian is easily grown in moist woodland shade in southern gardens and in some sun and light shade in northern gardens. Soil moisture must be maintained during dry periods. The unusual, closed "bottle" flowers always attract attention and last for weeks.

Geranium endressii
Endress's cranesbill
Europe. Flowers many, pink, petals notched, darker veins, trumpet-shaped, 1–1.5 in. (2.5–4 cm) long, above the leaves, on stems 12–18 in. (30–45 cm); June–September or later; rhizomatous, spreading; evergreen leaves green, 2–6 in. (5–15 cm) long, 5-lobed, and again divided and unevenly toothed. Zones 4–7. LS to WS. Any moist soil. Flowers appear over a long period, and the leaves make a dense groundcover. Good plant for dry shade in southern gardens and for more sun in northern gardens. Seeds around.

'Wargrave Pink' ('Wargrave Variety') is taller than the species and has salmon-pink flowers and petals more deeply notched; to 24 in. (60 cm).

Geranium maculatum
Wild geranium
Eastern North America. Flowers shallowly bowl-shaped, lavender to rose-purple, sometimes white, 1–1.5 in. (2.5–4 cm) across, in loose clusters above the leaves; April–June; rhizomatous, 12–24 in. (30–60 cm) tall; leaves 4–5 in. (10–13 cm) wide, grayish green, spotted, deeply toothed lobes. Zones 4–8. LS to WS. Any moist, well-drained to dry soil. The native wild cranesbill is well suited for moist woodland shade south and some sun and light shade north. It self-sows abundantly. Heat tolerant in southern gardens.

'Album' has white flowers, sometimes with a very pale pinkish cast.

Geranium renardii
Eastern Europe to the Caucasus. A widely available species in commerce as improved cultivars. Summer-flowering. Best in dry shade in southern gardens, more sun in northern gardens.

Geranium endressii 'Wargrave Pink'

Geranium renardii 'Terra Franche' (Tony Avent)

Gillenia trifoliata

Goodyera pubescens

Hakonechloa macra
'Aureola'

'Terra Franche', flowers violet, leaves fuzzy, deeply lobed, grayish green.

'Whiteknights' flowers white with a pale lavender background hue and dark lilac veins in early summer; leaves grayish green, deeply lobed.

Gillenia trifoliata
Bowman's root

Eastern North America. Flowers in open clusters above the leaves, white or pinkish, to 1.5 in. (4 cm) across, star-shaped; May–July; rhizomatous, 24–36 in. (60–90 cm) high; leaves 3-parted, green, toothed, to 4 in. (10 cm) long. Zones 4–7. LS to MS. Dry and moist, well-drained soils. A native that deserves to be grown more in gardens. Its white or pinkish flowers are produced on a graceful and dainty stalk. It adapts easily to different soil conditions. Occasionally offered under its synonym *Porteranthus trifoliatus*.

Goodyera pubescens
Downy rattlesnake plantain

North America. Flowers very small, green, insignificant, upright flower spikes; June–August; leaves evergreen, in a basal rosette, 3–4 in. (8–10 cm) long, dark grayish green with conspicuous network of silvery white principal veins and narrower cross veins. Zones 6–8. MS to FS. Moist, gritty, well-drained, acidic soil. Attractive four-season beauties for gardens without snow cover. For best effect, plant in groups, up close, and in a prominent spot to reveal its beauty. Expands into large colonies in time.

Hakonechloa macra
Hakone grass

Japan. Flowers and seedpods terminal, in loose, irregular clusters; culms wiry, smooth, green, arching, 20–26 in. (50–65 cm) long, leaf blades 6–12 in. (25–30 cm) long, to 0.6 in. (1.5 cm) wide, linear lance-shaped, light to medium green; rhizomatous, slowly expanding, 12–16 in. (30–40 cm) tall. Zones 5–8. Some sun, LS to WS. Moist soil. A graceful, elegant grass for a multitude of uses in shady gardens. It makes a spectacular accent plant. The leaf blades remain on the plant and provide winter interest.

'Alboaurea', leaf blades striped with ivory-white and some yellow; little green.

'Albovariegata' is similar but with no yellow in the leaves.

'Aureola', leaf blades mostly bright yellow, with a few thin, green stripes; excellent in nothern and southern gardens (see photo on page 194).

Helleborus argutifolius
Corsican hellebore

Mediterranean. Flowers many, light green, bowl-shaped, facing down, to 2 in. (5 cm); December–May; evergreen; overwintering flowerstalks to 4 ft. (1.2 m) tall and 36 in. (90 cm) wide; leaves divided into shiny dark green, leathery, spiny margined leaflets, 3–8 in. (8–20 cm) long. Zones 6–9. Sun, LS to MS. Neutral, dryish soil. An attractive, low-maintenance species that produces overwintering, leafy flowering stems and is evergreen. Marvelous winter interest in southern gardens.

'Janet Starnes' has shorter leaves that are attractively speckled whitish green.

Helleborus argutifolius

Helleborus cyclophyllus
Grecian hellebore

Balkans. Flowers faintly scented, green to yellowish green, saucer-shaped, facing down, 2–3 in. (5–8 cm) on stems 22 in. (55 cm) tall; January–April; deciduous, 16–18 in. (40–45 cm) tall and wide; leaves basal, divided into light green, conspicuously veined, leathery leaflets, the two outer leaflets divided again into leaflike lobes with finely toothed margins. Zones 6–9. Sun, LS to MS. Neutral, dryish soil. Deciduous, but with great leaf interest. Very heat-tolerant once established.

Helleborus foetidus
Stinking hellebore

Europe. Flowers many, to 48, pale green, bell-shaped, drooping, in clusters on erect, over-wintering stems to 32 in. (80 cm) tall; December–April; leaves evergreen, divided into first light then darker or grayish green, leathery, shiny leaflets, the two outer leaflets divided again into leaflike, lance-shaped lobes; leaves slightly fetid when crushed. Zones 6–9. Sun, LS to MS. Heat

tolerant. A variable species that colonizes by seed. One of the best species for the garden. In mild winter areas it begins flowering in early December, carrying on until May.

'Bowles' Form', leaves more finely divided; plant larger and vigorous.

'Green Giant', plant taller.

'Green Gnome' ('Sierra Nevada Form'), a dwarf to 8 in. (20 cm) tall.

'Italian Form', like 'Bowles' Form' but more floriferous.

'Miss Jekyll' ('Miss Jekyll's Scented Form'), flowers scented.

'Piccadilly', flowerstalks tinted red; leaves dark with grayish overlay.

'Ruth', leaves dark green, deeply cut, turning reddish in autumn.

'Sienna', leaves darker than the type.

'Sopron', leaves metallic, glossy dark green.

'Tros-os-Montes', flowers green; leaflets deeply serrated.

'Wester Flisk', flowers yellowish green, edged in reddish brown.

Helleborus cyclophyllus with hosta

Helleborus lividus

Mediterranean. Flowers green inside, flushed pinkish outside, bell-shaped, drooping, in clusters on erect, overwintering stems to 18 in. (46 cm) tall; December–April; leaves evergreen, divided into grayish green, leathery leaflets. Zones 6–9. Sun, LS to MS. Heat-tolerant and a variable species. Many offerings appear to be hybrids of *Helleborus argutifolius* × *H. lividus* (syn. *H.* ×*sternii*, which see).

Helleborus niger
Christmas rose

Alps. Flowers white with green center to 3.5 in. (9 cm) across, on purplish overwintering stems; December–March; 12 in. (30 cm) tall and wide; leaves divided into evergreen, dark green, leathery, shiny, leaflets. Zones 3–6. Sun, LS to MS. Neutral to alkaline dryish soil. A wonderful alpine hellebore that requires cool summers so is best in gardens from zone 6 north. This species produces some of the largest flowers.

Var. *angustifolius*, leaflets narrower, flowers smaller and white.

Blackthorn Group, flowers with pink buds, opening white, turning pink; stems dark.

'Flore Roseo', flowers pink.

'Foliis Variegatis', leaves variegated with cream in spring.

Var. *humilifolius*, leaves smaller on green stems, flowers larger.

Subsp. *macranthus*, flowers huge, to 4.5 in. (11 cm) across.

Helleborus foetidus

Helleborus lividus

'**Marion**', flowers double, with up to 25 petals.

Var. *oblongifolius*, a very long central leaflet that narrows abruptly toward its base.

'**Potter's Wheel**' ('Ladham's Variety'), flowers white with a green eye, large, 4–5 in. (10–13 cm) across; leaves very dark green.

'**Praecox**' (All-Saints-Day Christmas rose), flowers earlier.

Var. *stenopetalus*, lobes very narrow.

'**Trotter's Form**', flowers pure white, very long-lasting.

Helleborus odorus
Fragrant hellebore

Balkans, Greece. Flowers faintly scented, green, saucer-shaped, facing out, to 3 in. (8 cm), in clusters on overwintering stems; January–April; 16–18 in. (40–45 cm) tall and wide; leaves evergreen, basal, dark green, leathery, to 16 in. (40 cm) across, divided into leaflets, the two outer leaflets divided again into leaflike segments with toothed margins. Zones 6–8. Sun, LS to WS. Neutral to alkaline soil. An impressive hellebore with great leaf interest. Well worth growing.

Helleborus orientalis
Lenten rose

Balkans to the Caucasus. Flowers greenish white, to 3 in. (8 cm) across, on overwintering, branching stems, to 24 in. (60 cm) tall and 20 in. (50 cm) wide; leaves divided into dark green leaflets, leaflets again divided into segments. Zones 3–8. Sun, LS to MS. Any alkaline or acidic soil. The type and its subspecies are seldom available. Many hybrids under the names *Helleborus* ×*hybridus* or *H.* ×*orientalis* are widely available and very popular. Most are selected for flower color, but their nodding flower habit makes it hard to see the colors. Look for hybrids that show viewable color on the back of the flower. All of the named hybrids are of a stature similar to that of the typical species.

Subsp. *abchasicus*, flowers tinted with red.

'**Amethyst**', flowers mauve with dark edges; stems reddish purple.

'**Blowsy**', flowers creamy yellow.

'**Blue Spray**', flowers blackish purple; stems dark purplish green.

'**Citron**', flowers yellow outside with a rose-pink haze inside.

'**Dawn**', flowers pale, shiny pink, later turning coppery red.

'**Dusk**', flowers purple with blackish veins and speckles toward tips.

'**Eco Golden Eye**', flowers purple with darker veins.

'**Garnet**', flowers deep purplish red, veined darker purple.

'**Günter Jürgl**', flowers fully double, facing out, green with pink streaks on the back, pinkish speckled with darker pink inside, floriferous.

Subsp. *guttatus*, flowers white, spotted with red or purple.

Millet Hybrids, flowers white, pink, or red.

'**Nocturne**', flowers blackish purple, not opening flat.

'**Parrot**', flowers yellow, hanging down.

'**Queen of Night**', flowers nodding, deep purple, shiny on the back.

'**Snow Queen**', flowers fully double, white flushed green at the base.

'**Ushba**' ('Usba'), flowers smaller, pure white with off-white veins.

Helleborus ×*sternii*

Garden hybrid (*Helleborus argutifolius* × *H. lividus*). Flowers few, greenish, flushed with pink, on overwintering stems; December–April; clumping, of differing proportions; leaves grayish green, veins marked in greenish white, toothed, spiny margins or entire. Zones 6–9. Some sun, LS. Any alkaline soil. An extremely variable group of garden hybrids with a mixture of features resembling either one or the other parent. Of easy culture.

'**Blackthorn**' (Blackthorn Strain), flowers green flushed with pink on purple stems; leaves marbled with silvery gray, giving a smoky appearance; small.

'**Boughton Beauty**' (Boughton Beauty Strain), flowers green flushed with pink on purplish pink stems; leaves dark grayish green with conspicuous marbling; plants larger.

Helleborus odorus in bloom

Helleborus orientalis
(white-flowered form)

Helleborus ×*sternii*

Hepatica acutiloba
Sharp-lobed hepatica
Eastern North America. Flowers solitary on a stem, lavender, but also blue, pink, or white, sometimes purple, to 1 in. (2.5 cm); March–April; herbaceous, clumping; leaves green, to 3 in. (8 cm), lobed, with pointed tips. Zones 4–8. LS to FS. Any neutral to alkaline soil. In commerce several color varieties are offered. In the wild it hybridizes with the round-lobed *Hepatica americana*.

'Eco Royal Blue', flowers blue.

Hepatica americana
Round-lobed hepatica
Eastern North America. The widespread, native liverwort is similar in habit and culture to *Hepatica acutiloba*, except the leaves are lobed with rounded tips and it has fewer flowers, mostly pinkish blue, but also lavender or white. Also grows on acidic soils, where it usually has bluish flowers.

Hepatica maxima
Japan and Korea. Similar in habit and culture to *Hepatica acutiloba*, except it has very large, evergreen leaves to 4 in. (10 cm); flowers are light pink and less showy. Zones 6–8. Alkaline, moist soil. A variable species.

Hepatica nobilis
European hepatica
Europe. Similar in habit and culture to *Hepatica acutiloba*, except leaves sometimes mottled with grayish green, lobed with pointed tips. Herbaceous.

'Alba', flowers white.

'Alba Plena', flowers double, white.

Var. *asiatica*, flower colors variable; leaves mottled with silvery gray.

'Caerulea' ('Coerulea'), flowers blue.

'Eco Blue Harlequin', flowers blue; leaves mottled in green shades.

Var. *japonica*, flowers star-shaped; leaves green, mottled with silvery gray or yellow. The Asian counterpart of the European hepatica.

'Marmorata', leaves marbled in silvery gray.

'Plena', flowers double, blue.

'Rosea', flowers pink.

'Rubra', flowers dark rosy red.

'Rubra Plena', flowers double, red to rosy red.

Hepatica transsilvanica
Transsylvanian hepatica
Southeastern Europe. Flowers solitary, on stems to 5 in. (13 cm) tall, mostly blue, but also white and pinkish white, to 1.5 in. (4 cm) across; March–April; rhizomatous, herbaceous; leaves green, sometimes mottled with grayish green, to 4 in. (10 cm) long, lobed with rounded tips. Zones 5–8. LS to FS. Fertile, moist, well-drained soil. A gardenworthy species, with large flowers and leaves. Can withstand dry conditions better than the other species. The creeping rhizomes provide a spreading habit.

'Buis', flowers silvery cornflower-blue.

'Ellison Spence', flowers double, silvery blue; very floriferous.

Heuchera americana
Rock geranium
Eastern North America. Flowers insignificant, yellowish green; April–June; evergreen, clumping; leaves heart-shaped in a basal rosette, first mottled with purplish brown, later all green, shiny, leathery, lobed, toothed, 3–5 in. (8–13 cm). Zones 4–8, Some sun, LS to FS. Moist, fertile, neutral soil. Hardy in northern gardens. Very heat-tolerant. The best species for southern gardens. The leaves are the glory of these great foliage plants.

'Chocolate Veil', leaves to 6 in. (15 cm), deep brown with a purplish cast, veined silvery gray, purple underneath.

'Dale's Silver' ('Dale's Selection', 'Dale's Variety'), leaves mottled silvery gray; tall, to 30 in. (75 cm).

'Eco Running Tapestry', leaves to 6 in. (15 cm), green, heavily veined in dark purplish brown.

'Garnet', leaves medium green, with reddish brown veins.

'Persian Carpet', leaves burgundy red, with dark purplish brown edges and veins, tinted silvery gray in spots.

Hepatica acutiloba 'Eco Royal Blue' (Don Jacobs)

Hepatica maxima (Lynne Harrison)

Heuchera americana 'Pewter Veil' with *Hosta* 'Blue Cadet' in bloom

'**Pewter Veil**', leaves silvery gray, with purplish cast and gray veins.

'**Ruby Veil**', leaves ruby-red, with a network of silvery gray veins.

'**Velvet Night**', leaves very dark, velvety, greenish black shaded with purple.

Heuchera cylindrica
Poker alumroot

Western North America. Habit and culture similar to *Heuchera americana*, except flowers May–July; semi-evergreen; leaves hairy, dark green mottled with lighter green, 1–3 in. (2.5–8 cm). Best for northern gardens.

'**Alba**', flowers creamy white.

'**Green Ivory**', flowers whitish, with green bases.

'**Green Marble**', flowers greenish, leaves light green marbled.

'**Hyperion**', scapes very short, with pinkish red flowers.

'**Siskiyou Mountains**', a cute dwarf with scapes to 4 in. (10 cm) and a small leaf mound.

Heuchera micrantha
Crevice alumroot

Western North America. Flowers small, yellowish white; June–July; evergreen to semi-evergreen, clumping; leaves in a basal rosette, gray-green, 1–3 in. (2.5–8 cm) across, heart-shaped, lobed, each lobe scalloped. Zones 4–8, Some sun, LS to FS. Moist, fertile, neutral soil. Good for western and northern gardens. Does not like summer heat in southern gardens.

'**Chocolate Ruffles**', large, cocoa-brown leaves with heavily ruffled margins that reveal the purple underside.

'**Lace Ruffles**', ruffled leaves with white variegation.

'**Palace Purple**' ('Powis Purple'), deep purplish red leaves, to 6 in. (15 cm) across (see photo on page 180).

'**Pewter Moon**', leaves marbled with pewter, maroon underside; flowers pinkish.

Heuchera sanguinea
Coralbells

Southwestern United States to Mexico. Flowers large, bell-shaped, to 0.5 in. (1 cm) long, red, on flowerstalks to 20 in. (50 cm); May–June; evergreen to semi-evergreen, mat-forming; leaves in a basal rosette, dark green, 0.8–3 in. (2–8 cm) across, kidney- to heart-shaped, lobed, toothed. Zones 3–6. Some sun, LS to MS. Moist, fertile, neutral soil that does not dry out. In nature grows on moist shady rocks. It does not grow well in the heavy, acid clay soils of southern gardens, but can be tried in improved soil.

'**Alba**', flowers white.

'**Coral Cloud**', flowers coral-red; leaves shiny and crinkled.

'**Firesprite**', flowers bright rose-red.

'**Frosty**', flowers bright red; leaves variegated with silvery white.

'**Grandiflora**', flowers white, very floriferous.

'**Jack Frost**', flowers rose-red; leaves overlaid in silvery white.

Heuchera villosa 'Autumn Bride'

'**Pearl Drops**', flowers white flushed with pink; arching stems.

'**Red Spangles**', flowers crimson-red, late.

'**Schneewittchen**' ('Snow White'), flowers pure white.

'**Splish Splash**', flowers rose-pink; leaves splashed in creamy white.

'**White Cloud**', flowers white; leaves green mottled with silvery white.

'**Winfield Pink**', flowers clear pink.

Heuchera villosa

Southeastern United States. Habit and culture similar to *Heuchera americana*, except flowers white, showy; leaves large, scalloped, hairy, to 6 in. (15 cm). Zones 4–8. This native is at home on shady southeastern cliffs. An excellent plant for southern gardens. Its larger leaves make an imposing mound.

'**Autumn Bride**', leaves large, lime green; flowers in autumn.

'**Purpurea**', leaves large, purple.

Heuchera cultivars

Most average 24–36 in. (60–90 cm) in height, and, depending on location, flower during early or late summer. Most have green leaves with bright colored overlays.

'**Bloom's Coral**' ('Bloom's Variety'), flowers coral-red.

'**Can-Can**', flowers red; leaves silvery white with green veins, ruffled margins.

'**Carmen**', flowers dark red.

'**Champaign Bubbles**', flowers pink; leaves with silvery white overlay.

'**Chatterbox**', flowers rose-pink.

'**Freedom**', flowers rose-pink, floriferous, late.

'**Gloriana**', flowers dark pink.

'**Gracillima**', flowers pink, early.

'**Green Ivory**', flowers greenish white.

'**Huntsman**' ('Dennis Davidson'), flowers bright red on short stems.

'**Jubilee**', flowers light pink, early.

'**June Bride**', flowers snow-white.

'**Lady Romney**', flowers light pink.

'**Leuchtkäfer**' ('Firefly'), flowers fragrant, vermilion-red.

'**Mary Rose**', flowers deep pink.

'**Matin Bells**', flowers bright red.

'**Mint Frost**', flowers pinkish red; leaves silvery with olive-green veins.

'**Mint Julep**', flowers red; leaves mint-green with silvery overlay.

'**Monet**', flowers red; leaves large, green splashed with white.

'**Mt. St. Helens**', flowers cardinal-red.

'**Oakington Jewel**', flowers red; leaves greenish bronze.

'**Petite Pearl Fairy**', flowers pink; leaves splashed silvery white, dwarf.

'**Plum Puddin'**', flowers pink; leaves burgundy-red, silvery white between veins.

'**Pretty Polly**', flowers light pink.

'**Regal Robe**', flowers white, leaves silver with lavender.

'**Ring of Fire**', flowers red; leaves green with silvery white overlay and a thin orange-red margin.

Heuchera 'Plum Puddin'

'**Rosamundi**', flowers coral-pink.

'**Ruby Ruffles**', flowers red; leaves ruby-red with a silvery white overlay in leaf center, wrinkled and ruffled showing the purple underside.

'**Silberregen**' ('Silver Rain'), flowers pure white.

'**Snow Angel**', flowers rose-pink; leaves with silvery white splotches.

'**Taff's Joy**', flowers pink; leaves variegated cream and tinged pink.

'**Torch**', flowers dark scarlet-red.

'**Velvet Knight**', flowers red; leaves dark purple with veins outlined in red.

'**Weserlachs**' ('Weser Salmon'), flowers salmon-pink.

'**Whirlwind**', flowers pinkish red; leaves coppery, wrinkled, and ruffled.

'**White Marble**', flowers white; leaves green, mottled silvery white.

×*Heucherella*
Foamy bells

Garden hybrids (*Heuchera* × *Tiarella*). Some sun, LS to FS. Their floriferous and dense flowering habit is more like *Tiarella*. Because they are sterile, this group of hybrids must be propagated by division. ×*Heucherella alba* has white flowers without stolons. ×*Heucherella tiarelloides* has pink flowers on reddish flowerstalks and is stoloniferous.

'**Bridget Bloom**', flowers rich pink, floriferous; leaves marbled gray.

'**Kimono**', flowers yellowish white, floriferous.

'**Pink Frost**', flowers pink, floriferous; leaves green suffused with silvery white.

'**Silver Streak**', flowers creamy white, floriferous; leaves purple marked with silvery white.

'**Snow White**', flowers snow-white; leaves green suffused with silvery white.

×*Heucherella* 'Kimono' (Tony Avent)

HOSTA

Cultivation for all species and cultivars is similar. Zones 3–7. Most are not vigorous from zone 8 south. Some sun to WS in northern gardens. Some morning sun and LS to MS in southern gardens. Moist, fertile, deep and well-drained soil. Slowly spreading clumps. Provide supplemental water during drought periods.

Hosta kikutii

Southern Japan. Flowers white, funnel-shaped, to 2 in. (5 cm) long; July–August; flowerstalk to 20 in. (50 cm), leaning; clump 18 in. (45 cm) across, 10 in. (25 cm) high; leaves 7–9 in. (18–23 cm) long and 3–4 in. (8–10 cm) wide, green,

lance-shaped, flat with closely spaced, sunken veins. Excellent for southern gardens with hot, dry summers.

Forma *leuconota* has bluish green leaves with a powdery white coating underneath (see photo on page 10).

Var. *polyneuron* has wider leaves with many sunken veins.

Var. *yakusimensis* has smaller leaves, narrowly lance-shaped.

Hosta longipes

Japan. Flowers purple or white suffused with purple, bell-shaped, to 2 in. (5 cm) long; August–October; flowerstalk to 12 in. (30 cm), leaning; clump

Hosta kikutii f. *leuconota*
with *Blechnum spicant*
(foreground)

Hosta montana
'Aureomarginata'
(Hans Hansen)

dome-shaped, 18 in. (45 cm) across, 12 in. (30 cm) high; leaves 5–6 in. (13–15 cm) long and 3–4 in. (8–10 cm) wide, green, heart-shaped, flat with closely spaced, sunken veins; leaf and flowerstalks purple-spotted. This variable species is matchless for hot-summer gardens with long periods of drought (see photo on page 176).

'Urajiro' has near white leaf undersides.

Hosta montana

Japan. Flowers whitish, funnel-shaped, to 3 in. (8 cm) long; June–July; flowerstalk to 4 ft. (1.2 m), erect; clump 5 ft. (1.5 m) across, 4 ft. (1.2 m) high; leafstalks long, leaves green, to 12 in. (30 cm) long and 7 in. (18 cm) wide, heart-shaped. A highly variable species with many different forms in cultivation.

'**Aureomarginata**', size similar to the species; leaves green with broad, irregular golden yellow margin.

Forma *macrophylla*, huge clump 6 ft. (1.8 m) across, 4 ft. (1.2 m) high; leaves to 18 in. (45 cm) long, 12 in. (30 cm) wide, arching, broadly heart-shaped, deeply ribbed and furrowed at veins, dark green. This huge mountain hosta grows on elevated meadows and at the edge of forests.

'**On Stage**' ('Choko Nishiki'), size smaller than the species; leaves 9 in. (23 cm) long and 6 in. (15 cm) wide, arching, heart-shaped, with yellow center turning a light green later, with a streaky,

Hosta montana
f. *macrophylla*
(Hans Hansen)

Hosta 'On Stage'
(Hans Hansen)

Hosta plantaginea 'Aphrodite' (flower)

irregular dark green margin. Some morning sun helps to bring out the bright yellow color and retain it longer.

Hosta nigrescens

Central Japan. Flowers white, funnel-shaped, to 2 in. (5 cm) long; July–August; flowerstalk to 6 ft. (1.8 m), straight and erect; clump 30 in. (75 cm) across, 24 in. (60 cm) high; leaves 10–12 in. (25–30 cm) long, 7–9 in. (18–23 cm) wide, very dark green, glaucous. The black hosta is not actually black, but its sprouts are near dull black initially.

'Elatior' is much larger, with bright, shiny green leaves.

'Tall Boy', a hybridized form of the type, has green leaves and very tall flowerstalks, to 7 ft. (2 m).

Hosta plantaginea
August lily

China. Flowers largest in the genus, white, very fragrant, funnel-shaped, to 5 in. (13 cm) long with a spread of 3 in. (8 cm); August; flowerstalk to 30 in. (75 cm), leaning; clump 30 in. (75 cm) across, 20 in. (50 cm) high; leaves 7 in. (18 cm) long, 5 in. (13 cm) wide, heart-shaped, glossy light green.

The best fragrant hosta with the showiest flower. Requires considerable sun and high summer temperatures for flowering. The only night-bloomer in the genus, it opens flowers late in the afternoon, and their fragrance is most noticeable during evening. Does not tolerate drought well.

'Aphrodite', flowers double.

'Ming Treasure', leaf margins white.

'Venus' flowers double, stamens have developed into petals.

Hosta rectifolia

Japan. Flowers purple, funnel-shaped, to 2 in. (5 cm) long; July–September; flowerstalk to 38 in. (95 cm), erect; clump 24 in. (60 cm) across, 20 in. (50 cm) high; leaves 10 in. (25 cm) long and 3–5 in. (8–13 cm) wide, dark green, smooth and shiny, lance-shaped and slightly wavy, erect, with uniform transition to leafstalk.

'Kifukurin Tachi' has a creamy yellow margin that fades to white.

'Ogon Tachi' is yellow-leaved.

Hosta sieboldiana

Cultivated origin. Flowers glossy white, bell-shaped, 2 in. (5 cm) long; June–July; flowerstalk to 24 in (60 m), upright; clump 50 in. (1.3 m) across, 30 in. (76 cm) high; leaves 18 in. (45 cm) long and 12 in. (30 cm) wide, held on short, upright leafstalks, bluish gray, heart-shaped. Flowers often beneath leaves. This is the ubiquitous and classic European hosta and probably of garden origin. Over one hundred named cultivars are in the trade, all similar in habit.

Hosta ventricosa

China, Korea. Flowers dark purple-striped, expanding bell-shaped, to 2.5 in. (6 cm) long, fragrant; June–July; flowerstalk to 36 in. (90 cm), smooth, green, leaning; clump 36 in. (90 cm) across, 24 in. (60 cm) high; leaves 10 in. (25 cm) long and 8 in. (20 cm) wide, dark glossy green, heart-shaped, waves on the margin and twisted tip. An excellent specimen plant and landscape hosta for mass plantings and borders. It comes true, so seed propagation is easy.

Hosta venusta

Korea. Flowers few, lavender, funnel-shaped, to 1.5 in. (4 cm) long; July–August; flowerstalk 8–10 in. (20–25 cm), straight and with ridges; clump 6 in. (15 cm) across, 3 in. (8 cm) high; leaves 1 in. (2.5 cm) long and wide, satiny dark green, broadly heart-shaped, leaf margin wavy. A highly variable species. The clone in commerce represents but one of many different variants, some with lance-shaped leaves, others with much larger leaves, all recently found on Cheju Island.

'Suzuki Thumbnail', 'Thumbnail', and 'Tiny Tears' are selected smaller forms.

Hosta yingeri

Korea. Flowers light purple, spider-shaped, to 1 in. (2.5 cm) long and across, not one-sided, but all around the stem; August–September; flowerstalk to 24 in. (60 cm), straight but leaning; clump 18 in. (45 cm) across, 8 in. (20 cm) high; leaves 7 in. (18 cm) long and 3 in. (8 cm) wide, dark glossy green, elliptic, flat with heavy substance. The spidery flowers are unique among hostas and make a delightful late-summer display.

Hosta cultivars

All have similar flowers, funnel- or bell-shaped, purple to lavender, unless noted. Blooming time is June-July, unless noted. Being primarily a foliage plant, clump and leaf sizes are emphasized.

'**Abba Dabba Do**', clump dome-shaped, usually 36 in. (90 cm); leaves heart-shaped, 10 in. (25 cm) long and 7 in. (18 cm) wide, olive-green, leaf margin yellow.

'**Allan P. McConnell**', clump 18 in. (45 cm) across, 8 in. (20 cm) high; leaves heart-shaped, 3 in. (8 cm) long and 2 in. (5 cm) wide, dark green, margin white.

'**Ani Machi**' ('Geisha'), clump 10 in. (25 cm) across, 4 in. (10 cm) high; leaves 4 in. (10 cm) long and 2 in. (5 cm) wide, yellowish green with an irregular, dark green margin, heart-shaped but twisted and curved along the midrib and the tip curled under.

'**Antioch**', clump 36 in. (90 cm) across, 20 in. (50 cm) high; leaves 10 in. (25 cm) long and 8 in. (20 cm) wide, medium green, with white margin, heart-shaped.

'**August Moon**', flowers whitish, clump 30 in. (75 cm) across, 20 in. (50 cm) high; leaves 6 in. (15 cm) long and 5 in. (13 cm) wide, yellow, roundish heart-shaped, cupped, crinkled (see photo on page 34).

'**Birchwood Parky's Gold**', clump 30 in. (75 cm) across, 18 in. (45 cm) high; leaves 5 in. (13 cm) long and 4 in. (10 cm) wide, yellow, roundish heart-shaped, flat.

'**Blue Angel**', flowers white; clump 50 in. (1.3 m) across, 36 in. (90 cm) high; leaves 18 in. (45 cm) long and 12 in. (30 cm) wide, held horizontally on long, upright leafstalks, bluish gray, rugose, heart-shaped.

'**Blue Cadet**', clump dome-shaped, 28 in. (70 cm) across, 18 in. (45 cm) high; leaves 5 in. (13 cm) long and 4 in. (10 cm) wide, glaucous blue-green, heart-shaped, cupped (see photo on page 132).

'**Blue Moon**' ('Halo'); clump dome-shaped, 10 in. (25 cm) across, 6 in. (15 cm) high; leaves 3 in. (8 cm) long and 2 in. (5 cm) wide, glaucous blue-green, heart-shaped, flat.

'**Blue Wedgwood**' ('Blue Wave'); clump dome-shaped, 24 in. (60 cm) across, 14 in. (35 cm) high; leaves 6 in. (15 cm) long and 5 in. (13 cm) wide, glaucous blue-green, heart-shaped with a wedge-shaped outline, puckered.

'**Bold Ribbons**', clump 24 in. (60 cm) across, 16 in. (40 cm) high; leaves 6 in. (15 cm) long and 4 in. (10 cm) wide, medium dark green with white margin, heart-shaped.

'**Brim Cup**', flowers white, clump 16 in. (40 cm) across, 12 in. (30 cm) high; leaves 6 in. (15 cm) long and 5 in. (13 cm) wide, medium dark green with white margin, heart-shaped. Leaves are attractively cupped, but in some gardens, excessive cupping leads to tears in the margin.

'**Buckshaw Blue**', flowers white; clump 18 in. (45 cm) across, 12 in. (30 cm) high; leaves 6 in. (15 cm) long and 4 in. (10 cm) wide, blue-green, heart-shaped, flat. One of the bluest hostas. Holds it color longer than most.

'**Candy Hearts**', flowers white; clump 28 in. (70 cm) across, 16 in. (40 cm) high; leaves 6 in. (15 cm) long and 5 in. (13 cm) wide, grayish green with a bluish cast, heart-shaped, flat.

'**Chinese Sunrise**', clump 28 in. (70 cm) across, 16 in. (40 cm) high; leaves 6 in. (15 cm) long and 3 in. (8 cm) wide, beautiful yellow color with a narrow green margin in spring, green later, lance-shaped.

'**Christmas Tree**', flowers white; clump 36 in. (90 cm) across, 20 in. (50 cm) high; leaves 10 in. (25 cm) long and 6 in. (15 cm) wide, medium green, with white to creamy white margin, heart-shaped, wrinkled.

'**Crispula**', clump 36 in. (90 cm) across, 24 in. (60 cm) high; leaves 10 in. (25 cm) long and 7 in. (18 cm) wide, dark green with a regular white margin, smooth, heart-shaped, with a twisted, sharp tip.

Hosta 'Antioch' (left center) featured with variegated auralia (*Acanthopanax sieboldianus* 'Variegatus'), dwarf conifers (*Chamaecyparis obtuse* 'Nana'), and Japanese maples (*Acer shirasawanum* 'Aureum').

Hosta 'Blue Angel' (background) with *H.* 'Midas Touch' (front left) and *H.* 'Tokudama Flavocircinalis' (front right), edged by *H.* 'Gold Edger'

Hosta 'Blue Cadet' with *Dryopteris erythrosora*

'Decorata', clump 30 in. (75 cm) across, 12 in. (30 cm) high; leaves 6 in. (15 cm) long and 3 in. (8 cm) wide, dark green with a regular white margin, smooth, heart-shaped.

'Donahue Piecrust', flowers white; clump 30 in. (75 cm) across, 24 in. (60 cm) high; leaves 10 in. (25 cm) long and 7 in. (18 cm) wide, dark green, with distinct regular piecrust margins, heart-shaped.

'Elegans' (*Hosta sieboldiana* 'Elegans'). Garden origin. Flowers glossy white; clump 50 in. (1.3 m) across, 36 in. (90 cm) high; leaves 18 in. (45 cm) long and 12 in. (30 cm) wide, held on long, upright leafstalks, bluish gray, heart-shaped. A continual favorite in gardens.

'Fire and Ice', clump 36 in. (90 cm) across, 24 in. (60 cm) high; leaves 8 in. (20 cm) long and 5 in. (13 cm) wide, heart-shaped, dark green with very wide, irregular white margin and some streaking to the leaf midrib.

'Fortunei Albomarginata', clump 36 in. (90 cm) across, 24 in. (60 cm) high; leaves 10 in. (25 cm) long and 7 in. (18 cm) wide, dark green with a regular white margin, smooth, heart-shaped. An inexpensive, attractive, and easy-care landscape cultivar.

'Fortunei Aureomarginata' ('Ellerbroek', 'Golden Crown'); clump 36 in. (90 cm) across, 24 in. (60 cm) high; leaves 10 in. (25 cm) long and 7 in. (18 cm) wide, dark green with a regular yellow margin, smooth, heart-shaped. A classic.

'Fragrant Bouquet', flowers white, fragrant; clump 4 ft. (1.2 m) across, 20 in. (50 cm) high; leaves 9 in. (23 cm) long and 8 in. (20 cm) wide, heart-shaped, yellowish green with creamy white margin. One of the best variegated and fragrant hostas.

'Francee', clump 36 in. (90 cm) across, 24 in. (60 cm) high; leaves 8 in. (20 cm) long and 5 in. (13 cm) wide, heart-shaped, dark green with nar-

Hosta 'Francee'

row white margin. A distinguished, much-tested garden hosta that holds its leaf color, looking marvelous from spring until autumn.

'Ginko Craig', clump 10 in. (25 cm) across, 4 in. (10 cm) high; leaves dark green with a white margin, lance-shaped.

'Gold Standard', clump 36 in. (90 cm) across, 20 in. (50 cm) high; leaves 8 in. (20 cm) long and 5 in. (13 cm) wide, heart-shaped, yellow with a dark green margin. This classic hosta retains its parent's vigor and fast increase (see photo on page 147).

'Golden Bullion', clump 28 in. (70 cm) across, 14 in. (35 cm) high; leaves 6 in. (15 cm) long and 4 in. (10 cm) wide, heart-shaped, yellow, puckered and slightly cupped.

'Golden Sculpture', flowers whitish; clump 5 ft. (1.5 m) across, 32 in. (80 cm) high; leaves 15 in. (38 cm) long and 10 in. (26 cm) wide, rounded, heart-shaped, yellow, cupped and puckered, with distinct leaf tip.

'Golden Tiara', clump 24 in. (60 cm) across, 14 in. (35 cm) high; leaves 4 in. (10 cm) long and 3 in. (8 cm) wide, flat, green, heart-shaped, with a neat yellowish green margin that bleaches to near creamy white in sun.

'Great Expectations', flowers white; clump 40 in. (1 m) across, 24 in. (60 cm) high; leafstalks white, green-margined; leaves 9 in. (23 cm) long and 7 in. (18 cm) wide, broadly heart-shaped, dimpled and rippled, margins slightly upturned, sharp tip, emerging chartreuse turning to creamy white, with dark bluish green, irregular margin, with streaking toward midrib (see photo on page 18).

'Green Fountain', July–August; clump 36 in. (90 cm) across, 26 in. (65 cm) high; leaves 10 in. (25 cm) long and 3 in. (8 cm) wide, dark green, smooth and shiny, lance-shaped, cascading and slightly wavy. Good in hot southern gardens.

'Guacamole', flowers white, fragrant; clump 4 ft. (1.2 m) across, 24 in. (60 cm) high; leaves 10 in. (25 cm) long and 8 in. (20 cm) wide, heart-shaped, yellowish green with medium green margin. Among the best variegated and fragrant hostas.

'Halcyon' (Hosta 'Tardiflora' × H. 'Elegans'). Flowers white; clump dome-shaped, 32 in. (80 cm) across, 18 in. (45 cm) high; leaves 7 in. (18 cm) long and wide, upright on strong leafstalks, glaucous, pronounced blue-green, heart-shaped, flat; a popular garden plant.

'Honeybells' (Hosta plantaginea × H. sieboldii). Flowers almost white, fragrant; August; clump 4 ft. (1.2 m) across, 24 in. (60 cm) high; leaves 11 in. (28 cm) long and 8 in. (20 cm) wide, light green, heart-shaped, flat, laxly arching. A vigorous plant with fragrant flowers. Sun-tolerant and an old standby.

'Inniswood', flowers white; clump 4 ft. (1.2 m) across, 24 in. (60 cm) high; leaves 10 in. (25 cm) long and 8 in. (20 cm) wide, broadly heart-shaped, dimpled, yellow with irregular, wide green margin.

'Invincible', flowers white, slightly fragrant; clump 20 in. (50 cm) across, 10 in. (25 cm) high; leaves 5 in. (13 cm) long and 3 in. (8 cm) wide, broadly heart-shaped, smooth, glossy, rich green, sharp tip. This is one of the best glossy leafed hostas.

'June', clump dome-shaped, 30 in. (75 cm) across, 18 in. (45 cm) high; leaves 6 in. (15 cm) long and 4 in. (10 cm) wide, glaucous, with a yellowish center and irregular blue-green margin with streakings toward the midrib, heart-shaped, flat. Considered among the best variegated cultivars.

'Kabitan' (Hosta sieboldii 'Kabitan'); clump 10 in. (25 cm) across, 6 in. (15 cm) high; leaves 5 in. (13 cm) long and 1 in. (2.5 cm) wide, bright yellow with a narrow green margin, smooth, lance-shaped.

'Krossa Regal', clump erect, vase-shaped, 40 in. (1 m) across, 36 in. (90 cm) high; leaves 9 in. (23 cm) long and 5 in. (13 cm) wide, glaucous blue-green, heart-shaped, wavy, with long leafstalks erect. A classic hosta with architectural stature. An excellent garden plant.

'Lancifolia', clump 30 in. (75 cm) across, 12 in. (30 cm) high; leaves 6 in. (15 cm) long and 2–3 in. (5–8 cm) wide, dark green, smooth and

Hosta 'Love Pat' with ferns and blooming *Rodgersia sambucifolia*

Hosta 'Paul's Glory' (left) and 'Sultana' (right) with blooming *Rodgersia henrici*

shiny, lance-shaped and slightly wavy. A classic cultivar for edgings and mass planting.

'Love Pat', flowers white, clump 32 in. (80 cm) across, 18 in. (45 cm) high; leaves 7 in. (18 cm) long and wide, upright on strong leafstalks, glaucous, pronounced blue-green, heart-shaped, deeply cupped, intensely puckered. An excellent hybridized form of 'Tokudama'.

'Opipara' ('Bill Brincka'); clump 24 in. (60 cm) across, 15 in. (38 cm) high; leaves 7–9 in. (18–23 cm) long and 4 in. (10 cm) wide, dark green with a wide yellow margin, smooth and shiny, elliptic, round-tipped and slightly wavy.

'Pandora's Box', clump 10 in. (25 cm) across, 4 in. (10 cm) high; leaves 2 in. (5 cm) long and 1.5 in. (4 cm) wide, pure white center with green streaks and with dark green margin, broadly heart-shaped.

'Patriot', clump 36 in. (90 cm) across, 24 in. (60 cm) high; leaves 8 in. (20 cm) long and 5 in. (13 cm) wide, heart-shaped, dark green with very wide, irregular white margin and some streaking to the leaf midrib.

'Paul's Glory', flowers whitish lavender; clump 32 in. (90 cm) across, 24 in. (60 cm) high; leaves 7 in. (18 cm) long and 5 in. (13 cm) wide, ovate heart-shaped, slightly dimpled, emerging chartreuse, turning yellowish white or creamy white, with dark bluish green, irregular margin. An outstanding garden plant.

'Pearl Lake', clump 30 in. (75 cm) across, 18 in. (45 cm) high; leaves 5 in. (13 cm) long and 4 in. (10 cm) wide, grayish green with a bluish cast, heart-shaped, flat. A floriferous classic.

'Regal Splendor', clump dome-shaped, 40 in. (1 m) across, 36 in. (90 cm) high; leaves 12 in. (30 cm) long and 7 in. (18 cm) wide, glaucous blue-green with creamy yellow margin that turns creamy white, heart-shaped, wavy.

'Sagae', clump 4 ft. (1.2 m) or more across, 31 in. (79 cm) high; leaves 10–12 in. (25–30 cm) long and 8–9 in. (20–23 cm) wide, broadly heart-shaped, wavy with undulating margin, glaucous surface and underside, soft olive-green with irregular, wide yellow margin. A popular cultivar. Among the best variegated landscape hostas.

'Shade Fanfare', clump 24 in. (60 cm) across, 16 in. (40 cm) high; leaves 8 in. (20 cm) long and 7 in. (18 cm) wide, heart-shaped, flat, yellowish green center with a yellowish to creamy white margin.

Hosta 'Sagae'

Hosta 'Spritzer' with *H.* 'Undulata Albomarginata' (lower left)

'Shining Tot', July–August; clump 6 in. (15 cm) across, 2 in. (5 cm) high; leaves 1–2 in. (2.5–5 cm) long and 0.5 in. (1 cm) wide, glossy dark green, broadly heart-shaped, wavy leaf margin. One of the most popular tiny hostas.

'Spilt Milk', flowers glossy white; clump 50 in. (1.3 m) across, 25 in. (63 cm) high; leaves 10 in. (25 cm) long and 9 in. (23 cm) wide, held on short, upright leafstalks, bluish gray with white streaks and misting, heart-shaped. A delicate and unique variegation.

'Spritzer', July–August; clump 36 in. (90 cm) across, 26 in. (65 cm) high; leaves 10 in. (25 cm) long and 3 in. (8 cm) wide, dark green with green streaks extending into a yellow center, smooth and shiny, lance-shaped, cascading and slightly wavy. Good in hot southern gardens.

'Striptease', clump 36 in. (90 cm) across, 24 in. (60 cm) high; leaves 8 in. (20 cm) long and 6 in. (15 cm) wide, heart-shaped, narrow yellow center with a wide dark green margin and white streaks in the junction between center and margin.

'Sum and Substance', flowers whitish; clump 8 ft. (2.4 m) across, 32 in. (80 cm) high; leaves 16 in. (40 cm) long and 14 in. (35 cm) wide, but usually somewhat smaller, yellow, rugose, corrugated, and sometimes twisted, heart-shaped, with heavy substance, white pruinose back. This colossal cultivar needs some sun to go from chartreuse to yellow. Tops in popularity for a long time. It grows well in northern and in hot, humid southern gardens.

'Sun Power', July–August; clump erect vase-shaped, 36 in. (90 cm) across, 30 in. (75 cm) high; leaves 10 in. (25 cm) long and 7 in. (18 cm) wide, yellowish green to yellow, heart-shaped, wavy, with long leafstalks. Popular for its architectural stature and bright color.

'Tardiflora', flowers September–October; clump 18 in. (45 cm) across, 10 in. (25 cm) high; leaves 3–6 in. (8–15 cm) long and 2–3 in. (5–8 cm) wide, glossy dark green, leathery, heart-shaped.

'Tokudama', flowers whitish; clump 24 in. (60 cm) across, 14 in. (35 cm) high; leaves 8 in. (20 cm) long and 7 in. (18 cm) wide, rounded heart-shaped, cupped, puckered and dimpled, glaucous, bluish green.

Hosta 'Sum and Substance' (left) and *H.* 'Blue Dimples' (lower right) backed by *H.* 'Gold Standard' and variegated azaleas

Hosta 'Sun Power'
shines behind a border
of green hostas

Hydrastis canadensis

Hydrophyllum
virginianum
in bloom

'Tokudama Aureonebulosa', flowers whitish; clump 24 in. (60 cm) across, 14 in. (35 cm) high; leaves 8 in. (20 cm) long and 7 in. (18 cm) wide, rounded heart-shaped, puckered and dimpled, glaucous, with mottled yellowish green center and an irregular, streaky bluish green margin.

'Tokudama Flavocircinalis', flowers whitish; clump 36 in. (90 cm) across, 18 in. (45 cm) high; leaves 9 in. (23 cm) long and 6 in. (15 cm) wide, broadly elliptic with heart-shaped base, puckered and dimpled, glaucous bluish green, margin yellow and 1.5 in. (4 cm) wide (see photo on page 141). Larger than 'Tokudama Aureonebulosa' and more showy.

'Undulata', clump 24 in. (60 cm) across, 18 in. (45 cm) high; leaves 6–7 in. (15–18 cm) long and 3–4 in. (8–10 cm) wide, broadly elliptic with heart-shaped base and twisted tip, streaky white in the center, margin irregular, dark green with yellowish green and celadon streakings. An old classic still popular.

'Undulata Albomarginata', clump 28 in. (70 cm) across, 18 in. (45 cm) high; leaves 6–7 in. (15–18 cm) long and 3–4 in. (8–10 cm) wide, broadly elliptic with heart-shaped base, dark green with an irregular margin of creamy white to white. Long in cultivation. Among the best inexpensive variegated hostas. Easy to grow and vigorous in northern and southern gardens.

'Whirlwind', clump 16 in. (40 cm) across, 10 in. (25 cm) high; leaves 6 in. (15 cm) long and 3 in. (8 cm) wide, heart-shaped but contracted and twisted, with a viridescent yellowish green center and an irregular dark green margin.

Hydrastis canadensis
Goldenseal

Eastern North America. Flowers solitary, greenish white; flowerstalk green, hairy, 12–16 in. (30–40 cm); April–May; rhizomatous; leaves on the stem, 2, heart-shaped outline but lobed, irregularly cleft and toothed, dark green, 6–8 in. (15–20 cm) long, deeply furrowed wrinkled all over; red berries. Zones 3–8. WS to MS. Moist, well-drained, acidic soil. Ephemeral flowers, but the rich green, heavily crinkled leaves add much texture to the shady garden.

Hydrophyllum virginianum
Virginia waterleaf

Eastern North America. LS to WS. flowers several, above the leaves, drooping, white or dark violet, bell-shaped, with long, hairy filaments; stem 12–30 in. (30–75 cm); May–August; rhizomatous, creeping; leaves divided into leaflets, 2–5 in. (5–13 cm) long, gray to green, lance-shaped, lobed and toothed. Zones 3–7. WS to MS. Always moist, but well-drained soil. Engaging and unusual flower buds curled over like a scorpion's tail. Divided leaves are attractively mottled with gray early and turn all green later.

Iris cristata
Crested iris

Eastern North America. Flowers violet-blue sometimes white, crested with white or yellow ridges, solitary, atop a flowerstalk, 2.5 in. (6 cm) long; April–May; rhizomatous, mat-forming; leaves flat, lance-shaped, green, sheathing the stem,

Iris cristata 'Powder Blue Giant' (Tony Avent)

Iris tectorum flowers

'Shenandoah Sky', flowers medium blue, crests yellow, center patch white; stems to 6 in. (15 cm) tall; leaves to 7 in. (18 cm) tall.

'Vein Mountain', flowers bright pale blue, crests orange, center patch white bordered by dark purple, usually one-flowered; stems shorter, to 5 in. (13 cm) tall; leaves to 8 in. (20 cm) tall.

Iris foetidissima
Stinking iris

Europe. Flowers dull purple, lilac, or topaz tinged with yellow, 2–3 in. (5–8 cm) across, several on branched flowerstalk to 36 in. (90 cm) tall; June–July; rhizomatous, vigorous; leaves ever-green, flat, lance-shaped, green, in fan-shaped tufts, malodorous when crushed, to 30 in. (75 cm) long; showy scarlet seeds. Zones 7–9. LS to FS. Well-drained neutral to slightly acidic soil. A good iris for southern gardens and grown in part for the ornate seed clusters rather than the flow-ers. Evergreen leaves provide welcome green color during the off-season. Very heat-tolerant but appreciates supplemental water during dry summers.

'Citrina', flowers yellow veined in pale lilac.

'Fructoalba', seeds white.

'Lutescens', flowers pure yellow.

'Variegata', leaves striped creamy white or pale yellow. Eye-catching in the shady garden.

Iris tectorum
Japanese roof iris

China. Flowers blue-lilac, sometimes white, to 4 in. (10 cm) across, with frilly white crests, spotted purple; May–June; rhizomatous, rapid spreader; leaves flat, lance-shaped, sheathing the stem, 12–14 in. (30–35 cm) long and to 1 in. (2.5 cm) wide. Zones 4–8. Morning sun, LS in northern gardens, WS to MS in southern gardens. Thrives on neglect. Adapts to a variety of soils. Shade- and heat-tolerant.

'Alba', flowers white with yellow streaks on the falls.

'Variegata', leaves streaked and striped with creamy white.

5–8 in. (13–20 cm) long and 0.6–1 in. (1.5–2.5 cm) wide, short at bloom time but elongating after flowering. Zones 4–8. Morning sun, LS in northern gardens, WS to MS in southern gar-dens. Any soil. A shade-tolerant iris and a good garden plant. Tolerant even of some neglect.

'Alba', flowers white.

'Eco Purple Pomp', flowers very dark violet, crests bright yellow brushed with orange.

'Powder Blue Giant', flowers very large, pale blue, to 3.5 in. (9 cm) across, crests yellow, center patch white bordered with dark blue; leaves larger, to 12 in. (30 cm) tall.

Jeffersonia diphylla
Twinleaf

North America. Flowers solitary, above the leaves, to 1 in. (2.5 cm) across, white, star-shaped, on stems, 5–16 in. (13–40 cm) tall; April–May; clumping; leaves basal, 3–6 in. (8–15 cm) across, grayish green, deeply cleft along the centerline. Zones 5–7. MS to FS. Moist, humusy soil. An excellent native for northern and southern gardens. Long-lived, but it takes time to mature. It flowers briefly, but the unusual leaves carry on until autumn.

Jeffersonia dubia
Asian twinleaf

Eastern Asia. Similar in habit and culture to *Jeffersonia diphylla*, except smaller; flowers, usually blue or lavender-blue, not above the leaves.

Forma *alba* is a naturally occurring white-flowered variant. Zones 5–8.

Kirengeshoma palmata
Yellow waxbells

Southern Japan. Flowers yellow, in clusters, nodding, tightly tubular, bell-shaped with five fleshy,

Jeffersonia diphylla fruit

Jeffersonia dubia
(Lynne Harrison)

Kirengeshoma palmata
with *Hosta* 'Amanuma'

Lamium galeobdolon
'Hermann's Pride'

overlapping petals, to 1.5 in. (4 cm) long on flowerstalks 4–5 ft. (1.2–1.5 m); June–July; clumping, rhizomatous; leaves opposite, mapleleaf-shaped, light green, toothed and lobed, 4–8 in. (10–20 cm) long. Zones 5–8. LS to MS. Moist, acidic soil. An excellent plant with long-lasting, waxy, yellow bells that provide an unforgettable show. The maplelike leaves provide texture.

Lamium galeobdolon
Yellow archangel

Eurasia. Flowers brown-spotted yellow, large-lipped, tubular, to 0.8 in. (2 cm) long, in false whorls around stem; June–July; rhizomatous and stoloniferous, vigorously spreading; to 24 in. (60 cm) high; leaves heart-shaped, to 2.5 in. (6 cm) long, toothed, medium green often mottled with silvery gray, on stolonlike branches. Zones 4–8. LS to FS. Any moist soil. A quickly spreading, mat-forming groundcover that can be invasive in the border. Unsightly where the soil dries out. Still sold under the old synonym *Lamiastrum galeobdolon*.

'Florentinum' ('Variegatum', 'Type Ronsdorf'), leaves silvery gray with green margins.

'Hermann's Pride', leaves smaller, silvery gray-green with conspicuous darker green veins.

'Silver Angel', leaves silvery gray-green.

Lamium maculatum
Spotted deadnettle

Eurasia. Similar in habit and culture to *Lamium galeobdolon*, except flowers purple, sometimes pink or white; June–July; lower growing to 8 in. (20 cm) high; leaves 1–3 in. (2.5–8 cm) long.

'Album', flowers white; leaves silvery white mottled.

'Argenteum', flowers reddish; leaves silver-gray mottled.

'Aureum' ('Gold Leaf'), flowers pink; leaves yellow with white center.

'Beacon Silver' ('Beacon's Silver', 'Silbergroschen'), flowers pale pink to lilac; leaves silvery gray with a thin green margin.

'Pink Nancy', flowers pink; leaves silvery gray with thin green margin.

'Shell Pink', flowers pink, floriferous; leaves green with white blotch.

'White Nancy', flowers pure white; leaves silvery gray with narrow green margin.

Ligularia dentata

Eastern Asia. Flowers daisylike, yellow to orange-yellow, flower heads to 4 in. (10 cm) across on green, multibranched flowerstalks to 4 ft. (1.2 m) tall; September–November; clumping to 36 in. (90 cm) wide and high; leaves basal, large, 12–18

Lamium maculatum 'Beacon Silver' with *Athyrium niponicum* var. *pictum* as underplantings for a potted *Hosta* 'Hadspen Blue'

in. (30–45 cm), rounded, kidney-shaped, toothed, first reddish purple then dark green to grayish green atop erect, green or red stems. Zones 4–7. Sun to LS. Very moist, fertile, well-drained soil. Best for northern gardens. Even with constant moisture, the large leaves wilt in southern gardens in summer.

'Dark Beauty', flowers vivid light orange; leaves dark maroon.

'Desdemona', flowers deep orange; leaves brownish green.

Ligularia stenocephala

Eastern Asia. Similar in habit and culture to *Ligularia dentata*, except the flowers are golden yellow and the narrow flower spikes taller, to 6 ft. (1.8 m) tall; August–September; the leaves are to 12 in. (30 cm) long, triangular in outline and deep, glossy green with the margins heavily toothed and serrated. Zones 4–7. Sun to LS. Always moist, fertile, well-drained soil. Best for northern gardens where constant moisture is a must.

Lilium martagon
Turk's cap lily

Eurasia to Siberia. Flowers slightly fragrant or malodorous, usually pendent, glossy pink, mauve, red, or maroon, spotted with purplish or blackish brown, sometimes white with or without spots, petals very strongly recurved, 2 in. (5 cm) across, in loose clusters on long, branched flowerstalks, 3–6 ft. (0.9–1.8 m) tall; July–September; plant bulblike, stem-rooting; leaves in whorls along the stem to 6 in. (13 cm) long, elliptic or lance-shaped. Zones 3–7. Some sun, LS to WS. Fertile, moist soil high in organic matter. Plant needs at least two hours of full sun. Difficult in zone 8 and warmer. The long-lasting flowers come earlier than those of other lilies.

Var. *albiflorum*, flowers white with pink spotting.

Var. *album*, flowers white, unspotted, smaller to 1.5 in. (4 cm) across, anthers yellow.

Var. *cattaniae*, flowers maroon, unspotted.

Lilium philadelphicum
Wood lily

Eastern North America. Flowers facing up, cup-shaped, orange with a yellowish throat, spotted purplish brown, 2 in. (5 cm) on stems 12–36 in. (30–90 cm) tall; June–August; plant bulblike; leaves in whorls, lance-shaped. Zones 3–7. Some sun, LS to WS. Moist but well-drained soil. A magnificent, native "looking at you" wood lily. It requires a location that is drier than that of the American turk's cap lily. Often considered difficult because it is given too much moisture.

Lilium superbum
American turk's cap lily

Eastern North America. Flowers nodding down, orange with crimson tips and spotted with purplish brown, recurved petals in turk's cap fashion, 2.5 in. (6 cm) long, on stems 3–9 ft. (0.9–2.7 m) tall; July–September; plant bulblike; leaves in whorls or alternate in the upper part, 4–5 in. (10–13 cm), lance-shaped. Zones 3–7. Some sun, . LS to WS. Constantly moist soil acid (pH of 5). This is the largest and best of the native lilies; needs two hours of full sun and does well in the moist woodland garden.

Liriope muscari
Lilyturf

China, Taiwan, Japan. Flowers small, many, bluish violet, in a spike, to 5 in. (10–13 cm) long, on a flowerstalk to 15 in. (38 cm) tall; July–September; clumping, rhizomatous, spreading; leaves evergreen, dark green, linear lance-shaped, wider toward the top, tip blunt, leathery, 10–18 in. (25–45 cm) long; berries black. Zones 6–10. LS to FS. Any acidic soil. Drought-tolerant. The ubiquitous southern lilyturf. Also sold as *Liriope platyphylla*.

'Christmas Tree' ('Munroe No. 2'), flowers pale lavender or lilac.

'Curly Twist', flowers deep lilac, shaded to burgundy; leaves twisted.

'Gigantea', probably a large selection of *Liriope muscari*.

Lilium superbum
(Sigi Schmid)

Liriope muscari
'Variegata'

'Gold Banded' ('Gold Band'), leaves yellow with dark green margins.

'Ingwersen', flowers deep violet; leaves dark green.

'John Burch', flowers bluish lavender; leaves yellow striped.

'Lilac Beauty', flowers deep lilac, floriferous.

'Majestic', flowers deep lilac, sometimes fused, flattened spike, on tall stems to 20 in. (50 cm), floriferous; leaves dark green.

'Monroe White' ('Munroe No. 1'), flowers larger, pure white, floriferous; leaves wide, dark green.

'Royal Purple', flowers bright purple, floriferous.

'Silver Dragon' ('Gin Ryu'), leaves streaked with white.

'Variegata', variable cultivar, flowers violet; leaves green with white or yellow margins and/or streaks.

'Webster Wideleaf', flowers purple on stems to 18 in. (45 cm); leaves dark green, wider than most cultivars, to 0.8 in. (2 cm) wide.

Lobelia cardinalis inflorescence

Lobelia cardinalis
Cardinal flower

North America. Flowers many, brilliant red, to 1.5 in. (4 cm) long, in a cluster to 14 in. (35 cm) long, on erect, green to reddish purple stalks 2–4 ft. (0.6–1.2 m) tall; July–September; clumping rhizomatous with offsets; leaves alternate, new growth purple, then bright green, lance-shaped, toothed, to 4 in. (10 cm) long; clumping. Zone 3, heat-tolerant to zone 9. Some sun, LS to WS. Moist, fertile soil. Self-seeds in the woodland garden. Its brilliant red flowers are a beacon in the garden and hummingbirds love it.

'Alba', flowers pure white.

'Angel Song', flowers bicolored, salmon and cream.

'Cotton Candy', flowers pinkish white.

'Rosea', flowers rose-pink.

'Ruby Slippers', flowers dark ruby-red.

'Summit Snow', flowers pure white.

Lobelia siphilitica
Great lobelia

Eastern North America. Similar in habit and culture to *Lobelia cardinalis*, except flowers bright blue, to 1 in. (2.5 cm) on stalks 2–5 ft. (0.6–1.5 m) tall; August–September.

'Alba', flowers pure white.

'Nana', flowers bright blue; to 36 in. (90 cm).

'Nana Alba', flowers pure white; smaller than type.

Lygodium japonicum
Climbing fern

Asia. Fronds deciduous, produced in opposite pairs on very long, vining stems; both fertile and sterile fronds are produced on the same stem; sterile leaves to 9 in. (23 cm), dark green, divided into smaller leaflets; fertile leaves shorter with fringed margins. Zones 6–9. WS to FS. Any moist soil. A climbing fern for vertical gardening. It looks delicate, but is robust and withstands heat and drought in southern gardens. Root-hardy with protection in zone 6 and deciduous but hardy in zone 7a.

Lygodium japonicum ascending a dogwood (*Cornus florida*)

Lysimachia congestiflora
Loosestrife

China. Similar in habit and culture to *Lysimachia japonica*, except leaves opposite or whorled, dark green, lance-shaped, to 2 in. (5 cm) long.

'Eco Dark Satin', flowers yellow with red throat; leaves dark, satiny green.

'Outback Sunset', flowers yellow with red throat; leaves medium green with yellow margin, tinged red in spring.

Lysimachia japonica

Eurasia. Flowers small, one to three facing up, yellow, cup-shaped to 0.5 in. (1 cm) across; June–August; stoloniferous and stem-rooting, mat-forming; leaves on trailing stems, light green, slightly hairy, roundish to 1 in. (2.5 cm) long. Zones 6–9. Some sun, LS to WS. Moist, well-drained soil. The typical form is rare in commerce, but its miniature form is widely planted.

'Minutissima'. Miniature moneywort. A dwarf form that spreads quickly, forming pretty mats of tiny leaves sprinkled with bright yellow flowers in spring. Evergreen in zone 7a.

Lysimachia nummularia
Moneywort

Eurasia, naturalized in North America. Similar in habit and culture to *Lysimachia japonica*, except flowers solitary, larger, to 0.8 in. (2 cm) across and leaves on trailing stems, light green, broadly rounded to 1 in. (2.5 cm) long. Zone 4, heat-tolerant to zone 8 as long as moisture is maintained. A quick groundcover in full sun but better behaved in the open woodland.

'Aurea'. Yellow moneywort, yellow creeping Jenny. A vigorous yellow-leaved selection.

Lysimachia punctata

Eurasia. Similar in habit and culture to *Lysimachia japonica*, except leaves opposite or whorled, dark green, lance-shaped, to 2 in. (5 cm) long.

'Alexander', flowers yellow with red throat; leaves medium green with yellow margin.

Lysimachia japonica 'Minutissima' flowers

Lysimachia nummularia 'Aurea' as a groundcover fronting hostas

Lysimachia punctata 'Alexander'

Maianthemum kamtschaticum
May lily

Eurasia, North America, West Coast. Flowers tiny, fragrant, white, on stems to 7 in. (18 cm); May–June; basal leaves to 6 in. (15 cm) long, green, elliptic; berries red. Zones 4–7. LS to FS. Moist, acidic soil. Variable and larger than the native *Maianthemum canadense*. Both make a tight, flowering, fragrant groundcover in the woodland garden. In spring, lovely, small clumps of white flowers brighten the green carpet.

Matteuccia struthiopteris
Ostrich fern

North America, Eurasia. Fronds 4–6 ft. (1.2–1.8 m) long and 12–18 in. (30–45 cm) wide, with large, erect shuttlecocks; sterile leaves rich dark green, deciduous, divided into many pairs of alternate leaflets composed of subleaflets, not opposite; fertile leaves to 24 in. (60 cm), stiff, hard, leathery, green turning brown; spreading by rhizomatous runners. Zones 3–8. LS to MS. Moist, fertile acidic or neutral soil. A large, stately fern for the woodland, its spreading habit is welcome by many gardeners. A number of catalogs list it as *Matteuccia pennsylvanica*.

Mazus reptans

Himalaya, China. Flowers like snapdragons, blue, lower lip white, red-spotted, 0.8 in. (2 cm) long, on prostrate flowerstalks; May to frost; prostrate, mat-forming, rooting stems; leaves in rosettes, green, 1.2 in. (3 cm) long, oval, toothed. Zones 5–8. Some sun to LS. Moist to dry, fertile soils. Low maintenance and will naturalize easily even in drier soils. One of the best spreading groundcovers under tall, open wildflowers and cobra lilies. It needs some sun to flower.

'Albus', white-flowered, is very attractive and fits anywhere.

Mertensia virginica
Virginia bluebells

Eastern North America. Flowers blue, nodding, trumpet-shaped, to 1 in. (2.5 cm) long;

Matteuccia struthiopteris with hostas

Mazus reptans 'Albus', a flowering groundcover

March–June; clumping; leaves deciduous, bluish green, basal, elliptic, deeply veined; stem leaves smaller; stems 24 in. (60 cm) tall. Zones 3–7. Some sun, LS to WS. Moist, well-drained, alkaline soil. Hard to mix with acid-loving plants but deserves a spot in the garden. Pretty in spring but dormant in summer, so consider the bare spot. Sometimes offered under its synonym *Mertensia pulmonarioides*.

'Alba', flowers white.

'Rubra', flowers pinkish.

Milium effusum
Millet

North America, Eurasia. Flowers tiny, in yellowish spikes; May–June; clumping, tufted; leaves strap-shaped, flat, shiny green, erect but arching, to 18 in. (45 cm) long and 0.2–0.5 in. (0.5–1 cm) wide. Zones 6–9. LS to MS. Moist soil. A good grass for shady corners.

'**Aureum**' ('Bowles' Golden Grass') is widely available and has bright yellow blades that turn light green later. Comes true from seed.

Mertensia virginica

Milium effusum
'Aureum'

Mitchella repens
as a groundcover

'Variegatum', with leaves irregularly striped with white, is not robust and needs more sun than shade.

Mitchella repens
Partridgeberry
North America. Flowers terminal, white, in pairs, 0.8 in. (2 cm) long, facing up; May–July; prostrate, mat-forming; leaves shiny dark green, veins greenish white, sometimes white, to 0.8 in. (2 cm) long, oval; berries red. Zones 5–9. LS to MS. Moist to dry soils. A trailing ever-green groundcover that can be stepped on with no ill effect. Rugged and maintenance-free, it will naturalize. The twin flowers produce one two-eyed berry which hangs on for another season, so berries and flowers can be seen at the same time.

Forma *leucocarpa* has white berries.

Mukdenia rossii
China, Korea. Flowers small, bell-shaped, to 0.2 in. (0.5 cm), white, rarely pink, many in clusters above the leaves, on flowerstalks to 18 in. (45

Mukdenia rossii

cm) tall; May–June; clumping, rhizomatous; slowly spreading; leaves green, lobed, toothed, to 7 in. (18 cm) long and 6 in. (15 cm) wide. Zones 6–7. LS to WS. Constantly moist soil. This species can be rather difficult in gardens with hot, dry summers if the soil dries out. It has bloomed and returned yearly in an ever-moist and cool, shady spot in zone 7a.

'Crimson Fans', leaves remain red all summer.

Nothoscordum bivalve
False garlic

Eastern North America. Flowers yellow, funnel-shaped, in a cluster on stalks to 18 in. (45 cm) tall; April–May and September–October; herba-ceous, clumping; basal leaves straplike, green, to 12 in. (30 cm) long. Zones 5–7. Some sun, LS to WS. Any soil. This elegant native should find a place in every wildflower garden. It withstands very hot and dry summers and is well adapted to southern gardens. Given a warm autumn,

false garlic will re-bloom frequently starting in September.

Omphalodes cappadocica
Navelwort

Mediterranean. Flowers small, blue with white centers; April–June; clumping, rhizomatous, erect to ascending, to 10 in. (25 cm) tall; leaves evergreen, basal, green with conspicuous veins, heart-shaped. Zones 6–8. LS to FS. Moist, fertile soil. The best garden species, being evergreen and a more bushy plant does not spread. No white-flowered forms are known.

'Anthea Bloom', flowers bright blue, in up-right sprays.

'Cherry Ingram', flowers deep blue, larger than the species.

'Lilac Mist', flowers lilac-pink to mauve, larger than the species.

'Parisian Skies', flowers azure blue, shining.

'Starry Eyes', flowers bright sky-blue, nar-rowly outlined with white.

Omphalodes verna

Omphalodes verna
Blue-eyed Mary

Southern Europe. Similar in habit and culture to *Omphalodes cappadocica*, except stoloniferous, spreading. May become invasive. In southern gardens the leaves are evergreen, but in northern gardens they may become deciduous.

'Alba' is a natural albino form with white flowers.

'Grandiflora' has flowers larger than the type, to 0.6 in. (1.5 cm).

Onoclea sensibilis
Sensitive fern

North America. Fronds triangular, 24–30 in. (60–75 cm) long and 12–15 in. (30–38 cm) wide, singly along the rhizome, erect; sterile leaves light green, deciduous, divided into pairs of light green leaflets; fertile leaves 12–24 in. (30–60 cm) tall, club-shaped, green turning brown, with beadlike lobes containing spore cases. Zones 4–9. LS to FS. Moist, fertile, acidic soil. Spreading rapidly by rhizomatous runners near the surface, this is an attractive fern no garden should be without it. Forms with red stems and coppery sterile fronds are offered.

Ophiopogon jaburan
Jaburan lily turf

Japan. Flowers small, many, white, bell-shaped, to 0.5 in. (1 cm) long, in tight clusters on stalks to 6 in. (15 cm) tall; August–September; rhizomatous, tufted, spreading; leaves evergreen, dark green, linear lance-shaped, to 24 in. (60 cm) long and 0.2–0.5 in. (0.5–1 cm) wide; berries violet. Zones 7–10. Some sun, LS to MS. Any moist, well-drained soil. Initially clump-forming, but spreading when established, with stolons terminating in new plantlets.

'Aureovariegatus', leaves green, striped with yellow.

'Caeruleus', flowers purplish blue, violet.

'Vittatus' ('Argenteovittatus', 'Javanensis', 'Variegatus'), leaves green, narrowly margined and striped with white.

Ophiopogon japonicus
Mondo grass

Japan, Korea. Similar in habit and culture to *Ophiopogon jaburan*, except flowerstalks 2–3 in. (5–8 cm) tall and leaves 8–12 in. (20–30 cm) long; berries blue. Spreads fast.

'Albus', flowers pure white.

'Compactus' ('Minor'), extremely dwarf, leaves short, curling, to 2 in. (5 cm) tall and 4 in. (10 cm) wide.

'Kyoto Dwarf' ('Intermedius'), very dwarf, to 4 in. (10 cm) tall and wide.

'White Dragon' ('Shiro Ryu'), leaves widely striped with white, little green showing in some leaves, to 12 in. (30 cm) long.

Onoclea sensibilis with *Woodwardia areolata* (bottom right), both showing sterile fronds

Ophiopogon japonicus 'Compactus'

Ophiopogon planiscapus 'Nigrescens'

Osmunda cinnamomea

Ophiopogon planiscapus

Japan. Similar in habit and culture to *Ophiopogon jaburan*, except flowers purplish white or pinkish white, 0.2 in. (0.5 cm) long; leaves 6–14 in. (15–35 cm) long and 0.2 in. (0.5 cm) wide; berries blue to blackish blue. Zone 6.

'Leucanthus' (*Ophiopogon leucanthus* of gardens), flowers pure white.

'Nigrescens' ('Arabicus', 'Black Dragon', 'Ebony Knight'), flowers pinkish; leaves black. An outstanding plant with leaves that contrast well with dwarf yellow hostas, yellow club moss (*Selaginalla kraussiana* 'Aurea'), and dwarf golden sweetflag (*Acorus gramineus* 'Minimus Aureus'). It comes true from seed and produces mostly black-leaved seedlings, although a few green seedlings show up.

Osmunda cinnamomea
Cinnamon fern

North America. Fiddleheads woolly, white; fronds to 36 in. (90 cm) tall, as much as 5 ft. (1.5 m); in clusters; sterile leaves light green, lance-shaped, divided into light green, leaflets; fertile leaves appear and wither first, to 39 in. (90 cm) tall, erect, club-shaped, pointed, forming a club-like mass of spore-holding leaflets, light green, later cinnamon-brown. Zones 4–9. LS to FS. Moist, fertile, acidic soil. This attractive fern is widely offered and no garden should be without it. The sterile fronds wither early so cut them to maintain a tidy appearance. Good in northern and southern gardens.

Osmunda claytoniana
Interrupted fern

Eastern North America. Fiddleheads woolly, white; sterile fronds 24 in. (60 cm) tall and 7 in. (18 cm) wide, vase-shaped, around taller fertile fronds to 36 in. (90 cm); sterile leaves light green, lance-shaped, light green pairs of leaflets; fertile leaves to 36 in. (90 cm) tall, fertile leaflets below, green turning brown, growing parallel to the stem, followed by sterile leaflets in lower part. Culture like *Osmunda cinnamomea*.

Oxalis regnellii

Osmunda regalis as an accent plant.

Osmunda regalis
Royal fern

Nearly cosmopolitan. Fiddleheads woolly, brown; fronds 3–6 ft. (0.9–1.8 m) tall; sterile leaves light green, erect, divided into widely spaced leaflets (looking much like a locust tree); subleaflets translucent light green, narrowly oblong; fertile leaflets light brown, densely clustered and contracted.

Culture like *Osmunda cinnamomea*. A truly majestic fern that must be carefully placed due to its large size. It does well in gardens with some sun and dappled shade but it will also grow in medium to woodland shade. Its size varies greatly depending on growing conditions. Constantly moist soil results in larger sizes.

'Crispa', crisped leaflets and subleaflets.

'Cristata', distinctly crested leaflets and subleaflets.

'Purpurascens', fronds flushed reddish bronze to purple in spring.

Var. *spectabilis* is sometimes sold as the native North American form.

'Undulata', subleaflets wavy-margined.

Oxalis regnellii

South America. Flowers small, white or pink, trumpet-shaped, on short stems above the leaves; April through summer; mat-forming, slowly spreading; leaves to 3 in. (8 cm), clover-like with three triangular leaflets, green or purple, sometimes multicolored, to 8 in. (20 cm) high. Zone 7a, but herbaceous; evergreen during mild winters in zone 7. LS to MS. Any moist, but well-drained soil. Also sold under the names *Oxalis regnellii* 'Triangularis' and *O. magellanica*. A fine groundcover for shady gardens in southern gardens, with reports of success into zone 6. It has a very long flowering period starting in early spring and continuing sporadically until early autumn (see photo on page 16).

Pachysandra procumbens
Allegheny spurge

Eastern North America. Flowers small, white, fragrant, many, on spikes 2–4 in. (5–10 cm) tall; April–May; clumping, slowly spreading; leaves 3–5 in. (8–13 cm) long, whorled around the stem, dull gray-green mottled with light brownish gray; stems first trailing along the ground, the terminal part becoming erect, holding leaves to 12 in. (30 cm) high. Zone 6, but herbaceous; evergreen in zone 7. WS to FS. Any moist soil. In spite of its rather slow growth, this attractive native is still the most gardenworthy pachysandra available.

'Eco Picture Leaf', leaves distinctly variegated in spring.

'Kingsville', leaves with distinct silvery markings.

Pachysandra terminalis
Japanese spurge

China, Japan. Sun, flowers small, white, not showy; May–July; rhizomatous, quickly spreading; evergreen, dark shiny green leaves 1–3 in. (2.5–8 cm) long on leafstalks to 12 in. (30 cm), in whorls around the stem or on short side branches Zones 4–8. LS to FS. Any but very dry soils. An al-

most maintenance-free species that grows into a dense groundcover and seems to live forever. Invasive in some situations. In a garden setting, it will grow so dense as to eliminate all other low-growing perennials, as well as weeds.

'Green Carpet', leaves darker green than the species.

'Green Sheen', leaves very glossy dark green.

'Silveredge' ('Silver Edge'), leaves with a thin, silvery white margin.

'Variegata', leaves with an irregular silvery white margin.

Pachysandra procumbens 'Eco Picture Leaf' (Don Jacobs)

Pachysandra terminalis

Paris polyphylla

Himalaya, eastern Asia. Flowers terminal, solitary, spiderlike, yellow, with threadlike petals to 3 in. (8 cm) above the leaves on flowerstalk to 6 in. (15 cm) tall; June–July; stems 12–36 in. (30–90 cm) tall; leaves with 8–12 leaflets, lance-shaped, whorled, bright green, 3–8 in. (8–20 cm) long; scarlet seeds. Zones 6–8. MS to FS. Moist, fertile soil. Cold hardiness depends on natural habitat in China. The mountain species from Sichuan tend to be hardy to zone 6 and those from Yunnan perhaps to zone 7a. Inquire as to original habitat. It adapts to hot summers in southern gardens if located in a cool, shady spot.

Var. *alba* is from western Yunnan, with almost white flowers.

Var. *nana* is a dwarf form from Sichuan.

Paris quadrifolia
Herb paris

Europe. Similar in habit to *Paris polyphylla*, except flowers bright yellow and stems 6–16 in. (15–40 cm) tall; scarlet to dark brown berries. Zones 5–8. LS to MS. Cool, moist soil. Of easy culture and quite heat-tolerant if planted in shade to keep the ground cool. This is the well-known European form that is hardier than most of the Asian species. Try this one first.

Paris verticillata

Eurasia, China, Korea, Japan. Similar in habit and culture to *Paris polyphylla*, except stems 8–16 in. (20–40 cm) tall; leaflets, tight on the stem or connected broadly lance-shaped, 3–5 in. (8–13 cm) long and 1.5–2 in. (4–5 cm) wide; berries large,

Paris polyphylla

Paris verticillata with opening flower bud

purple. Zones 6–8. LS to MS. Cool, moist soil. A variable species, but among the easiest to cultivate. Reasonably heat-tolerant in zone 7, if sited in a cool, moist, shady spot.

Peltoboykinia tellimoides

Southern Japan. Flowers small, shallowly bell-shaped, many in clusters, greenish yellow, flowerstalks to 38 in. (95 cm) tall; July–September; clumping, rhizomatous, spreading; leaf stems to 20 in. (50 cm); leaves basal, green, heart-shaped, lobed, toothed, 6–12 in. (15–30 cm) long and 4–10 in. (10–25 cm) wide. Zones 6–9. LS to MS. Moist, fertile soil. A good foliage plant for the natural shade garden. It is frequently sold as *Peltoboykinia watanabei*.

Peltoboykinia watanabei

Southern Japan. Similar in habit and culture to *Peltoboykinia tellimoides*, except it is larger, to 5 ft. (1.5 m); basal leaves more rounded and with deeper lobes, 15–24 in. (38–60 cm) long. Not for small gardens (see photo on page 6).

Peltoboykinia tellimoides

Persicaria
Ornamental knotweed

North temperate zone. Flowers insignificant; clumping; leaves elliptical, 3–8 in. (8–20 cm) long, usually lighter green with darker markings. Zones 5–8. Some sun, LS to WS. Moist soil. Cultivars listed here are suitable in northern and southern gardens. Also listed and sold under the generic names *Polygonum* and *Tovara*, some ornamental knotweed species have been specifically developed as foliage plants with beautiful foliage patterns but insignificant flowers. The species most frequently involved is *Persicaria virginiana*. Plants seed around and should not be used around delicate wildflowers, which might be overcome. In spite of this, they are colorful and widely planted.

'Brushstrokes', leaves yellowish green with a black chevron marking in the leaf center. It blooms in autumn.

'Lance Corporal', leaves yellowish green with a maroon chevron marking in the leaf center.

'Painter's Palette' (*Tovara virginiana*), leaves dark green with a black chevron marking in the leaf center and white and pink sections toward leaf tip.

'Red Dragon', leaves burgundy red with a silvery gray chevron marking in the leaf center.

'Silver Dragon', leaves silvery gray with a reddish margin.

Petasites albus
White butterbur

Eurasia. Flowers small, yellowish white, in dense clusters on thick stalks, 6–12 in. (15–30 cm) tall, arising before the leaves emerge; March–April; rhizomatous, widely creeping; leaves basal and umbrella-like, kidney-shaped, 6–16 in. (15–40 cm) across, green, with regular, toothed lobes, on stout, upright stems to 15 in. (38 cm) tall. Zones 5–8. Morning sun, LS to MS. Deep, evermoist, fertile soil. A gardenworthy plant, but it spreads vigorously by rhizomes so caution is advised. In short time it makes a very large accent group or groundcover for very large areas. Grow in containers in smaller gardens or plant in an inground, large plastic tub. Check for and remove stray runners every spring.

Persicaria 'Brushstrokes'

Petasites japonicus
Japanese butterbur

Eastern Asia. Similar in habit and culture to *Petasites albus*, except leaves larger, to 32 in. (80 cm), on stout leaf stems to 40 in. (1 m) tall. Zone 5. Very heat-tolerant as long as soil remains moist. Easily the most aggressive butterbur, it is for large gardens only. Check clumps every early spring and remove errant rhizomes.

Var. *giganteus* ('Giganteus') is huge—too large for smaller gardens. Its leaves are 4–5 ft. (1.2–1.5 m) across, rising on stout stems to 7 ft. (2 m).

'Variegatus'. Variegated butterbur. Leaves irregularly variegated with yellowish or creamy white.

Phegopteris connectilis
Narrow beech fern

Cosmopolitan. Fronds 12–14 in. (30–35 cm) tall, in rows along rhizome, erect, leaning with age; leaves deciduous; divided into pale green leaflets, 8–12 in. (20–30 cm) long and to 6 in. (15 cm) wide, again cut into lobed subleaflets. Zones 3–7. WS to FS. Moist soil. This fern is better suited for northern gardens and requires lots of moisture. In southern gardens it does poorly if the soil dries up but it in can be grown if planted in deep shade in a constantly moist location.

Phegopteris hexagonoptera
Southern beech fern

Eastern North America. Similar in habit and culture to *Phegopteris connectilis*, except a larger fern with fronds to 24 in. (60 cm) tall, tilting backward from an upright stalk; leaflets widest in the middle, to 16 in. (40 cm) long. Zones 4–8. Among the best ferns for southern gardens and holds its own further north. Very hardy and heat-tolerant.

Phlox divaricata
Woodland phlox

North America. Flowers many, in clusters, showy, trumpet-shaped, lavender-blue to pale violet and white, to 1.5 in. (4 cm) across; April–June; semi-evergreen, spreading, stem-rooting; erect to ascending, 10–15 in. (25–38

Petasites japonicus

Phegopteris hexagonoptera in the woodland

Phlox divaricata

cm) tall; leaves green, hairy, oval to lance-shaped, on the stem, opposite, to 2 in (5 cm) long. Zones 4–8. LS to WS. Moist, fertile soil. A shade-tolerant, widely planted, native not subject to mildew damage. It reseeds, producing seedlings with a mix of colors.

'Blue Dreams', flowers fragrant, lilac blue.

'Dirigo Ice', flowers icy pale blue.

'Fuller's White', flowers pure white.

'Louisiana Blue', flowers bluish purple; stems to 10 in. (25 cm).

'May Breeze', flowers fragrant, clear white; stems to 8 in. (20 cm).

Pinellia cordata

China, Korea. Spathe to 3 in. (8 cm) long on purple stem to 8 in. (20 cm); with light green tube, purple veined, with flaring, incurved hood, spadix with long appendage; June–July; petiole 6 in. (15 cm) tall, purple; leaves basal, lance-shaped, dark green with veins outlined in grayish to yellowish green, bright purple beneath, 3–5 in. (8–13 cm) long. Zones 6–8. Some sun, LS to WS. Moist, well-drained, fertile soil. The smallest but showiest of the pinellias. Its variegated, dark green leaves and purple stems are outstanding. The plant increases moderately via very small bulblets and seed.

Pinellia petadisecta
Green dragon

Western China. Spathe 4–6 in. (10–15 cm) long on green stem to 12 in. (30 cm), with lime-green tube, hood erect, tapering, green, spadix yellowish; June–July; petiole to 10 in. (25 cm) tall, green; leaves basal, finger-leaved, divided into lance-shaped segments, green, 4–7 in. (10–18 cm) long.

Culture same as for *Pinellia cordata*. Though not as showy, this species is much taller and looks great overtopping small hostas, ferns, and astilbes.

Pinellia tripartita

Southern Japan. Similar in habit and culture to *Pinellia petadisecta*, except spathe 3–4 in. (8–10 cm) long with green tube and whitish green hood, erect tapering, green outside, purple or green inside; leaves basal, with three oval segments, 3–8 in. (8–20 cm) long. A well-behaved pinellia that spreads slowly.

'Atropurpurea' has deep purple inside spathe.

'Golden Dragon' has leaves variegated with yellow splashes or all yellow.

'Polly Spout', a hybrid, is delicately pink within the spathe and the erect hood. Like the species, the spadix extension is up to 10 in. (25 cm) long. It stands out like a pink flag in the wildflower garden.

'Silver Dragon' has leaves variegated in silvery gray.

Plantago major 'Variegata'
Variegated plantain

Cosmopolitan. Flowers on a spike, insignificant; leaves basal, to 2 in. (5 cm), in a rosette, heart-shaped at the base, dark green, randomly variegated with lighter green and creamy yellow. Zones 5–8. Some sun, LS to WS. Any soil. Grows just about anywhere. Leaves are beautifully mottled with a lighter green and bright creamy yellow. Coming true from seed, it seeds around and lights up the garden here and there. Seedlings are easy to remove and everyone seems to want them.

Forma *contracta* is smaller than the typical species in all respects.

Platanthera chlorantha
Greater butterfly orchid

Europe; Flowers small, fragrant, greenish white, many in a loose cluster on an erect stem to 10–20 in. (25–50 cm) high; June–August; leaves basal, glossy green, conspicuously veined, 3–10 in. (8–25 cm) long, oval to elliptic, pointed tip, upper leaves bractlike, much smaller, sheathing stem. Zones 6–7. Some sun, LS to WS. Moist, usually boggy soil with a high content of peat; maintaining high acidity is essential. Widely cultivated in Europe. Occasionally seen in American gardens.

Pinellia cordata

Pinellia tripartita

Plantago major 'Variegata'

Platanthera ciliaris with *Hosta longipes* in bloom

Platanthera ciliaris
Yellow fringed orchid

North America. Similar in habit and culture to *Platanthera chlorantha*, except the flowers are bright, yellowish orange, not fragrant. This is one of the prettiest native orchids. Zone 7.

Platanthera grandiflora

North America. Similar in habit and culture to *Platanthera chlorantha*, except the flowers are larger, many, to 1 in. (2.5 cm) long, fragrant, light purple or lavender, on an erect spike to 4 ft. (1.2 m) high; June–August. Best for northern gardens. Zone 5.

Podophyllum difforme

China. Similar in habit and culture to *Podophyllum pleianthum*, except the flowers are elongated, bell-shaped with much longer lobes, borne just underneath the upper leaf junction, deep red to maroon; leaves deeply lobed to starfish shape, leathery, larger at 9–18 in. (23–46 cm) long and wide; bright to dark green or grayish green with central blotches and markings from silvery gray to almost cream. The color patterns are attractive and alike in a given plant, yet quite different from plant to plant; maroon to almost black clones are known; fruit small, berry-shaped, yellow when fully ripe. Zones 6–8. LS to MS. Moist, fertile soil. Evergreen in zone 7a. It is best to remove the old leaves before new growth starts. Some forms of this species are very colorful and attractive, and the large mound attracts attention. Unlike *Podophyllum pleianthum* this is a clumping species that does not spread.

'Kaleidoscope', leaves patterned with purplish, silver, and bronze.

Starfish Strain, leaf outlines pronounced starfish shaped.

Podophyllum hexandrum
Himalayan Mayapple

Himalaya to China. Flower solitary, bell-shaped, slightly nodding, borne in the leaf axil, to 2 in. (5 cm) across, waxy white; April–June; rhizomatous, spreading; stems to 18 in. (45 cm) tall; leaves rounded, lobed, margins toothed, 6–10 in. (12–25 cm) across, leaf usually mottled purple on green, turning all green. Zones 5–8. LS to MS. Moist, fertile soil. A good foliage plant for the natural shade garden. Many clones are in commerce with varying patterns of leaf variegation. Considerable variances should be expected but forms turn all green by summer.

Podophyllum peltatum
Mayapple

Eastern North America. Flower solitary, shallowly bell-shaped, white, fragrant, nodding, borne in the leaf axil, to 2 in. (5 cm) across, waxy white; April–June; rhizomatous, vigorously colonizing; stems to 12–24 in. (30–60 cm) tall; leaves on nonflowering stems solitary, on flowering stems 2, rounded, lobed with most lobes deeply cleft, margins toothed, 9–12 in. (23–30 cm) across, green. Zones 4–8. LS to MS. Moist, fertile soil. This native Mayapple forms huge colonies in

Podophyllum difforme 'Kaleidoscope'

Podophyllum peltatum underplanted with *Asarum canadense*

some wild areas. The pretty, white flowers are usually hidden underneath a solid canopy of leaves. In fertile and moist garden soil Mayapple grows quickly into a foot-tall (30-cm) deciduous groundcover.

Podophyllum pleianthum

China, Taiwan. Flowers in a cluster, maroon, nodding, odorous, on the leafstalk, 2–2.5 in. (5–6 cm) long; May–July; rhizomatous, spreading; stems stout, upright, to 18 in. (45 cm) tall; leaves on flowering stem, bright glossy green, 9–15 in. (23–38 cm) across, rounded, with very shallow lobes, margins with spaced teeth. Zones 6–8. LS to MS. Moist, fertile soil. Sensational, dark maroon flowers up close add to the spectacular glossy green leaves that remain fresh and green from the time they unfurl in spring until the first freeze cuts them down (see photo on page 225). Frequently sold as *Podophyllum versipelle*, but the latter has much smaller flowers and deeply lobed leaves.

Podophyllum versipelle

Tibet to China. LS to MS. flowers open, rounded and bell-shaped, on very long flower stalks, to 4 in. (10 cm) long, in a drooping cluster at the leaf base of the upper leaf, purplish brown or maroon, odorous; May–July; clumping, rhizomatous; stems to 18 in. (45 cm) tall; leaves bright glossy green similar of those to *Podophyllum pleianthum* but with much deeper lobes, 9–15 in. (23–38 cm) across. Zones 6–8. LS to MS. Moist, fertile soil. The beautiful purplish flowers and long-lasting, majestic leaves of this species add much to the garden.

Polemonium caeruleum
Jacob's ladder

Eurasia, western North America. Flowers many, usually blue, saucer-shaped climbing erect, branched leafy stems to 36 in. (90 cm) tall; May–July; clumping, herbaceous; leaves fernlike, divided into many small green to dark green leaflets to 1.5 in. (4 cm) long. Zones 3–6. Some

Podophyllum pleianthum with *Tiarella wherryi*

Podophyllum versipelle

sun to LS. Moist soil. Best for northern gardens with cool summers, but can be grown in zone 7 given medium shade and ever-moist soil. Attractive, but not long-lived, though it renews itself by seeding around.

'Brise d'Anjou', flowers lilac-blue; leaves margined with creamy white.

Var. *lacteum* ('Album'), flowers pure white

Polemonium reptans
Greek valerian

North America. Similar in habit and culture to *Polemonium caeruleum*, except that its numerous flowers are lavender-blue on cushions of attractive foliage; June–July; low growing, to 12 in (30 cm) tall. Being a native, it is longer lived than *P. caeruleum*.

'Album' has white flowers.

'Blue Pearl' has bright blue flowers.

'Lambrook Mauve' has lilac-blue flowers; mounds to 18 in. (45 cm).

Pollia japonica

Southern Japan to China. Flowers small, many, white, ball-shaped, in clustered whorls on straight stems to 4 ft. (1.2 m) tall; May–July; vigorously rhizomatous, spreading; leaves singular, glossy green, alternate, to 18 in. (45 cm) long and 2 in. (5 cm) wide, tapered toward both ends, slightly arching from the stem; berries bluish black.

Some sun, LS to MS. This species should be contained like bamboo; gardeners with plenty of room can grow it in the open, but its perimeter should be watched closely. An excellent potted companion when the container is placed among hostas, ferns, and astilbes. The flowers are long-lasting and the berries contrast well with the soft green leaves, making a nice show in autumn.

Polygonatum biflorum
Smooth Solomon's seal

North America. Flowers greenish white, to 1 in. (2.5 cm) long, hanging, bell-shaped; May–July;

Polemonium caeruleum

Pollia japonica with ferns, hostas, and *Heuchera micrantha* 'Palace Purple' (bottom left)

stems arching, hairless, to 7 ft. (2 m) tall; leaves single, alternate, green, to 6 in. (15 cm) long, lance-shaped; berries black. Zones 3–9. MS to FS. Moist, fertile soil. An extremely variable species with tall and short clones. Some grow to 8 ft. (2.5 m) but most are about 3 ft. (90 cm). The taller forms are useful as overtopping accents in hosta and fern plantings. The smaller forms, allowed to form colonies, make good background screens and groundcovers (see photo on page 32). Sold under several synonyms: *Polygonatum canaliculatum*, *P. commutatum*, and *P. giganteum*.

Polygonatum cirrhifolium
Himalaya. Flowers white, to 1 in. (2.5 cm) long, bell-shaped, in clusters in the leaf axils; May–July; stems erect, leaning, to 8 ft. (2.5 m) tall; leaves in whorls, green, narrowly lance-shaped, to 6 in. (15 cm) long, with coiled-under leaf tips ending in a twisting, threadlike structure by which the plant grasps a support; berries translucent red. Zones 6–8. MS to FS. Moist, fertile soil.

Polygonatum geminiflorum
Western China. Similar in habit and culture to *Polygonatum cirrhifolium*, except flowers creamy white, green-tipped, to 1 in. (2.5 cm) long, bell-shaped with flaring lobe tips; June–July; stems short, to 15 in. (38 cm) tall; leaves shiny green, broadly ovate, to 2 in. (5 cm) long; berries bluish. This species is among the smaller Asian Solomon's seals, with attractive white flowers (see photo on page 75).

Polygonatum humile
Dwarf Solomon's seal
China, Korea, Japan. Flowers white, to 0.5 in. (1 cm) long, bell-shaped, in clusters; May–June; stems erect, to 8 in. (20 cm) tall, with alternate, green leaves to 2 in. (5 cm) long, broadly ovate, to 1 in. (2 cm) wide; bluish black berries. Zones

Polygonatum biflorum

Polygonatum humile

Polygonatum odoratum
'Variegatum' bordering
a walk, underplanted
with blooming
Saxifraga veitchiana

Polypodium
polypodioides mature
and emerging fronds

Polypodium
virginianum

5–8. LS to MS. Moist soil. Given fertile soil, it spread fast so makes a good, low-growing, dainty groundcover. It goes dormant early if not supplied with supplemental water during hot, dry summers.

'Streaker', leaves irregularly striped yellow.

Polygonatum ×hybridum
Common Solomon's seal

Garden hybrid (*Polygonatum multiflorum* × *P. odoratum*). Flowers white, to 1 in. (2.5 cm) long, hanging, bell-shaped; May–July; stems erect, to 5 ft. (1.5 m) tall; leaves green, to 8 in. (20 cm) long, broadly lance-shaped; berries black, to 0.3 in. (8 mm) in diameter. Zones 5–8. LS to MS. Moist soil. This graceful addition to the garden has been around a long time and mixes well with ferns, hostas, and native wildflowers. The available plants are highly variable.

'Flore Pleno', double-flowered, slightly spreading lobes.

'Striatum', variegated sport with cream-striped leaves.

'Variegatum', very similar if not identical to 'Striatum'.

'Weihenstephan', an outstanding, larger size sterile form.

Polygonatum odoratum
Common Solomon's seal

Eurasia. Flowers greenish white, with green margins, 1 in. (2.5 cm) long, mildly lily-scented, bell-shaped; April–June; stems angular, arching to 32 in. (80 cm) tall; leaves alternate, green, to 6 in. (15 cm) long, broadly elliptic; berries black. Zones 5–8. LS to MS. Moist soil. One of the parents of *Polygonatum* ×*hybridum*. The green species is rarely seen in gardens, but its cultivars make up a majority of Solomon's seals seen (see photos on pages 31 and 39).

'Flore Pleno' is a double-flowered form.

'Gilt Edge' has a yellow leaf margin.

'Striatum' is a variegated sport with mostly white-striped leaves and a white margin on most leaves.

'Variegatum' is a variegated sport with varying, somewhat streaky, creamy white margins

and more articulated toward the tip of the leaf. The best-known and most appreciated Solomon's seal. Widely available.

Polygonatum verticillatum
Whorled Solomon's seal

Eurasia. Flowers white, green fringed, to 0.5 in. (1 cm) long, bell-shaped; May–June; stems erect, 4–8 ft. (1.2–2.5 m) tall; leaves stalkless, in whorls, green, narrowly lance-shaped leaves to 6 in. (15 cm) long, with the long leaf tips straight or pointed down; berries red. Zones 5–8. Some sun, LS to WS. Moist soil. This is the primary Eurasian form with whorled leaves, which sets it apart from Solomon's seals with alternate single or opposite leaves. Best for northern gardens with cool summers.

Var. *rubrum* ('Rubrum') has red stems and leaf petioles.

Polypodium polypodioides
Resurrection fern

North America. Fronds on separate erect stems, 4–8 in. (10–20 cm) high, leaf oblong, divided into pairs of dark green, leathery leaflets, alternate, sometimes almost opposite, 0.5–1 in. (1–2.5 cm) long. Zones 7–8. Some sun to WS. Moist soil. This fern "plays dead" during dry periods, looking dried and curled, but comes back to life when moisture returns. It is a widespread and variable species. In protected areas gardeners have had success into zone 6. Tolerates heat and drought.

Polypodium virginianum
American wall fern

North America, eastern Asia. MS to FS. Similar in habit and culture to *Polypodium vulgare*, except that fronds are smaller, 8–10 in. (20–25 cm) long and to 4 in. (10 cm) wide.

Polypodium vulgare
Wall polypody

Cosmopolitan. Fronds on separate erect stems, to 16 in. (40 cm) high; leaf lance-shaped, variable, 10–12 in. (25–30 cm) long and to 6 in. (15 cm) wide, divided into dark green, leathery leaflets, 0.8–2 in. (2–5 cm) long. Zones 4–8. Some sun to WS. Moist soil. Widespread and extremely variable, adaptable to many different habitats, including growing on walls. Tolerant of cold, heat, and drought.

Polystichum acrostichoides
Christmas fern

North America. Fronds to 36 in. (90 cm), in rosettes; fertile fronds taller, more erect; leaves first light green, later dark green, lance-shaped, narrow, to 32 in. (80 cm) long and 4 in. (10 cm) wide, divided into leaflets, lance-shaped and prominently eared at base. Zones 3–8. Some sun to WS. Moist soil. A popular fern with bright green young fronds that are beacons in the spring garden. Remove the old fronds to give new fronds room to rise. Christmas fern is excellent for very cold areas and provides evergreen fronds year-round in hot, dry summers in southern climates.

Polystichum polyblepharum
Japanese tassel fern

China, Korea, Japan. Fronds to 40 in. (1.0 m), forming funnel-shaped clumps; leaves leathery, glossy dark green, oblong lance-shaped, 18–32 in. (45–80 cm) long and 6–10 in. (15–25 cm) wide, divided into many oblong lance-shaped leaflets, to 5 in. (13 cm) long, again divided into showy subleaflets, eared at base and blunt, spiny-toothed and prickly tipped. Zones 5–8. Some sun to WS. Moist soil. One of the finest ferns for the natural green garden, it will naturalize and spread as an added benefit. In snow-free gardens, the fresh, glossy green fronds provide excellent winter color.

Polystichum setiferum
Soft shield fern

Europe. Fronds to 4 ft. (1.2 m), forming vase-shaped clumps; leaves leathery, dark green, oblong lance-shaped, 18–36 in. (45–90 cm) long and 6–10 in. (15–25 cm) wide; cut into lance-shaped leaflets to 4 in. (10 cm) long; again divided into spiny-toothed and prickly tipped sub-

leaflets. Zones 6–8. Some sun to WS. Moist soil. A popular fern for southern gardens. A multitude of cultivars are available, which have their fronds finely divided into a delicate, filigreed and/or plumose pattern of narrowed, leathery segments.

Divisilobum Group, fronds finely divided, each subleaflet further divided into sub-subleaflets, creating a delicate, filigreed pattern of narrowed, leathery segments, much finer than the excellent type.

'Lineare' ('Confluens'), very narrow leaves, leaflets at base missing.

Multilobum Group, fronds finely divided, similar to the Divisilobum Group but not narrowed or leathery.

Plumosodivisilobum Group, fronds more finely divided and overlapping at the base; each sub-subleaflet is further divided toward the base, while the segments toward the tip are narrowed, creating an ethereal, feathery appearance of great daintiness.

'Plumosum Bevis' ('Pulcherrimum Bevis', 'Pulcherrimum'), very narrow frond subsegments curving gracefully toward the tip. This very popular English cultivar appears to be sterile and must be propagated vegetatively.

Polystichum tsussimense
Dwarf holly fern

Tsushima Island. Fronds to 15 in. (38 cm) long and 5 in. (13 cm) wide, forming vase-shaped clumps; leaves leathery, dark green, oblong lance-shaped. Zones 6–8. Some sun to WS. Moist soil. Very similar in appearance and detail to Polystichum acrostichoides and particularly suited for smaller gardens.

Primula prolifera

Asia. Flowers small, tubular with spreading lobes at top, yellow and fragrant, arranged in several whorls on flowerstalks to 24 in. (60 cm) tall; May–July; semi-evergreen, clumping; leaves in a basal rosette, oval, crinkly, medium green, to 12 in. (30 cm) long. Zones 5–8. Some sun to MS. Moist, neutral soil. Best for northwestern gardens

*Polystichum
acrostichoides*

*Polystichum
polyblepharum*

*Polystichum
tsussimense*

but heat-tolerant in southeastern gardens if constant moisture and shade are provided. Also sold as *Primula helodoxa*.

Primula veris
Cowslip

Eurasia. Flowers small, up-facing, tubular with spreading lobes at top, deep yellow and fragrant, in clusters on flowerstalks to 9 in. (23 cm) tall; March–June; semi-evergreen, clumping; leaves in a basal rosette, oval, crinkly, medium green, to 8 in. (20 cm) long. Zones 3–7. Some sun to WS. Moist, acidic to neutral soil. This species and the similar *Primula vulgaris* are best for zone 6 north. Heat-tolerant to zone 7 if constant moisture and shade are provided.

Pteridium aquilinium
Bracken fern

Cosmopolitan. Fronds herbaceous, to 6 ft. (1.8 m) tall, sometimes taller, in rows along a rhizome; leaves 36 in. (90 cm) wide and long, bright green, divided into three equal subleaves, triangular in shape and composed of 12 to 20 tapered, variable leaflets; rhizomatous, widely creeping. Zones 3–8. Some sun to WS. Moist soil. This fern is included because it is a magnificent, architectural plant in the garden. Unfortunately, it is a strong fern that is aggressive and spreads far and wide. In small gardens confine it to a large, plastic tub sunk into the ground. Planted in the ground in larger woodland areas it shows its true splendor but needs constant watching. Consider it strongly invasive in cultivated garden areas and beds.

Primula prolifera

Primula veris

Pteridium aquilinium and the author in a forest near Uppsala, Sweden, 1984.

Pulmonaria angustifolia
Blue lungwort

Europe. Flowers small, funnel-shaped, bright blue, in forked clusters on flowerstalks 9–12 in. (23–30 cm) tall; March–May; deciduous, clumping; leaves in a basal rosette, bristly, medium to dark green, unspotted, to 16 in. (40 cm) long and 2 in. (5 cm) wide, elongated lance-shaped. Zones 3–7. Some sun to WS. Moist soil. Heat-tolerant to zone 7.

'Alba', flowers white; leaves dark green.

'Munstead Blue', flowers blue; leaves dark green, to 6 in. (15 cm).

'Rubra', flowers early, light red; to 10 in. (25 cm).

'Variegata', flowers blue; leaves variegated grayish white.

Pulmonaria longifolia
Longleaf lungwort

Europe. Flowers small, funnel-shaped, violet to purplish, on flowerstalks to 12 in. (30 cm); April–May; deciduous, clumping; leaves in a basal rosette, green spotted with grayish to silvery white, rarely all green, to 18 in. (45 cm) long and 2.5 in. (6 cm) wide, lance-shaped. Zones 3–7. Some sun to WS. Moist soil. Heat-tolerant to zone 7. Many named cultivars are available.

'Bertram Anderson', flowers bright blue; leaves green, marked strongly with white.

Subsp. *cevennensis*, flowers blue; long white-spotted leaves.

'Dordogne', flowers blue; leaves almost white; thin, white-spotted green margin.

'Little Star', flowers cobalt-blue; leaves green spotted silvery white.

'Roy Davidson', flowers blue; leaves spotted white, green margin.

Pulmonaria officinalis
Common lungwort

Europe. Flowers small, funnel-shaped, blue, in forked clusters on flowerstalks 9–12 in. (23–30 cm) tall; March–May; evergreen, clumping; leaves in a basal rosette, medium grayish green, irregularly spotted, splashed, or mottled with white, to 6 in. (15 cm) long and 4 in. (10 cm) wide, oval to elliptic. Zones 6–8. Some sun to WS. Moist soil. This is the ubiquitous, extremely variable lungwort from Europe.

'Alba', flowers white.

'Bowles' Blue', flowers small, blue to lilac-blue.

'Cambridge Blue' ('Cambridge'), flowers light blue; leaves mottled white, to 12 in. (30 cm).

'Sissinghurst White', flowers pure white; leaves large, to 20 in. (25 cm), dark green, spotted white.

Pulmonaria rubra
Red lungwort

Southeastern Europe. Similar in habit and culture to *Pulmonaria angustifolia*, except flowers red, March–May, some cultivars January–February; evergreen, clumping; leaves also unspotted, to 12 in. (40 cm) long and 4 in. (10 cm) wide, elliptic. Zones 5–8. Some sun to WS. Moist soil. The only species with red flowers.

'Albocorollata', flowers white.

'Berries and Cream', flowers red; leaves silvery with green margin.

Pulmonaria longifolia subsp. *cevennensis*

'Beth's Pink', flowers deep coral; leaves broader, mottled white.

'Raspberry Splash', flowers red; leaves spotted silvery white.

Pulmonaria saccharata
Bethlehem sage

Europe. Flowers small, funnel-shaped, bluish in clusters on flowerstalks 9–12 in. (23–30 cm) tall; March–May; evergreen, clumping; leaves in a basal rosette, grayish green, spotted or mottled silvery white, to 10 in. (25 cm) long and 4 in. (10 cm) wide, elliptic. Zones 4–8. Some sun to WS. Moist soil. The favored lungwort; heat-tolerant to zone 8 if kept moist.

'Alba', flowers large, pure white; leaves silvery white variegated.

'Argentea', flowers bluish; leaves entirely silvery white.

'Mrs. Kittle', flowers pale blue; leaves with green midrib, more white toward center and a white-spotted green margin.

'Mrs. Moon', flowers lilac, suffused red; leaves profusely spotted with silvery white.

'Reginald Kaye', flowers violet; leaves spotted silvery white.

Pulmonaria vallarsae

Europe. Similar in habit and culture to *Pulmonaria longifolia*, except flowers purple, March–May; deciduous, clumping; leaves narrowing abruptly to the leafstalk, hairy and shiny dark green, spotted with white, rarely all green or all silvery white, to 20 in. (50 cm) long and 5 in. (13 cm) wide, elliptic. Zones 6–8. Some sun to WS. Moist soil. Good for southern gardens.

'Margery Fish', flowers violet; leaves silvery white all over.

Pulmonaria cultivars

Zone 5; suitable into zone 8 if soil moisture is maintained. MS to FS.

'Beth Chatto', flowers dark blue; leaves heavily spotted with white.

'Coral Springs', flowers coral-red; leaves long, spotted with white.

'Excalibur', flowers pink; leaves silvery white, green margined.

'Majeste' ('Majesty'), flowers blue; leaves white, greenish undertone.

'Milky Way', flowers dark blue, early; leaves spotted with silvery white.

Pulmonaria 'Majeste' (Hans Hansen)

Ranzania japonica

Japan. Flowers solitary, rosy lilac; May–June; rhizomatous, spreading; leaves with three stalked, lobed leaflets, 3–5 in. (8–13 cm) long, rounded, bright green; white berries. A *Podophyllum* relative that adds bright green foliage texture to the garden. Zones 6–7. Some sun to WS. Moist soil.

Rheum palmatum
Chinese rhubarb

Northwestern China. Flowers small, red, in clusters on erect, branched flowerstalk to 6 ft. (1.8 m); May–July; clumping; leaves to 36 in. (90 cm) long, glossy dark green above, purplish red to red underneath; deeply lobed; bright red fruit. Zones 5–7. Some sun to LS. Moist, peaty soil. Best in northern gardens. Can be grown in southern gardens if given light shade and moist soil but will not grow as large.

'**Atrosanguineum**' ('Atropurpureum'), flowers pinkish; leaves crimson-red when young, fading to dark green above, remaining purplish green underneath.

'**Hadspen Crimson**', flowers red, giant stalks to 15 ft. (5 m); leaves huge, to 40 in. (1 m).

Rodgersia aesculifolia
Fingerleaf rodgersia

Western China. Flowers white, small, many in dense clusters on flowerstalks 4–6 ft. (1.2–1.8 m) tall; June–July; deciduous, clumping; leaves fingerlike, on red-brown stalks divided into dark green, leaflets with impressed, reddish veins, crinkled, 4–10 in. (10–25 cm) long. Zones 5–8.

Ranzania japonica
(Lynne Harrison)

Rodgersia aesculifolia
in autumn
(Allan Armitage)

Rheum palmatum 'Hadspen Crimson'

Sun, LS to FS. Deep, constantly moist soil. Best north of zone 6.

'Irish Bronze' has glossy, bright reddish bronze leaves.

Rodgersia henrici

Tibet to China. Similar in habit and culture to *Rodgersia aesculifolia*, except flowers red; flowerstalks 3–5 ft. (0.9–1.5 m) tall; June–July; somewhat smaller. This species differs from *R. aesculifolia* by having reddish flowers and longer and narrower leaves (see photo on page 144).

Rodgersia pinnata
Featherleaf rodgersia

Western China. Flowers white, in clusters on flowerstalks 3–4 ft. (0.9–1.2 m) tall; June–July; deciduous, clumping; leaves large, to 36 in. (90 cm), divided into several elliptic, dark green, bronze suffused leaflets, 8 in. (20 cm) long, arranged in opposite pairs along the stem. Zones 5–8. Sun, LS to FS. Deep, constantly moist soil. Best north of zone 6.

'Elegans', flowers rose-pink to pale pink in dense clusters on a stem to 36 in. (90 cm). A good garden form.

'Superba', flowers reddish pink; leaves and stems suffused with bronze in spring, later dark green.

Rodgersia podophylla

Korea, Japan. Flowers white, clustered on flowerstalks 4–7 ft. (1.2–2 m) tall; June–August; deciduous, clumping; leaves large, to 16 in. (40 cm), divided into glossy reddish bronze, later brownish green, fingerlike leaflets with deep lobes and intensely crinkled. Zones 5–8. Sun, LS to FS. Deep, constantly moist soil. Best north of zone 6.

'Rotlaub' ('Red Leaf') has brownish red new leaves.

Rodgersia sambucifolia

Western China. Similar in habit and culture to *Rodgersia pinnata*, except leaves smaller, to 30 in. (75 cm), divided into leaflets to 8 in. (20 cm) long, shaped similar to those of elderberry (*Sam-*

Rodgersia podophylla (Allan Armitage)

bucus spp.), medium to dark green, nonglossy, arranged in wider-spaced opposite pairs along the stem. The smallest of the rodgersias. Zone 7 when given supplemental water and a shady position (see photos on pages 144 and 197).

'Rothaut' ('Red Skin') has brownish red new leaves.

Rohdea japonica
Sacred lily

Southeastern China to Japan. Flowers small, greenish white, inconspicuous, in a dense cluster hidden in the leaf crown; near ground level; clumping; leaves in a basal rosette, arching, lance-shaped, dark glossy green, to 18 in. (45 cm) long and 1–2 in. (2.5–5 cm) wide, midrib keeled; berries red. Zones 7–9. LS to FS. Moist soil. This plant's tough constitution together with its beautiful, thick leathery leaves makes it ideal for winter gardens in southern climates. It adapts to pot culture, so in northern climates it can be potted and plunged during summer. Tolerates summer heat and drought.

'Aureostriata', leaves striped with yellow.

'Fuji-no-Yuki' ("snow of Mount Fuji"), leaves creamy white margined, to 12 in. (30 cm) long and 0.8 in. (2 cm) wide.

'Galle' ('Tyokkwina'). Narrow-leaved sacred lily. Leaves very narrow, to 18 in. (45 cm) long, 0.8–1 in. (2–1.5 cm) wide.

'Ganjaku', leaves deeply keeled, to 6 in. (15 cm) long, with thin, creamy white stripes, variable; clump to 6 in. (15 cm) high.

'Marginata', leaves dark green with narrow white margin.

'Mure Suzume', leaves short, with many white stripes, variable; dwarf, 4–6 in. (10–15 cm) tall and 6 in. (15 cm) wide.

'Striata', leaves dark green striped with white. Similar to but larger than 'Ganjaku'.

'Suncrest', leaves with yellowish striping in the leaf blade; variable. Distorted tissue forms the highly desired white dragon crest in leaf center.

'Washitakakuma', leaves dark green covered with large patches of white, often covering the entire lower portion of the leaf, with a green tip

Rohdea japonica 'Galle'

Rohdea japonica 'Washitakakuma'

Rohdea japonica 'Marginata' backed by *Hakonechloa macra* 'Aureola' (left) and astilbes

and green streaking into the white part; clump to 18 in. (45 cm) high.

'Yattazu Yan Jaku', leaves dark green blotched with variously sized patches of white; clump to 18 in. (45 cm) high.

Sanguinaria canadensis
Bloodroot

Eastern North America. Flowers solitary, white, open cup-shaped, to 1.5 in. (4 cm) across, on upright flowerstalk to 10 in. (25 cm), leaves curl around the flowerstalk; March–April; clumping, rhizomatous; to 8 in. (20 cm) high; leaves basal, kidney-shaped, 4–8 in. (10–20 cm) long, deeply lobed, dull bluish green; sap red. Zones 3–9. LS to FS. Moist, well-drained soil. This native flowers early and is ephemeral. In cool, shady areas the attractive, grayish leaves last well into early summer.

'Flore Pleno' ('Multiplex', 'Pleno'), flowers double.

'Rosea', flowers usually pink, unstable.

Saruma henryi
Pyramidal Chinese ginger

Western China. Flowers bright yellow to 0.8 in. (2 cm) wide; April–September; clumping; to 24 in. (60 cm) tall and 30 in. (75 cm) wide, stems branching; leaves to 5 in. (13 cm) long and wide, heart-shaped, shiny, light green at first, turning a dull dark green. Zones 5–8. LS to FS. Moist, well-drained soil. Heat-tolerant with supplemental water. This is a tall-growing wild ginger relative with a long flowering period and showy, yellow flowers.

Sasa veitchii
Kuma bamboo grass

Japan. Flowers inconspicuous; rhizomatous, vigorously spreading; culms slender, to 4 ft. (1.2 m) tall, leaves elliptic, 7–10 in. (18–25 cm) long, glossy dark green, soon developing yellowish white margins. Zones 6–9. LS to WS. Moist, well-drained soil. A good, variegated bamboo for the

Sanguinaria canadensis

Saruma henryi in bloom with *Acorus gramineus* 'Minimus Aureus'

Sasa veitchii

shady garden. As with all bamboos, its spreading habit must be watched and stray runners cut back in spring.

Sauromatum venosum
Voodoo lily

Africa, Asia. To 30 in. (75 cm) tall; malodorous; spathe constricted in center, tube 2–4 in. (5–10 cm) long, brownish purple; limb lance-shaped, 20–28 in. (50–70 cm) long, translucent yellow with many maroon spots, first erect then folding away, lying on the ground; spadix extension erect, maroon, to 18 in. (45 cm) long, slowly tapering toward blunt tip; leaf solitary, with 7–13, leaflets, to 18 in. (45 cm) wide, medium glossy green with grayish veins; fruit ball-shaped, covered with black seed. Zones 6–9. LS to WS. Moist but well-drained soil a must. An attractive and unusual addition to the garden. The weird but attractive floral display is brief but the attractive foliage lasts well into late summer. The tubers will survive outdoors in soil that does not freeze, so heavy mulching will extend its range.

Saxifraga stolonifera
Mother-of-thousands

Eastern Asia. Flowers white, spotted yellow or pink, 0.8 in. (2 cm), on slender green flower-stalk to 24 in. (60 cm); July–October; clumping, evergreen, spreading by thin, red stolons; leaves long-stalked, in a basal rosette, roundish, 1–3 in. (2.5–7.5 cm) across, grayish green with silvery gray veins, reddish beneath. Zones 7–9, zone 6 with some protection. LS to MS. Any soil. This is the ubiquitous mother-of-thousands plant known to many gardeners. In warm climates, it spreads all over the place and is removed where not wanted and transplanted or given away as a wonderful pass-along plant. Among the most easy-to-care plants in the garden, it makes an attractive, low-maintenance groundcover and has long-lasting flowers in spring (see photo on page 6).

'Eco Butterfly', flowers white; leaves yellow with a butterfly-like pattern of contrasting green.

'Tricolor' ('Magic Carpet'), flowers white; leaves dark green variegated with silvery gray, greenish white, and pink.

Saxifraga veitchiana

China. Similar in habit and culture to *Saxifraga stolonifera*, except that the leaves are a matte, unmarked dark green. Very tolerant of poor soils, heat, and drought, and easy to care for (see photo on page 182).

Sauromatum venosum

Saxifraga stolonifera in bloom

Saxifraga veitchiana in bloom with emerging *Rodgersia sambucifolia*

Selaginella braunii
Arborvitae fern

Western China. Stems erect, 12–18 in. (30–45 cm) tall, many-branched in the upper half, with branches forming erect fanlike blades with triangular outline; leaves evergreen, tiny, oval, dark green. Zones 6–8. LS to FS. This hardy, slow-spreading spike moss forms handsome, tightly bunched, upright clumps. Zone 6.

Selaginella kraussiana
Spreading clubmoss

South Africa, Azores. Stems 6–12 in. (15–30 cm) long, to 1 in. (2.5 cm) high, trailing, matting, and rooting along the way, much-divided and many-branched; leaves tiny, oval, bright green. Zones 7–9; hardy and evergreen in zone 7 with protection. LS to FS. Moist, fertile, acidic or neutral soil.

'**Aurea**'. Yellow club moss. Leaves very bright yellow when young, maturing to a greenish yellow.

'**Brownii**' ('Emerald Isle', *Selaginella brownii*), a compact form with dense growth habit forming cushiony mounds of bright emerald green, to 2 in. (5 cm) high and 8 in. (20 cm) wide.

'**Variegata**', leaves splashed with creamy white; mat-forming.

Selaginella uncinata
Peacock moss

China. Stems 12–24 in. (30–60 cm) long, to 1 in. (2.5 cm) high, trailing, matting and rooting along the way, much-divided alternately and many-branched; leaves tiny, oval, blue-green with a metallic sheen on new growth. Zones 7–9; hardy and evergreen in zone 7 with protection. LS to FS. Moist, fertile, acidic or neutral soil. It requires abundant moisture and colors best in woodland shade.

Shortia galacifolia
Oconee bells

Southern Appalachians. Flowers solitary, large, to 1 in. (2.5 cm) across, nodding, funnel-shaped, white, sometimes pinkish white, on a flowerstalk to 8 in. (20 cm); late March–May; evergreen, clumping; leaves basal, roundish, leathery, glossy bright green, to 3 in. (8 cm) across, with margins lobed and sharply toothed. Zones 6–7; MS to FS. Constantly moist, leafy, acidic soil. Remarkably

Selaginella braunii

Selaginella kraussiana
'Aurea'

Selaginella uncinata

Shortia galacifolia
(Don Jacobs)

heat-tolerant as long as soil is constantly moist. Procure from seed-propagated sources only.

Silene polypetala
Fringed campion

Southeastern North America. Flowers solitary or grouped along flowering tips ascending from the prostrate stems, large, 1.5–2 in. (4–5 cm) across, open and up-facing, fan-shaped, light to rose pink; April–May; evergreen, mat-forming, spreading by runners, mostly prostrate, 12–18 in. (30–45 cm) long; leaves opposite, along the stem, elliptic, light grayish green, 1–2.5 in. (2.5–6 cm) long, flat to the ground. Zones 6–9. Some sun to LS. Moist, well-drained soil. Available from seed propagated sources.

Smilacina japonica

Japan. Flowers creamy white to white, in nodding clusters; May–June; leaves green, covered with fine hairs, to 4 in. (10 cm) long; berries red. Zone 7. MS to FS. The Asian counterpart of our native false Solomon's seal.

'**Angel Wings**' has thin, white leaf margins.

Silene polypetala in bloom backed by *Adiantum pedatum* with emerging *Veratrum viride* (left center)

Smilacina japonica in bloom

'Halo' broad creamy white leaf margins that change to white later.

Smilacina racemosa
False Solomon's seal
Eastern North America. Flowers, tiny, white, many, in pyramidal cluster; May–June; stems arching, zigzagging, to 36 in. (90 cm) tall; leaves single, green, to 6 in. (15 cm) long, broadly lance-shaped and distinctly veined, downy beneath, wavy in the margins; berries red. Zones 4–8; LS to MS. Moist, well-drained, acidic soil. Very heat-

tolerant if watered during dry periods. Plant in a group for best effect.

Smilacina stellata
Starry Solomon's seal
Eastern North America. Flowers small, white, many in a cluster, up to 2 in. (5 cm) long; May–June; stems arching, to 6 in. (15 cm) tall, sometimes much shorter; leaves glaucous medium green, to 5 in. (13 cm) long, folded along the midrib, downy beneath; berries bright red. Zones 4–8; LS to MS. Moist, well-drained, acidic soil.

Smilacina racemosa in bloom

Smilacina stellata

Spigelia marilandica
Indian pink

Eastern North America. Flowers to 1 in. (2.5 cm) across and 2 in. (5 cm) long, upright, trumpet-shaped, scarlet outside, yellow inside, in clusters on a stem 12–24 in. (30–60 cm) tall; March–June; deciduous, clumping; leaves lance-shaped, green, 2–4 in. (5–10 cm) long, with smooth margins. Zones 6–10. Some sun to WS. Moist, well-drained, acidic soil. A dazzling native that deserves to be more widely grown. Tolerates heat in southern gardens as long as moisture is maintained.

Spiranthes cernua
Autumn ladies' tresses

North America. Flowers numerous, small, creamy white, fragrant, to 0.5 in. (1 cm) long, hoodlike, lower lip with yellow spot in center, flowers in spiraling rows on upright flower spikes, 6–24 in. (15–60 cm) tall; August–October; leaves in a basal rosette to 10 in. (25 cm) long, dark green, narrowly lance-shaped. Zones 3–10. Some sun to WS. Moist, well-drained, leafy, acidic soil. Among the easiest orchids for gardens. Expect considerable variability in commercially available plants.

    Var. *odorata*. Fragrant ladies' tresses. Flowers very fragrant.

Streptopus amplexifolius
White mandarin

Eurasia, North America. Flowers greenish white; May–July; stems arching, to 38 in. (95 cm), branched; leaves smooth green, toothed, to 5 in. (13 cm) long and 2 in. (5 cm) wide, lance-shaped and stem-clasping; berries red. Zones 3–10. Some sun to WS. Moist, well-drained, leafy, acidic soil. An autumn display of bright, yellow leaves and brilliant red fruit earn this plant a place in the garden.

Streptopus roseus
Rose mandarin

North America. Similar in habit and culture to *Streptopus amplexifolius*, except flowers rose colored, April–June. Zone 5.

Spiranthes cernua

Stylophorum diphyllum
Celandine poppy

North America. Flowers brilliant yellow, saucer-shaped, in clusters on erect, downy, leafy stems to 20 in. (50 cm) tall; March–May; herbaceous, rhizomatous; stem leaves dull, medium green, oval, each with incised lobes and deeply scalloped, 4–10 in. (10–25 cm) long; all other leaves basal, similar; sap yellow. Zones 5–8. Some sun to WS. Moist, well-drained, leafy, soil. Spreads by self-seeding but is easily controlled. This bright accent should be in every woodland garden (see photo on page 92).

Stylophorum lasiocarpum
Chinese wood poppy

Central and eastern China. Similar in habit and culture to *Stylophorum diphyllum*, except flowers

Spigelia marilandica in bloom

*Streptopus
amplexifolius* fruit

Stylophorum diphyllum

Stylophorum lasiocarpum fruit

drained, acidic, soil. No shade garden should be without this outstanding foliage plant. The deeply divided leaves look like they have been run through a shredder.

Syneilesis palmata
Palmate umbrella plant
Korea, Japan. Similar in habit and culture to *Syneilesis aconitifolia*, except leaves less deeply divided, bright medium green, and not glaucous. Very attractive.

Thalictrum aquilegiifolium
Common meadow rue
Eurasia. Flowers many, small, lilac, white or deep purple in showy clusters 3–5 in. (8–13 cm) wide, on flowerstalks 24–36 in. (60–90 cm), sometimes taller; April–June; clumping, deciduous; leaves divided into many oval, bluish green, lobed leaflets, toward the tip, to 1.5 in. (4 cm), resembling those of the columbine. Zones 5–8. Some sun to WS. Moist, well-drained soil. In all the several available cultivars, it is the showy flower filaments that provide color. The taller ones may need staking.

'Album' is fairly tall at 30 in. (75 cm), with white flowers that contrast well with its slate-gray foliage.

'Amy Jan' is an outstanding selection with yellow foliage throughout the season; flowers pink.

bright orange-yellow. This species has red sap. The leaves are frost-resistant, and the plant is heat-tolerant if provided with supplemental water.

Syneilesis aconitifolia
Shredded umbrella plant
Eastern Asia. Flowers many, pinkish, in clusters on erect stems to 4 ft. (1.2 m) tall; July–September; herbaceous, rhizomatous, spreading; leaves on leafstalks to 24 in. (60 cm) tall, like Mayapple; at first covered with silky, white hair, to 12 in. (30 cm) across, deeply divided into lobes, each lance-shaped, grayish green, slightly glaucous. Zones 5–7. Some sun to WS. Moist, well-

Thalictrum dioicum
Early meadow rue
North America. Similar in habit and culture to *Thalictrum aquilegiifolium*, except flowerstalks 10–24 in. (25–60 cm) tall; April–May. An excellent foliage plant for southern gardens, it is equally suited to northern gardens, growing well into zone 4, although it will be cut down there by the first hard freeze. The flowers are mediocre, but in southern gardens the foliage holds up well into late autumn.

Thalictrum filamentosum
Korea. Flowers many, white, in showy clusters, on smooth, leafy flowerstalks 18 in. (45 cm) tall;

Syneilesis aconitifolia

Syneilesis palmata

Thelypteris noveboracensis

Thalictrum filamentosum var. *tenerum*

April–May; clumping, deciduous; leaves compound, divided into matte green leaflets. The frothy white flower heads are compact and very long-lasting. Zone 5. Some sun, LS to WS.

Var. *tenerum* is a lower-growing form of this handsome species, of garden origin, with a leaf mound of 12 in. (30 cm). Equally well suited in northern and southern gardens.

Thelypteris noveboracensis
New York fern
Eastern North America. Fronds to 18 in. (45 cm) tall and 6 in. (15 cm) wide, in tufts; leaves deciduous, yellowish green, divided into pairs of leaflets; the lower leaflets diminish in size toward the bottom and are cut into subleaflets with rounded, blunt-pointed lobes. Zones 3–8. Some sun, LS to MS. Moist, well-drained soil. This fern has delicate, narrow fronds of light green that brighten shady corners.

Thelypteris palustris
Marsh fern
Eurasia, North America. Fronds to 24 in. (60 cm) tall and 6 in. (15 cm) wide, fertile fronds more erect and taller; leaves deciduous, yellowish green, divided into leaflets, the lower pairs shorter than the center leaflets; leaflets cut into blunt-tipped lobes. Zones 2–8. Some sun, LS to MS. Moist, well-drained soil. This fern develops fronds throughout the summer. Old and new

fronds mingle, providing an ethereal display. For best effect, plant several together.

Tiarella cordifolia
False miterwort, foamflower
Eastern North America. Flowers many, white, sometimes tinged pink, small, in a feathery cluster on leafless stems 6–12 in. (15–30 cm) tall; April–June; evergreen leaves in a basal rosette, similar to red maple leaves (*Acer rubrum*), dull green with the veins outlined in red, 1.5–3 in. (4–8 cm) long. Zones 3–8. LS to MS. Moist, well-drained soil. This species has the best white flowers in the genus.

'Cygnet', flowers white, buds rose-colored; leaves deeply lobed and cleft, almost star-shaped, deep green with purple along the midrib.

'Dark Eyes', flowers white; leaves green marked with a large blotch of black; clumping.

'Eco Eyed Glossy', flowers white, fragrant; leaves medium green, very glossy.

'Eco Running Tapestry', flowers white; leaves medium green with dark, sometimes red veining; stoloniferous.

Thelypteris palustris

Tiarella cordifolia 'Eco Running Tapestry'

Tiarella cordifolia 'Eco Slick Rock' in bloom

'**Eco Slick Rock**' ('Slick Rock'), flowers pinkish, fragrant; leaves deeply cleft, dark green; smaller than the species and spreads vigorously by stolons.

'**Elizabeth Oliver**', flowers white; leaves deeply lobed, green with a blackish purple pattern.

'**Filigree Lace**', a garden hybrid (*Tiarella cordifolia* × *T. trifoliata*); flowers white; leaves lacy, blackish green patch at base.

'**Heronswood Mist**', flowers white; leaves blotched and marbled with stable, creamy white variegation.

'**Iron Butterfly**', flowers white; leaves larger than the type and more deeply cleft and broadly marked with purplish black along the midvein.

'**Marmorata**', flowers deep purple to maroon; leaves first tinged bronze, later turning dark green with purple spots.

'**Ninja**', flowers white tinged pink; leaves deeply lobed, dark green and marked in the center with blackish purple, in autumn turning dark purple.

Tiarella wherryi
Wherry's foamflower

Eastern North America. A nonstoloniferous, more southern form of *Tiarella cordifolia* and very similar in habit and culture. Also sold under the synonym *T. cordifolia* var. *collina*. Zone 5. (See photo on page 178).

'**Bronze Beauty**', flowers white tinged pink; leaves reddish bronze.

Tiarella wherryi

Tradescantia 'Sweet Kate'
(Tony Avent)

'Dunvegan', flowers white tinged pink, on short stems to 6 in. (15 cm); leaves deeply cleft and lobed, medium green.

'Eco Maple Leaf', flowers white tinged pink, fragrant; leaves mapleleaf-shaped, medium green, marked darker along the veins with red.

Tradescantia ohiensis
Spiderwort, trinity
Eastern North America. Similar in habit and culture to *Tradescantia virginiana*, except smaller, on stems to 30 in. (75 cm) tall.

'Alba' has white flowers and blue stamens.

Tradescantia virginiana
Common spiderwort
Eastern North America. Flowers numerous in clusters violet-blue, sometimes pink or white, 1–2 in. (2.5–5 cm) on top of stems to 36 in. (90 cm) tall; April–July; clumping; leaves on the stem, green, narrowly lance-shaped to 15 in. (38 cm) long and 1.5 in. (4 cm) wide. Zones 4–8. LS to MS. Moist, well-drained soil. The petals do not drop off but turn into a jellylike liquid (see photo on page 8).

'Sweet Kate' ('Blue and Gold') has bright yellow foliage with deep blue flowers.

Tricyrtis affinis
Japan. Flowers whitish, with purple markings inside, saucer-shaped, up-facing, to 1 in. (2.5 cm); September–October; clumping, to 24 in. (60 cm); leaves elliptic, dark green with large brownish spots, to 3 in. (8 cm) long. Zones 4–8. LS to MS. Moist, well-drained soil.

Tricyrtis flava
Japan. Similar in habit and culture to *Tricyrtis affinis*, except flowers yellow, with purple markings inside; leaves larger, to 6 in. (15 cm) long, elliptic, uniform bright green.

'Chabo' has short stems to 8 in. (20 cm) covered with dark purple leaves, which provide a stunning contrast to the large yellow flowers.

Var. *nana* differs only by its smaller size.

Tricyrtis affinis

Tricyrtis flava

Tricyrtis formosana 'Amethystina'

Tricyrtis formosana
Formosan toad lily

Taiwan. Flowers whitish, with purple markings inside, increasingly darker toward center, facing up, to 1 in. (2.5 cm); September–October; rhizomatous, spreading, deciduous; stems 30 in. (75 cm) tall; erect; leaves stem-clasping, elliptic, shiny light green, to 3 in. (8 cm) long. Zones 6–9. LS to MS. Moist, well-drained soil. Very showy flowers.

'Amethystina' has lavender flowers with intense purple spotting.

'Gates of Heaven' ('Ogon') is smaller and has bright yellow leaves.

'Samurai'. Striped toad lily. Leaves with narrow, white margins.

'Variegata' has distinctly gold-margined leaves.

Tricyrtis hirta
Japanese toad lily

Japan. Flowers whitish, spotted with lavender, up-facing, in leaf axils, 1 in. (2.5 cm) across; August–October; deciduous, clumping; stems arching, to 24 in. (60 cm) tall; leaves stem-clasping, elliptic, medium green to 5 in. (13 cm) long. Zones 4–9. LS to MS. Moist, well-drained soil. The leafy stems of Tricyrtis hirta arching here and there among hostas, astilbes, and ferns are extraordinary. The species naturalizes in the garden due to its habit of spreading abundant seed.

'Alba' has white flowers.

'Albomarginata' has leaves with a narrow white margin.

'Amanagawa', a garden hybrid (Tricyrtis perfoliata × T. hirta). Flowers light yellow, with a few speckles; leaves green with brown speckles.

'Kohaku', garden hybrid; flowers white, spotted with dark purple and with yellow throats.

'Lilac Towers' is similar to the type but has larger lilac flowers.

Var. masamunei is much like the species but devoid of all hair.

'Miyazaki' is smaller, to 12 in. (30 cm) tall, leaves all green.

'Miyazaki Gold', leaves with narrow, yellow margin.

'Togen' ('Tojen'), garden hybrid. Flowers whitish lavender, spotted with light purple and with yellow throat; clumping, 4 ft. (1.2 m) tall; leaves very large, medium green, stem-clasping, to 12 in. (30 cm) long and 4 in. (10 cm) wide. This gigantic hybrid is the grandest of all toad lilies but needs staking.

'White Towers', white flowers and pink stamens. Similar to 'Alba'.

Tricyrtis latifolia
Broadleaf toad lily

Japan. Similar in habit and culture to Tricyrtis formosana, except flowers light yellow, with deep purple spots inside, up-facing, 1 in. (2.5 cm) across; August–October; clumping; stems to 30 in. (75 cm) tall, very erect; leaves stem-clasping,

Tricyrtis hirta flowers

Tricyrtis 'Togen'

Tricyrtis hirta 'Albomarginata'

Tricyrtis macrantha var. *macranthopsis* flowers

Tricyrtis macropoda in bloom

rounded, dark green, to 6 in. (15 cm) long and 4 in. (10 cm) wide. Zones 5–9. LS to MS. Moist, well-drained soil.

Var. *makinoana* has more hairs on the stems and beneath the leaves.

Tricyrtis macrantha

Japan. Flowers deep yellow, bell-shaped, pendent, richly spotted inside with reddish purple, to 1 in. (2.5 cm) long in clusters in the upper leaf axils; September–October; clumping; stems to 24 in. (60 cm), arching, becoming pendulous; leaves elliptic, dark green to 5 in. (13 cm) long. Zones 7–9. LS to MS. Moist, well-drained soil.

Var. *macranthopsis*. Japan. Similar to the type, but the flowers are larger, to 2 in. (5 cm) long, emerging in the leaf axils and at ends of branches; stems to 4 ft. (1.2 m) long. LS to MS. The exquisite drooping flowers are spectacular, the largest in the genus.

Tricyrtis macropoda

Japan, Korea. Similar in habit and culture to *Tricyrtis formosana*, except flowers whitish, purple spotted inside, with petals drooping, downward-facing; clumping, to 36 in. (90 cm) tall.

Tricyrtis oshumiensis

Japan. Flowers yellow, nearly without spots, up-facing, in the outer leaf axils, 1 in. (2.5 cm) across; August–October; clumping; stems 30 in. (75 cm) tall; leaves stem-clasping, medium green, to 4 in. (10 cm) long. Zones 7–9. LS to MS. Moist, well-drained soil.

Trillium catesbaei
Catesby's trillium

Eastern North America. Flowers stalked, nodding halfway, large, 2–3 in. (5–8 cm) across, white, pink, or rose; April–June; clumping, 8–20 in. (20–50 cm) tall; leaves to 4 in. (10 cm) long, elliptic, whorled. Zones 7–9. LS to MS. Moist, well-drained, acidic soil. A good garden form for southern gardens with acidic soil. It is attractive and long-lived.

Tricyrtis oshumiensis flower

Trillium catesbaei

Trillium cernuum
Nodding trillium
Eastern North America. Flowers stalked, nodding below the leaves, small, 1.5 in. (4 cm) across, white or pink, rarely dark pink, recurved; April–June; clumping, 8–24 in. (20–60 cm) tall; leaves to 6 in. (15 cm) long, diamond-shaped, whorled. Zones 3–7. LS to MS. Moist, well-drained, acidic soil. Very hardy.

    Forma *album* has white flowers.

Trillium chloropetalum
Giant trillium
Western North America. Flowers sessile, fragrant, 2–4 in. (5–10 cm) long, white, yellow, maroon, purplish red; February–April; clumping, 8–24 in. (20–60 cm) tall; leaves green, mottled brown, 3–7 in. (8–18 cm) long and wide, rounded diamond-shaped, whorled. Zones 7–9. LS to MS. Moist, well-drained soil. Not suitable for the East, as it rises and blooms very early, so is often damaged by late freezes.

Trillium cuneatum
Whippoorwill toadshade
Eastern North America. Flowers sessile, 2.5 in. (3–6 cm) long, maroon, green, yellow; March–April; clumping, 6–18 in. (15–45 cm) tall; leaves overlapping, dark green mottled lighter to grayish green, 3–7 in. (8–18 cm) long, elliptic, whorled. Zones 6–9. LS to MS. Moist, well-drained soil. This southern trillium has long been incorrectly sold as *Trillium sessile*. It is extremely variable and its yellow-flowered forms are often mistaken for *T. luteum*. An excellent garden trillium with strikingly variegated leaves and a choice of flower colors. It is well adapted to hot, dry summers given supplemental water.

Trillium erectum
Purple trillium, wakerobin
Eastern North America. Flowers long-stalked, outward-facing, large, to 3 in. (8 cm) across, maroon, purple, or white, rarely yellow; April–June; clumping, 8–24 in. (20–60 cm) tall; leaves 2–8 in. (5–20 cm) long, diamond-shaped, bright green.

Zones 4–9. LS to MS. Moist, well-drained, acidic soil. A robust trillium for gardens. Variable.

    Var. *album* has white flowers.

    Forma *luteum* has greenish yellow petals.

Trillium flexipes
Bent trillium
Eastern North America. Flowers stalked, held above the leaves, large, to 3 in. (8 cm) across, white, rarely maroon; April–June; clumping, 8–20 in. (20–50 cm) tall; leaves bright green, 3–10 in. (8–25 cm) long, diamond-shaped, overlapping. Zones 4–9. LS to MS. Moist, well-drained, neutral to alkaline soil. This large species has long-lasting flowers and leaves. Its flowerstalk has a kneelike bend, facing the flower outward.

Trillium grandiflorum
Great white trillium
Eastern North America. Flowers stalked, held above the leaves, very large, 3–4 in. (8–10 cm) across, white, fading to pink; April–June; clumping, 6–12 in. (15–30 cm) tall; leaves 6–8 in. (15–20 cm) long, diamond-shaped, dark green, whorled. Zones 4–9. LS to MS. Moist, well-drained, acidic soil. This is the best trillium for gardens. It is large-flowered and has leaves that carry on until early autumn. It likes slightly acidic soil but does well in circumneutral soils.

    'Eco Double Gardenia', flowers many-petaled and with petals wavy, turning pinkish.

    'Flore Pleno', flowers double, white.

    'Green Mutant', flowers green with white margin.

    'Smith's Double' ('Variety Plena'), flowers double.

    'Snow Bunting', flowers multipetaled (so-called stacked double).

Trillium kurabayashii
Western whippoorwill toadshade
Western North America. Similar in habit and culture to and the western equivalent of *Trillium cuneatum*. Usually too early for gardens in the East, where it is exposed to damage by late freezes.

Trillium cuneatum (bottom) with *T. luteum*

Trillium erectum

Trillium grandiflorum, showing new white flowers and older ones fading to pink, with red *T. sulcatum* (Don Jacobs)

Trillium lancifolium

Trillium lancifolium
Lance-leaved trillium

Eastern North America. Flowers sessile, small, erect, maroon or yellowish brown; April–May; leaves lance-shaped to 4 in. (10 cm) long and 1 in. (2.5 cm) wide, dark green mottled with lighter green, often slanted down. Zones 6–7. LS to MS. Moist, well-drained, acidic soil. A unique trillium with long, lance-shaped leaves that emerge very early in southern climates and thus are exposed to damage by late freezes.

Trillium luteum
Yellow toadshade

Eastern North America. Flowers sessile, lemon-like fragrance, 1.2–3 in. (3–8 cm) long, shades of yellow (only); April–May; clumping, 6–16 in. (15–40 cm) tall; leaves overlapping, dark green mottled with lighter green to grayish green, 3–7 in. (8–18 cm) long, elliptic, whorled. Zones 5–7. LS to MS. Moist, well-drained, acidic soil. Widely available. The only sessile mountain trillium that produces yellow flowers exclusively. It can be rec-

Trillium luteum in bloom

ognized by its lemon fragrance (see photo on page 215). In hot southern gardens, the yellow-flowered forms of *Trillium cuneatum* are better choices.

Trillium ovatum
Western white trillium
Western North America. Similar in habit and culture to and the western equivalent of *Trillium grandiflorum*. The showiest western trillium, it is usually too early and not hardy enough for northeastern climates. Zone 6. Needs slightly alkaline soil to grow well in southeastern climates.

Trillium recurvatum
Prairie trillium
Eastern North America. Flowers sessile, petals erect with tips bent inward, 2 in. (2–5 cm) long, maroon or clear yellow; March–May; clumping, 6–18 in. (15–45 cm) tall; leaves dark green mottled strongly with lighter green or grayish green, 7 in. (18 cm) long elliptic, whorled. Zones 5–7. LS to MS. Moist, well-drained, neutral to alkaline

soil. Widespread and variable over its large habitat. A good garden plant in eastern North America. It requires a more alkaline soil than the southern trilliums so add dolomitic limestone when planting.

Trillium sessile
Sessile trillium, toadshade
Eastern North America. Flowers sessile with spicy fragrance, erect, 1.5 in. (4 cm) long, maroon, reddish brown to greenish yellow; March–May; clumping, 3–10 in. (8–25 cm) tall; leaves overlapping, dark green, mottled, 4 in. (10 cm) long, elliptic, whorled. Zones 4–7. LS to MS. Moist, well-drained soil. With supplemental water, this trillium adapts well to hot, dry summers. Unfortunately, it is smaller than and not as prominent as some other species.

Trillium sulcatum
Southern red trillium
Eastern North America. Flowers stalked, held above the leaves, slightly drooping, to 2.5 in. (6

Trillium sessile

Trillium vaseyi in bloom

Tupistra chinensis leaves

cm) across, maroon, red, pink, or creamy yellow; April–May; clumping, 6–28 in. (15–70 cm) tall; leaves dark green, 6–8 in. (15–20 cm) long, diamond-shaped, whorled. Zones 4–7. LS to MS. Moist, well-drained soil. This large trillium has the widest range of flower colors in the genus, from near black, to red, yellow, and white (see photo on page 215).

Trillium vaseyi
Sweet trillium

Eastern North America. Flowers stalked, held at or below the leaves, to 4 in. (10 cm) across, crimson, maroon-red, brownish red; April–June; clumping, 6–24 in. (15–60 cm) tall; leaves 4–8 in. (10–20 cm) long and often wider, diamond-shaped, dark green, whorled. Zones 6–7. LS to MS. Moist, deep, well-drained, acidic soil. This stately species has the largest flowers in the genus. Unfortunately, they are nodding and so do not show their full beauty from above. Plant them up on a slope, where the flowers can be observed from the path below. It is well adapted to hot southern gardens, if planted in deep shade and given deep, acidic, woodland soil and sup-

plemental water. Its foliage lasts well into early autumn—a great garden plant.

Tupistra chinensis
China ruffled lily

Southern China. Flowers small, inconspicuous, in a cluster near ground level; evergreen in areas with mild winter, clumping; to 24 in. (60 cm) high and wide; leaves in a basal rosette, upright and arching, narrowly lance-shaped, medium matte green, to 24 in. (60 cm) long, deeply keeled, ruffled. Zones 6–7. LS to MS. Well-drained soil. The great foliage adds texture wherever it is planted.

Uvularia grandiflora
Large-flowered bellwort

Eastern North America. Flowers yellow, 2 in. (5 cm) long, hanging, bell-shaped with twisted tips; April–May; rhizomatous, slowly creeping; to 32 in. (80 cm) tall; leaves pierced by the stem, green, to 5 in. (13 cm) long, elliptic. Zones 4–8. LS to MS. Moist, well-drained soil. The largest species in the genus, it has spreading rhizomes that in-

Uvularia grandiflora

Uvularia perfoliata flower

Vancouveria hexandra

crease its clump size. Its large flowers are showy and it makes a splendid accent plant in the shady border. Even after flowering, the leafy clumps add to the composition of the garden. Given plenty of water, the clumps last until late summer or early fall.

Uvularia perfoliata
Bellwort, strawbells
Eastern North America. Flowers pale yellow, 1 in. (2.5 cm) long, hanging, bell-shaped with twisted tips; April–June; clumping; stems to 24 in. (60 cm) tall; leaves pierced by the stem, medium green, to 3 in. (8 cm) long, elliptic. Zones 4–8. LS to MS. Moist, well-drained soil. A smaller version of *Uvularia grandiflora*.

Uvularia sessilifolia
Sessile bellwort
Eastern North America. Flowers pale greenish yellow, 1 in. (2.5 cm) long, hanging, narrowly bell-shaped, tips flaring; April–June; rhizomatous, widely creeping; stems to 16 in. (40 cm) tall; leaves stem-clasping, yellowish green, to 3 in. (8

cm) long, elliptic. Zones 4–8. LS to MS. Moist, well-drained soil. Smaller and more delicate than other bellworts.

'Cobblewood Gold', yellow leaves, much brighter than the species.

Vancouveria hexandra
Inside-out flower
Western North America. Flowers small, many, nodding, white, spotted red on leafless stems 10–18 in. (25–45 cm); May–June; deciduous, rhizomatous, spreading; leaves to 16 in. (40 cm) long, divided into many light green, heart-shaped, lobed leaflets to 1 in. (2.5 cm) long. Zones 5–8. LS to MS. Moist, well-drained, leafy soil. A ferny looking groundcover with flowers.

Veratrum album
European white hellebore
Eurasia. Similar in habit and culture to *Veratrum viride*, except flowers whitish, in clusters on a branched flowerstalk to 6 ft. (1.8 m) tall; July–August. Zones 5–8. Some sun, LS to WS. Moist, deep, well-drained soil.

Uvularia sessilifolia in bloom

Veratrum album (Allan Armitage)

Veratrum viride with hardy geraniums and *H. sieboldiana* (Allan Armitage)

Veratrum viride
White hellebore
North America. Flowers small, inconspicuous yellowish green, in clusters on a branched flower-stalk 3–7 ft. (0.9–2 m) tall; May–July; clumping; leaves basal, arching, lance-shaped, light green, 6–12 in. (15–30 cm) long, pleated (see photo on page 200). Zones 3–8. Some sun, LS to WS. Moist, deep, well-drained soil.

Vinca major
Greater periwinkle
Eurasia. Similar in habit and culture to *Vinca minor* but more shrubby, with prostrate as well as erect stems, to 18 in. (45 cm). Zone 7. Some sun, LS to MS. Best for southern gardens. This quickly spreading plant makes a good groundcover for large areas.

Vinca minor
Lesser periwinkle
Eurasia. Flowers purplish blue with a white center, 1–1.2 in. (2.5–3 cm) across; April–May; evergreen, trailing, mat-forming; 4–8 in. (10–20 cm) high; leaves lance-shaped, glossy dark green. Zones 3–8. Some sun, LS to WS. Moist, deep, well-drained soil. The ubiquitous groundcover.

'**Alba Variegata**' ('Alba Aureovariegata'), flowers white; leaves with light yellow margin.

Vinca major
as groundcover

Vinca minor in bloom
(Allan Armitage)

Viola blanda

Viola pedata (Allan Armitage)

'Argenteovariegata' ('Variegata'), flowers violet to lilac-blue; leaves with white to creamy white margin.

'Azurea Flore Pleno' ('Azureaplena', 'Caerulea Plena', 'Caeruleoplena'), flowers blue, double.

'Multiplex' ('Alpina', 'Double Burgundy'), flowers reddish plum-purple, double.

'Plena', flowers blue, double.

Viola blanda
Sweet white violet
North America. Flowers white, purple-veined, spurred; leaves green, heart-shaped, lobed and pointed, to 2.5 in. (6 cm); evergreen, self-seeds freely. Zones 2–7. Some sun, LS to WS. Any fertile, well-drained soil.

Viola canadensis
Canada violet
North America. Flowers fragrant, inside white, outside, yellow center; leaves green, heart-shaped, to 2.5 in. (6 cm); evergreen, self-seeds freely. Zones 2–7. Some sun, LS to WS. Any fertile, well-drained soil.

Viola labradorica
Labrador violet
Northeastern North America. Flowers violet to purple, spurred; leaves green, kidney-shaped, toothed, to 1.5 in. (4 cm); semi-evergreen, self-seeds freely. Zones 2–7. Some sun, LS to WS. Any fertile, well-drained soil. This is probably one of the better violets for somewhat shady gardens. Spreads actively. In southern gardens it lingers in summer, but revitalizes with cooler weather.

Viola pedata
Bird's foot violet
Eastern North America. Flowers large, to 1.4 in. (4 cm) across, beardless, upper petals deep blue-violet, lower pale violet or whitish, veined; March–June; leaves fan-shaped, lobed, toothed; semi-evergreen, clumping, not invasive. Zones 4–8. Some sun, LS to WS. Any fertile, well-drained soil. The best violet for the shady wild-

Viola pubescens var. *eriocarpa* with *Podophyllum pleianthum*

flower garden. Moisture is essential during hot, dry weather.

'Artist's Palette', flowers with whitish violet lower petals with a dark center stripe.

'Bicolor', flowers bicolored, dark and light violet.

Viola pubescens
Downy yellow violet
Eastern North America. Flowers yellow with purple veins; leaves on the stem, green, downy, heart-shaped, scalloped, to 5 in. (13 cm) long; clumping, self-seeds freely. Zones 4–7. Some sun, LS to WS. Any fertile, well-drained soil.

Viola variegata

Var. *eriocarpa*. Smooth yellow violet. Common in eastern North America. Has a few basal leaves and a hairless stem.

Viola variegata
Variegated violet

East Asia. Flowers violet; leaves kidney-shaped, silvery gray with dark green patches between veins, reddish purple beneath, to 0.8 in. (2 cm); herbaceous, clumping, spreading, self-seeds freely. Zones 6–7. Some sun, LS to WS. Any fertile, well-drained soil.

'Dancing Geisha', flowers light violet or white; leaves silvery gray variegated, toothed.

Var. *niponica* (frequently mislabeled *Viola koreana*) is the form most seen in commerce; it has beautifully variegated, cyclamen-like leaves of silvery green with dark grayish green fields between the veins.

'Syletta', flowers pale violet; leaves variegated.

Wasabia japonica

Waldsteinia fragarioides
Barren strawberry

Eastern North America. Flowers yellow, on branched stem, to 0.8 in. (2 cm) across, cup-shaped; April–June; strawberry-like, mat-forming; leaves divided into leaflets, green, hairy, rounded, scalloped, 1–2 in. (2.5–5 cm) long and wide. Zones 3–6. Some sun, LS to MS. Any fertile, well-drained soil.

Waldsteinia ternata

Eurasia. Flowers bright yellow, to 0.8 in. (2 cm) across; April–June; semi-evergreen, mat-forming; leaves divided into leaflets, green, hairy, rounded, scalloped, 1–2 in. (2.5–5 cm) long and wide.

Wasabia japonica

Eastern Asia. Flowers white, on stalks to 12 in. (30 cm); May-June; herbaceous, clumping; leaves basal, on 6 in. (15 cm) stalks, dark shiny green, kidney-shaped, heart-shaped, toothed, 5–7 in. (13–18 cm) long and to 6 in. (15 cm) wide. Zones 3–6. Some sun, LS to FS. Makes a good groundcover.

Woodwardia areolata
Netted chain fern

Eastern North America. Sterile and fertile fronds separate; sterile fronds deciduous, taller, oval, green, to 24 in. (60 cm) tall, cut into pairs of leaflets to 3 in. (8 cm) long; fertile fronds remaining through winter, cut into much more contracted leaflets with margins rolled over the chainlike rows of spore cases. Zone 5. Some sun, LS to FS. Always moist soil of any kind. Tolerant of heat and drought.

Woodwardia virginica
Virginia chain fern

Eastern North America. Fronds deciduous, to 5 ft. (1.5 m) but usually shorter, in clusters; leaves yellowish green in spring, dark green later, lance-shaped, broadest in the middle, pointed at top, to 4 ft. (1.2 m) long and 10 in. (25 cm) wide; cut into pairs of closely spaced, opposite, leaflets; subleaflets rounded at tip. Zones 3–7. Some sun, LS to FS. Any moist, fertile soil. Quite heat-tolerant.

Woodwardia areolata fertile fronds

USDA HARDINESS ZONE MAP

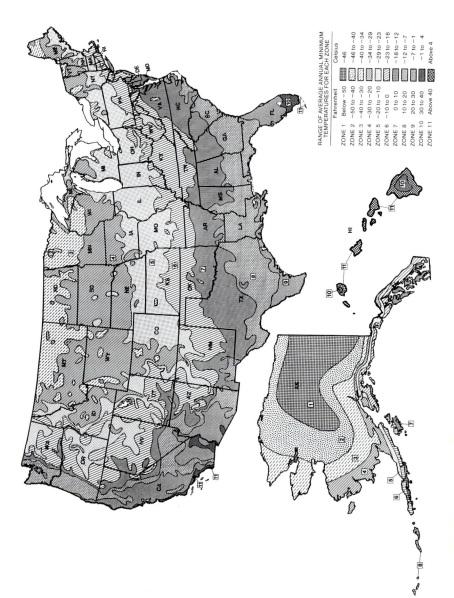

	RANGE OF AVERAGE ANNUAL MINIMUM TEMPERATURES FOR EACH ZONE	
	Fahrenheit	Celsius
ZONE 1	Below −50	−46
ZONE 2	−50 to −40	−46 to −40
ZONE 3	−40 to −30	−40 to −34
ZONE 4	−30 to −20	−34 to −29
ZONE 5	−20 to −10	−29 to −23
ZONE 6	−10 to 0	−23 to −18
ZONE 7	0 to 10	−18 to −12
ZONE 8	10 to 20	−12 to −7
ZONE 9	20 to 30	−7 to −1
ZONE 10	30 to 40	−1 to 4
ZONE 11	Above 40	Above 4

EUROPEAN HARDINESS ZONE MAP

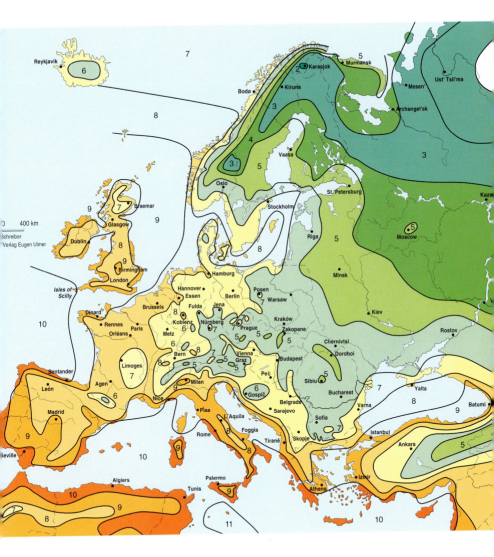

NURSERY SOURCES

This is a partial list, limited to nurseries in the United States, Canada, and the United Kingdom that specialize in perennials for shady gardens or that offer hard-to-find plants. Catalogs or lists are available from most. No endorsement is intended, nor is criticism implied of sources not mentioned.

Canada

Ashley Gardens
525-535 Road 7
Leamington, Ontario N8H 3V8
(519) 326-1968
http://www.ashleygardens.ca

Ego's Farm Market & Greenhouses
596 Horseshoe Valley Road, East
Coldwater, Ontario L0K 1E0
(705) 326-9922
http://www.egosgardencentre.com

Humber Nurseries
8386 Highway #50, RR # 8
Brampton, Ontario L6T 3Y7
(905) 798-8733
http://www.gardencentre.com

Minter Country Garden
10015 Young Road Street
Chilliwack, British Columbia V2P 4V4
(604) 792-6612
http:// www.mintergardens.com

Parkway Gardens
1201 Oxford Street
London, Ontario N6H 5E1
(519) 657-7360

Patrick Studio
18 Haendel Street
Kirkland Quebec H9H 4Y9
(514) 695-8399
http://www.thegurugarden.com

Sipkens Nurseries
3261 London Line
Wyoming, Ontario N0N 1T0
(519) 542-8353
http://www.spikensnurseries.com

Thimble Farms
175 Arbutus Road
Salt Spring Island, British Columbia V8K 1A3
http://www.thimblefarms.com

United Kingdom

Ann and Roger Bowden
Sticklepath
Okehampton
Devon EX20 2NL
+ 44 (0)1837 840481
http://www.hostas-uk.com

Burlingham Gardens
31 Main Road
North Burlingham
Norfolk NR13 4TA
+44 (0)1603 716615
http://www.wildflowers.co.uk

Church Farm
Westgate, Rillington
Malton
North Yorkshire YO17 8LN
+44 (0)7813 327886
http://www.ornamentalgrass.co.uk

Fern Nursery
Grimsby Road
Binbrook
Lincolnshire LN8 6DH
+44 (0)1472 398092
http://www.fernnursery.co.uk

Goldbrook Plants
Hoxne
Eye
Suffolk IP21 5AN
+44 (0)1379 668770

Kernock Park Plants
Pillaton
Saltash
Cornwall PL12 6RY
+44 (0)1579 350561
http://www.kernock.co.uk

Kintaline Farm Plant Centre
Benderloch (by Oban)
Argyll PA37 1QS, Scotland
+44 (0)1631 720223
http://www.kintaline.co.uk

Park Green Garden Nurseries
Wetheringsett
Stowmarket
Suffolk IP14 5QH
+44 (0)1728 860139
http://www.parkgreen.co.uk

Penlan Perennials
Penrhiwpal, Llandysul
Ceredigion SA44 5QH, Wales
+44 (0)1239 851244
http://www.penlanperennials.co.uk

Pennard Plants
3, The Gardens—East Pennard
Shepton Mallet
Somerset BA4 6TU
+44 (0)1749 860039
http://www.pennardplants.com

South Shropshire Meadow
Brays Tenement
Welshpool SY21 8JY
+44 (0)1938 580030
http://www.southshropshiremeadow.co.uk

The Vicarage Gardens
Carrington
Manchester M31 4AG
+44 (0)1617 752750
http://www.vicaragebotanicalgardens.co.uk

The Weird and Wonderful Plant Company
Fenton Barns Industrial Units
Drem
North Berwick EH39 5BW
+44 (0)1620 850755
http://www.weirdandwonderfulplant.co.uk

Whitehall Garden Centre—Lacock
Corsham Road
Chippenham
Wiltshire SN13 OEF
+44 (0)1249 730204
http://www.whitehallgardencentre.co.uk

United States

Ambergate Gardens
8730 Country Road 43
Chaska, Minnesota 55318
(952) 443-2248
http://www.ambergategardens.com

André Viette Farm & Nursery
P.O. Box 1109
Fishersville, Virginia 22939
(800) 575-5538
http://www.viette.com

Arrowhead Alpines
1310 North Gregory Road
Fowlerville, Michigan 48836
(517) 223-3581
http://www.arrowheadalpines.com

Asiatica
Box 270
Lewisberry, Pennsylvania 17339
(717) 938-8677
http://www.asiaticanursery.com

Bluestone Perennials
7211 Middle Ridge Road
Madison, Ohio 44057
(800) 852-5243
http:www.bluestoneperennials.com

Boehlke's Woodland Gardens
5890 Wausaukee Road
West Bend, Wisconsin 53095
(262) 675-2740

Busse Gardens
17160 245th Avenue
Big Lake, Minnesota 55309
(763) 263-3403
http://www.bussegardens.com

Camellia Forest Nursery
125 Carolina Forest Road
Chapel Hill, North Carolina 27516
(919) 968-0504
http://www.camforest.com

Carroll Gardens
444 East Main Street
P.O. Box 310
Westminster, Maryland 21157
(800) 638-6334
http://www.carrollgardens.com/

Collector's Nursery
16804 NE 102nd Avenue
Battle Ground, Washington 98604
(360) 574-3832
http://www.collectorsnursery.com

Fancy Fronds Nursery
P.O. Box 1090
Gold Bar, Washington 98251
(360) 793-1472
http://www.fancyfronds.com

Forestfarm Nursery
990 Tetherow Road
Williams, Oregon 97544
(541) 846-7269
http://www.forestfarm.com

Garden in the Woods
Hemenway Road
Framington, Massachusetts 01701
(508) 877-7630
http://www.newfs.org

Garden Vision
63 Williamsville Road
Hubbardston, Massachusetts 01452
(978) 928-4808

Gardens of the Blue Ridge
Box 10
Pineola, North Carolina 28662
(828) 733-2417
http://gardensoftheblueridge.com

Greer Gardens
1280 Good Pasture Island Road
Eugene, Oregon 97401
(541) 686-8266
http://www.greergardens.com

Heronswood Nursery
7530 NE 288th Street
Kingston, Washington 98346
(360) 297-4172
http://www.heronswood.com

Lee Gardens
25986 Sauder Road
Tremont, Illinois 61568
(309) 925-5262

Mid-Atlantic Wildflowers
Star Route, Box 226
Gloucester Point, Virginia 23062
(804) 642-4602

Munchkin Nursery & Gardens
323 Woodside Drive NW
Depauw, Indiana 47115
(812) 633-4858
http://www.munchinnursery.com

Native Gardens
5737 Fisher Lane
Greenback, TN 37742
(865) 856-0220

Naylor Creek Nursery
2610 West Valley Road
Chimacum, Washington 98325
(360) 732-4983
http://naylorcreek.com

Niche Gardens
1111 Dawson Road
Chapel Hill, North Carolina 27516
(919) 967-0078
http://www.nichegdn.com

Piccadilly Farm
1971 Whippoorwill Road
Bishop, Georgia 30621

Plant Delights Nursery
9241 Sauls Road
Raleigh, North Carolina 27603
(919) 772-4794
http://www.plantdelights.com

Prairie Moon Nursery
Route 3, Box 1633
Winona, Minnesota 55987
(507) 452-1362
http://www.prairiemoon.com

Putney Nursery
P.O. Box 265, Route 5
Putney, Vermont 05346

Robyn's Nest Nursery
14324 206th Street SE
Snohomish, Washington 98296
(425) 486-6919
http://www.robynsnestnursery.com

Roslyn Nursery
211 Burrs Lane
Dix Hills, New York 11746
)631) 643-9347
http://www.roslynnursery.com

Russel Graham
4030 Eagle Crest Road NW
Salem, Oregon 97304

Seneca Hill Perennials
3712 County Route 57
Oswego, New York 13126
(315) 342-5915
http://www.senecahill.com

Shady Oaks Nursery
Box 708
Waseca, Minnesota 56093
(507) 835-5033
http://www.shadyoaks.com

Siskiyou Rare Plant Nursery
2825 Cummings Road
Medford, Oregon 97501
(541) 772-6846
http://www.srpn.com

Tower Perennial Gardens
4010 East Jamieson Road
Spokane, Washington 99223
(509) 448-6778
http://www.towerflower.com

Wade and Gatton Nurseries
1288 Gatton Rocks Road
Bellville, Ohio 44813
(419) 886-2094
http://www.wadegardens.com

Wayside Gardens
1 Garden Lane
Hodges, South Carolina 29695
(800) 213-0379
http://www.waysidegardens.com

We-Du Nurseries
Route 5, Box 724
Marion, North Carolina 28752
(828) 738-8300

Weston Nurseries
Box 186, Route 135
Hopkinton, Massachusetts 01748
(508) 435-3414
http://www.westonnurseries.com

White Flower Farm
P.O. Box 50, Route 63
Litchfield, Connecticut 06759
(800) 503-9624
http://www.shepherdseeds.com

Woodlanders
1128 Colleton Avenue
Aiken, South Carolina 29801
(803) 648-7522
http://www.woodlanders.net

Yucca Do Nursery
P.O. Box 907
Hempstead, Texas 77445
(979) 826-4580
http://www.yuccado.com

GLOSSARY

alternate of leaves or branches, arranged in two ranks along the stem

apex the tip of a leaf or the growing point of a stem or inflorescence

basal of leaves, arising at ground level directly from the rhizome or on a very short, sometimes buried stem

bract a modified, protective leaf usually subtending the flower or clothing the flower stalk

bulblet a small bulblike growth arising from a leaf axil

cleft of a leaf, cut almost to the center

clumping of a plant, remaining as a slowly increasing clump, not spreading

crest of a flower, usually a toothed ridge on a flower, as in iris or orchids

culm the stem of grasses

deciduous a plant that sheds its leaves annually, as opposed to evergreen

divided of leaves, signifying a compound leaf that is twice or thrice divided into leaflets and subleaflets as in fern fronds or compound leaves of astilbes

ephemeral a plant with a short life cycle that ends in early dormancy, usually before onset of summer as in many native wildflowers

fall usually a drooping petal in the iris flower

frond the leaf of a fern composed of the stipe (stem) and the leaf blade; fertile fronds carry spore cases, sterile fronds lack spore cases

glaucous coated with a fine bloom, giving a whitish or bluish green appearance as in hosta leaves

herbaceous of plants whose aboveground structures disappear at the end of a growing season, usually in autumn, as in hostas

hybrid a plant created by cross-breeding two genetically dissimilar parents

incised of leaves with a sharply indented leaf margin

inflorescence the complete arrangement of flowers and flowering parts on a flower stalk

keel, keeled of leaves with a sunken or deeply impressed midrib, as the keel of a boat

leaflets the first division of a compound leaf; see divided

lip of a flower, forming specialized parts as in the dead nettles, an upper one, frequently hooded, and a lower one made up of fused petals to provide a platform for pollinators

lobed of leaves, divided into usually rounded segments separated by clefts

mat-forming forming a low, matlike, dense groundcover with leaves

opposite usually of leaves that are attached to a stem at the same point but on opposite sides

ovate egg-shaped in outline

petiole a leaf stalk

pleated a leaf surface arranged in folds like those of a fan

prostrate lying flat on the ground

rhizomatous growing from a rhizome, which is a horizontal, usually underground swollen stem that often spreads by sending out roots and shoots

rosette a circular cluster of leaves that radiate from a center at or close to the ground, as in the dandelion

sepal part of a flower, usually bractlike and green, but often petal-like and colorful

sessile stalkless or almost stalkless

spadix a fleshy, often clublike spike bearing minute flowers

spathe a leaflike, tubular bract (spathe tube) that encloses or subtends a flower cluster or spadix, as in the jack-in-the-pulpit; the spathe often has a hoodlike spathe limb

spur a modified petal of a flower that forms a tubular or saclike extension, as in columbines

stalk a stem that supports a plant part such as a flower, flower cluster, or leaf

stem-clasping usually a leaf that clasps the stem with its basal lobes

stolon, stoloniferous a shoot that bends to the ground or that grows horizontally at ground level or just above the ground and produces roots and shoots

striate of leaves that are striped, grooved, or ridged

subleaflets the second division of a compound leaf; see divided

terminal a flower, leaf, or other plant part growing or appearing at the end of a stem, branch, or stalk

toothed having small, notched, toothlike projections

tuber a swollen, fleshy, usually underground stem of a plant, bearing buds from which new plant shoots arise

tufted a dense clump of leaf stalks or culms of grasses

whorl an arrangement of three or more leaves, petals, or other plant organs radiating from a single point along a stalk

FURTHER READING

General references for shade and perennials

Armitage, Allan M. 2000. *Armitage's Garden Perennials: A Color Encyclopedia*. Portland, Oregon: Timber Press.

Druse, Ken. 1992. *The Natural Shade Garden*. Portland, Oregon: Timber Press.

Ellis, Barbara. 2001. *Taylor's Guide to Perennials*. Boston: Houghton Mifflin.

Harstad, Carolyn. 2003. *Got Shade?* Bloomington: Indiana University Press.

Hinkley, Daniel J. 1999. *The Explorer's garden: Rare and Unusual Perennials*. Portland, Oregon: Timber Press.

Rice, Graham. 1995. *Hardy Perennials*. Portland, Oregon: Timber Press.

Schenk, George. 1991. *The Complete Shade Gardener*. Portland, Oregon: Timber Press.

Schmid, W. George. 1991. *An Encyclopedia of Shade Perennials*. Portland, Oregon: Timber Press.

Epimedium (cpf--check size vs italic heads to follow)

Probst, Darrell R. N.D. Epimediums. Annual comprehensive listing of epimediums in cultivation. Hubbardstone, Massachusetts: Garden Vision.

Stearn, William T. 2002. *The Genus Epimedium*. Portland, Oregon: Timber Press.

Ferns

Hoshizaki, Barbara J., and R. C. Moran. 2001. *The Fern Grower's Manual*. Portland, Oregon: Timber Press.

Mickel, John T. 2003. *Ferns for American Gardens*. Portland, Oregon: Timber Press.
Geranium
Bath, Trevor, and Joy Jones. 2004. *The Gardener's Guide to Growing Hardy Geraniums*. Portland, Oregon: Timber Press.

Helleborus

Ahlburg, Marlene. 1993. *Hellebores*. London: Batsford.

Mathew, Brian. 1989. *Hellebores*. Worcestershire, United Kingdom: Alpine Garden Society.

Rice, Graham, and E. Strangman. 2001. *The Gardener's Guide to Growing Hellebores*. Portland, Oregon: Timber Press.

Hosta

Aden, Paul. 1992. *The Hosta Book*. Portland, Oregon: Timber Press.

Grenfell, Diana. 2004. *The Color Encyclopedia of Hostas*. Portland, Oregon: Timber Press.

Grenfell, Diana. 1996. *The Gardener's Guide to Growing Hostas*. Portland, Oregon: Timber Press.

Schmid, W. George. 1991. *The Genus Hosta: Giboshi Zoku*. Portland, Oregon: Timber Press.

Zilis, Mark. 2000. *The Hosta Handbook*. Rochelle, Illinois: Q&Z Nursery.

Iris

Glasgow, Karen. 1997. *Irises: A Practical Gardening Guide*. Portland, Oregon: Timber Press.

Lilium

Jefferson-Brown, Michael, and Harris Howland. 2002. *The Gardener's Guide to Growing Lilies*. Portland, Oregon: Timber Press.

McRae, Edward Austin. 1998. *Lilies: A Guide for Growers and Collectors*. Portland, Oregon: Timber Press.

Orchids

Cribb, Phillip. 1997. *The Genus Cypripedium*. Portland, Oregon: Timber Press.

Cribb, Phillip, and Christopher Bailes. 1989. *Hardy Orchids*. Portland, Oregon: Timber Press.

Keenan, Philip E. 1998. *Wild Orchids Across North America*. Portland, Oregon: Timber Press.

Trillium

Case, Frederick W., Jr., and Roberta B. Case. 1997. *Trilliums*. Portland, Oregon: Timber Press.

Jacobs, Don L., and Robert L. Jacobs. 1997. *Trilliums in the woodland garden—American Treasures*. Decatur, Georgia: Eco-Gardens.

INDEX